The supernatural in early modern Scotland

Manchester University Press

Alexander Runciman, *The Witches Showing Macbeth the Apparitions*, c.1772 (National Galleries of Scotland).

The supernatural in early modern Scotland

Edited by
Julian Goodare and **Martha McGill**

Manchester University Press

Copyright © Manchester University Press 2020

While copyright in the volume as a whole is vested in Manchester University Press, copyright in individual chapters belongs to their respective authors, and no chapter may be reproduced wholly or in part without the express permission in writing of both author and publisher.

Published by Manchester University Press
Oxford Rd, Manchester M13 9PL
www.manchesteruniversitypress.co.uk

British Library Cataloguing-in-Publication Data
A catalogue record for this book is available from the British Library

ISBN 978 1 5261 3442 4 hardback
ISBN 978 1 5261 6714 9 paperback

First published 2020
Paperback published 2023

The publisher has no responsibility for the persistence or accuracy of URLs for any external or third-party internet websites referred to in this book, and does not guarantee that any content on such websites is, or will remain, accurate or appropriate.

Typeset by Newgen Publishing UK

Contents

List of figures		vii
Contributors		viii
Acknowledgements		x
Abbreviations		xi
1	Exploring the supernatural in early modern Scotland *Julian Goodare and Martha McGill*	1
2	The elrich poems: the supernatural and the textual *Janet Hadley Williams*	25
3	Emotional relationships with spirit-guides in early modern Scotland *Julian Goodare*	39
4	Experiencing the invisible polity: trance in early modern Scotland *Georgie Blears*	55
5	The ninety-nine dancers of Moaness: Orkney women between the visible and invisible *Liv Helene Willumsen*	72
6	Angels in early modern Scotland *Martha McGill*	86
7	Scottish political prophecies and the crowns of Britain, 1500–1840 *Michael B. Riordan*	107

8 Astrology and supernatural power in early modern
   Scotland 127
   Jane Ridder-Patrick

 9 Fallen spirits and divine grace: sermons and the
   supernatural in post-Reformation Scotland 144
   Michelle D. Brock

10 The uses of providence in early modern Scotland 160
   Martha McGill and Alasdair Raffe

11 The invention of Highland Second Sight 178
   Domhnall Uilleam Stiùbhart

12 The pagan supernatural in the Scottish Enlightenment 204
   Felicity Loughlin

13 Eighteenth-century Scotland and the visionary
   supernatural 221
   Hamish Mathison

Index 239

Figures

	Frontispiece: Alexander Runciman, *The Witches Showing Macbeth the Apparitions*, c.1772 (National Galleries of Scotland)	ii
5.1	Looking over the Bay of Creekland (foreground) to the outjutting headland of Moaness, Hoy, Orkney (Simon Butterworth/Getty Images)	75
6.1	Richard Cooper, *An Ascending Angel*, c.1800 (National Galleries of Scotland)	87
6.2	Detail from a sacrament house at Deskford Church, Moray, 1551 (David Ross, www.britainexpress.com)	89
6.3	Detail from Alexander Macleod's tomb at St Clement's Church, Rodel, Harris, 1528 (Atlantide Phototravel/ Getty Images)	90
6.4	Detail from the painted ceiling of St Mary's Chapel, Grandtully, Perthshire, c.1636 (BCS/Alamy Stock Photo)	93
6.5	Gravestone in Greyfriars Kirkyard, Edinburgh, 1614 (Ryan McGoverne www.ryanmcgoverne.co.uk)	94
7.1	Prophecies with the badge of Scotland (British Library Board, Cotton Vespasian E.VIII, fo. 29^r)	113
7.2	Reconstruction of the evolution of the texts of *The Whole Prophesie* (image created by Michael B. Riordan)	115
7.3	The HEMPE prophecy (*The Whole Prophesie of Scotland*, Edinburgh, 1615, sig. A4^r)	115

Contributors

Georgie Blears is a trainee at American law firm Latham & Watkins. She studied intellectual and cultural history in medieval and early modern Europe at the University of Edinburgh, and her chapter in this book arose from her honours dissertation.

Michelle D. Brock is Associate Professor of History at Washington and Lee University. She is author of *Satan and the Scots: The Devil in Post-Reformation Scotland, c.1560–1700* (Routledge, 2016) and co-editor of *Knowing Demons, Knowing Spirits in the Early Modern Period* (Palgrave Macmillan, 2018). She is currently working on religious life in Covenanted Scotland.

Julian Goodare is Emeritus Professor of History at the University of Edinburgh. He is director of the online Survey of Scottish Witchcraft, and his most recent book is *The European Witch-Hunt* (Routledge, 2016). He is currently working on various aspects of witchcraft and popular culture in Scotland and Europe.

Janet Hadley Williams is Honorary Lecturer in English and Drama at the Australian National University. She has edited *Sir David Lyndsay: Selected Poems* (ASLS, 2000), *A Companion to Medieval Scottish Poetry* (D. S. Brewer, 2006, with Priscilla Bawcutt) and *'Duncane Laideus Testament' and Other Comic Poems in Older Scots* (Scottish Text Society, 2016).

Felicity Loughlin is Research Fellow in History at the University of St Andrews. She has published on the classical scholarship of Thomas Blackwell (1701–57) in the *Records of the Scottish Church History Society*. Her research interests lie in the intellectual, religious and cultural history of early modern Europe.

Martha McGill is British Academy Postdoctoral Fellow at the University of Warwick, where she is pursuing a project on 'Bodies, Selves, and the Supernatural in Early Modern Britain'. She is author of *Ghosts in Enlightenment Scotland* (Boydell, 2018).

Hamish Mathison is Lecturer in English at the University of Sheffield. He has published widely on eighteenth-century Scottish literature, book history and print culture. Recent work includes 'On Robert Burns: Enlightenment, Mythology and the Folkloric', in *The Voice of the People*, ed. Matthew Campbell and Michael Perraudin (Anthem, 2012).

Alasdair Raffe is Senior Lecturer in History at the University of Edinburgh. He is author of *The Culture of Controversy: Religious Arguments in Scotland, 1660–1714* (Boydell, 2012), *Scotland in Revolution, 1685–1690* (Edinburgh University Press, 2018) and numerous articles on religion, politics and ideas in early modern Scotland.

Jane Ridder-Patrick is an independent scholar whose doctorate from the University of Edinburgh focused on astrology in early modern Scotland. She specialises in the psychological and medical applications of astrology, and her books include *A Handbook of Medical Astrology* (Penguin/Arkana, 1990).

Michael B. Riordan recently graduated from the University of Cambridge with a doctorate examining mystical and prophetic traditions in early modern and Enlightenment Scotland. He is working on a monograph on the religious culture of moderate episcopacy, *The Moral Reformation in Scotland, 1660–1730*, to be published by Oxford University Press.

Domhnall Uilleam Stiùbhart is Senior Lecturer at Sabhal Mòr Ostaig, University of the Highlands and Islands. He has edited *The Life and Legacy of Alexander Carmichael* (Islands Book Trust, 2008) and has published widely on the history, literature, ethnology and oral tradition of the Scottish Gàidhealtachd.

Liv Helene Willumsen is Professor Emerita of History at the University of Tromsø – the Arctic University, Norway. Her specialism is witchcraft trials in Scotland and northern Norway, and her books include *Witches of the North: Scotland and Finnmark* (Brill, 2013). She is currently researching transference of demonological ideas across Europe.

Acknowledgements

This volume was planned at the University of Edinburgh, where both of the editors were then based. Within the university we are particularly grateful to its Institute for Advanced Studies in the Humanities. We also gratefully acknowledge the financial support of the Strathmartine Trust. Professor Colin Kidd and Professor Alasdair A. MacDonald have been helpful. Finally, we are grateful for the support and advice provided by the editorial staff at Manchester University Press.

Abbreviations

BL	British Library, London
DOST	*Dictionary of the Older Scottish Tongue* (in the Dictionary of the Scots Language, online at www.dsl.ac.uk)
EUL	Edinburgh University Library
L&P Henry VIII	*Calendar of Letters and Papers, Foreign and Domestic of the Reign of Henry VIII*, ed. J. S. Brewer *et al.*, 21 vols (HMSO: London, 1864–1932)
Maitland Misc.	*Miscellany of the Maitland Club*, 4 vols (Edinburgh: Maitland Club, 1833–47)
NLS	National Library of Scotland, Edinburgh
NRS	National Records of Scotland, Edinburgh
ODNB	*Oxford Dictionary of National Biography* (2004)
RPS	*Records of the Parliaments of Scotland*, ed. Keith M. Brown *et al.* (St Andrews, 2007, online at www.rps.ac.uk)
SHR	*Scottish Historical Review*
SHS	Scottish History Society
Spalding Misc.	*Miscellany of the Spalding Club*, 5 vols (Aberdeen: Spalding Club, 1841–52)
STS	Scottish Text Society

1

Exploring the supernatural in early modern Scotland

Julian Goodare and Martha McGill

> Upon a tyme the faierie elves
> Having first array'd themselves
> They thought it fit to cloath their king
> In robs fit for revelling
> He had a cobweb shirt more fin[e]
> Then ever spider yet did spin
> Bleach'd in the whytening of the snow
> When the northern winds did blow.

This quotation is from a poem that circulated in seventeenth-century England and Scotland. In sixty-four lines, the poem describes the elaborate outfits donned by the fairy king and queen in preparation for a 'revel'.[1] Humorous in tone, it explores the fairies' fantastical environment in colourful detail. There was no expectation that its fairies should be taken seriously. But the poem may have echoed genuine folkloric stories, and this may have been one reason for its success. There was nothing innately incredible in a world of magical possibilities.

For early modern Scots, supernatural forces were real and present. People disagreed about how these forces might manifest themselves, but throughout the period from 1500 to 1800 there were men and women who might perceive the supernatural in a whirlwind, or a dream, or the shimmer of a neighbour's eye. The supernatural was familiar. But it also – by definition – broke the laws by which the world generally operated. In thinking, talking and writing about supernatural forces, Scots were fashioning a reality that could never fully be known through experience or the evidence of the senses. Within this reality, there was no *logical* reason why fairies might *not* be out on snowy days, bleaching their shirts. To determine what was and was not possible, early modern Scots might look to theology, or metaphysics, or – for the common people – folkloric tradition. They were unlikely to find any clear consensus on the questions of when natural became supernatural, or legitimate supernatural belief became superstition – but that did not stop them exercising both their intellects and their imaginations in exploring the supernatural.

Sources on the early modern Scottish supernatural are varied. The contributors to this book draw on material including records from witch trials, accounts of visionary experiences, ministers' and antiquarians' descriptions of folk belief, religious and philosophical treatises, university lectures, sermons, songs, diaries, cheap pamphlets and artworks. Each of these source types was created to serve specific purposes. Some offer sober, reasoned explorations of the nature and capabilities of magical beings; others are sensationalised or romanticised. Many accounts straddle the boundary between fact and fiction. Ballads, folk tales and stories from pamphlets might be considered mere entertainment, but might also be believed or half-believed. Surveying different time spans, social groups, geographical areas and types of source material, the chapters in this book reveal a rich variety of ways in which early modern Scots imagined the world's magical potential.

Academic interest in the supernatural has surged in the last few decades. Influential studies on patterns of belief in Europe have demonstrated how the study of the supernatural can reflect on broader historical trends. Euan Cameron's survey of the changing understandings of 'superstition' is particularly relevant here, showing how intellectuals policed the boundaries of correct belief.[2] There have been studies of demonic possession and of 'discernment of spirits' – the process by which good and bad spirits were differentiated.[3] Julian Goodare's study of witch-hunting sets it in the context of broader processes including folk belief and magical practice.[4] Edward Bever's study of the 'realities' of 'witchcraft and popular magic' should be noted particularly for the way in which it, too, ranges beyond witchcraft and opens up a realm not of 'belief' but of magical action and experience.[5]

England has also been well surveyed. Keith Thomas's celebrated *Religion and the Decline of Magic* (1971) covered a wide range of supernatural beliefs, and demonstrated the value of devoting serious scholarly attention to topics such as fairies, ghosts and popular magical rituals.[6] The witch trials have consistently attracted scholarly attention, and in recent years especially, there has been a proliferation of studies exploring other supernatural phenomena in depth.[7] Thomas argued for the 'decline of magic' amid the rise of new philosophies and technologies, particularly in the seventeenth century.[8] However, the more recent trend has been to underline the persistent cultural importance of supernatural beliefs in early modern England, and to stress the perpetual entanglement of science, religion and magic.

Most of the recent scholarship on England has focused on specific supernatural powers or beings. One exception is Darren Oldridge's *The Supernatural in Tudor and Stuart England* (2016), which encompasses divine interventions, the Devil, angels, goblins, ghosts and occult (or hidden) powers. Oldridge contests the idea that supernatural beliefs were superseded by a scientific outlook in his period. He does, however, argue that ways of thinking about the supernatural changed, particularly in three respects. First, there was a 'reformation of spirits': Protestants excluded non-biblical supernatural beings from the officially sanctioned cosmos. Second, there was a fresh emphasis on the invisible, incorporeal and interior manifestations of supernatural forces. Third, the doctrine of divine providence took on new importance as 'the dominant model for explaining the operation of supernatural powers'.[9]

Some of the chapters in this book identify similar patterns. Particularly relevant to Oldridge's arguments, as we shall see, are Michelle D. Brock's chapter on sermons after the Reformation, and Martha McGill and Alasdair Raffe's chapter on providence. But Scotland did not always follow the same patterns as England. In the late seventeenth century, accounts of wondrous manifestations of providence declined in England, but proliferated in Scotland.[10] Scotland had its own church, and distinct intellectual and literary traditions. The witch-hunts were significantly more severe; Scotland executed about ten times more witches by head of the population than England.[11] Folkloric beliefs also differed by region. Compared to England, Scotland placed more emphasis on fairies. Second Sight, discussed in this book by Domhnall Uilleam Stiùbhart, was particularly associated with Scotland. Work such as Oldridge's is valuable for Scottish historians, but we cannot assume that English trends replicated themselves across the border.

When it comes to work on Scotland specifically, orthodox religion – and, especially, the impact of the Reformation – has been widely discussed.[12] The witch-hunts have proved a popular topic, in part because of the relative richness of the surviving source material.[13] Recent work has also focused on fairies, Second Sight, the Devil, folk belief and ghosts.[14] Again, most studies discuss particular beliefs in isolation, rather than looking at several together. A notable exception is Lizanne Henderson's edited collection *Fantastical Imaginations* (2009).[15] The essays in that book range from the late medieval period to the present day and cover a wide range of topics, demonstrating the vitality and variety of the Scottish supernatural. The present book builds on the foundations laid down by Henderson's collection, offering a specific focus on the early modern period – a time when religious and intellectual change was calling into question old sureties about the operations of the supernatural world.

This book is concerned with any beings or forces that transcended the natural order. This includes the 'faierie elves' of the poem at the start of this chapter, as well as other kinds of spirits. It encompasses occult (or hidden) knowledge, and magical powers. Early modern Christianity also had prominent aspects that one cannot avoid characterising as 'supernatural': a creator God who intervened in the world, a Devil who also intervened in the world and who tempted humans to sin, life after death for humans – either in Heaven or Hell – and spirits in the form of angels and demons. There is no denying that these Christian phenomena were 'supernatural'. As the impact of the Scottish Reformation has been covered in previous literature, we have aimed to avoid duplication by focusing specifically on what was *supernatural* about Scottish Protestantism. We have also placed relatively little emphasis on the Scottish witch-hunts. Some of the chapters draw on evidence generated by the witch trials, but this is in order to gather information about topics other than witchcraft. We have aimed so far as possible to take discussion of the Scottish supernatural in new directions.

In defining 'supernatural' so broadly, we are following common usage, while deviating from the pattern set down by Stuart Clark in his influential *Thinking with Demons*. Clark points out that early modern demonologists distinguished between the 'supernatural' and the 'preternatural'. God, and his unmediated actions, would be described as supernatural. Other spirits (with the possible exception of angels) were understood to be preternatural. Extraordinary occurrences that happened by the agency of created beings, or through the patterns of nature, were also interpreted as preternatural.[16] The division between supernatural – God and his miracles – and preternatural – wonders and created spirits – was important in theological and philosophical writing. It will therefore be considered in some of the chapters in the book, particularly those on providence, sermons and astrology. However, when discussing folk culture it is unnecessary, and perhaps even misleading, to differentiate between supernatural and preternatural. Elite debates were inaccessible to the vast majority of Scotland's population, and there is no evidence that ordinary men and women made use of this categorisation.

To define the early modern supernatural, it may help to ponder the question of what was considered 'natural'. Students at Scottish universities studied natural philosophy. This encompassed lectures on matter, the planets, light, sound, motion, time and the workings of human and animal bodies. More obviously supernatural topics were reserved for metaphysics courses, which dealt with spirits, including God. However, the division between natural and metaphysical topics was not always obvious from a modern standpoint. The human mind was understood to be a spiritual substance, and was generally a topic within metaphysics. The soul, however, was discussed in natural philosophy courses until the eighteenth century, following an Aristotelian tradition of interpreting the soul in physical terms. Crossover between lectures on natural philosophy and metaphysics was common, highlighting the difficulties of drawing stark divisions between natural and supernatural.

In the early modern period, just as much as today, people did not comment explicitly on the ordinariness of their everyday experience. The question of what was 'natural' was directly addressed only in a negative context: something was 'natural' by virtue of not being supernatural. James VI debated whether the nightmare experience, 'the Mare, which takes folkes sleeping in their bedds', was to be attributed to 'spirites', but decided that it was 'but a naturall sicknes'.[17] Early modern Scots seem to have reasoned that 'if you don't see this every day', or 'if you can't produce an everyday explanation for it', then it was 'not natural' and thus probably supernatural. A similar process of reasoning operates today. The question may thus arise: who has authority to decide what is natural and what is supernatural?[18]

Today, what is normal or natural is defined by science. There is nothing unscientific about the concept of large marine animals, and no basic scientific assumptions would be violated if a large marine animal were to be found in Loch Ness. However, a common-sense approach to the way in which the Loch Ness Monster is discussed indicates that belief in such a monster is in fact paranormal; the belief operates in similar ways to belief in more obviously paranormal phenomena such as telepathy.[19] The present book does not address 'paranormal' questions directly, because modern discourse on the paranormal is framed in scientific or at least quasi-scientific terms that lack precise early modern equivalents.

The search for fabulous beasts, known today as 'cryptozoology' and exemplified by tales of the Loch Ness Monster, nevertheless finds early modern parallels.[20] Sixteenth-century Scotland inherited a medieval literary tradition of 'barnacle geese' – not the modern birds of that name, but legendary geese engendered from barnacles growing on wood. The birds' legend may have been connected with the fact that some species of wild geese were never observed to build nests or raise young (they did so on migration to the Arctic, but bird migration was unknown before modern times). A description of Scotland published in 1458 ascribed barnacle geese particularly to Scotland, and described them growing on trees, hanging from their beaks.[21]

In 1527, Hector Boece, the humanist principal of Aberdeen University, attempted to revise the story of barnacle geese. He cited information from a friend of his – not necessarily to be taken literally – to argue that the geese were engendered from worms within seaweed, through the power of the ocean.[22] Boece's use of phrases like *'rei miraculo'* (by this miraculous thing) and *'incomparabili'* (wonders) shows that he thought that barnacle geese were something out of the ordinary.[23] The point for us is that barnacle geese, as understood by sixteenth-century intellectuals like Boece, transcended the currently accepted boundaries of how birds were supposed to behave. By introducing worms into the story he may have been attempting to bring it within the scope of natural explanations;

worms were traditional exceptions to the rule that living creatures could not generate spontaneously.[24]

The difference between the modern paranormal and the early modern supernatural is mainly to do with the frame of reference. Today's paranormal beliefs operate within a scientific frame, so believers assume that they have to cite scientific evidence. Early modern supernatural beliefs operated within a religious frame, and had to be validated by religious evidence. If you encountered what appeared to be a spirit, you asked yourself, not 'What is the scientific evidence for spirits?' but 'How can I categorise this spirit within an orthodox framework?' The Bible provided a much-quoted passage of guidance on this: 'Believe not every spirit, but try the spirits whether they are of God' (1 John 4:1). A spirit sent from God would behave in godly ways and bring godly messages. However, if you encountered what appeared to be a spirit, and if you tried to decide whether it was a godly or an ungodly spirit, you had already entered a supernatural mode of thinking.

Judgements about the boundary between natural and supernatural often had broader personal or political implications. John Maitland, second Earl and later first Duke of Lauderdale, was a believer in demonic possession, and regretted what he saw as an atheistical trend to deny the reality of spirits. Hence his interest in the case of an uneducated woman from the Scottish borders who was possessed by a Latin-speaking demon, which he described as credible in 1659 in a letter to the English theologian Richard Baxter. However, Lauderdale was also ready to recognise cases of fraudulence, especially where Catholics were concerned. In the same letter he recalled how he had once travelled to Loudun, France, to see the notorious group of demonically possessed nuns there, only to find them 'nothing but wanton Wenches singing baudy Songs in *French*'.[25]

When Philip Standsfield, of Newmills, Haddingtonshire, was accused in 1688 of having murdered his father, one of the points of evidence raised against him was that when he touched the corpse it 'did (according to God's usual method of discovering murders) blood afresh upon him, and defiled all his hands, which struck him with such a terror, that he immediately let his father's head and body fall with violence, and fled from the body'. The idea that the dead would bleed in the presence of their murderers was of long standing. The defence advocate took a sceptical stance, arguing that it was 'but a superstitious observation, without any ground either in law or reason', and citing the *Practica Criminalis* of the respected German jurist Benedict Carpzov (1635). But the influential prosecuting advocate, Sir George Mackenzie, argued for divine and indeed directly 'miraculous' intervention:

> Some chirurgions and friends ... having raised the body, did see it bleed miraculously upon his [Philip's] touching it. In which God

Almighty himself was pleased to bear a share in the testimonies which we produce; that Divine Power, which makes the blood circulat during life, has oft-times, in all nations, opened a passage to it after death, upon such occasions, but most in this case.[26]

Here, interpretations of events were clearly guided by particular agendas.

Thus, in deciding what was normal and what was unusual, and whether something unusual was unusual to the point of being *supernatural*, there was a complex mixture of considerations at play. In the examples above, the stakes could be high. Lauderdale defended true Protestant supernaturalism in the face of Catholic fraudulence. In the case of Philip Standsfield, the confirmation of supernatural involvement led to an execution. Self-interest, or the interest of a particular community, inevitably influenced how people made sense of unusual events. Relevant, too, were factors such as religious beliefs, levels of education and prior experience. The boundaries between natural and supernatural were continually drawn and redrawn, and for men and women across the social spectrum, encounters with the supernatural might be full of uncertainties.

In this book, the term 'belief' is generally used in the modern sense, to indicate a conviction of the reality of a particular being or force, or the truth of a certain proposition. For much of our period, however, this is not how the term was understood. Wilfred Cantwell Smith has highlighted how understandings of the term 'belief' have changed over time. Originally, 'to believe' was to pledge loyalty. It was a promise of action, as much as of faith. People believed in other people. It was only in the late seventeenth century, Smith argues, that there was a shift towards believing in propositions. He continues:

> The affirmation 'I believe in God' used to mean: 'Given the reality of God as a fact of the universe, I hereby pledge to Him my heart and soul. I committedly opt to live in loyalty to Him. I offer my life to be judged by Him, trusting His mercy'. To-day the statement may be taken by some as meaning: 'Given the uncertainty as to whether there be a God or not, as a fact of modern life, I announce that my opinion is "yes". I judge God to be existent'.[27]

To be part of the early modern Christian 'community of believers' was thus to live a godly life. Unbelievers were guilty of a spiritual crime, but not necessarily of denying the reality of God. Thus, early modern statements of belief were often more about what one *did* than how one thought about things.

Jeanne Favret-Saada's anthropological study of witchcraft in rural France is also relevant here. The men and women she interviewed knew that belief in witchcraft was treated as a sign of ignorance, and claimed no interest in the topic. They would, nevertheless, seek the services of 'unwitchers' in cases of illness. Abstract questions of belief were of minimal relevance; protection against sickness or misfortune was the matter of importance.[28] This practice-oriented approach to the supernatural world has early modern parallels. In his 1703 *Description of the Western Islands of Scotland*, Martin Martin detailed a community custom from Lewis. Around Halloween the inhabitants of the island collectively brewed a vat of ale and tossed a cup into the sea as a tribute to a god called Shony. Thereafter, the community drank, danced and sang together all night. Martin wrote that this ceremony had been 'believ'd to be a powerful means to procure a plentiful crop', but that ministers had more recently – and with much difficulty – convinced the locals to give up the tradition.[29] For Martin, this was a story about false beliefs, subsequently corrected. But this is really a story about a practice. For the villagers, the issue at stake was the protection of crops, not abstract questions about Shony's ontological status vis-à-vis the Christian God. The question of beliefs becomes marginal.

Another problem with the word 'belief' relates to the division between beliefs and knowledge. Smith argues that by the nineteenth century, a clear opposition had developed between beliefs and knowledge. Knowledge is correct and certifiable. The term belief, by contrast, implies doubtfulness or error. Thus, we speak of the *belief* that the earth is flat and the *knowledge* that the earth is round.[30]

This distinction was present in the early modern period too. The following story was recorded by the pioneer ethnographer Edward Lhuyd, who visited the Highlands in 1699–1700: '[The Highlanders] believe that there are in the freshwater lochs creatures which they call *tarbh-uisge* (or *tarbh-feirigh*) (water-bulls) and *each uisge* (water-horses); and that these serve the (ordinary) cows and mares; and the calves that come from them are hornless (lacking ears), but what ears there are, are red.'[31] Lhuyd was writing about *other people's* belief in water-horses, a belief that he almost certainly did not share, and thus bracketing off their 'belief' as something inherently unlikely or untrue. He made no attempt to denigrate the 'beliefs' that he recorded, but there is something questionable in the process of defining as 'beliefs' the customs and propositions that we do not share. It is unsatisfactory to say that other people have beliefs about water-horses, but we don't.

While Lhuyd used the term 'belief' in the modern sense, for most early modern men and women the difference between belief and knowledge depended more on *how* people knew things than on whether they were doubtful. People did not believe in everyday things. They knew about them from direct, unarguable experience. The supernatural realm was a matter of *belief* because it was generally unknowable by ordinary, everyday experience. But here, too, we run into lexical difficulties.

Consider the following illustration. The people in the Highlands did not 'believe' in the existence of wrens. The wren, though a small and shy bird, was recognisable through the everyday senses. But people did hold certain beliefs about wrens. Again, we can cite a story recorded by Lhuyd: 'There are twelve feathers in a wren's tail, and one of them is very lucky, but they do not know which one. And in one wing there is a lucky one, and in the other an unlucky one; but it is not known which wing, or which feather.'[32] This story is a good illustration of a supernatural belief because it emphasises people's awareness about the limits of what was knowable. These lucky and unlucky feathers were unknowable by ordinary means, and the story had uncertainty built into its structure – 'it is not known which wing, or which feather'. But we again see the clumsiness of the term 'belief'. The story was about what was knowable, not about what was believable.

Early modern men and women speculated about the supernatural world, and their notions of the supernatural translated into practical actions. But this does not necessarily mean that their concepts of the supernatural can be marshalled into anything we might refer to as a 'belief system', with all the implications of coherence, consistency and commitment, on an abstract level, to a particular world view. It is with this caveat in mind that we set out to explore the tangle of supernatural ideas that emerges from early modern Scottish source material.

As a starting point, we look to imaginative explorations of the supernatural world. Poetry and drama drew on religious and folkloric traditions, but might also subvert them. In the fairy poem discussed earlier in this chapter, familiar and unfamiliar are blended. The fairies are clothed in the stuff of nature, and move through a tiny world of insects, arachnids and molluscs. They have recognisably human concerns: on being presented with a waistcoat lined with 'humming bees soft plush', the king frets that he will get too hot. At the same time, the fairies are an aberration. When the fairy king and queen realise that they might overheat, they adopt solutions that would not readily spring to the human mind. The king replaces his bee-fur waistcoat with a yet more curious garment 'made of downie hair / New taken from ane Eunuchs chin'. The queen adopts an even more striking solution: she fans herself with the cooling air of a lady's scoff, or disdainful laugh. As spiritual beings, fairies are able to use non-material things as though they were physical.

The account of the fairy king's attire continues:

> His hat was all of Ladyes Love
> So wondrous light that it wold move
> If any gnat or humming flie
> did beat the air in passing by
> About it went a wreath of pearle
> Fall'n from the eyes of some poor girle
> Pinch'd because she had forgot
> To leave clean water in her pot.

In pinching a slovenly girl, the fairies are behaving in a normal, if rude, human fashion. But in fashioning a wreath from her tears, they are performing transformative magic beyond human capability. A hat made of ladies' love similarly defies the laws of materiality (and includes a dose of casual misogyny: ladies' love was 'light' because women were fickle). When early modern men and women talked about magic that they believed fairies or witches had performed, the acts they described were relatively mundane: changing the weather, harming or healing livestock and humans, predicting future events, finding lost or stolen goods. Even shape-shifting, while dramatic, turned one familiar thing (a human form) into another familiar thing (an animal form). This was a kind of magic that was easily pictured. The fairy poem, on the other hand, tested the limits of the human imagination; the act of making hats out of love belonged in the realm of poetry.

Hats of love and wreaths of tears are romantic notions. The fairies are further distanced from the everyday world in the following description of the queen's attire:

> Her gown was party collered fair
> The rain-bow gave't a dip
> Perfumed by ane amber air
> Breath'd from a virgins lip
> The shift was all of morning dawn
> When phebus did but peep
> And by a poets pencil drawn
> In Thetis Lap asleep.

Here the poem exhibits the Renaissance literary tradition of allusion to Greece. The references to the sun god Phoebus and the sea nymph Thetis place the fairies in a world of classical mythology, obscuring their presence within contemporary Scottish folklore. It is also notable that the fairies of the poem are associated with symbols of chastity. The king is clad in his coat of eunuch hair. The queen wears a modest white veil, the perfume of a virgin's lip and shoes made – alarmingly – of 'maidenhoods'. This contrasts with folk legends, in which fairies readily had sex with humans: examples can be seen in the chapters by Julian Goodare and Michael B. Riordan. There may well have been something knowing in the poem's allusion to the fairies' symbols of chastity; after all, fairies were believed to be deceptive. Nevertheless, the vision of fairies that emerges from the poem seems to be positioned against the folkloric narratives that may have inspired it.

Comedic – often bawdy – literary explorations of the supernatural were common in the Renaissance and the eighteenth century. Further study of supernatural elements in seventeenth-century Scottish literature is required; most of this literature was written either in standard

English or in Latin, and neither of these languages has attracted much scholarly attention.[33] The preliminary suggestion can be made that the exquisite prettiness of the poem's tiny fairies represents a retreat from the wider-ranging exploration of the supernatural previously found in sixteenth-century literature. From the late sixteenth to the late seventeenth centuries, when the witch trials were at their height, there was less appetite for irreverent explorations of the supernatural.[34]

The ordering of chapters within this book is partly chronological, but we have also sought to illustrate a movement from popular to elite culture. Several of the early chapters deal unambiguously with the supernatural in popular culture, while later chapters tend to engage more with intellectual ideas of the supernatural. It is in some of these later chapters that we see more change and development; changes in popular culture tend to be slower and more gradual, and thus harder for scholars to pinpoint.

The chapters by Janet Hadley Williams and Hamish Mathison deal, respectively, with the beginning and end of our period of analysis, when fiction was freer to explore and exploit the dramatic potential of the supernatural. In 'The elrich poems: The supernatural and the textual' (Chapter 2), Hadley Williams discusses a group of late fifteenth- and early sixteenth-century Older Scots poems that offer fantastical, humorous excursions into the supernatural world. The magical events and beings in the poems are simultaneously familiar and strange, comic and threatening. They are also frustratingly difficult to fully comprehend. Records of the poems often post-date the times of composition by decades. Scribal omissions or errors impede our efforts to recapture the poets' original meanings. In some cases, the poems' original forms were consciously altered. This happened particularly in the wake of the 1560 Reformation, when scribes removed or changed references to Catholic beliefs and practices. Hadley Williams demonstrates the complexity of recovering ideas of the supernatural that were recorded only in incomplete or otherwise problematic ways. Her chapter also reveals how even burlesque poetry was tailored to conform with religious orthodoxy.

With Hamish Mathison's 'Eighteenth-century Scotland and the visionary supernatural' (Chapter 13) we move forward in time. As Mathison demonstrates, fictional evocations of the supernatural had a significant role to play as Scottish people evaluated the implications of the 1707 Union with England. In eighteenth-century poetry, apparitions representing past generations warned of a Scottish future blighted by the loss of independence. Describing encounters with spirits or muses of Scotland, writers including Allan Ramsay and Robert Burns deployed a language of seeming: the visionary supernatural was *like* or *as if*, but never wholly discernible. By this means, they depicted Scottishness itself as an elusive force, immune to critical scrutiny, but also fundamentally insubstantial. These literary explorations constituted a distinctive mode of negotiating Scottish identity in the eighteenth century. Mathison's chapter shows how fictional explorations of the supernatural could both reflect, and help to form, political realities.

Dramatic, romanticised depictions of supernatural worlds became more common in the late eighteenth century, amid the rising popularity of gothic literature and James Macpherson's Ossian poetry.

The frontispiece of the present book features an image of Macbeth encountering the witches, by the Edinburgh-born painter Alexander Runciman, dating from 1771 or 1772. It illustrates Act IV, Scene 1 of Shakespeare's play, when Macbeth meets the witches for the second time. The setting is a cave; outside we see the outline of Macbeth's castle. Two witches drop toads and insects into a winged cauldron, placed within a magic circle. In the foreground, a horrified Macbeth is confronted by the armoured head that warns him to beware of Macduff. Behind the cauldron rises a skeletal figure who might be the third witch or the goddess Hecate. There is also a motley gathering of human-like figures, perhaps the 'elves and fairies in a ring' mentioned by Hecate (line 42). An owl, a bat and a winged skull fly overhead and a skeletal horseman makes an entrance at one side, recalling Salvator Rosa's well-known image of Saul and the Witch of Endor (*c*.1668).

The image implies the impossibility of containing the supernatural. The cauldron, which should be part of the everyday material world, has sprouted wings and clawed feet. Macbeth occupies the foreground, dressed as a warrior, but shrinks back helplessly from the witches' phantasms. The looming figure in the background bears vials billowing with fumes, which in turn seep into an eclipse above Macbeth's castle. Once unleashed, the supernatural forces of the image cannot be kept to the confines of the cave; their intrusion leaves a subtle poison lingering in the atmosphere. In a world where supernatural powers remained credible, it was similarly impossible to keep the threat of other-worldly evil fixed within the realm of art or stories. One early nineteenth-century commentator suggested that humankind could never overcome fear of the supernatural, as the menace of invisible forces was too deeply rooted in the human imagination. 'Human flesh', the commentator wrote, 'will creep to the end of time at the witches of Macbeth'.[35]

While the threat of supernatural evil was compelling, so too was the promise of protection. Within this volume, Martha McGill's 'Angels in early modern Scotland' (Chapter 6) assesses conceptions of good angels, drawing on sources including plays, songs and visual imagery, as well as accounts of angelic visitations. The angels evoked in ministers' sermons were different from those on Renaissance painted ceilings, and different again from Christsonday, an angelic guide described by an accused witch from sixteenth-century Aberdeenshire. At the same time, there are potentially instructive continuities. In theory, angels represented the nice side of the supernatural. They were humankind's protectors and guardians, beings of pure goodness, the counterpart to demons. However, McGill's chapter demonstrates the prominence of frightening angels for early modern Scots. Sword-wielding angels stand ready to punish the wicked, while angels with 'hydous voce' and 'terribyll Trumpat' herald a fiery Judgement Day.[36] Protective angels were certainly recognised, but it was only in the eighteenth century that the idea of the distant, loving guardian figure became dominant. Representations of angels fed into a broader understanding of the supernatural world as a gravely serious matter: the fate of one's soul demanded constant attention.

Depictions of the supernatural within art and literature reveal how people thought about magical forces and beings, and how these ways of thinking changed over time. These representations might have evocative resonances for early modern Scots. In a universe underpinned by powerful spiritual forces, fictionalised depictions reflected genuine beliefs.

A sharp contrast might nevertheless be drawn between fictionalised accounts of the supernatural and direct personal experiences of it. We have argued above that one defining feature of the supernatural was that it was not knowable through ordinary experience. Yet some people had experiences that were very much out of the ordinary – and such experiences may well have fed into fictional accounts. It is also necessary to study direct, personal experiences of the 'supernatural' in their own right.

Personal experience is the topic of Georgie Blears's chapter, 'Experiencing the invisible polity: Trance in early modern Scotland' (Chapter 4). Drawing on insights from medical, psychiatric and anthropological literature, Blears identifies the symptoms of trance states in many early modern people's stories of encounters with the supernatural. Overwork, undernourishment, disease and particular sleeping patterns all made trance experiences more likely, while early modern Scots' animist world view meant that individuals who had trances often understood their experiences to involve encounters with spirits. Working mainly with the accounts of accused witches and second-sighted seers, Blears identifies cases both of involuntary trances, and of trances that might have been deliberately provoked to gain privileged knowledge or skills. Blears's chapter demonstrates the value of supplementing social and cultural explanations for supernatural experiences with explanations based on modern-day medical knowledge. By recognising and understanding early modern people's experience of trance, we can come to appreciate how, for some individuals, the supernatural was real from a neurobiological perspective.

Julian Goodare's chapter 'Emotional relationships with spirit-guides in early modern Scotland' (Chapter 3) also examines how some early modern Scots experienced the supernatural realm. Goodare focuses on visionaries who had relationships with spirit-guides. He pays particular attention to Alison Pearson from Fife, who was tried in 1588 and had a spirit-guide called William Simpson. The authorities assumed that people like Pearson had been meeting with the Devil, but Pearson, like other visionaries, interpreted her spirit-guide as a ghost who associated with fairies. Spirit-guides had mysterious magical powers, but Goodare demonstrates that they were understood in familiar terms. Visionaries' relationships with their spirit-guides mirrored established human relationships, most notably the patron/client relationship. Furthermore, these were relationships with a significant emotional element. The visionaries felt varied emotions towards their spirit-guides, with fear being most prominent. They also attributed emotions to their guides, including sympathy and anger. The visionaries normalised their relationships with their spirit-guides, and however we might understand their experiences, the emotional dimensions were genuine.

In early modern Scotland, the Christian religion – which for most of our period took an assertively Protestant form – had cultural authority. Some visions, wonders and supernatural beings fell within the boundaries of orthodox Christianity. Some hovered at the borderline and might be judged orthodox or unorthodox by different individuals, or at different points in time. Other beliefs, particularly those that were associated with Catholicism or paganism, were considered wholly unacceptable by educated authorities. Within folk culture, however, the divide between orthodox and unorthodox was often supplanted by the divide between good and bad. Common folk tended to think that *good* spirits were, or should be, orthodox. We sometimes see kirk sessions going along with this, but at other times we see them taking a more theologically austere approach whereby they defined virtually all spirits encountered by the common folk as demons or the Devil, and condemned any negotiation, however benevolent in intent, with any of them.

There was also an important divide in elite culture between the 'superstitious' and the 'demonic'. This was a subdivision within the division between orthodox and unorthodox. Once it was decided that a ritual or other such act was unorthodox, the question became: how unorthodox was it? Was it a minor sin, and thus 'superstitious', or did it arise from a pact with the Devil, thus making it 'demonic'? At what point did an unorthodox ritual become demonic? Was it to do with the nature of the ritual – e.g. herbs versus words – or with the person's level of understanding of what they were doing – e.g. could you be forgiven through ignorance? The level of understanding question was probably addressed at least in part in the way that a criminal court would address it today: ignorance of the law is no excuse, and a crime is an act that any reasonable person, educated or not, ought to recognise as a crime. A pact with the Devil, in particular, was always assumed to be a deliberate act.

Michelle D. Brock's chapter, 'Fallen spirits and divine grace: Sermons and the supernatural in post-Reformation Scotland' (Chapter 9), shows how ministers after the Reformation educated their parishioners about legitimate supernatural belief. The supernatural, as outlined in sermons, was a body of knowledge and forces that humans were incapable of comprehending in their terrestrial state, subject to original sin. The elect nevertheless had a duty to aspire to better understanding. Ministers emphasised two themes, both related to how the supernatural featured in human lives: Satan's perpetual presence and influence, and the possibility of redemption through communion with God. There were mentions of demons in sermons, and angels made occasional appearances, but non-biblical beings like fairies were conspicuously absent. Sermons offered an unparalleled opportunity to educate early modern men and women about proper understandings of the supernatural, and to focus attention on God and the Devil. Parishioners were encouraged to think of the supernatural as a continual presence, but only in approved forms.

Liv Helene Willumsen's chapter on 'The ninety-nine dancers of Moaness: Orkney women between visible and invisible' (Chapter 5) takes the opposite vantage point, examining a story that circulated within folk culture. The story described a dance involving ninety-nine individuals that took place on the Orkney island of Hoy. It was mentioned as part of the interrogation for witchcraft of Barbara Bowndie in 1643, but it had been discussed locally for at least a decade previously. Willumsen approaches the account of Bowndie's interrogation through close reading, teasing out information from the language used in the record. Her chapter demonstrates the conflict between the demonological ideas of the interrogators and the folkloric vision of the dance seemingly shared by Orkney women. The folkloric conception of the dance reflects animistic conceptions of the landscape. The interrogators sought to demonise the magical forces that Bowndie located in the natural environment, a reading that Bowndie later rejected. Willumsen's chapter highlights the tensions that arose when men and women of different social groups endeavoured to talk together about the invisible forces lurking at the edge of their communities.

Jane Ridder-Patrick's 'Astrology and supernatural power in early modern Scotland' (Chapter 8) demonstrates the complexity of determining when orthodox became unorthodox, or superstitious practices became demonic. Astrology linked the natural and supernatural worlds, imbuing the movements of the planets with occult (that is, hidden) significance. It was generally divided into two branches: natural astrology, which dealt with topics such as the weather and agriculture, and judicial astrology, which made more wide-ranging predictions. The former was generally endorsed, and the latter rejected, or treated with suspicion. But even legitimate astrological knowledge could be dangerous if it fell into the wrong hands. Learned men practised astrology, and it was taught in universities until the late seventeenth century. The popular practice of astrology was rare, but the authorities condemned it as superstitious if it occurred. In the eighteenth century, astrology was usually dismissed by educated people, who increasingly understood celestial events in natural terms. Nevertheless, belief and interest in astrology persisted outside the intellectual mainstream. Orthodox and unorthodox; legitimate, superstitious and demonic: these were fluid categories that changed over time, and were used differently in reference to the practices of people from different social groups.

While the three chapters described above all highlight points of tension between elite and popular culture, prominent Scottish supernatural beliefs were shaped both by learned discourse and by folklore. Domhnall Uilleam Stiùbhart's 'The invention of Highland Second Sight' (Chapter 11) demonstrates this cultural overlap. The concept of Second Sight, he shows, was adapted from theology into popular belief, and was influenced along the way by covenanting culture and by Freemasonry. Second Sight is commonly described as an involuntary clairvoyant ability, and is associated particularly with the Scottish Highlands. Stiùbhart argues that this understanding of the phenomenon emerged during the early modern period. In the wake of the Reformation, supernatural encounters were demonised. In response, diverse beliefs about divination and communication with spirits were subsumed into the category of Second Sight, an involuntary – and therefore defensible – ability. Strikingly, Stiùbhart also shows that Lowland narratives played a key role in the invention of Second Sight, although it ended up being depicted as a uniquely Highland phenomenon by outsiders. This would be further emphasised when Highland culture was romanticised in the eighteenth and nineteenth centuries. The chapter thus demonstrates the complex blend of influences moulding notions of the supernatural.

Understandings of the supernatural evolved over the course of the early modern period. The Reformation redefined the boundaries of orthodoxy, resulting in a period of negotiation between kirk authorities and local communities. In the seventeenth century, the Scientific Revolution spurred a re-evaluation of supernatural forces in elite circles. At the same time, interest in 'remarkable providences' flourished, and a fear of radical new philosophies meant that folk beliefs were increasingly rehabilitated in order to demonstrate the reality of the world of spirits. In the eighteenth century, Enlightenment thinkers placed a fresh emphasis on finding natural explanations for extraordinary experiences, while early romantic and gothic works explored the emotive power of supernatural themes.

Meanwhile, the witch-hunts emerged, reached their zenith and declined again. Changes and continuities in conceptions of the supernatural between 1500 and 1800 are discussed by several chapters of this book.

According to Max Weber's famous 'disenchantment' thesis, the supernatural world view went into decline after the Reformation. Disenchantment is often understood to refer to the diminishing importance of magic within culture; thus, works on the 're-enchantment of the world' have argued for the significance of magic within spheres including art, music, the media and entertainment.[37] For Weber, disenchantment was a more specific concept. The world was disenchanted if it was understood to operate according to logical, predictable laws. One need not have recourse to 'mysterious, incalculable forces' to explain why any given event had come about. Protestantism was a crucial stepping stone in the journey towards a disenchanted world because it placed the responsibility for salvation on the individual, leading to 'the complete elimination of salvation through the Church and the sacraments'.[38] Magical rituals thus lost their power and indeed came to be viewed with suspicion, as distractions from true religious feeling.

There are valuable elements in Weber's thesis. Western society has certainly come to place more faith in scientific laws, rather than the influence of magical forces, as a means of understanding the workings of the universe. There were important developments here in the early modern period, although they more obviously arose from the intellectual changes of the Scientific Revolution and the Enlightenment than from the religious transformations of the sixteenth century. Ridder-Patrick's chapter demonstrates how the development of mathematics and Newtonian physics encouraged the idea that the movement of the planets followed natural laws, pushing astrology out of the university syllabus. Also significant is the end of the witch trials, a development that can be partly attributed to the rise of mechanical philosophy, which had no room for active demons.[39] As the eighteenth century progressed, intellectual culture increasingly adopted naturalistic explanations for phenomena that were previously interpreted as supernatural. The ecclesiastical and secular authorities ceased strictly to control representations of the supernatural. As highlighted above, the comic and emotive potential of witches, apparitions, demons and fairies was explored in poetry, paintings, short stories and drama. This development attests to the continued cultural value of the supernatural, but was possible only because aspects of the supernatural world were not taken as seriously as they had been a century previously.

At the same time, the narrative of disenchantment remains debatable in many of its details. Michael D. Bailey has rejected the idea that the Protestant Reformation marked a critical juncture, but instead of shifting the focus to the seventeenth and eighteenth centuries he has moved it back to the late middle ages. He argues that disenchantment must be understood as a 'profoundly gradual transition' that received particular impetus in the fifteenth century, when authorities increasingly challenged 'superstitious' practices.[40] Bob Scribner has similarly argued against the importance of Protestantism as a turning point, although on different grounds: he challenges the idea that Protestantism disentangled magic from religion, citing examples of the continued importance of ritual within Protestant culture.[41] Alexandra Walsham has proposed that instead of a linear process of disenchantment, there were continual 'cycles of desacralization and resacralization' in early modern England.[42]

Euan Cameron, while accepting much of this, has pointed out that Scribner paid more attention to the often limited effects of the Reformation on the ground than to the theology that drove it. Offering a Scottish example, he points out that although many ordinary Scots continued to visit holy wells after the Reformation, 'it would be bizarre to suggest that holy wells formed an inherent part of the Scots Calvinist belief-system'. Cameron thus reasserts the idea that the Reformation introduced dynamic forces of change to the world of early modern European thought. Endorsing the idea of 'cycles' of supernaturalism, he adds that the 'resacralization' of the late seventeenth century was in its own way a linear movement, brought about by the breakdown of scholastic Aristotelianism. Overall, there may not have been a decline of magic, but there was a decline of the *fear* of magic.[43]

Several chapters in the present book engage with the disenchantment thesis in various ways. While certain ways of talking about the supernatural fell out of fashion in the eighteenth century, it remained usual to understand the world through reference to supernatural forces operating in ways that humans could not necessarily discern or predict. Three chapters relating to these topics are discussed below. There is also particularly relevant material in four chapters previously discussed above. Martha McGill's chapter demonstrates that stories of angels persisted in Protestant society, but that depiction of angels softened in the eighteenth century, in line with Cameron's suggestion that the magical world became less intimidating. Michelle D. Brock's chapter on sermons brings out the restrictions that Protestant ministers sought to apply to their parishioners' understanding of the supernatural, while Domhnall Uilleam Stiùbhart's chapter on Second Sight underlines how the Reformation encouraged rethinking of categories of supernatural belief. Jane Ridder-Patrick's chapter on astrology illustrates one intellectual consequence of the decline of Aristotelianism.

Martha McGill and Alasdair Raffe's 'The uses of providence in early modern Scotland' (Chapter 10) discusses a doctrine of central importance to Scottish religious culture. 'General providence' was God's design for the universe, drawn up at the Creation, while 'special providences' were his subsequent spontaneous interventions. Pious Scots were primed to identify God's hand in the world around them, and events ranging from the wondrous to the mundane might be interpreted in providential terms. Ministers used the doctrine of providence to refute atheists, and to comfort parishioners in the face of misfortunes. Providences demonstrated God's support for particular religious or political causes. Finally, historians recounted Scotland's past in providentialist terms, showing how God had steered the fate of the nation. With the arrival of Enlightenment, special providences were dropped from high intellectual discourse, but the doctrine of general providence remained important. Whereas earlier accounts of providence had emphasised the religious conflict prefiguring the apocalypse, Enlightenment thinkers framed providence in more optimistic terms, as a divine force ensuring social progress. Providence was also put to new political uses, justifying projects such as empire-building. Discussions of providence changed to suit evolving social circumstances, but, throughout the early modern period, the doctrine imbued everyday events with supernatural significance.

Michael B. Riordan's 'Scottish political prophecies and the crowns of Britain, 1500–1840' (Chapter 7) similarly stresses the usefulness of the supernatural, exploring the value of prophecy within political culture. Riordan focuses on prophecies attributed to figures from Europe's past, especially those collected in the *Whole Prophesie of Scotland* published in 1603. At sixteenth-century Tudor and Stewart courts, prophecies were used to claim that the reigning monarch was destined to unite Britain under one crown. This occasionally caused diplomatic problems – James V was forced to disavow prophecy when promises of a Scottish Catholic takeover antagonised Henry VIII – but the use and adaptability of prophecy persisted, even after the Union of Crowns was achieved by James VI. In the eighteenth century, Jacobites and Whigs drew on the same prophecies to make opposite arguments. It was only in the nineteenth century that prophecies lost their place in political discourse, chiefly because antiquarians had cast doubt on their origins. In the early modern period, prophecies retained credibility because they drew upon a legitimate theological tradition and were attributed to venerated ancient figures. The persistence of political prophecy demonstrates sustained faith in supernatural inspiration.

The final chapter to discuss here is Felicity Loughlin's 'The pagan supernatural in the Scottish Enlightenment' (Chapter 12), which examines how eighteenth-century thinkers engaged with ancient pagan concepts of the supernatural. Loughlin focuses in particular on discussions about pagan oracles, gods and the afterlife. In the case of the oracles, she traces a changing interpretative trajectory. In the late seventeenth and early eighteenth centuries, intellectuals often interpreted the oracles as demonic, and used them to prove the reality of the world of spirits. This altered around the mid-eighteenth century: it became usual to understand the oracles in naturalistic terms, as human impostures. As a result, the oracles disappeared from scholarly discussions of the supernatural realm.

However, eighteenth-century thinkers continued to take an interest in pagan conceptions of gods and the afterlife. The orthodox Christian view was that pagans had not enjoyed divine revelation, so their ideas about the supernatural were relevant to an important eighteenth-century question: could humans ascertain religious truths through reason alone, or was revelation necessary? The possibility that religion could be founded on reason was a radical argument associated with deists; most Scottish Enlightenment thinkers opposed it and stressed the necessity of revelation. Incorrect pagan supernaturalism thus became a way to vindicate correct Christian supernaturalism. The supernatural was discussed in carefully regulated ways, but forces beyond nature remained crucially important in teaching humankind about how the world worked.

> The revells ended she put off
>   Because her grace was warm
> She fan'd her with a Ladyes scoff
>   And so she catch'd no harm.

In this anticlimactic way, the fairy poem concludes. For sixty-two lines the fairies have prepared for a party. The sixty-third line tells us merely that with the revels over, the fairy queen undresses. The grand event itself remains hidden, a matter for the reader's speculation. In exploring the early modern Scottish supernatural, we are perpetually faced with omissions of this sort. Written accounts offer blinkered views, being tailored to satisfy particular agendas or to accord with religious orthodoxy. Nevertheless, the surviving material shows that early modern Scottish discourses on the supernatural ranged widely. The boundaries between natural and supernatural, or orthodox and unorthodox, were in continual flux. The supernatural consistently provided Scots with a way of understanding topics including the natural environment, physical and emotional well-being, current events and visions of the past and future. In exploring the early modern supernatural, this book has much to reveal about how early modern men and women thought about, debated and experienced the world around them.

Notes

1 The earliest version of this poem, c.1626, has been attributed to the English poet Simeon Steward. The Scottish version quoted here, with substantial alterations and additions, was recorded in a notebook by Alexander Robertson, Episcopalian minister of Fortingall, in the 1690s; he also produced

a Latin translation. See St Andrews University Library, MS 36225, notebook of Alexander Robertson, 1676–93, pp. 107–11. A similar Scottish version was seemingly set down in the late seventeenth century by the Edinburgh physician Archibald Pitcairne, who apparently produced Latin translations of his own, and his versions were subsequently published. See *A Description of the King and Queene of Fayries, Their Habit, Fare, Their Abode, Pompe, and State* (London, 1634; Rosenbach Museum and Library, Philadelphia, STC2 21512.5), pp. 1–3, reproduced in editorial notes to Archibald Pitcairne, *The Latin Poems*, ed. John MacQueen and Winifred MacQueen (Assen: Royal van Gorcum, 2009), pp. 447–8. One version is Walter Dennestone [Archibald Pitcairne?], *ΜΟΡΜΟΝΟ-ΣΤΟΑΙΣΜΟS sive Lamiarum Vestitus* ([Edinburgh?], 1691), reproduced in Pitcairne, *The Latin Poems*, pp. 276–88; another version is [Archibald Pitcairne?], *A Poem on the King and Queen of Fairy* (London, [1670?]), reproduced in James Watson, *Choice Collection of Comic and Serious Scots Poems*, ed. Harriet Harvey Wood, 2 vols (Woodbridge: STS, 1977–91 [1706–11]), II, pp. 91–7.
2 Euan Cameron, *Enchanted Europe: Superstition, Reason, and Religion, 1250–1750* (Oxford: Oxford University Press, 2010). This work, like many others in the field, is indebted to Stuart Clark, *Thinking with Demons: The Idea of Witchcraft in Early Modern Europe* (Oxford: Clarendon, 1997).
3 Brian P. Levack, *The Devil Within: Possession and Exorcism in the Christian West* (New Haven, CT: Yale University Press, 2013); Clare Copeland and Jan Machielsen (eds), *Angels of Light? Sanctity and the Discernment of Spirits in the Early Modern Period* (Leiden: Brill, 2012); Helen Parish (ed.), *Superstition and Magic in Early Modern Europe: A Reader* (London: Bloomsbury, 2015); Jennifer Spinks and Dagmar Eichberger (eds), *Religion, the Supernatural and Visual Culture in Early Modern Europe* (Leiden: Brill, 2015); Michelle D. Brock, Richard Raiswell and David R. Winter (eds), *Knowing Demons, Knowing Spirits in the Early Modern Period* (Basingstoke: Palgrave Macmillan, 2018).
4 Julian Goodare, *The European Witch-Hunt* (London: Routledge, 2016), ch. 5.
5 Edward Bever, *The Realities of Witchcraft and Popular Magic in Early Modern Europe: Culture, Cognition and Everyday Life* (Basingstoke: Palgrave Macmillan, 2008).
6 Keith Thomas, *Religion and the Decline of Magic: Studies in Popular Beliefs in Sixteenth- and Seventeenth-Century England* (London: Weidenfeld & Nicolson, 1971).
7 To give just a few examples, James Sharpe, *Instruments of Darkness: Witchcraft in England, 1550–1750* (London: Hamish Hamilton, 1996); Malcolm Gaskill, *Witchfinders: A Seventeenth-Century English Tragedy* (Cambridge, MA: Harvard University Press, 2007); Jonathan Barry, *Witchcraft and Demonology in South-West England, 1640–1789* (Basingstoke: Palgrave Macmillan, 2012); Alexandra Walsham, *Providence in Early Modern England* (Oxford: Oxford University Press, 1999); Darren Oldridge, *The Devil in Early Modern England* (Stroud: Sutton, 2000); Nathan Johnstone, *The Devil and Demonism in Early Modern England* (Cambridge: Cambridge University Press, 2006); Owen Davies, *Popular Magic: Cunning-Folk in English History* (London: Hambledon Continuum, 2007); Sasha Handley, *Visions of an Unseen World: Ghost Beliefs and Ghost Stories in Eighteenth-Century England*

(London: Pickering & Chatto, 2007); Laura Sangha, *Angels and Belief in England, 1480–1700* (London: Pickering & Chatto, 2012).
8 Thomas, *Religion and the Decline of Magic*, ch. 22.
9 Darren Oldridge, *The Supernatural in Tudor and Stuart England* (London: Routledge, 2016), esp. pp. 153–6 (quotation at p. 155).
10 Walsham, *Providence in Early Modern England*, pp. 333–4; William E. Burns, *An Age of Wonders: Prodigies, Politics and Providence in England, 1657–1727* (Manchester: Manchester University Press, 2002), ch. 6 and conclusion.
11 James Sharpe, 'Witch-hunting and witch historiography: some Anglo-Scottish comparisons', in Julian Goodare (ed.), *The Scottish Witch-Hunt in Context* (Manchester: Manchester University Press, 2002), pp. 182–97, at p. 182.
12 Useful studies include Michael Lynch, 'Preaching to the converted? Perspectives on the Scottish Reformation', in A. A. MacDonald, Michael Lynch and Ian B. Cowan (eds), *The Renaissance in Scotland: Studies in Literature, Religion, History and Culture Offered to John Durkan* (Leiden: Brill, 1994), pp. 301–43; Julian Goodare, 'Scotland', in Bob Scribner, Roy Porter and Mikuláš Teich (eds), *The Reformation in National Context* (Cambridge: Cambridge University Press, 1994), pp. 95–110; Margo Todd, *The Culture of Protestantism in Early Modern Scotland* (New Haven, CT: Yale University Press, 2002); Jane E. A. Dawson, *Scotland Re-formed, 1488–1587* (Edinburgh: Edinburgh University Press, 2007); John McCallum (ed.), *Scotland's Long Reformation: New Perspectives on Scottish Religion, c.1500–c.1660* (Leiden: Brill, 2016).
13 Christina Larner, *Enemies of God: The Witch-Hunt in Scotland* (London: Chatto & Windus, 1981); Goodare, *The Scottish Witch-Hunt in Context*; Julian Goodare, Lauren Martin and Joyce Miller (eds), *Witchcraft and Belief in Early Modern Scotland* (Basingstoke: Palgrave Macmillan, 2008); Brian P. Levack, *Witch-Hunting in Scotland: Law, Politics and Religion* (Abingdon: Routledge, 2008); Julian Goodare (ed.), *Scottish Witches and Witch-Hunters* (Basingstoke: Palgrave Macmillan, 2013).
14 Lizanne Henderson and Edward J. Cowan, *Scottish Fairy Belief: A History* (East Linton: Tuckwell, 2001); Michael Hunter (ed.), *The Occult Laboratory: Magic, Science, and Second Sight in Late Seventeenth-Century Scotland* (Woodbridge: Boydell, 2001); Michelle D. Brock, *Satan and the Scots: The Devil in Post-Reformation Scotland, c.1560–1700* (London: Routledge, 2016); Lizanne Henderson, *Witchcraft and Folk Belief in the Age of Enlightenment: Scotland, 1670–1740* (Basingstoke: Palgrave Macmillan, 2016); Martha McGill, *Ghosts in Enlightenment Scotland* (Woodbridge: Boydell, 2018).
15 Lizanne Henderson (ed.), *Fantastical Imaginations: The Supernatural in Scottish History and Culture* (Edinburgh: John Donald, 2009).
16 Clark, *Thinking with Demons*, esp. ch. 10.
17 James VI, *Daemonologie*, in his *Minor Prose Works*, ed. James Craigie (Edinburgh: STS, 1982), pp. 1–56, at p. 48 (bk 3, ch. 3).
18 Peter Lamont, *Extraordinary Beliefs: A Historical Approach to a Psychological Problem* (Cambridge: Cambridge University Press, 2013), pp. 223–4 and *passim*.

19 Christopher C. French and Anna Stone, *Anomalistic Psychology: Exploring Paranormal Belief and Experience* (Basingstoke: Palgrave Macmillan, 2014), pp. 7–9.
20 Cf. Tea Krulos, 'Cryptozoology: the hunt for hidden animals and monsters', in Dennis Waskul and Marc Eaton (eds), *The Supernatural in Society, Culture, and History* (Philadelphia, PA: Temple University Press, 2018), pp. 190–209.
21 Alasdair M. Stewart, 'Hector Boece and "claik" geese', *Northern Scotland*, 8 (1988), 17–23, at p. 18.
22 *Ibid.*
23 Hector Boece, *Scotorum Historiae a Prima Gentis Origine* (Paris, 1527), 'Scotorum Regni Descriptio', fo. xv^r.
24 Matthew Cobb, *The Egg and Sperm Race: The Seventeenth-Century Scientists Who Unraveled the Secrets of Sex, Life, and Growth* (London: Free Press, 2006), ch. 3.
25 Richard Baxter, *The Certainty of the Worlds of Spirits, and Consequently, of the Immortality of Souls, of the Malice and Misery of the Devils and the Damned* (London, 1691), pp. 83–4, 89 (original emphasis). For the Loudun nuns see Levack, *The Devil Within*, e.g. pp. 3–4, 6–8.
26 William Cobbett, T. B. Howell and T. J. Howell, *Cobbett's Complete Collection of State Trials and Proceedings for High Treason*, 34 vols (London: R. Bagshaw, 1809–26), XI, no. 354, cols 1371–420, esp. 1376–7, 1380, 1387, 1402–3, 1409, 1417 (quotations at cols 1376, 1380, 1417).
27 Wilfred Cantwell Smith, *Belief and History* (Charlottesville: University of Virginia Press, 1977), pp. 41–8 (quotation at p. 44).
28 Jeanne Favret-Saada, *Deadly Words: Witchcraft in the Bocage*, trans. Catherine Cullen (Cambridge: Cambridge University Press, 1980 [original French ed. 1977]). For a useful introduction to anthropological debates on the issue of 'belief', see Byron J. Good, *Medicine, Rationality and Experience: An Anthropological Perspective* (Cambridge: Cambridge University Press, 1993), ch. 1.
29 Martin Martin, *A Description of the Western Isles of Scotland* (London, 1703), pp. 28–9.
30 Smith, *Belief and History*, pp. 58–67 (quotation at p. 65).
31 J. L. Campbell and Derick Thomson, *Edward Lhuyd in the Scottish Highlands, 1699–1700* (Oxford: Clarendon, 1963), p. 56. Quotations from Lhuyd are the editors' translations from the Welsh language in which he recorded his notes.
32 *Ibid.*, p. 67.
33 For a recent exception see A. A. MacDonald, *George Lauder (1603–1670): Life and Writings* (Cambridge: D. S. Brewer, 2018). Lauder did not write about the supernatural, however.
34 Julian Goodare, 'Fantasy and humour in Scottish witchcraft literature', *Bottle Imp*, 24 (2018), www.thebottleimp.org.uk/2018/12/fantasy-and-humour-in-scottish-witchcraft-literature (accessed 1 June 2020).
35 'The Devil's elixir', *Blackwood's Edinburgh Magazine*, July 1824, 55–67, at p. 56.
36 Sir David Lindsay of the Mount, *Works*, ed. Douglas Hamer, 4 vols (Edinburgh: STS, 1931–36), 'Ane Dialog betwix Experience and ane Courteour', I, p. 364, lines 5588, 5594.

37 For examples and discussion, see Simon During, *Modern Enchantments* (Cambridge, MA: Harvard University Press, 2002); Gordon Graham, *The Re-Enchantment of the World: Art versus Religion* (Oxford: Oxford University Press, 2007); Joshua Landy and Michael Saler (eds), *The Re-Enchantment of the World: Secular Magic in a Rational Age* (Palo Alto, CA: Stanford University Press, 2009); Allison P. Coudert, 'Rethinking Max Weber's theory of disenchantment', in Albrecht Classen (ed.), *Magic and Magicians in the Middle Ages and the Early Modern Time: The Occult in Pre-Modern Sciences, Medicine, Literature, Religion, and Astrology* (Berlin: De Gruyter, 2017), pp. 705–39; Michael Saler, 'Modernity and enchantment: a historiographic review', *American Historical Review*, 111 (2006), 692–716.

38 Max Weber, 'Science as a vocation', in H. H. Gerth and C. Wright Mills (eds), *From Max Weber: Essays in Sociology* (New York: Oxford University Press, 1946), p. 139; Max Weber, *The Protestant Ethic and the Spirit of Capitalism*, trans. Talcott Parsons (London: Routledge, 1992 [1930]), p. 61.

39 Michael Wasser, 'The mechanical world-view and the decline of witch-beliefs in Scotland', in Goodare *et al.*, *Witchcraft and Belief*, pp. 206–26.

40 Michael D. Bailey, 'The disenchantment of magic: spells, charms, and superstition in early European witchcraft literature', *American Historical Review*, 111 (2006), 383–404.

41 Robert W. Scribner, 'The Reformation, popular magic, and the "disenchantment of the world"', *Journal of Interdisciplinary History*, 23 (1993), 475–94.

42 Alexandra Walsham, 'The Reformation and "the disenchantment of the world" reassessed', *Historical Journal*, 51 (2008), 497–528.

43 Cameron, *Enchanted Europe*, pp. 10–14, 247–85 (quotations at p. 13). We regret that publication schedules did not allow us to engage with the most recent contribution to this debate: Michael Hunter's insightful *The Decline of Magic: Britain in the Enlightenment* (New Haven, CT: Yale University Press, 2020). Hunter reasserts the idea that there was a decline of magic and locates it around the second quarter of the eighteenth century. He makes a compelling case that rising scepticism about magic owed more to the influence of humanist freethinking than to scientific developments.

2

The elrich poems: the supernatural and the textual

Janet Hadley Williams

Literature in Older Scots includes a group of poems, mostly anonymous, that employs supernatural phenomena for burlesque or satiric purposes. Aptly called 'elrich fantasyis',[1] they include Roule's 'Devyne poware of michtis maist', *The Gyre Carling*, 'My gudame wes a gay wyf', 'God and Sanct Petir', 'The Crying of ane Playe', Lichtoun's 'Quha doutis dremis is bot phantasye?' and *Lord Fergus Gaist*.[2] In their 'comic supernaturalism'[3] and inventive mixed reference to popular traditions, romances, classical literature, magic, witchcraft and church ritual, the poems have much to interest those concerned to document and explain beliefs and cultural attitudes in early modern Scotland.[4] Yet our understanding is hampered in various ways. Little is known of the poems' authors, beyond their undoubted imaginative and poetic skills. Even less is known of the poems' textual difficulties. Only a few scholars have paid close attention to these fantasies;[5] their challenges remain hidden.

Textual matters thus are the focus of this chapter, but it is useful to look first at the term used to describe this type of writing, *elrich*. To the authors of the fantasies and their contemporaries, the word had many shades of meaning. Things 'elrich' could be 'connected with, proceeding from, suggestive of, elves or supernatural beings', such as incubi, or the king and queen of fary. They could also be 'weird, strange, or uncanny'.[6] What was elrich was above all 'other-worldly'.[7]

Use of the word could change an everyday creature, place or item into something apart. In some poems, the result is disorienting, strange, yet often also comic.[8] Lichtoun's 'Quha doutis dremis is bot phantasye?', for example, plays with the scholarly interest of the times in the causes and types of dreams and visions and in their roles in the interpretation of the past and future.[9] The poem opens with the dreamer-narrator recalling his state of ecstasy after his 'spreit was reft' (2) and his wits had left him (4). Seemingly visionary incidents occur without preamble or logic.

One such is an encounter with a pound keeper and his herd on a misty morning. The narrator awakens in a bed of mint to the sound of the pound keeper's 'elrich horne' (58). As if in response, three white whales appear in a green meadow beside the dreamer. Immense, man-eating creatures, they are tethered, impossibly, by grasshoppers' hair (59–61). Wearing a coat of ant skins, and equipped with a club made from a board from Noah's Ark, the keeper drives the herd of whales into a clearing, where one of them swallows him (77–8). Later, after harvest time, when the 'hirdis [shepherds] draif thame hame' (80), one whale threatens to swallow the narrator. He flees in alarm, only to fall and then awaken to a rawly amusing yet comforting reality, 'in ane henslaik [hen's dust bath]' (85), 'betuix ane picher and the wall' (86).

'My gudame wes a gay wyf' offers another instance of an other world that is strange yet familiar. Again, the narrative is disorienting, but the humorous aspect is uppermost. Said to have died of thirst, Kittok sets off confidently to Heaven. On her way she wanders off the highway, and arrives at 'ane elriche well' (8). In folklore, wells could be 'points of contact between the [known] world and settings for supernatural adventures'.[10] Here, too, in this story about the narrator's grandmother, the elrich well is a signal that she has passed into a strange other world, where anything can happen and nothing is verifiable. Thus Kittok meets everyday creatures there, a newt and a snail, but they are in a bemusing configuration, the first riding on the second. Even more fantastically, the gudame hails them and, it is stated, until evening 'raid ane inche behind the taill' (12). The question of 'which tail?' arises. The larger creature is sitting on the smaller. When, furthermore, the sense of 'behind' is considered closely, the conclusion must be that if Kittok is an inch behind the tail, either tail, she is not mounted at all. To travel with the two creatures, she can employ nothing but the slippery silvery mucus of the snail trail. The following aside, 'Sa scho had hap to be horsit [conveyed] to hir herbry' (14) draws attention to the absurdity. The status of the 'ailhous neir hevin' (15), where the three spend the night, is similarly vague, and Kittok's entry to Heaven is so irregular that God himself laughs.

Use of the word *elrich* also could be linked to matters of fear and superstition, often in opposition or response to then-orthodox religious beliefs. In *Sir Colling the Knycht*, it is the 'alreche svord' (134, 187), won in battle from the 'alreche knycht' (96, 102),[11] that equips the 'kirsin [Christian]' (10) Sir Colin to defeat the dark power of a three-headed giant (152–5).[12] In the prologue to Book VI of his translation of Virgil's *Aeneid* (1513), Gavin Douglas imagines a detractor who sees Virgil simply as pagan, his work 'ful of leys and ald ydolatryis', of 'gaistis and elrich fantasyis'; who condemns those paying heed to 'browneis' and 'bogillis' as 'mangit [misguided]', influenced by 'dremys or dotage in the monys cruke [waning moon], / Vayn superstitionys aganyst our richt beleve' (6 Prol. 10, 17, 18–22).[13] This person uses 'elrich' to signal a deep suspicion of 'hyd sentence' (13) and of experience beyond the known, the rational or approved Christian belief.

The dark comedy of some elrich fantasies exploits this fear of the other and of its demonic origins. Roule's 'Devyne poware of mychtis maist', for example, is a mock excommunication of thieves who stole 'fyve fat geis' with 'capounis, hennis, and uther foulis' (13–14). Because the poem draws on the language and form of an actual cursing, in which a person could be condemned, terrifyingly, to suffer 'all the plagis and pestilence that ever fell on man or beist',[14] the tone and subject matter (horrifying illnesses, attacks by devils in hellish surroundings) of this parodic excommunication is frequently deeply alarming as well as derisively comic.

Fear is also present, but less overtly, in *Lord Fergus Gaist*. It is concerned mainly with conjuring a spirit, a ritual performed in real life by those clergy considered qualified to do it. Such rites, Richard Kieckhefer notes,[15] were used when a spirit was thought to be in pain or troubled, but the ghost of Fergus is irritating and meddlesome. He clucks 'lyk a corne myll' (81) and steals from Abraham both his 'quhorle [spindle fly wheel]' and 'quhum quham [trifling ornament]' (75). The speaker-practitioner, boasting of his learning, exposes his ignorance: the books he mentions are two school texts (12). His list of ingredients for the conjuring spell includes those that are comic, such as 'tod tailis ten thraif [stooks]' (18). These and other details establish that the poem is a spoof, yet the accompanying instructions cause unease: many of them, such as the casting of 'the grit haly watter' (19) and the incantatory words to be spoken to the spirit to discover whether it is of God's law or the Devil's (48–60), parody real religious ritual. A darker undertow thus remains, despite the humorous 'patter patter' (20) of pseudo-erudition, of the surreally persistent presence of the ghost, his marriage to 'the Spenyie fle' (87) and the mention of their unlikely progeny, 'Orpheus king and Elpha quene' (93). Teasingly, this last startling twist takes the poem into another supernatural world just as it concludes.

Such oppositions of comic disorientation and a darker, threatening humour are far from clear-cut, as the *The Gyre Carling* demonstrates. This poem (of which more later) is at one level a romance parody, telling of the courtship of the gyre carling, a giant witch. Her would-be lover is so enamoured of her 'lawchand lippis' (6) that he gathers an army of moles to besiege her tower, although the use of this burrowing animal with poor vision humorously signals limited success with siege weaponry. On another level, however, the poem is a dark battle between two supernatural powers, the 'devilische deme [lady]' (27) and the king of fary, in which the gyre carling, by the use of trickery and demonic magic, is the victor.

For soundly based study, it is worth remembering that, from small clues within them, the fantasies are thought to have been composed during the later 1400s and early 1500s.[16] No authorial manuscripts are known to survive; the poems have come down to us chiefly in two anthologies compiled much later, the Bannatyne Manuscript (B), completed by 1568, and the Maitland Folio Manuscript (MF), by 1586.[17] Written in 'time of Papistrie and blindenesse',[18] or, in less emotive terms, during the reigns of James IV (1489–1513) and James V (1513–42), the fantasies have become linked by their context to the last years of Mary's reign and most of James VI's Scottish reign (1567–1603).

Like most extant remnants of late medieval Scottish poetry, the elrich poems have suffered textual degradation. For them, however, the difficulties created by what might be called time-slip – the survival in late manuscript miscellanies of these pre-Reformation works – have been compounded by their distinct linguistic originality, impossible juxtapositions and tricky subject matter of other worlds and beings, engaging in activities as difficult to pin down as shape-shifting and magical trickery. When, for instance, the narrator of 'Quha doutis dremis is bot fantasye?' can mend his hurt head in such amusingly novel ways as drinking from a well dry for seven years and leaping three times, it becomes more difficult to weigh the evidence relating to the cause of his injury. Did he fall on the 'kirne [churn]' of cream (20), as in the MF version of the poem, or the 'know [hillock]' of cream as in B? Adoption of B's version, it could be argued, would admit the possibility of parodic allusion, the hillock of cream understood as a reference to the 'fairy hills' recorded in other literary and ethnographical contexts.[19] The MF's churn, by contrast, would make sense, yet in doing so would clash with the poem's 'impossibilities' elsewhere. Which of these late textual differences is closer to the now-lost original poem's use of supernatural elements remains problematic.

Some effects of time-slip can be traced more precisely in those fantasies where it is possible to examine what later scribes changed when the words or usages they copied were to them unintelligible, old-fashioned or unacceptable to Protestants. Scholars in more recent times, consulting those altered later versions, can be led to false conclusions about the references to the supernatural. The effects are readily evident in the few instances where an elrich poem has survived not only as a text in a late miscellany, but in an early one as well, allowing changes to be compared. One instance where the composition date of the poem is close to that of the compilation date of the manuscript containing it, is *The Maner of the Crying of ane Play*, c.1512–15,[20] preserved in the Asloan Manuscript of c.1515–25.[21]

The Asloan text opens with the cry, 'harry harry hobillschowe'. By the time of B this has become 'Hiry hary hubbilschow'. Some scholars, referring only to this later text, assume that the words refer to a person, 'hary Hubbilschow'. They link this man to the mention of 'blynd hary' (10) a few lines on, and see him as either the poem's author or the Crier, someone who can assume many forms, including that of writer, Blind Harry.[22] For these scholars, the supposed Hary's arrival '[w]ith the quhorle wynd' (4) is a sign that he belongs with those supernatural creatures who often travelled in eddies and whirlwinds,[23] but recourse to the earlier Asloan text corrects these impressions. There, the opening words, 'harry harry', denote rapid movement, and the following word, 'hobbillschowe', a state of 'confused uproar'.[24] The sense becomes clear: somewhat like today's flash mobs, the enigmatic Crier arrives with a sudden commotion of action and sounds to draw attention to his presence among those who also happen to be at Edinburgh's Market Cross – 'Se quha is cummyn nowe' (2). Only then does he begin his entertaining elrich 'Crying'.

More often, elrich texts survive in late miscellanies only. Disentangling sense and interpreting the role of the supernatural become more challenging. The descriptions of devils' chins or beards, as preserved in the two late texts of Roule's 'Devyne poware of michtis maist', are both confusing. Without the help of an earlier, or less corrupt, text, neither 'bludy dungis' (B, 200) nor 'blaudis of longis' (MF, 220) can add reliably to the store of information about such demonic figures.[25] Source texts available to the copyists might have been imperfect, or careless copying could be to blame, as seems to be the case for *The Gyre Carling*. The only known text, in B, records how the giant ogress of the title threatens to use 'a fals cast' (30) to carry away North Berwick Law. The next line, which should have told more of this magic, does not follow. The incomplete couplet in this distinctive thirteen-line alliterative stanza betrays a missing piece that can only be returned, inadequately, by conjecture. At any stage, flawed transmission can impede understanding.

It is possible to tease out evidence of a different kind of alteration to some elrich poems – omissions that are deliberate – and to observe how these are linked in various ways to the times or events contemporaneous with the late manuscripts in which they are found. In the MF's longer version of 'Devyne poware', copied in the 1580s, the inclusive list of diseases and unpleasant medical conditions that is part of the curse culminates in 'elf schot' (68).[26] This sudden stabbing pain, in either cattle or men, had long been known.[27] A late tenth-century metrical charm to alleviate the affliction associates the delivery of the pain with the *hægtessan*, variously translated as 'witch wives',[28] 'mighty women'[29] and 'not human witches but powerful and malevolent supernatural females'.[30] The charm recognises elf-shot's malign magic, and the existence of supernatural powers and beings thought to be responsible for it, then counters them with a pre-Reformation piety, as the end, 'May the Lord help you', shows.[31] By placing 'elf schot' at the climax of the curse-list of diseases, the author of 'Devyne poware' shows an understanding of the power of these associations. That understanding is borne out by the references to 'elf schot' in witch trials held only slightly later, which associate it with the Devil and treat it as the work of human witches.³² Bannatyne, however, copying his version of the poem in the later 1560s just after the Witchcraft Act of 1563 had criminalised 'witchcraftis, sorsarie and necromancie',³³ ended that section of the poem a few lines earlier, with the unpleasant, but more common, ailments, 'The kanker and the kattair' (66). His striking omission of 'elf schot' is an example of textual interference as response to contemporary events.

Bannatyne's version of 'Devyne poware' contains further, more direct, evidence of a reaction to religious change.³⁴ Whereas the conservative MF's text refers to the possibility of forgiveness for the confessed sinner, of a person '[t]hat will schryf thame with thair curat' (85), the line in B is rearranged to omit 'shryf', in accord with the Reformist removal of penance from among the sacraments.³⁵ Later in the B text, the thieves are described as 'wickit' (177), not 'cursit', as in MF (193). The additional details of punishments in the latter version, 'Quhair with the dewill Jakkis and Jokkis / Salbe bordourit and buttonit als, / In sing that thai war menswore and fals' (196–8),³⁶ are deleted. With those reworkings, Bannatyne has reduced both the old church's role, and the severity of the thieves' condemnation. Viewed together, these changes argue that the scribe of MF's version either copied an older text than B's, or (the distance of another twenty years lessening the urgency for Protestantisation) copied more faithfully the text that both had. The poem version of most interest to historians or literarians thus might differ.³⁷

More oblique responses to the changed times, which alter the role of the supernatural, are discoverable when the Asloan manuscript's *Crying of ane Play* is compared with the later Bannatyne's, where the title is *Ane litill Interlud of the droichis* [dwarf's] *pairt of the play* (fos 11ᵛ–12ʳ).³⁸ Whether or not this title alludes ironically to the Crier's claims of descent from giants, the greater emphasis placed on the dwarf's 'pairt', as that of an actor, associates the figure with court entertainments rather than with a supernatural other world.³⁹ In the same way, the use of 'littill Interlude' emphasises the dramatic, while also suggesting that the lines are an excerpt from something larger.⁴⁰ The version in B is indeed shorter, shorn of the explicit references in the earlier Asloan text that tie the work to Edinburgh and its civic and mercantile interests, and identify it as advance publicity for a play associated with Robin Hood May games.⁴¹ Arguably, Bannatyne's generalising adjustments both fit the interlude for the 'mirry' section of his manuscript and reflect the impact of the Marian act of 1555 that prohibited participation in such festivities.⁴²

In the methodology employed and the predominant themes in the late manuscripts, other effects of time-slip are revealed. These offer glimpses of how the elrich poems were regarded by their later copyists and readers. In the MF, poems by Sir Richard Maitland (1496–1586), with a couple by his son, John (James VI's chancellor), and the many by William Dunbar form the greater part of the compilation, as far as can be established from the manuscript's disarranged state.[43] The emphases are thus on family piety, personal behaviour and aspects of court life.

The two elrich fantasies included in MF, Lichtoun's 'Quha doutis?' and Roule's 'Devyne poware', have been placed in a group of diverse works, including those by Dunbar, Lydgate, Douglas, Henryson, Stewart and the anonymous *Christis Kirk on the Grene* and *The Freiris of Berwik*. Within this group, Roule's poem is surrounded by moralising material; preceded by a poem made of proverbs, 'Mony man makis ryme and luikis to na ressoun', and followed by one of instruction, with the opening, 'My sone gif yow to the court will ga', and colophon, 'ffinis how the father teichit his sone'.[44] Between them, untitled, Roule's work also contributes to this manuscript's loose but persistent interest in how a man should live his life.

In this context in MF, Roule's first lines are deeply serious, intimidating the sinner by calling on the highest authorities to condemn, as in the real-life excommunication: 'Devyne poware of michtis maist / Of father, sone, and halie gaist'. Only later when the crime is announced – a bathetic revelation of the theft of 'fyve fat geis' and other poultry (13–14) – does the tone become blackly comic. Even then, there is uncertainty: similar crimes were taken seriously and were the subjects of near-contemporary legislation.[45] The vivid list of distinctive and named devils later in the poem continues this ambivalence, rivalling the threatening matter of actual cursings, encompassing every aspect of the sinner's life – 'sittand', 'eittand', 'drynkand', 'walkand', 'slepand', within and without the house and 'fra hayme'.[46]

Very different is the place of Roule's poem in Bannatyne's manuscript. After some false starts, the young merchant with literary interests completed his ambitious five-part project within a concentrated period, 'in tyme of pest' (fo. 375ʳ).[47] He placed Roule's poem with others, including several more elrich fantasies, in the part of the volume he called 'ballettis mirry and uther solatius consaittis [merry songs and comforting notions]'.[48] A reductive rubric, almost certainly added by Bannatyne himself, precedes the poem:[49] 'Heir followis the cursing of Schir Johine Rowlis / Upoun the steilaris of his fowlis'. There is an expectation of comedy in its easy allusion to cursing and a hint that one of the Catholic Church's most solemn procedures, which meant damnation when carried out, is no longer taken seriously in post-Reformation Scotland.[50]

Bannatyne's 'mirry' subtitle has had an observable influence on other elrich poems within this part. *Lord Fergus Gaist* illustrates. Its instructions for the conjuration, including the use of a magic circle; the burning (in a dog's ear) of specific, if often impossible, ingredients (the bottom of an old sieve, the tail of an infertile sow, 36, 39); the casting of holy water; incantations; and an ambivalent instruction ('with your left heill it sane [bless/kick?]', 65), are at odds with contemporary legislation condemning the 'havy and abominabill superstitioun' of those who use necromancy.[51]

Both the old church's sanction of these sometimes fraudulent practices and the inadequacies of those who carry them out are traditional anti-fraternal targets;[52] but the poem's place in the 'mirry' part of Bannatyne's late miscellany has enabled it to serve both comic and reformist ends.

So, too, the placing of *The Gyre Carling* in the 'mirry' part of B helps to ameliorate the poem's new relevance in post-Reformation Scotland. The giant ogress is opposed by the powerful 'king of fary' who comes with 'elffis mony ane' and 'all the doggis fra Dumbar ... to Dumblane' (14, 16)[53] to besiege her tower. In turn, the gyre carling uses her own supernatural skills to evade him. She bewitches the Haddington hens so that they will not lay, threatens the removal by magic of her earlier creation, North Berwick Law, then changes herself into a sow, crossing the 'Greik sie' (20) to marry Mahomyte. By that trickery she eludes the fary king and becomes 'quene of Jowis' (25). When *The Gyre Carling* was composed in the late 1400s, the eating of Christian flesh, Jewishness, the sow metamorphosis and Muhammed were all related to, or forms of, Antichrist.[54] By the later 1500s they were potentially also aligned with the witchcraft practices receiving new notice. Bannatyne's comic classification helps to emphasise the romance themes mentioned earlier, but he also distances himself from this group of 'mirry' poems, it is worth noting, by stating that they are 'set furth be divers ancient poyettis [composed by various poets of times long past]' (fo. 97r).

The late manuscript locations of the elrich fantasies have increased the potential for false relationships to be created between an assumed composition date and authorship, influencing the way in which the supernatural in these poems is interpreted. An elrich fantasy in B has the humorous prefacing couplet (again probably an addition of the compiler): 'How the first Helandman of god was maid / of Ane hors turd in argylle as is said'. It is followed by a poem titled 'Ane anser to ane helandmanis Invective / maid be alex[r] montgomry' (B, fo. 163r). This is one of the manuscript's later, undated, additions,[55] but proximity has encouraged the attribution of both poems to Montgomerie[56] and the assumption – an error – that like his datable work, and also possibly 'Ane anser to ane helandmanis Invective', the preceding elrich poem on the first Highlandman was composed in the 1580s or 1590s.[57] Although both poems make use of traditional stereotypes, only the latter uses the supernatural for humorous purposes. Writing at an earlier time, its author delights in the quick, fantastically impossible exchanges on earth between God, the saint and the newly created Highlandman (instantly a sinner, in parody of innocent Adam).[58] It is deeply unlike the Montgomerie-ascribed verse that flytes in a single voice and remains in an everyday world.[59] That poem's alliterative thirteen-line stanza is most deftly used to hurl abuse at a person named 'Finlay, son of Black Duncan MacFadyen', deriding his Highland clothing, diet, poverty, heritage, deceit and, above all, language,[60] this stance in keeping with Scottish government policies at the probable time of its composition.

In this instance it is worth keeping the distinction, blurred by the late manuscript locations, between Montgomerie's poems and those of the elrich poets, when considering the use of the supernatural. In the first invective of the *Flyting* (c.1580),[61] Montgomerie asserts that his opponent Polwart's work, unlike his own, is old-fashioned and unoriginal, borrowed from Lyndsay and Chaucer (45), but Montgomerie himself borrows from the literary past. In his narrative-invective of Polwart's monstrous birth and Fates' prophecies,[62] he responds with a list of ills and diseases that draws repeatedly on those in Roule's 'Devyne poware'. Later, describing Nicneven and her company, Montgomerie looks again to that earlier poem, borrowing details of the modes of transport adopted by Roule's 'Greit Baliall' (177) and his company.[63] Yet he puts these borrowings to new use. He does not mock the practice of excommunication, brought into disrepute by its use for trivial offences, which appears to be one of Roule's aims.[64] He does not set one fantasy world against another, even more terrible one, as Roule does when he speaks of 'feyndis phantesy', qualifying with, 'In court nocht with the quene of fary' (233–4). By linking Roule's disease and devil terms to prophecy, evil witchlore, witches and their dealings with fairyland, Montgomerie addresses preoccupations of his own time.[65]

It is not easy to draw useful conclusions from an examination of the textual aspects of these early elrich fantasies; the relationships between them and the later sixteenth-century manuscript miscellanies containing them are highly varied. Yet these interactions need to be considered if we are to understand the reception of the supernatural in early modern Scotland. Establishing, from these late versions, the texts that best represent the word choice and beliefs of their late fifteenth-century authors is almost impossible. What little can be traced of the poems' textual histories, especially of the scribal interventions – due to anything from an incomplete source, miscopying or deliberate additions and omissions because of new legislation or change in religious practice – is unfortunately patchy and, when it exists, not always clear. Unexpectedly, the findings focus attention on the late versions. Altered in various ways as they are, they yield valuable clues, signalling the need for caution, but assisting our understanding of attitudes to the supernatural in the later, not the earlier, sixteenth century.

Notes

1 See Priscilla Bawcutt, 'Elrich fantasyis in Dunbar and other poets', in J. Derrick McClure and Michael R. G. Spiller (eds), *Bryght Lanternis: Essays on the Language and Literature of Medieval and Renaissance Scotland*

(Aberdeen: Aberdeen University Press, 1989), pp. 162–78, at pp. 162–5; Priscilla Bawcutt, *Dunbar the Makar* (Oxford: Clarendon, 1992), pp. 257–61.

2 For texts, see Janet Hadley Williams (ed.), *'Duncane Laideus Testament' and other Comic Poems in Older Scots* (Edinburgh: STS, 2016); *The Asloan Manuscript*, ed. W. A. Craigie, 2 vols (Edinburgh: STS, 1923–25), II, pp. 149–54 ('The Crying'). For full discussion of Dunbar's contributions, and their differences (a 'dark and sinister' tone that only Roule's poem matches; greater attention to the shape of the narrative), see Bawcutt, *Dunbar the Makar*, pp. 260–92. Numbers in parentheses in the text of this chapter denote line numbers of the poems quoted.

3 C. S. Lewis, *English Literature in the Sixteenth Century, Excluding Drama* (Oxford: Oxford University Press, 1954), p. 71.

4 See, for example, J. A. MacCulloch, 'The mingling of fairy and witch beliefs in sixteenth and seventeenth century Scotland', *Folklore*, 32 (1921), 227–44; Lizanne Henderson and Edward J. Cowan, *Scottish Fairy Belief: A History* (East Linton: Tuckwell, 2001); Julian Goodare, Lauren Martin and Joyce Miller (eds), *Witchcraft and Belief in Early Modern Scotland* (Basingstoke: Palgrave Macmillan, 2008); and Julian Goodare, 'Boundaries of the fairy realm in Scotland', in Karin Olsen and Jan R. Veenstra (eds), *Airy Nothings: Imagining the Otherworld of Faerie from the Middle Ages to the Age of Reason: Essays in Honour of Alasdair A. MacDonald* (Leiden: Brill, 2013), pp. 139–69, at pp. 164–6.

5 See Bawcutt, 'Elrich fantasyis'; Bawcutt, *Dunbar the Makar*, pp. 257–92; Keely Fisher, 'Eldritch comic verse in Older Scots', in Sally Mapstone (ed.), *Older Scots Literature* (Edinburgh: John Donald, 2005), pp. 292–313; Janet Hadley Williams, 'James V, David Lyndsay, and the Bannatyne Manuscript poem of the Gyre Carling', *Studies in Scottish Literature*, 26 (1991), 164–71; Janet Hadley Williams, 'The "silken schakillis" of Lichtoun's Dream', *Journal of the Northern Renaissance*, 4 (2012), http://northernrenaissance.org (accessed 24 January 2013).

6 See *DOST*, s.v. *Elrich(e, elrage*, adj.

7 Alaric Hall, 'The etymology and meanings of *Eldritch*', *Scottish Language*, 26 (2007), 16–22.

8 Cf. Emily Lyle, *Fairies and Folk: Approaches to the Scottish Ballad Tradition* (Trier: Wissenschaftlicher Verlag, 2007), p. 1 (speaking of the ballad tradition): 'We have to retain a nuanced awareness of the operation of fiction even in a community where the boundary of what was regarded as fact differed from that of the present day.'

9 See Geoffrey Chaucer, *The Riverside Chaucer*, ed. Larry D. Benson (Oxford: Oxford University Press, 1987), notes, with references, to *The House of Fame*, pp. 977–8.

10 Juliette Wood, 'Lakes and wells: mediation between the worlds in Scottish folklore', in Dietrich Strauss and Horst W. Drescher (eds), *Scottish Language and Literature, Medieval and Renaissance: Fourth International Conference 1984 Proceedings* (Frankfurt am Main: Peter Lang, 1986), pp. 523–32, at p. 526.

11 See *DOST*, s.v. *Elrich(e*, wherein *Alreche* is recorded as a variant.

12 See Rhiannon Purdie (ed.), *Shorter Scottish Medieval Romances* (Woodbridge: STS, 2013), pp. 104–11, and the valuable editorial notes of Lyle, *Fairies and Folk*, pp. 84–109.

13 *Virgil's 'Æneid' Translated into Scottish Verse by Gavin Douglas*, ed. David F. C. Coldwell, 4 vols (Edinburgh: STS, 1957–64).
14 See *St Andrews Formulare, 1514–1546*, ed. Gordon Donaldson and C. Macrae, 2 vols (Edinburgh: Stair Society, 1942–44), I, no. 229, p. 270.
15 Richard Kieckhefer, *Magic in the Middle Ages* (Cambridge: Cambridge University Press, 1989), pp. 73–5.
16 See Hadley Williams, *Comic Poems*, pp. 4, 9, 13, 16, 18–19, 22, 25.
17 NLS, Adv. MS 1.1.6 (Bannatyne Manuscript); Cambridge, Magdalene College, Peypsian Library 2553 (Maitland Folio Manuscript). Other texts are scattered: Cambridge University Library, Ll.5.10 (Reidpeth Manuscript), contains a partial text of Roule, 'Devyne poware', fos 32^v–33^v; NLS, MS 16500 (Asloan Manuscript), contains the longer text of 'The maner of the crying of a playe', fos 240^r–242^v; the print of 'My gudame' is bound with the Chepman and Myllar prints: William Beattie, *The Chepman and Myllar Prints: Nine Tracts from the First Scottish Press, Edinburgh 1508: A Facsimile* (Edinburgh: Edinburgh Bibliographical Society, 1950), pp. 192–3.
18 See James VI, *Daemonologie*, in his *Minor Prose Works*, ed. James Craigie (Edinburgh: STS, 1982), pp. 1–56, at p. 45 (bk 3, ch. 2).
19 See, for instance, *Sir Colling the Knycht*, in Purdie, *Shorter Romances*, line 56; Michael Hunter (ed.), *The Occult Laboratory: Magic, Science and Second Sight in Late Seventeenth-Century Scotland* (Woodbridge: Boydell, 2001) p. 85.
20 This is established from internal evidence. See David Parkinson, 'The entry of Wealth in the Middle Scots "Crying of ane Playe"', *Modern Philology*, 93:1 (1995), 23–36; also Keely Fisher, 'The Crying of ane Playe: Robin Hood and maying in sixteenth-century Scotland', *Medieval and Renaissance Drama in England*, 12 (1999), 19–58, at pp. 19–20. For a differing view, see Henderson and Cowan, *Scottish Fairy Belief*, pp. 45, 49–50.
21 See Catherine van Buuren, 'John Asloan and his manuscript: an Edinburgh notary and scribe in the days of James III, IV and V (c.1470–c.1530)', in Janet Hadley Williams (ed.), *Stewart Style, 1513–1542* (East Linton: Tuckwell, 1996), pp. 15–51, at pp. 50–1.
22 See Henderson and Cowan, *Scottish Fairy Belief*, p. 49; Keely Fisher, 'Comic Verse in Older Scots' (DPhil thesis, University of Oxford, 1999), p. 143.
23 Fisher, 'Comic Verse', p. 143, who cites the testimony of Bessie Dunlop at her trial (1576); Robert Pitcairn (ed.), *Ancient Criminal Trials in Scotland*, 3 vols (Edinburgh: Bannatyne Club, 1833), I, part ii, p. 53.
24 See *DOST*, s.vv. *Hiry-hary*, interj. and *Hubbilschow, Hobillschowe*, n.
25 See *DOST*, s.vv. *Dung*, n.^{2} and *Blad, Blaud*, n.^{1}; *Lung, Long, Loung*, n. MF's collocation may be translated as 'fragments of lung'.
26 See *DOST*, s.vv. *Elf-Shot*, n., senses 1 and 2; *S(c)hot*, n.^{1}, senses 2 and 10; *OED*, s.v. *elf-shot*, n., referring to John Jamieson's *Etymological Dictionary of the Scottish Language*, 'Disease, supposed to be produced by the immediate agency of evil spirits'.
27 Alaric Hall, 'Getting shot of elves: healing, witchcraft and fairies in the Scottish witchcraft trials', *Folklore*, 116 (2005), 19–36; Alaric Hall, *Elves in Anglo-Saxon England: Matters of Belief, Health, Gender and Identity* (Woodbridge: Boydell, 2007), pp. 108–18; Jacqueline Simpson, 'On the ambiguity of elves', *Folklore*, 122 (2011), 76–83.

28 Elliott van Kirk Dobbie (ed.), *The Anglo-Saxon Minor Poems* (London: Routledge and Kegan Paul, 1942), pp. 122–3 (BL, MS Harley 585, 175ʳ–176ᵛ); *Leechdoms, Wortcunning and Starcraft of Early England*, ed. Thomas Oswald Cockayne, with a new intro. by Charles Singer, 3 vols, 1864–66; rev. ed. (London: Holland, 1961), III, pp. 52–5.
29 Hall, *Elves*, p. 2.
30 Simpson, 'Ambiguity of elves', p. 79.
31 See further, Priscilla Bawcutt, '"Holy words for healing": some early Scottish charms and their ancient religious roots', in Luuk Houwen (ed.), *Literature and Religion in Late Medieval and Early Modern Scotland: Essays in Honour of Alasdair A. MacDonald* (Leuven: Peeters, 2012), pp. 127–43, who notes that the use of charms for 'woundes or maladie of men or beestes' was tolerated by the church, because, as Chaucer's Parson acknowledges, with a good outcome God will receive 'the moore feith and reverence'; Chaucer, *Riverside Chaucer, Canterbury Tales*, X, pp. 609–14.
32 Henderson and Cowan, *Scottish Fairy Belief*, pp. 77–9, and related references.
33 *RPS*, A1563/6/1; and further, Julian Goodare, 'The Scottish witchcraft act', *Church History*, 74 (2005), 29–67.
34 On the topic of editorial intervention in response to religious change, see further A. A. MacDonald, 'Poetry, politics, and Reformation censorship in sixteenth-century Scotland', *English Studies*, 64 (1983), 410–21, especially pp. 416–20.
35 The Confession of Faith (1560), cap. xxi, in John Knox, *History of the Reformation in Scotland*, ed. William Croft Dickinson, 2 vols (London: Nelson, 1949), II, pp. 268–9 (Appendix VI); see also *DOST*, s.v. Schrive, Schrif(e, v.
36 'Where, with the devil, Jacks and Jocks / Shall be bound and also restrained, / In sign that they were guilty of perjury, and false.'
37 See further, Julia Boffey, 'The Maitland Folio Manuscript as a verse anthology', in Sally Mapstone (ed.), *William Dunbar, 'The Nobill Poyet': Essays in Honour of Priscilla Bawcutt* (East Linton: Tuckwell, 2001), pp. 40–50, at pp. 43–5.
38 Bannatyne's text is 136 lines; Asloan's 165 lines.
39 The use of dwarfs in court entertainments had a long tradition; cf. Richard Holland, *The Buke of the Howlat*, ed. Ralph Hanna (Woodbridge: STS, 2014), lines 649–50, recording that the 'littill we wran' took the part of the dwarf in the court procession of the emperor's bird retainers. Alternatively, since the words 'elves' and 'dwarves' were sometimes used interchangeably, see Ármann Jakobsson, 'Beware the elf! A note on the evolving meaning of *Álfar*', *Folklore*, 126 (2015), 215–23, at p. 216; Euan Cameron, *Enchanted Europe: Superstition, Reason, and Religion, 1250–1750* (Oxford: Oxford University Press, 2010), p. 268.
40 On Bannatyne's use of the word 'Interlude': Janet Hadley Williams, 'George Bannatyne's "sertane mirry interludis" and Sir David Lyndsay's play', *Medieval English Theatre*, 37 (2015), 27–40, at p. 29.
41 See lines 138–44, Asloan text. For overviews, see Anna Jean Mill, *Mediaeval Plays in Scotland* (Edinburgh: St Andrews University Publications, 1927), pp. 21–35; E. Patricia Dennison, 'Robin Hood in Scotland', in Julian Goodare and Alasdair A. MacDonald (eds), *Sixteenth-Century Scotland: Essays in Honour of Michael Lynch* (Leiden: Brill, 2008), pp. 169–88.

42 *RPS*, A1555/6/41.
43 See further, Priscilla Bawcutt, 'The earliest texts of Dunbar', in Felicity Riddy (ed.), *Regionalism in Late Medieval Manuscripts and Texts: Essays Celebrating the Publication of 'A Linguistic Atlas of Late Medieval English'* (Woodbridge: D. S. Brewer, 1991), pp. 183–98, at pp. 190–3; Boffey, 'The Maitland Folio Manuscript', pp. 40–50.
44 'Mony man' is on pp. 139–40; 'How the father' on pp. 148–52.
45 *RPS*, 1535/21, 'Off brekaris of yardis and orchartis'.
46 *St Andrews Formulare*, I, no. 229, p. 269.
47 See Bawcutt, 'The earliest texts', pp. 194–6.
48 See *The Bannatyne Manuscript: National Library of Scotland Advocates' MS 1.1.6.* [Facsimile], intro. Denton Fox and William A. Ringler (London: Scolar Press in association with The National Library of Scotland, 1980), pp. ix–xvii; fos 97^r–211^r.
49 The poem versions diverge in the last lines, which could serve as descriptive colophons or titles: Maitland Folio: 'Roullis conscience' (286); Bannatyne: 'Rowllis cursing' (266).
50 See further, Donaldson and Macrae, 'Introductory note', in *St Andrews Formulare*, I, p. xx; William Dunbar, *Poems*, ed. Priscilla Bawcutt, 2 vols (Glasgow: Association of Scottish Literary Studies, 1998), 'Doverrit with dreme' (B11), I, pp. 71–2.
51 On these, see further, Kieckhefer, *Magic in the Middle Ages*, pp. 151–75.
52 Penn R. Szittya, *The Antifraternal Tradition in Medieval Literature* (Princeton, NJ: Princeton University Press, 1986); *Colloquies: Collected Works of Erasmus*, trans. and annotated by Craig R. Thompson, vol. 39 (Toronto: Toronto University Press, 1997): 'Exorcism, or the spectre', pp. 531–44.
53 The dog, because of its reputation as a magic animal, was hated by the Jews; see Beryl Rowland, *Animals with Human Faces: A Guide to Animal Symbolism* (Knoxville: University of Tennessee Press, 1973), p. 59.
54 On 'Mahoun [Muhammed]' as the Devil, the Jew as evil, and the sow's links to lechery and evil bestiality, see Dunbar, *Poems*, 'Off Februar the fyiftene nycht' (B47), pp. 6, 27, 109, 145, 208, 227; *A Ballat of the Abbot of Tungland* (B4), pp. 1–8, 29–32; and 'Off Februar the fyiftene nycht' (B47), pp. 67–78; also Rowland, *Animals with Human Faces*, pp. 41–2, and R. K. Emmerson, *Antichrist in the Middle Ages* (Manchester: Manchester University Press, 1981). Note also the poem's opening line, a reference to the fourteenth-century epic English poem, *The Siege of Jerusalem*.
55 On these, see Fox and Ringler, 'Introduction', *Bannatyne Manuscript* [facsimile], p. xvi.
56 See further, Hadley Williams, *Comic Poems*, pp. 25–6. Reference to Argyll, where God and St Peter stroll, coupled with Polwart's gibe in the *Flyting* that Montgomerie spent part of his upbringing there, might also have been influential. Alexander Montgomerie, *Poems*, ed. David Parkinson, 2 vols (Edinburgh: STS, 2000), I, *Invective VIII*, pp. 5–8, 14.
57 Other poems attributed to him, from Bannatyne's draft manuscript: 'Robert [Alexander] montgomerie', 'Ane godlie ballat', pp. 49–50; 'montgumry', 'The first pshalme' [*sic*], p. 51; 'montgumry', 'The xxiii sphalme [*sic*] translait be him', pp. 51–2; and 'montgomery', 'Lyik as the dum solsequium', pp. 52–3.

58 The poem turns on a traditional joke: see Hadley Williams, *Comic Poems*, pp. 26–7.
59 The source of the title, like those mentioned earlier, is uncertain.
60 See David Murison, 'Linguistic relationships in medieval Scotland', in G. W. S. Barrow (ed.), *The Scottish Tradition: Essays in Honour of Ronald Gordon Cant* (Edinburgh: Scottish Academic Press, 1974), pp. 71–83, at pp. 79, 81; Margaret A. Mackay, 'The Alliterative Tradition in Middle Scots Verse' (PhD thesis, University of Edinburgh, 1975), pp. 489–91, for discussion and translation.
61 See Montgomerie, *Poems*, I, pp. 141–75.
62 On the 'weird sisters', see Jacqueline Simpson, '"The weird sisters wandering": burlesque witchery in Montgomerie's *Flyting*', *Folklore*, 106 (1995), 9–20, at p. 11.
63 Cf. for example, Roule, 'Devyne poware', pp. 42–66; Montgomerie, *Poems*, *Invective II*, pp. 62–74 (on which see further p. 8 in the same volume); Roule, pp. 177, 180; and Montgomerie, *Invective II*, p. 159.
64 See Knox's report of the sermon on cursing by Friar William Arth and the responses to it: Knox, *History*, I, pp. 15–16.
65 These were matters in which James VI was interested, and later publicly involved. See James VI, *Poems*, ed. James Craigie, 2 vols (Edinburgh: STS, 1955–58), I, p. 81; James VI, *Daemonologie*, pp. 6, 24–36.

3

Emotional relationships with spirit-guides in early modern Scotland

Julian Goodare

What would it feel like to be visited frequently by a companion from another world? Or even to be taken away to visit another world? In early modern Scotland, there is a good deal of evidence for visionaries who experienced relationships with spirits. These visionaries were ordinary people who had extraordinary experiences, and who often gained special powers as a result. Most of the visionaries, though not all, were women. Most of the spirits were fairies or ghosts. The ghosts were usually experienced as male, while the fairy queen was important to several visionaries. Fairies and ghosts were often related; several visionaries had a ghost as a main spirit-guide, but the ghost associated with fairies and introduced the visionary to fairyland.

Here I am particularly interested in the emotions that were involved in the relationship. What emotions did the human experient feel, or express, towards the supernatural spirit? And what emotions did the spirit feel, or express, towards the human experient? Answers to the latter question depend, of course, upon how the human experienced or understood the spirit's emotions. The story that we are told is about a relationship between two people – yet this remarkable relationship was enacted entirely within one person's head.

The other person in the relationship – the supernatural being – is therefore also remarkable. Historians, no matter how respectful we may wish to be towards the beliefs of the people we study, do not take supernatural beings to be autonomous historical actors. Yet the visionary encounters presented to us by the sources are not just 'stories' or 'folklore'. These encounters represent lived, felt experience for the human visionaries.

In a previous paper I have introduced 'visionaries' as a distinct category of people who experienced encounters with spirits.[1] The evidence mostly comes from witchcraft trials in which the interrogators assumed that they were dealing with a witch who had met the Devil, but it is clear that this is not how the visionaries themselves had experienced their relationship before their arrest. I outlined the modalities of the experience – people *saw*, *heard* and often *touched* the spirit, and conducted two-way discussions with it. I discussed power aspects of the relationship – the spirit-guide often exercised power over the visionary, sometimes in an unwelcome and abusive way, but also sharing their power with the visionary so as to enable the latter to become a magical practitioner. And I briefly outlined a connection with psychological studies of hallucinations and other visions.[2] In the present chapter I would like to use these findings as a starting-point for a further enquiry, focusing on a central question about the relationship. The human visionary and the spirit had an *emotional* engagement with each other. How did their emotional relationship work?

Explicit interest in emotions as a topic of study has begun only recently among historians. Other disciplines have been studying emotions for much longer, and historians have thus sought to draw on insights from these disciplines. The main disciplines drawn on so far have been anthropology and psychology.[3] In addition, sociology has something to offer, as will be seen in what follows. Psychology is particularly useful for the present enquiry. History is a social science, while some psychology focuses more on the interior state of the individual.[4] These interior states are not readily accessible to historians, who tend to focus on social interactions and social structures.

As has become usual, I study emotions in a flexible and pragmatic way, rather than insisting on an exclusive and definite list of emotions. I generally use a mainstream 'appraisal' theory of emotions: thus an emotion is something that you feel and express in response to a situation that you are appraising. By contrast, if you are happy or sad in an empty room, that is a mood, not an emotion. The historical evidence usually gives us emotions rather than moods, in that the evidence tends to record events – expressions of emotion in situations. Some psychologists study emotions in non-social situations – a much-discussed example concerns the person on a remote hillside who suddenly encounters a snake;[5] but historians study *social* situations, in which the 'appraisal' of the situation involves the person in reacting to their relationships with other people.

Some of the most ambitious and influential historians of emotion have sought to study expressions of emotions, or even of a specific emotion, throughout a given society. The *emotion itself* is the object of study. These historians have thus sought out evidence for their chosen emotions in a variety of social contexts. Some have even addressed questions of how specific emotions change as society changes, sometimes over long periods of time, or have argued for changing emotional regimes as motors for broader historical change.[6] My approach in this chapter is less ambitious, at least as regards the 'history of emotions' as a discrete topic. My sources do not lend themselves to the study of emotional change over time, nor do they usually go into detail about how the emotions were articulated. Nor am I studying *emotions themselves* throughout early modern society; I am studying visionaries and their social context, of which their emotions form only a part.

What I can do with my sources, however, is to take the study of emotions in a fresh social and psychological direction. Many of the situations that my visionaries were 'appraising' did not directly involve other *people*; they involved *spirits* that were regarded both as like people and as unlike them. And hardly any of the emotions in this chapter were 'expressed' at all, at least as that term is usually understood. Instead the visionaries experienced the emotions – both their own emotions and the emotions of their spirit-guide – as part of an interior process of fantasising and self-discovery. The issue of fantasy deserves fuller treatment than it can receive here, but psychologists recognise that some people are 'fantasy-prone' and live much of their lives in fantasy worlds that they experience vividly.[7] Although fantasies do not have to involve the supernatural, these visionaries all took their fantasies into other worlds. The emotional aspect of this process is hard to reconstruct, but it can be noted that there is a distinct emotional dimension to fantasy-proneness.[8] A historical analysis of these emotional relationships, informed by psychological and sociological studies, should be of comparative and methodological interest.

Several of the themes in this chapter can be opened up by a case study of one visionary, Alison Pearson, whose relationship with her spirit-guide can be reconstructed in detail. Later sections of the chapter will discuss themes in the visionary experience, and evidence from further visionaries will be adduced as and when appropriate.

Alison Pearson was a magical practitioner – a folk healer and diviner – who lived in Boarhills, apparently a typical rural settlement on the east coast of Fife. The main evidence comes from the record of her trial for witchcraft on 28 May 1588.[9] Her dittay (indictment) is mostly recorded in the third person, but it seems to be close to her own original statements. One first-person expression survives, 'quhene we heir the quhirll-wind', evidently reproducing her original voice. The narrative rambles from point to point in a way that an orally delivered confession would have been likely to do. The scribe has added a superficial appearance of topical organisation by inserting the word 'Item …' from time to time, but has not attempted a systematic reorganisation. The introduction accuses Pearson of 'Invocatioun of the spreits of the Dewill', but this is clearly separate from her confession. The interrogators make no attempt to force her to confess to conventional encounters with the Devil. Malefice against neighbours, too, is entirely absent. Overall, Pearson's story is so individual that it cannot have arisen from stereotyped answers to leading questions. Its rambling nature leaves a few loose ends, but the outline of a coherent narrative can nevertheless be recovered.

Pearson was probably aged about thirty-five at the time of her trial. She had practised as a magical practitioner for the past sixteen years, in and around the nearby town of St Andrews. She seems not to have had a husband or children, but her extended family was important to her, at least in her visions. She was respected enough for Patrick Adamson, archbishop of St Andrews, to consult her in 1584 about his health, though this followed a previous episode in 1583 in which the archbishop and others had investigated her for witchcraft.[10] Her cures included herbal remedies, but also – more suspiciously to the authorities – magical rituals. And she learned her cures by consulting a spirit-guide.

Pearson's encounters with spirits took several forms, but her main spirit-guide was the ghost of her uncle, William Simpson, her mother's brother. There is a slight ambiguity about this relationship; Pearson first called him 'hir cousing and moder-brotheris-sone', meaning her first cousin on her mother's side, and later 'hir guidschyre-sone', meaning her grandfather's son. A satirical poem by Robert Sempill against the archbishop in 1584, narrating a burlesque version of Pearson's medical treatment of him, called her spirit-guide 'Williame Symsoune, hir mother brother'.[11] Pearson said that Simpson was a young man, only six years older than herself. She clearly respected and looked up to him; she referred to him as 'Mr William Sympsoune', a title appropriate for a university graduate, and described him as 'ane grit scoller and doctor of medicin'. However, her experience was of 'the visioune and forme of Mr William Sympsoune'. Although the record never said explicitly that Simpson was dead, Pearson never seems to have met him in person. Either he had died as a very young man before her first encounter with him, or else he had never existed outside her imagination. As we shall see, she thought of him as living with the fairies.

Pearson related that her first encounter with Simpson occurred when she was aged twelve, suffering from an illness that took the power from her hand and foot. She 'reparit' (travelled) to him 'in Lowtheane, within the toun of Edinburghe', and he healed her; she then spent the next seven years coming and going between there and her home, during which time she was 'helpit of her seiknes' – the initial cure was evidently incomplete. Here it may be noted that Pearson's age of thirty-five at trial is inferred from her initial age of twelve, plus this seven-year period, plus her later sixteen-year career as a magical practitioner. Pearson, as we shall see, later narrated being carried to 'Lowtheane' by the fairies, and her journeys to visit Simpson probably had a similar visionary character.

Pearson had a story to tell about Simpson's career. If Simpson had ever really existed, then this story may have originated with things she had been told by her mother or other family members. Simpson, as we have seen, was six years older than Pearson, which would put his date of birth at about 1547. He had been born in Stirling, and his father had been the king's smith. We know that King James V, who had had much work done on Stirling Castle, had died in 1542. So far, so plausible, therefore, though blacksmiths were sometimes associated with magic. But Simpson had been 'tane away fra his fader be ane mann of Egypt, ane gyant, being bot ane barne, quha had him away to Egypt with him, quhair he remanit to the space of tuell yeiris or he come hame agane' (taken away from his father when he was only a child by a man of Egypt, a giant, who took him to Egypt, where he remained for twelve years before he came home again). There were gypsies, known as 'Egyptians', in sixteenth-century Scotland; they too were sometimes associated with magic. But this 'gyant' was clearly not human, and Pearson evidently thought of 'Egypt' as an abode of magical beings. Simpson presumably learned his skills there, since it was soon after his homecoming that he healed Pearson. Her chronology thus indicated that Simpson had been taken to 'Egypt' about the time of her own birth.

While Simpson was away in 'Egypt', his father died 'for opining of ane preist-buik and luking uponne it'. This episode was clearly connected to the Reformation, which had initially occurred in 1560, when Pearson was aged about seven. The saying and hearing of mass became criminal offences, but the death penalty was prescribed only for a third offence and was never exacted in practice; even priests were banished from the realm at worst. This story about Simpson's father sounds like a child's fantasy, coupled with a magical reverence for the written word.

Pearson also had a visionary relationship with the fairies – collectively, and, in two cases, individually. She never used the word 'fairies', but her term for them, 'guid nychtbouris' (good neighbours), was a recognised fairy euphemism, and her experiences included several fairy motifs. She mentioned 'hanting and repairing with the gude nychtbouris and Quene of Elfame, thir divers yeiris bypast'. She initially said that she did not know how long she had had this relationship, but she then added that it had been seven years since she had last seen the queen, and that she had been 'ewill handlit' (ill-treated) in the fairy court for seven years. These periods of seven years were probably not precise; seven could be a round number in magical terms. The two periods may have coincided, in that Pearson may have meant that the disappearance of the queen happened around the time when the fairies began to ill-treat her. However, there was a sense in which Pearson thought that the fairies had always ill-treated her, as we shall see. Quite possibly her relationship with the fairies had begun at around the same time as her career as a magical practitioner.

Pearson's first encounter with the fairies was traumatic. She went to 'Grange-mure', which from its name was probably somewhere wild rather than cultivated, with other 'folkis that past to the Mure'. There she collapsed and had a vision of a man in green (a fairy colour), who told her that he would do her good if she would be 'faithfull'. This might in theory have been a positive offer, but Pearson did not experience it thus. She reacted with fear, crying for help, but nobody came – a nightmarish motif. She then tried to negotiate with him: 'scho chargeit him, "In Godis name and the low he levit one," that if he come in Godis name and for the weill of hir saull, he sould tell' (she demanded to him 'In God's name, and by the law he lived by', that, if he came in God's name and for the good of her soul, he should tell [her]). Fairies were known to have ambivalent morality; they might either help or harm. And there were various different kinds of spirits. Many initial encounters with spirits were scary because the visionary did not know whether the spirit was positive or not.[12]

The initial vision ended at this point, but the man in green later returned. In describing this second vision of him, Pearson called him 'ane lustie mane' – a strong or vigorous man – with many men and women with him. Again she reacted with fear, blessing herself and praying. But she was carried away by the fairies, further than she could tell; she added that she was carried to Lothian, which, as we have seen, she evidently thought of as a magical place. She saw piping and merriment and good food, and wine puncheons and wineglasses – luxury items to a peasant. She does not seem to have shared in the feast. She also, on this or a later occasion, saw the fairies making salves (ointments) for healing, using pans and fires and gathering herbs before sunrise as she herself did. The fairies did not impart healing skills to her, however; rather she attributed all her skill to Simpson's teaching.

Pearson's emotion of fear was justified. The fairies proved cruel and demanding, tormenting her severely for speaking to other people about them. One of them beat her on her first visit to them, so that she lost all strength in one of her sides; the blow left a blue and discoloured mark, which she did not feel but could see. This may indicate that her injury was real, but her experience of receiving it certainly involved fantasy. The fairies' action had a dreamlike lack of logic; they were supposedly punishing her for revealing their secrets, yet on her first visit to them she had not yet had an opportunity to do so. Evidently Pearson could not fathom their motives.

The suffering continued during Pearson's later encounters with the fairies. These encounters were of three kinds. In the first kind of encounter, the fairies came to her at home. Sometimes they tried to carry her away again, but more often they simply visited her – sometimes once a week. They were sometimes fearsome, and she wept when they came. On the last time when she spoke to others about them, they punished her by beating her worse than before; she lost all strength in her side, and was bedridden for twenty weeks. Sometimes the fairies sat beside her and promised that she would prosper if she was faithful to them – the same demand made by the man in green on her first encounter; but they also threatened that they would martyr her if she spoke of them. These simultaneous promises and threats are intriguing, but Pearson, again as in a dream, could not make the commitment that the fairies demanded.

William Simpson was connected with later occasions when the fairies threatened to carry Pearson away, and these occasions formed her second kind of fairy encounter. He himself lived with the fairies, having been carried away by them out of Middle-Earth. This phrase provides a further indication of the location of Pearson's 'Egypt' – it, too, was beyond Middle-Earth (the everyday world between Heaven and Hell). Simpson was a ghost, but ghosts could associate with fairies, as we shall see other ghostly spirit-guides doing. Pearson sometimes experienced Simpson visiting her shortly before the fairies were due to appear. On these occasions she would be fearful, but he would warn her and protect her. When they heard the whirlwind blow in the sea, they would know that the fairies were on their way. (Boarhills was on the coast, but these were presumably envisioned whirlwinds rather than real ones.) Simpson would bid her keep herself safe and bless herself, so that she was not taken away by them again. She added that one-tenth of the fairies were taken each year to Hell – a traditional motif also found elsewhere in folk culture.[13]

Pearson also experienced a third kind of fairy encounter. She mentioned that she would sometimes be securely in her bed, but would not know where she would be by morning. This evidently alludes to episodes of sleepwalking. Unfortunately she gave no further details.

As well as Simpson – a positive figure – and the man in green – a negative figure – Pearson also envisioned the fairy queen. The queen was more remote than the other two spirit-guides, but generally positive. She presided over a court that contained many of Pearson's own relatives – 'freindis [i.e. relatives] in that court quhilk wes of her awin blude'. These relatives were kind and well acquainted with the queen, and Pearson thought that they might have helped her – but it does not seem that they had actually done so. Moreover, her relationship with them had broken down. She mentioned that these relatives were 'all away now', and that she had no wish to visit them 'eftir the end'. She did not elaborate on what this 'end' had been, but it may have been connected with the end of her relationship with the queen, whom, she said, she had not seen for seven years. She seems to have been sad about this. Pearson may have thought of the fairy queen in the way that early modern peasants sometimes thought of their king: as a remote but ultimately kind and just figure who would right their wrongs if he only knew of them.

Alison Pearson was just one of several visionaries with spirit-guides in early modern Scotland. It is not practical to narrate all their individual stories in detail. Instead I will turn now to a thematic analysis, commenting from time to time on Pearson's case but also bringing in the cases of other visionaries who, between them, may be able to tell us something of what was typical. The search for typicality should not exclude a recognition of the individuality of each visionary's experience, but common themes do emerge. How did the visionaries form and negotiate their relationship with their spirit-guide? What emotions did they experience? And what emotions did they attribute to the spirit-guide? Questions like this will arise periodically during the following analysis.

What was the structure of the relationship between the human visionary and the spirit-guide? To answer this, it may be necessary to ask a related question. What were the human analogues of the relationship? Here it may help to begin by suggesting that the simplest analogue is that of a relationship between two friends. As a model, this has the advantage of flexibility, not requiring a formally recognised social or legal framework – unlike marital or master–servant relationships, for instance. Alison Pearson's relationship with William Simpson was described as 'familiaritie', meaning intimacy, close association or friendship. His protection of her against the fairies in the whirlwind is an example of friends supporting each other against enemies.[14]

However, these were not friendships between equals. The spirit-guide was always more powerful than the visionary. We can approach closer to an understanding of their relationship by considering patrons and clients. Patron–client relationships were common in early modern society.[15] Crucially, the patron–client relationship was expressed in terms of friendship, even though it was not one of equality. Powerful patrons needed less powerful clients, and clients needed more powerful patrons. Some people were both patrons of less powerful people below them *and* clients of more powerful people above them; thus, someone at a lower social level might be able to persuade their immediate patron to intercede for them at a higher level, in theory all the way up to the royal court. The framing of the patron–client relationship as one of 'friendship' meant that, although patrons might command clients, they would be more likely to make requests – even though these might be requests that could not be refused. Indeed some clients had little practical choice in forming their relationship with their patron.

Patron–client relationships in early modern society were often connected with kin relationships. An aristocrat headed a network of kinsfolk, mostly cousins of some kind, who recognised their loyalty to the head of the 'house'. Similar relationships could be formed by non-kinsfolk; sometimes patron and client exchanged written 'bonds' that created a relationship equivalent to that assumed to exist between the patron and his less powerful cousins.[16] These relationships of patronage, service and dependence have mainly been studied among aristocrats, but the processes also operated at lower social levels.

The patron–client model can be seen in several visionaries' relationships. Elspeth Reoch, in Orkney in 1616, encountered two slightly sinister fairies, but the head of the household in which she was serving advised her to trust them, as they were his kinsfolk. Reoch later experienced her spirit-guide John Stewart calling himself her 'kinsman'.[17] Alison Pearson's William Simpson was her uncle, and she had other relatives in the fairy court, who, she hoped, would intercede on her behalf with the fairy queen – a characteristic thing for patrons to do. And, as with other clients, the visionaries were not always free agents in choosing their spirit-guides – Pearson and Reoch certainly were not.

The visionary's relationship with her or his spirit-guide was also comparable, though more distantly, with a human's relationship with God. God was kind, and the human was grateful for God's kindness. The human *thanked* God, and, if pious, might try actively to *serve* God, but did not *help* God; God was assumed not to need human help. Similarly, the spirit-guide did not need human help; the main thing that it wanted from the visionary was committed loyalty. Most early modern Scots, including most of the visionaries, would have regarded it as blasphemous to compare a spirit-guide with God, but a few parallels can be detected. Andrew Man, in Aberdeenshire in 1597, described the angel Christsonday, one of his spirit-guides, as 'Goddis godsone'.[18] Jean Brown, in Wigtownshire in 1706, had three unnamed spirit-guides, and she explicitly said that 'these spirits are her maker and she would serve and beleeve her maker'.[19] These spirits were 'three men', and her relationship with them was a sexual one; but 'being interrogat anent the worshiping of these spirits, she confesses the worshiping of th[e]m and th[a]t he is the God that made heaven & earth'.[20] Probably she was thinking idiosyncratically of the Holy Trinity. Brown may come the nearest to a visionary who loved her spirits, in that she assertively protested her loyalty to them when the minister told her that they were wicked and deceitful.

Bessie Dunlop, in Ayrshire in 1576, exemplifies a more typical attitude to a spirit-guide. In her case this was a ghost, Thom Reid. Her interrogators asked her what Reid's motive was for coming to her. In answer to this, Dunlop related a conversation that she had experienced with him. Reid had reminded her of a visit she had previously received from a 'stout woman' (strong woman), and revealed that this had been his own mistress, the Queen of Elphen (fairyland). Because Dunlop had offered hospitality to the incognita visitor, she, as a reward, had commanded Reid to wait on her and do her good.[21] Lizanne Henderson has discussed this aspect of Dunlop's story in detail.[22] She rightly recognises the visit from the Queen of Elphen as a folkloric motif, and argues that it relates to two connected motifs from Stith Thompson's *Motif-Index of Folk Literature*: N825.3.1 'Help from old beggar woman' and N826 'Help from beggar'.[23] However, the source does not mention begging; the story is really about being rewarded for hospitality, a motif in many folk tales. Arguably the relevant motifs from Thompson are F330 'Grateful fairies' (especially the subcategory F332 'Fairy grateful for hospitality') and Q45 'Hospitality rewarded'. Dunlop's transaction with the queen was important, as Henderson has shown, but it was one of reciprocity with a putative equal, not of superiority over a destitute beggar. Indeed the 'stout woman' was transformed from an equal to a superior as soon as Reid revealed her royal identity. Reid himself, as Dunlop's regular patron, was an intermediary between her and the queen.

Was there compromise, or give and take, in the relationship? Here we have to remember the inequality of power; a spirit-guide could be demanding. Again Bessie Dunlop offers examples. She refused some of Reid's demands, notably his demand to renounce Christianity and his indirect offer of sex. Reid nevertheless continued to cooperate with her and guide her; he was often masterful in his dealings with her, but he allowed her some autonomy.

These were instrumental relationships, formed for specific social and even material purposes. Sociologists have discussed 'pure relationships', which people form to maximise mutual self-actualisation – to become better or fuller people, rather than to achieve a task. Pure relationships have been argued to be characteristic of the modern world.[24] Pure relationships have also been argued to be abstractions based on an 'ideology of late modernity', never entirely achievable in practice because 'A relationship will bring emotional satisfactions and dissatisfactions in more or less equal measure'.[25] This debate need not concern us directly, but considering the 'pure relationship' as an ideal type may help us to recognise our visionaries' distance from it. Romantic love features in many pure relationships, but visionaries did not express romantic love for their spirits, nor did the spirits express such love for them. They may have taken pleasure in each other's company, but that was not the purpose of the relationship.

Let us analyse further the emotions involved in these relationships. How did the emotions operate? An 'appraisal' approach to emotions involves both cognition and evaluation. During a social interaction, we work out what the other person has said or done (cognition), and experience positive or negative assessments of its significance for us (evaluation). Our own expression of emotion in response to the situation may also lead us to experience that emotion as more concrete; having articulated and even perhaps named the emotion, we have committed ourselves to it. This has led William M. Reddy to coin the term 'emotive' for the combined process of appraisal and concrete expression.[26]

What, then, were the main situations requiring appraisal? The visionary's first encounter with their spirit-guide was a key moment; most of the visionaries spoke about this. This may partly reflect the interests of the interrogators, who wanted to know the circumstances in which a witch made a pact with the Devil. However, the stories of encounter and appraisal, and of formation of a relationship, were clearly important stories to the visionaries themselves. The visionaries' accounts of how they had formed the relationship bore little or no resemblance to conventional witchcraft narratives about the Devil, which is one indication among many that their accounts were not shaped by leading questions from the interrogators. Several of the visionaries' stories of formation of the relationship involved doubt, fear and hesitation.

At this point it may be mentioned that some relationships with the Devil, as constructed by interrogators who guided suspects more firmly towards conventional witchcraft confessions, have certain parallels with spirit-guide relationships. The Devil could offer help at a traumatic moment, for instance. There were probably complex three-way influences here. To some extent, the relationship between witch and Devil was constructed like the relationship between visionary and spirit-guide. To some extent, both these relationships were constructed (independently) like relationships between two real people, as has been discussed above for the visionaries.[27] And to some extent, the relationship between visionary and spirit-guide may have been constructed like the relationship between witch and Devil. However, the idiosyncratic nature of these visionaries' accounts makes it unlikely that the accounts have been distorted by the interrogators' preconceptions in ways relevant to the present study.[28]

Further emotionally charged situations requiring appraisal often arose when the visionary was introduced to a wider and scarier world of spirits. Thom Reid took Bessie Dunlop to the fairy court on his fourth visit to her, warning her of the danger of speaking to anyone there. She collapsed on her return, apparently from stress.[29] Isobel Haldane, in Perth in 1623, experienced abduction by the fairies, from whom she was grateful to be rescued by her spirit-guide, a grey-bearded man who may have been a ghost.[30]

In some of these situations, the visionary *needed* the spirit. Their initial state of despair or trauma invited an intervention from the supernatural world. Later, perhaps more routinely, the visionaries acted as magical practitioners and needed to summon or otherwise consult their spirit. As for the spirit's need for the visionary: the spirit often found itself appraising a situation in which it hoped for, but was not necessarily confident of receiving, the visionary's loyalty and commitment. This is noticeable in Pearson's encounter with the man in green, where his frustration in dealing with her agonised twists and turns is palpable.

What of specific emotions themselves? The clearest emotion that emerges from all this is fear. Some visionaries said a good deal about this emotion. They formed a relationship with their spirit-guide by conquering their fear of it, and some never entirely freed themselves of their fears. Bessie Dunlop was 'sumthing fleit' (rather afraid) at the end of her first meeting with Thom Reid, when he disappeared through a hole in the dyke that was too small for a human.[31] However, she became accustomed to Reid's visits. Pearson was often fearful, as we have seen. Andrew Man was 'not effrayit' to go among the elves; thus, they *were* frightening, but he was able to manage his fear.[32] Ronald Hutton has discussed fear of fairies in the 'Celtic' societies of the British Isles, including the Scottish Highlands; he argues that fairies were known throughout the British Isles but were feared more by the Highlanders and other Celtic peoples.[33] The present evidence comes from the Lowlands, but Hutton's argument is one of degree: fairies were feared everywhere, but only in the Highlands did this fear overtake the fear of witches. Dealing with a spirit-guide in early modern Scotland was a scary business.

Related to fear, there were emotions of trust and distrust. Isobel Watson, in Perthshire in 1590, frequently experienced being taken by the fairies, often dancing with them once a month. But, when a fairy offered Watson an oatcake, her aunt (who was also present) 'forbad hir' to take it, 'bidding hir gif thair meat to the gress and grein eard' (telling her to give their food to the grass and green earth). Like Alison Pearson, Watson periodically suffered beatings by the fairies.[34]

The visionaries did not just express emotions of their own: they also attributed emotions to their spirit-guides. The sources are reticent here, but there is enough evidence to show that these emotions existed. They can be divided broadly into positive and negative emotions.

The first positive emotion to mention is sympathy. Elspeth Reoch's spirit-guide explicitly professed concern for her welfare; even when he deprived her of the power of speech, this was to prevent her being 'hurt'.[35] Bessie Dunlop's spirit-guide was sympathetic to her when they first met, offering reassurance in her despair. Visionaries often experienced their spirit-guide as wanting to look after them in some way.

Sexual desire may perhaps be considered a positive emotion. Several visionaries experienced their spirit-guide as desiring them, or (less positively) as wishing to dominate them sexually. Elspeth Reoch submitted to the sexual advances of her main spirit-guide, much as she seems to have done to those of the real men in her life. Jean Brown valued her sexual relationship with her spirits. Bessie Dunlop, as we have seen, experienced Thom Reid as making a pass at her, though she rejected him. Andrew Man had a long-standing sexual relationship with the fairy queen, while recognising that she might also have sex with other men if she desired them.[36] The idea of the husband–wife relationship provided material upon which some of these relationships could be modelled, thus supplementing or overlapping with the main patron–client model mentioned above.

More negatively, there is much evidence for angry spirit-guides. Reoch's two spirits argued with each other when she first encountered them. Thom Reid was 'verrie crabit' (very angry) with Bessie Dunlop when she refused to go to fairyland with him. On another occasion he told her, 'Bessie, thow hes crabit God' (Bessie, you have angered God), and advised her to 'mend' her relationship with God.[37] Finally, there are Alison Pearson's violent fairies, who punished her for speaking of them; she thus attributed emotions of anger and jealousy to them.

A conclusion to all this may begin by stressing that these narratives of interpersonal relationships are told in a completely straightforward way. One person said this, the other said that. It seems perfectly intelligible – until we remind ourselves that one 'person' in the relationship was actually a ghost or a fairy or some other spirit. Which means that, in today's terms, the entire 'relationship' is best understood as having taken place inside one person's head.

Nevertheless, visionaries' accounts of their experiences evidently made sense to them – and we can now see that they were grounded in the social realities of the early modern period. The spirits, no matter how imaginary, were just like real people. Or, rather, they were like real *spirits*, which were quite like people but which by definition were understood as being different from people in some ways. Fantasy beings are more readily understood if they behave, not simply like humans, but like fantasy beings as these are culturally understood.[38]

The spirits were experienced as different from humans in various ways, largely to do with their supernatural powers. Some of these were mechanical matters, such as their ability to appear and disappear – but other differences had emotional aspects. The main point was that the spirit-guide was omniscient about the visionary – a point that most visionaries seem to have taken for granted and experienced as reassuring. Some spirit-guides operated by different moral rules, notably the fairy queen whose sexual promiscuity Andrew Man recognised as normal for her. More often, however, as with Alison Pearson, the spirit-guide was inscrutable or capricious in ways that the visionary found troublesome.

Mainstream studies of emotions assume that emotions are expressed. However, the emotions being studied here remained within the thought processes of individual visionaries; they were a kind of story that the visionaries told, first to themselves, then to their clients, and, finally, under harrowing circumstances, to the interrogators questioning them about witchcraft. These were emotions that were *culturally understood* in early modern Scotland, thus enabling visionaries to experience fantasised stories that employed these emotions. This is why we find visionaries encountering characters who were culturally recognised in their society, like the fairy queen, and why we find them constructing relationships that were familiar in their society, like patron–client relationships.

The problem of the non-expression of these emotions can be investigated further with reference to the work of William M. Reddy, an influential historian theorising emotions with reference to psychological studies. He usually focuses on the immediate, verbal expression of emotion. However, Reddy also recognises the past-tense expression of emotions such as 'I was angry at you'. Such statements, Reddy argues, are genuine 'emotives' – his term for emotional expressions that feed back into creating and defining the emotions that they express. They define the person's present emotional state, if only by contrast with the past, and clarify the person's understanding of their own past.[39] Similarly, the visionaries narrated their emotions, and those of their spirit-guide, to their interrogators; this past-tense narration of their emotions to their interrogators thus helped to construct a new phase of their emotional understanding of themselves. However, this phase was brief; Alison Pearson and most of the other visionaries discussed in this chapter were executed for witchcraft soon after they made their confessions. We want to know what the visionaries' confessions tell us about their lives and experiences before they were arrested, not about the effect of their confessions on their emotional state.

This leads on to the question of the psychological processes by which visionaries constructed their experiences. In addition to fantasy (mentioned above), it is likely that hallucinations were also involved in at least some cases.[40] There may also have been an element of false memory, which leads people to 'remember' experiences that they have never had.[41] Such memories can be implanted by interrogators – but these interrogators were asking about the Devil, not about ghosts nor about the fairy queen. In Alison Pearson's case there is independent, prior evidence of her relationship with her spirit-guide. Most of what we know of it comes from her retrospective narrative made during her interrogation in 1588, but the satirical poem of 1584 (discussed above) shows that she was already talking about, and using, the relationship at that date.

Overall, therefore, it is fascinating to see the detailed and various ways in which these visionaries understood and experienced, not only their own various emotions, but also the various emotions of their supernatural partners. We may think that these partners had no existence outside the visionaries' own minds, but that is not how they themselves construed their experience. Their navigation of their complex and demanding two-way relationships formed an important aspect of their lives. The emotions of supernatural beings are a deeply human subject.

Notes

1 Julian Goodare, 'Visionaries and nature spirits in Scotland', in Bela Mosia (ed.), *Book of Scientific Works of the Conference of Belief Narrative Network of ISFNR, 1–4 October 2014, Zugdidi* (Zugdidi: Shota Meshkia State Teaching University of Zugdidi, Georgia, 2015), pp. 102–16.

2 For a further study that develops this aspect of the topic, examining some of the same cases as the present chapter, see Georgie Blears, 'Experiencing the invisible polity: trance in early modern Scotland', Chapter 4 this volume. For a study of trauma and psychosis among these visionaries, see Julian Goodare, 'Away with the fairies: the psychopathology of visionary encounters in early modern Scotland', *History of Psychiatry*, 31 (2020), 37–54.
3 Jan Plamper, *The History of Emotions: An Introduction*, trans. Keith Tribe (Oxford: Oxford University Press, 2015).
4 Laura A. Griner and Craig A. Smith, 'Contributions of motivational orientation to appraisal and emotion', *Personality and Social Psychology Bulletin*, 26 (2000), 727–40.
5 Plamper, *History of Emotions*, pp. 2–3, 204, 212–13.
6 William M. Reddy, *The Navigation of Feeling: A Framework for the History of Emotions* (Cambridge: Cambridge University Press, 2001); Barbara H. Rosenwein, 'Worrying about emotions in history', *American Historical Review*, 107 (2002), 821–45.
7 Sheryl C. Wilson and Theodore X. Barber, 'The fantasy-prone personality: implications for understanding imagery, hypnosis, and parapsychological phenomena', in Anees A. Sheikh (ed.), *Imagery: Current Theory, Research, and Application* (New York: Wiley, 1983), pp. 340–87.
8 Russell J. Webster and Donald A. Saucier, 'I believe I can fly: re-examining individual differences in imaginative involvement', *Imagination, Cognition and Personality*, 30 (2011), 425–45.
9 Robert Pitcairn (ed.), *Ancient Criminal Trials in Scotland*, 3 vols (Edinburgh: Bannatyne Club, 1833), I, part ii, pp. 161–5. Subsequent quotations concerning Pearson are from this passage.
10 D. J. Parkinson, '"The Legend of the Bishop of St Androis Lyfe" and the survival of Scottish poetry', *Early Modern Literary Studies*, 9 (2003), online.
11 James Cranstoun (ed.), *Satirical Poems of the Time of the Reformation*, 2 vols (Edinburgh: STS, 1891–93), I, p. 365.
12 Julian Goodare, 'Boundaries of the fairy realm in Scotland', in Karin E. Olsen and Jan R. Veenstra (eds), *Airy Nothings: Imagining the Otherworld of Faerie from the Middle Ages to the Age of Reason* (Leiden: Brill, 2014), pp. 139–69, at pp. 153–8.
13 Emily Lyle, *Fairies and Folk: Approaches to the Scottish Ballad Tradition* (Trier: Wissenschaftlicher Verlag, 2007), pp. 128–31.
14 Lynn Jamieson, *Intimacy: Personal Relationships in Modern Societies* (Cambridge: Polity, 1998), pp. 77–8.
15 Keith M. Brown, *Noble Power in Scotland from the Reformation to the Revolution* (Edinburgh: Edinburgh University Press, 2011), pp. 61–88.
16 Jenny Wormald, *Lords and Men in Scotland: Bonds of Manrent, 1442–1603* (Edinburgh: John Donald, 1985).
17 *Maitland Misc.*, II, pp. 188–9.
18 *Spalding Misc.*, I, p. 120. For more on Andrew Man and Christsonday, see Martha McGill, 'Angels in early modern Scotland', Chapter 6 this volume.
19 Henry Paton (ed.), *The Session Book of Penninghame, 1696–1724* (Edinburgh: privately printed, 1933), p. 164.

20 Stirling Council Archives, A1081 Allanton & Touch Collection, Bundle 4, Box 2, confession of Jean Brown, 1706. I am grateful to Stirling Council Archives for advice on this document and for permission to quote from it.
21 Pitcairn, *Trials*, I, part ii, pp. 56–7.
22 Lizanne Henderson, 'Witch, fairy and folktale narratives in the trial of Bessie Dunlop', in Lizanne Henderson (ed.), *Fantastical Imaginations: The Supernatural in Scottish History and Culture* (Edinburgh: John Donald, 2009), pp. 141–66.
23 Stith Thompson (ed.), *Motif-Index of Folk Literature*, 6 vols, 2nd ed. (Copenhagen: Rosenkilde & Bagger, 1955–58).
24 Derek Layder, *Intimacy and Power: The Dynamics of Personal Relationships in Modern Society* (Basingstoke: Palgrave Macmillan, 2009), pp. 10–13.
25 Ian Craib, 'The sociology of the emotions', in Ian Craib, *Experiencing Identity* (London: Sage, 1998), pp. 105–15, at p. 114.
26 Reddy, *Navigation of Feeling*, pp. 96–111.
27 For the construction of the witch–Devil relationship as paralleling Scottish irregular marriage, see Lauren Martin, 'The Devil and the domestic: witchcraft, quarrels and women's work in Scotland', in Julian Goodare (ed.), *The Scottish Witch-Hunt in Context* (Manchester: Manchester University Press, 2002), pp. 73–89.
28 Goodare, 'Visionaries and nature spirits', pp. 103–4.
29 Pitcairn, *Trials*, I, part ii, pp. 52–3.
30 *The Register of the Privy Council of Scotland*, 2nd series, vol. 8, ed. P. Hume Brown (Edinburgh: HMSO, 1908), p. 353.
31 Pitcairn, *Trials*, I, part ii, p. 52.
32 *Spalding Misc.*, I, p. 122; cf. Reddy, *Navigation of Feeling*, p. 103, for further discussion of the claim 'I am not afraid'.
33 Ronald Hutton, 'Witch-hunting in Celtic societies', *Past and Present*, 212 (Aug. 2011), 43–71, at pp. 50–60.
34 NRS, CH2/722/2, minutes of presbytery of Stirling, 1589–96, pp. 21–5.
35 *Maitland Misc.*, II, p. 189.
36 *Spalding Misc.*, I, pp. 119–21.
37 Pitcairn, *Trials*, I, part ii, pp. 53, 52.
38 Jeffrey E. Foy and Richard J. Gerrig, 'Flying to Neverland: how readers tacitly judge norms during comprehension', *Memory and Cognition*, 42 (2014), 1250–9.
39 Reddy, *Navigation of Feeling*, p. 105.
40 Vanessa Beavan, John Read and Claire Cartwright, 'The prevalence of voice-hearers in the general population: a literature review', *Journal of Mental Health*, 20 (2011), 281–92; Frank Larøi, 'The phenomenological diversity of hallucinations: some theoretical and clinical implications', *Psychologica Belgica*, 46:1/2 (2006), 163–83; Angela Woods, Nev Jones, Ben Alderson-Day, Felicity Callard and Charles Fernyhough, 'Experiences of hearing voices: analysis of a novel phenomenological survey', *Lancet Psychiatry*, 2 (2015), 323–31.
41 Christopher C. French and Anna Stone, *Anomalistic Psychology: Exploring Paranormal Belief and Experience* (Basingstoke: Palgrave Macmillan, 2014), pp. 141–2.

4

Experiencing the invisible polity: trance in early modern Scotland

Georgie Blears

> It may be supposed not repugnant to Reason or Religion to assert ane invisible polity, or a people to us invisible, having a Commonwealth, Laws & Oeconomy, made known to us but by some obscure hints of a few admitted to their Converse.
>
> (Robert Kirk, c.1689)[1]

In early modern Scotland, as in the rest of Europe, there was an entrenched belief that humanity's terrestrial world existed alongside 'ane invisible polity'. This chapter is about those few exceptional people who developed a relationship with this spiritual other world, whether by receiving spiritual visitors, travelling to unknown places or acquiring information inaccessible to their human peers. I posit that there was a critical factor enabling the development of these relationships with the supernatural realm: the altered state of consciousness known as trance.

Historians have traditionally assumed that reports of supernatural experiences were no more than superstitious stories, and have focused primarily on what these stories can tell us about such issues as gender, religion and community conflict. Psychoanalytical theory has furnished another line of enquiry; Diane Purkiss and Lyndal Roper have suggested that the fantasy elements of witchcraft confessions served as vehicles for repressed emotion.[2] There is value in both of these approaches, but they risk becoming reductionist. More recently, as the discipline of history has begun to catch up with the 'cognitive revolution' taking hold in other fields, scholars including Emma Wilby, Owen Davies, Julian Goodare, Éva Pócs and Gábor Klaniczay have sought to understand the experiential foundation of supernatural beliefs.[3] This approach is most fully expounded by Edward Bever's *The Realities of Witchcraft and Popular Magic in Early Modern Europe*, which sets out to demonstrate how early modern supernatural experiences were real from a neurobiological perspective.[4] Bever acknowledges the value of cultural historians' analyses of the social function of supernatural stories, but argues that neurocognitive explanations for supernatural experiences also deserve 'a place at the table'.[5] His work has proved controversial, with some regrettably polarised positions being taken by some participants in the debate including Bever himself. His most recent critic, Michael Ostling, does, however, acknowledge the value of the neurocognitive approach and seeks to 'build bridges between culturalist and neurobiological approaches'.[6] Tom Webster is one of several scholars to have questioned what, exactly, we learn by retrospectively diagnosing early modern men and women.[7] This chapter aims to demonstrate that by using modern medical, psychiatric and anthropological literature to confirm that early modern Scots experienced trance, and to understand how or why they did so, we can uncover information about their lives that would otherwise go unnoticed.

Discerning incidents of trance has been integral to a number of scholars' arguments. Éva Pócs argues that magical practitioners used trance to contact supernatural beings; Carlo Ginzburg demonstrates how the *benandanti* visionaries employed trance to allow their souls to engage in night battles; and in his explication of the Scottish seely wight cult, Julian Goodare suggests that its human members entered into trances.[8] However, few scholars have attempted to understand the phenomenon or how it was experienced. Emma Wilby is an exception. In two important books, she reconstructs a number of likely cases of trance-induced visionary experiences.[9] Without taking away from Wilby's important contribution, her almost exclusive use of anthropological studies of shamanic trance to guide her search for early modern trance experiences is limiting. Shamanic trance constitutes its own distinct form of trance in that it uniquely involves all three of the following: voluntary control over trance, interplay with audience and post-trance memory.[10] Early modern Scots experienced trance in a wide variety of ways, most of which do not fit within this model.

Possible trance experiences appear in numerous early modern accounts of the supernatural, and it has not been possible to survey all of them here. Future scholarship might profitably engage with the accounts of prophetic visionaries, who accessed the supernatural realm in what certainly appear to have been trance states, sometimes 'falling dead' or becoming 'speechlesse'.[11] Also potentially relevant are the states of altered consciousness that could be experienced during orthodox Christian prayer or rituals such as communion. However, this chapter will concentrate on the accounts of accused witches and second-sighted seers, which offer rich descriptions of encounters with the supernatural world.

These sources are not exempt from problems. The testimonies of accused witches frequently reflect elite ideas elicited through coercive interrogation questions. I therefore focus on reports that contain enough details beyond the interrogators' own interests to convince us that these details really were told by the accused. Early modern treatises on the prophetic abilities of second-sighted seers are also problematic, having been written by men who were setting out in search of supernatural phenomena in order to rebut the mechanical world view being expounded by contemporary Cartesians.[12] These accounts do, nevertheless, throw up some likely examples of trance. By considering the experience of trance as it emerges from these sources, we can come to understand how the 'invisible polity' was experienced as a complete reality by certain people in early modern Scotland.

What can modern medical and anthropological studies tell us about the human propensity to experience trance? For the larger part of its modern medical and psychiatric history, trance was studied through a pathological lens, as a dissociative disorder symptomatic of psychological trauma. Clinicians and psychiatrists generally focused on the most extreme types of trance, including possession trance, catatonic trance and absence seizures.[13] The symptoms of these severe trances include any number of the following: derealisation (the feeling that one's surroundings are not real), depersonalisation (detachment from the self), loss of consciousness, rigidity of body, unresponsiveness to external stimuli, behaviours beyond one's immediate control and distortion of time perception.[14]

More recently, the American Psychiatric Association has recognised a separate category of non-pathological trance, opening the floodgates for numerous studies of normative dissociative phenomena.[15] It is now widely accepted that trance can be a voluntary or pleasurable experience, and that dissociative trance can take place frequently throughout the day. Daydreaming, 'highway hypnosis' and 'getting lost' in a book or film are all experiences that involve subtle derealisation and depersonalisation.[16]

This shift away from the pathological bias towards dissociative trance mirrors anthropological discussions of the subject. Anthropologists commonly agree that the ability to generate visionary phenomena while in trances is a universal feature of the mind, commonly experienced.[17] In a 1960s study of 488 societies worldwide, Erika Bourguignon found that 90 per cent displayed trance.[18] Sheryl Wilson and Theodore Barber suggest that a number of individuals – perhaps as many as 4 per cent of the population – have such strong hallucinatory and hypnotic abilities that they can '"see", "hear", "smell", "touch" and fully experience whatever they fantasize'. By becoming immersed in such hallucinatory fantasies, these fantasy-prone people will 'lose either partial or complete awareness of time and place' in an experience that is 'characteristic of hypnosis or trance'.[19] In a similar vein, Tanya Luhrmann has shown how evangelical Christians' use of kataphatic, or 'imagination rich', prayer allows them to experience mental images with such sensorial potency as to convince them that they are talking and walking with God.[20]

This chapter builds on these insights, approaching trance as a common dissociative phenomenon that might be voluntary or involuntary; that might be linked to trauma, but might also develop naturally in fantasy-prone individuals; and that might be of long or short duration, with symptoms ranging from the mild to the dramatic. By taking this broad approach, we can develop a fuller understanding of why and how early modern Scots could experience the supernatural.

'Trance' was a recognised concept in early modern Scotland. The *Dictionary of the Older Scottish Tongue* cites numerous uses of the term 'trance' (also 'traunce' or 'trauns'), defined as any of the three following phenomena: (i) an abnormal state of mind, typically of excitement, ecstasy or terror; (ii) a state of semi-consciousness between sleeping and waking; and (iii) a state of complete unconsciousness.[21] Many pre-industrial conditions would have been conducive to experiencing trance, including chronic undernourishment, physical toil, long working hours, ingestion of hallucinogenic plant toxins like ergot and exposure to high levels of disease. Moreover, early modern Scotland was committed to an animist world view.[22] As Rebecca Seligman and Laurence J. Kirmayer have demonstrated, in cultural contexts where spirit communication is valued, there will be 'increased opportunities to experience dissociative phenomena like trance'.[23] Combining the belief in spirit communication with the heightened psychological and physical stresses on early modern people, we can assume that trance-induced visionary experiences would have occurred with greater frequency than they do in present-day Western societies.

Reference to trance can be found in William Dunbar's poem 'Fasternis evin in Hell' (*c.*1507):

> OFF Februar the fyiftene nycht
> Full lang befoir the dayis lycht
> I lay in till a trance;   [*I fell into*
> And than I saw baith hevin and hell.[24]

The poetic trance or dream-vision was a literary motif, but Dunbar's lines do demonstrate a cultural understanding that trances might occur in the night or during unusual conditions of sleep.

Grizell Love, a Presbyterian visionary who saw other-worldly beings while awake in bed, also displayed some understanding of what was meant by a trance. On one occasion in 1661, Love wrote that angels appeared to her while 'laying in my bed neither sleeping nor in a trance'. Love's explicit denial that she had entered any trance was probably an attempt to forestall accusations of religious enthusiasm.[25] However, she was clearly aware of the potential to fall into trances in the period between sleep and wakefulness.

In order to find real trance experiences, we turn first to the early modern Scottish witch trial records. Trance is mentioned explicitly in some reports, although rarely discussed in detail. The synod of Aberdeen complained in 1675 that people 'under the pretence of trance' were 'goeing uith these spirits commonlie called the faeries', a statement that at most makes the connection between trance and visionary experiences.[26] Margaret Wallace, in Glasgow in 1622, was said to have experienced a 'suddane transe or diseis that she had tane the day befoir'.[27] In 1643, the minister of Tibbermore reported that Jean Crie, a widow in his parish, had come to 'lay in trance for certain days'. Crie's trances were seemingly induced by an eating disorder: suffering under a 'melancholic disease', she had 'fasted 17 or 18 weeks'.[28] However, Wallace's and Crie's own voices are missing from the records; we get no sense of how they experienced their trances.

The most detailed report that explicitly mentions trance is the indictment of John Fian, who was tried in 1591. Fian's state of 'extasies and transis' was directly linked to his experience of being 'transportit to mony montanes, as thocht throw all the warld', and to the more general feeling he described of having 'his spreit tane'.[29] Some classic symptoms of trance are present in these descriptions of flight. Fian seems to have experienced intense derealisation and a degree of depersonalisation, as well as likely distortion of time perception and unresponsiveness to external stimuli.

Other reports do not explicitly mention trance, but do include descriptions of flight either to the witches' sabbat or to fairyland, and are sufficiently individualised to be credible. In these cases, we can use the similar descriptions of how people felt suddenly detached from their bodies and immediate surroundings to suggest that they too were experiencing trance. Several individuals described experiences strongly suggestive of derealisation and depersonalisation. In 1678, Isobel Elliot reported how 'she left her bodie in Pencaitland, and went in the shape of a corbie, to Laswade'. In 1662, Isobel Gowdie confessed how ''ve vold flie away, quhair ve vold, be ewin as strawes wold flie wpon an hie-way'. In 1612, Bessie Henderson was reported to have been 'carried by the said green kirtles wherever they pleased'.[30]

What is particularly interesting about these descriptions of flight, with the potential exception of Bessie Henderson given that the description was not her own, is the suggestion that these women believed that they were flying in spirit rather than in body. This is clearly specified in Elliot's case, since it is said that she 'left her bodie in Pencaitland'. It is also suggested by Gowdie, who reported how members of her coven would 'put boosomes [i.e. brooms] in our bed with our husbandis, till ve return again to them'.[31] Taken literally, this suggests that Gowdie flew physically, leaving behind a fake magical body with a view to fooling her husband. However, it is equally feasible to suggest, as Emma Wilby does, that Gowdie was making recourse to subtle body lore, believing there to be a mode of herself that was detached from her physical body and able to roam the world with spirits.[32]

If the latter is more reflective of Gowdie's understanding of her own experience, we can suggest that what she was undergoing was catatonic trance. Catatonic trance causes muscular rigidity and decreased sensitivity, resulting in a conscious awareness of the weight of one's body in contrast to the lightness of one's spirit. Lacking a neurobiological understanding of catatonic trance states, Gowdie and perhaps also Elliot were rationalising their experiences in the only way available to them: through subtle body lore. A suggestion of how these trances might have appeared to onlookers is offered in King James VI's *Daemonologie* (1597); James reports how the bodies of certain magical practitioners would appear 'senselesse' and 'as it were a sleepe' at the times they claimed to have had visions.[33]

In descriptions of visits from other-worldly beings, rather than flight to other-worldly locations, it is more difficult to discern trance experiences. We generally lack the most obvious symptoms of trance: derealisation, depersonalisation, unresponsiveness to outside stimuli, rigidity of body or distortion of time perception. In the absence of any mention of these symptoms, and given the often completely naturalistic descriptions of spirits, it is not surprising that these visionary encounters have on occasion been confused for empirically real events or people. A prime example of this is Bessie Dunlop's 1576 confession. Her detailed description of Thom Reid as 'ane honest wele elderlie man' who was 'gray bairdit' and dressed in a 'gray coitt with Lumbard slevis of the auld fassoun' made Robert Pitcairn, the first editor of her trial record, question whether this was not in fact a real person, 'some heartless wag, acquainted with the virtues and use of herbs'.[34] While lifelike descriptions like this almost convince us of the reality of Dunlop's encounters, the illusion is broken by fantastical anomalies that give us an insight into her dreamlike state of consciousness. We see, for instance, how Thom Reid was able to enter a space that no 'erdlie man culd haif gane throw'.[35] A similar interplay between realistic descriptions and slips of fantastical detail permeates the confessions of Janet Boyman (1572), Alison Pearson (1588), Andrew Man (1597–98) and Elspeth Reoch (1616).[36]

It is also notable that Bessie Dunlop, Alison Pearson, Andrew Man and Elspeth Reoch appear to have experienced their visions in hypnagogic states – that is, in the transitional state between sleep and wakefulness. Dunlop was visited by Thom Reid while she was 'lyand in child-bed-lair'; Pearson 'wald be in hir bed hail and seir' when she saw the fairy queen; Reoch was tormented by a fairy man who 'wald never let her sleip'; and Man, after a night of being with the fairies and Christsonday, would 'find [him] self in a moss on the morne'.[37] Trance is a 'betwixt and between' state that falls in between waking consciousness and rapid eye-movement (REM) sleep, often involving phases of what neurologist James H. Austin has called 'micro-REM dreaming while awake'.[38]

Early modern Western Europeans might have been particularly susceptible to night-time trances. It was usual for sleep to be divided into two intervals, with an hour or more of 'quiet wakefulness' generally taking place around midnight.[39] In a controlled experiment, Thomas Wehr recreated pre-industrial sleep patterns and found that the intervening period of wakefulness possessed an 'endocrinology all of its own'.[40] The experiment's participants exhibited heightened levels of prolactin, a hormone that also enables chickens to sit contentedly atop their eggs for extended periods of time. This led the participants towards 'an altered state of consciousness not unlike meditation'.[41]

Thus, by paying attention to the time when visionary experiences were reported to have taken place, we may very well uncover likely experiences of trance. It is probably no coincidence that fairy and witch visits were commonly said to take place at midnight.[42] Returning to the testimony of Dunlop, Pearson, Man and Reoch, we can suggest that they entered trance states in periods of intervening wakefulness, which subsequently allowed their conscious or unconscious thoughts to generate vivid and self-propelling illusory narratives.

Dunlop, Pearson, Man and Reoch experienced their hallucinations through a number of senses other than sight, and evidently believed them to be real. This rules out the possibility that their experiences were dreams that took place in REM sleep states, as opposed to in trances. The research conducted by Wilson and Barber into the ability of what they term 'fantasy-prone personalities' sheds light on this particular issue. Like our accused witches, Wilson and Barber's fantasy-prone subjects 'experience[d] a reduction in orientation to time, place, and person that is characteristic of hypnosis or trance'. In this state they would 'experience their fantasies at hallucinatory intensities ("as real as real") in all sense modalities'.[43]

Isobel Gowdie offers a particularly useful example of how early modern visions could be experienced in all sense modalities. Gowdie, we can recall, reported travelling to the witches' sabbat, leaving a 'boosome' behind for her husband. She experienced this visually, seeing the Devil and other witches; there was an auditory element, as indicated when she repeated a verbal formula 'thryse ower'; a touch element was manifested through imagined pain, as evidenced in her reports of how the Devil 'wold be beatting and scurgeing ws all wp and downe'; and there may even have been taste and smell elements, as implied by references to feasting.[44]

In the case of Wilson and Barber's fantasy-prone subjects, the power of experiencing hallucinations as 'real as real' was such that 85 per cent of the subjects would 'confuse their *memories* of their fantasies with their *memories* of actual events'. On occasion, individuals would even put themselves in harm's way.[45] One of the fantasy-prone subjects found herself in the middle of a traffic-filled street, believing all the while that she had been 'walking with her imaginary pet lamb through an imaginary meadow'.[46] An almost direct parallel for this experience was recorded in the trial of Andrew Man: 'Thou grantis the elphis will mak the appear to be in a fair chalmer [chamber], and yit thow will find thy self in a moss on the morne; and that thay will appear to have candlis, and licht, and swordis, quihilk wilbe nothing els bot deed gress and strayes [straws].'[47] Alison Pearson and Janet Cowie (Elgin, 1646) were reported to have had very similar experiences.[48]

These accused witches' experiences can certainly be classed with the 'real as real' hallucinations experienced in trance states by as many as 4 per cent of people in our present-day population. However, we should also consider sleepwalking as a possible cause. This would not mean categorising the experiences of Andrew Man, Alison Pearson and Janet Cowie as something markedly different from trance; rather, it would demonstrate yet another way that trance was experienced in early modern Scotland. Often defined as a half-waking trance, sleepwalking is a combination of sleep and wakefulness that takes place as a result of arousals during slow-wave sleep at the beginning of the night.[49] It is the fact that this very particular altered state of consciousness takes place during slow-wave sleep (the deepest sleep within non-rapid eye movement) that ambulation, dream-like visionary narratives and high-performance tasks are possible.[50] This contrasts with the earlier experiences of trance we have isolated, which appear to have taken place in hypnagogic states.

Thus, having already observed a trance that was induced by nourishment deprivation, likely examples of catatonic trance and probable instances of fantasy-driven trance taking place in hypnagogic states, we have now perhaps fallen upon another type of trance that involves an until now elusive trance symptom: behaviours beyond one's conscious control. All of these experiences exhibit the fundamental trance symptoms of derealisation and depersonalisation, while also involving a variety of other respective symptoms. This indicates that there was variation in the type and depth of trance that was experienced in early modern Scotland.

We can now turn to the literature on the Scottish seers, to observe instances of trance at the more normative end of the spectrum. Although we should be careful not to distinguish categorically between the trance experiences of accused witches and those of seers, it is possible to observe some general differences.

Seers most usually seem to have experienced trance spontaneously while awake. Their trances were short in duration, with the corresponding vision being more akin to a flashing image than a film-like narrative. The experience of Duncan Campbell is representative. Writing in the late seventeenth or early eighteenth century, the minister John Fraser reported that Campbell was 'one morning walking in the Fields' when 'he saw a dozen of men carrying a Bier, and knew them all but one, and when he looked again, all was evanished.'[51] The fact that seers' visions took place during an 'awaking sense' (as the minister Robert Kirk termed it), and did not usually last long, marks a clear difference from the trance-induced visions we have thus far encountered.[52]

In accounting for this difference, and also demonstrating that trance was still likely at the core of the seers' visions of future events, we can consider that many of these visions seem to have been triggered by monotonous focus. Evidence for this comes most clearly from Robert Kirk's *The Secret Commonwealth* (1692): 'The sight is of noe long duration, only continueing so long as they can keep their eye steady without twinkling. The hardy therefor fix their look, that they may see the longer, But the timorous see only glances, their eyes alwayes twinkling at the first sight of the object.'[53] Kirk's hypothesis for how seers experienced their visions is highly indicative of trance, and it gains credibility from the likelihood that he himself experienced some of the trances that he discussed. In a modern study, Richard J. Castillo writes that trance-induced yogic meditation 'has its key dynamic in a narrowed focus of attention'. This involves 'holding the attention of the participating self on a certain object', whether that be 'a visual image; an image in the mind; a particular sound ... or any external object'. Monotonous focus enables the brain to 'block cognition of external reality and allow a mental image to dominate the conscious awareness of the individual'.[54]

Returning to the literature on the seers, we find many descriptions that indicate the use of this trance-inducing technique. One widely reported case from 1653 concerned a servant who was digging when he had a vision of 'an armie of English-men leading of horses'. The servant was said to have 'look[ed] very attentively at the middle of a very high hill', which he 'gazed att so stedfastly'.[55] It would appear that the seer unintentionally induced trance by cultivating a monotonous focus, probably assisted by the rhythmic process of digging. This indicates that normative experiences of trance – similar, perhaps, to modern-day experiences of 'highway hypnosis' – were also experienced in early modern Scotland.

Having isolated a number of instances where trance seems to have been at the core of a person's supernatural experience, we can now turn to the question of whether individuals exercised any degree of control over their trances. While trance was often involuntary, there are a few cases where we can discern an impressive level of control.

A key example is Janet Boyman, an individual of particular importance to this chapter owing to her position among the seely wights, a Scottish shamanistic cult whose human members are likely to have entered into trances.[56] Boyman's confession of having been 'subject to fairies' certainly implies, as Goodare notes, that 'she had experienced travelling in spirit with the fairies – probably involuntarily, but evidently in trance'.[57] We lack the evidence to examine these trance-induced visionary night flights in detail. There is, however, extensive evidence that Boyman intentionally induced trance in order to be visited by spirits. Summarising Boyman's testimony, her indictment stated:

Ye past thairwith to ane well under Arthours Saitt thatt rynnis southwert, quhilk ye call ane elrich well and thair maid incantatioun and invocatioun of the evill spreitis quhome ye callit upoun for to come to yow and declair quhat wald becum of that man and thair come thaireftir first ane grit blast lyke a quhirll wind and thaireftir thair come the schaip of ane man.[58]

We do not get any hint that Boyman used dance, music or drumming, the standard trance-inducing methods employed by ritualistic shamans. Her choice of Arthur's Seat is potentially revealing. It is possible that in this quiet and wide-open space, Boyman would sit and focus herself in a meditative state before calling upon the spirits in service of her clients.[59] Additionally, as Goodare has shown, there appears to have been a 'formula' to Boyman's self-proclaimed 'craft', involving patterned behaviours such as verbal formulae, specific timings and even a ritual action. She went to Arthur's Seat 'at the none tyde in the day and thair maid your prayaris ye haldand evir the thowme of your rycht hand lukkin in your neith' (at noon, there you made your prayers, while holding the thumb of your right hand inside your fist).[60] Similar to Boyman's invocation of the spirits through what appear to be intentionally induced trances was Andrew Man's ability to have 'rasit' Christsonday and the fairy queen 'be the speking of the word *Benedicite*'. Man's genuine belief that 'this word *Benedicite* rasit the Dewill, and *Maikpeblis* laid him againe' would indicate that much like Boyman, Man used a personally developed technique that induced trance.[61] However, it is important not to overstate the level of control exercised by these individuals. Although Boyman could call upon spirits, there were restrictions; she told one desperate client that she could 'do [her husband] na guid at that tyme Because it was past halow evin [Halloween]'.[62]

Both Boyman and Man experienced trance visions repeatedly over an extended period. Boyman 'confessit that ye haif sene twentie tymes the evill blast' – the whirlwind blast that preceded the appearance of the spirits she communicated with. Man reported having been first visited by the 'Quene of Elphen' when he was 'bot a young boy', and thereafter for 'about thrette yeris'.[63] Possibly pertinent to Man's case is present-day research into the ability of young children to use dissociative techniques such as trance to conjure up an 'ideal companion' for themselves. This companion is created to offer the child 'unconditional love, approval, support, and advice in a world that otherwise was unstable, unsupportive and cruel'.[64] Perhaps this is what the fairy queen was to the 'young boy' Andrew Man. She appeared to him in his 'motheris hous', as a woman that 'promesit to the[e], that thow suld knaw all thingis, and suld help and cuir all sort of seikness'.[65] Interestingly, the fairy queen seems to have been something of a supporting figure in Alison Pearson's life as well;

Pearson talked of the 'kynd freindis' she had in fairyland and her 'gude acquentance of the Quene of Elphane'.[66]

Studies have demonstrated that children who use dissociative techniques, often as self-preservation from stress or trauma, continue this tendency into their adult life, making them more prone to falling into spontaneous or intentionally induced trances.[67] This propensity to experience trance is not necessarily pathological.[68] Luhrmann has emphasised how people might actively learn to 'treat what the mind imagines as more real than the world one knows', a dimension that makes the experience very different from trauma-induced psychosis.[69] It would certainly seem that Andrew Man had this ability, conjuring up the fairy queen and his 'engell' Christsonday whenever he wished and having many pleasant experiences while in 'cumpanie with thame'.[70] We could hypothesise that Man had an enjoyable childhood propensity for trance-induced fantasising, and learned over time how to exert a greater degree of control over when he entered into trances. However, the same cannot be said of Alison Pearson. Pearson's visionary experiences were initially positive; she found 'guid friendis' at the fairy court, a healing companion in the form of William Simpson and an ally in the fairy queen. But there was a point when her experiences ceased to be pleasurable.[71] Pearson came to feel 'tormentit' by the fairies, and was left without the power of her left side after one visit to them.[72] It is recognised within psychiatric literature that initially non-pathological experiences of trance, if deployed too frequently in response to psychological trauma, can damage neural circuits and subsequently make chronic psychosis more likely.[73] The difference between Man's and Pearson's experiences of trance underlines the fact that trance was experienced in a number of ways, and did not necessarily remain static over time.

Further supporting this conclusion is the manner in which a number of seers seem to have learned to exert control over what had likely begun as spontaneous experiences of trance. In the late seventeenth century, an unnamed Strathspey divinity student reported the case of a man who 'used ordinarily by looking to the fire, to foretell what strangers would come to his house'.[74] In an even clearer indication of intentionally induced trance, we see in some reports how seers would use a 'science ... called *slinnenacd*' (shoulder-blade): 'looking into [a] bone they will tell if whoredome be committed in the Ouners house; what money the Master of the sheep had, [and] if any will die out of that house for that moneth'.[75] These seers had perhaps realised the potential of cultivating monotonous focus, and were using objects to further harness their ability to enter into trances and consequently receive visions that could aid the community.

Some authors believed there to be a hierarchy of seers. This is indicated in a story that Martin Martin reported in 1703, in which he described how 'the novice mentioned above, is now a skillful seer'.[76] What seems to have allowed the individual to upgrade from the status of novice to 'skillful seer' was, as Kirk indicates, an improved ability to master the fix of one's gaze: where the 'hardy therefore fix their look, that they may see the longer', the 'timorous only see glances, their eyes alwayes twinkling'.[77] We can conjecture from this that just as Janet Boyman and Andrew Man learned over time to enter intentionally into trances through personalised processes, a handful of seers learned how to employ monotonous focus in order to experience trance-induced visions.

While cases demonstrating conscious trance inducement were exceptional, the majority of the trance-induced visions we have surveyed contain enough coherence, lucidity and self-determination for us to suggest that trances did not just happen *to* the individuals in question. The plainest manifestation of the agency that individuals had within their trances is the near-uniform search for healing abilities and answers about the future. Margaret Wallace, Jean Crie and John Fian seem to have fallen into trances involuntarily, but all made good use of the experience. Wallace was able to cure a baby and enable a man to walk again; Crie had 'attained to great skill of all diseases, and of things to come, so that there is great resort of the people to her'; Fian learned how to predict when and by what means people would die.[78] Bessie Dunlop would enter into her trances with a pre-prepared list of questions for her spirit-guide, Thom Reid: 'quhen sundrie persounes cam to hir to seik help for thair befit, thair kow or yow, or for ane barne that was tane away with ane evill blast of wind, or elf-grippit, sche gait and sperit at Thome, Quhat mycht help thame?'[79] (When a number of persons came to her to seek help for their benefit, their cow or ewe, or for a child that was taken away by an evil blast of wind, or afflicted by elves, she went and asked Thom, What could help them?) Vision quests were conditioned by cultural beliefs and societal needs. Given that early modern minds were impregnated with fairy lore from a young age, and anxieties about disease and the future were prevalent, it should come as no surprise that during experiences of trance we find them receiving insights into the future and healing advice from spirit-guides like Thom Reid. This stands as evidence that trance was not just imposed upon early modern people; some of them managed to wrest control within their trances, using the experience to address personal or community concerns.

Early modern Scots experienced trance in varied ways. This chapter has identified examples of catatonic trances, fantasy-driven trances occurring in hypnagogic states, trances involving behaviours outside of one's conscious control (sleepwalking), and normative, everyday trances, caused by intense absorption. A number of individuals seem to have developed the ability to enter voluntarily into trances. Even in the majority of cases where we cannot identify such a level of control, trances did not just happen *to* individuals; some were able to exert a degree of control *within* their trances by shaping what they saw and learned in their visions.

Trances might be unpleasant experiences; interaction with the supernatural world was fraught with dangers. However, trances also performed important functions in early modern Scotland, providing individuals with a means to service their community or indulge in fantasy escapism.

As we can see from the frequency of visions about fairies, healing and seeing into the future, the phenomenon of trance is conditioned by social and cultural context just as much as by neurobiological processes. Rather than focusing on one of these approaches to the exclusion of the other, this chapter has shown how neurobiological brain functions worked together with social and cultural context to create very real visionary experiences. The medical, psychiatric and anthropological literature helps us to understand the intensity of trance symptoms that a number of early modern people experienced. This means it is no longer tenable to disregard their experiences as superstitious nonsense, or even to confine ourselves to psychoanalytical interpretations. In answer then to what retrospective diagnosis can do for the historian, it brings us closer to the early modern people we study; it forces us to acknowledge the degree to which the 'invisible polity' would have been experienced as a very real place, its spiritual populace acting as virtually tangible friends and tormenters to a number of people in early modern Scotland.

Notes

1 From Robert Kirk's London diary (1689–90), quoted in Michael Hunter (ed.), *The Occult Laboratory: Magic, Science, and Second Sight in Late Seventeenth-Century Scotland* (Woodbridge: Boydell, 2001), p. 17.
2 Diane Purkiss, 'Sounds of silence: fairies and incest in Scottish witchcraft stories', in Stuart Clark (ed.), *Languages of Witchcraft: Narrative, Ideology and Meaning in Early Modern Culture* (Basingstoke: Macmillan, 2001), pp. 81–98; Lyndal Roper, *Witch Craze: Terror and Fantasy in Baroque Germany* (New Haven, CT: Yale University Press, 2004).
3 Emma Wilby, *The Visions of Isobel Gowdie: Magic, Witchcraft and Dark Shamanism in Seventeenth-Century Scotland* (Brighton: Sussex Academic Press, 2010); Emma Wilby, *Cunning Folk and Familiar Spirits: Shamanistic Visionary Traditions in Early Modern British Witchcraft and Magic* (Brighton: Sussex Academic Press, 2005); Owen Davies, 'The nightmare experience, sleep paralysis, and witchcraft accusations', *Folklore*, 114 (2003), 181–203; Margaret Dudley and Julian Goodare, 'Outside in or inside out: sleep paralysis and Scottish witchcraft', in Julian Goodare (ed.), *Scottish Witches and Witch-Hunters* (Basingstoke: Palgrave Macmillan, 2013), pp. 121–39; Éva Pócs, *Between the Living and the Dead: A Perspective on Witches and Seers in the Early Modern Age*, trans. Szilvia Rédey and Michael Webb (Budapest: Central European University Press, 1999); Éva Pócs and Gábor Klaniczay (eds), *Communicating with the Spirits* (Budapest: Central European University Press, 2005); Gábor Klaniczay, 'The process of trance: heavenly and diabolic apparitions in Johannes Nider's *Formicarius*', in Nancy van Deusen

(ed.), *Procession, Performance, Liturgy, and Ritual: Essays in Honor of Bryan R. Gillingham* (Ottawa: Institute of Mediaeval Music, 2007), pp. 203–58.
4 Edward Bever, *The Realities of Witchcraft and Popular Magic in Early Modern Europe: Culture, Cognition and Everyday Life* (Basingstoke: Palgrave Macmillan, 2008).
5 Edward Bever, 'Culture warrior: a response to Michael Ostling's review essay on *The Realities of Witchcraft and Popular Magic in Early Modern Europe*', *Preternature*, 5 (2016), 112–20, at p. 113.
6 Michael Ostling, 'Secondary elaborations: realities and rationalization of witchcraft', *Preternature*, 4 (2015), 203–10; Michael Ostling, 'Anti-anti-culturalism: a response to Edward Bever's "Culture warrior"', *Preternature*, 5 (2016), 237–41, at p. 237. For an earlier debate see Michael D. Bailey, Stuart Clark, Richard Jenkins, Rita Voltmer, Willem de Blécourt, Jesper Sørensen and Edward Bever, 'Contending realities: reactions to Edward Bever, *The Realities of Witchcraft and Popular Magic in Early Modern Europe: Culture, Cognition, and Everyday Life*', *Magic, Ritual, and Witchcraft*, 5 (2010), 81–121.
7 Tom Webster, '(Re)possession of dispossession: John Darrell and diabolical discourse', in John Newton and Jo Bath (eds), *Witchcraft and the Act of 1604* (Leiden: Brill, 2008), pp. 91–111, at pp. 106–10.
8 Pócs, *Between the Living and the Dead*; Carlo Ginzburg, *The Night Battles: Witchcraft and Agrarian Cults in the Sixteenth and Seventeenth Centuries*, trans. John and Anne Tedeschi (London: Routledge & Kegan Paul, 1983 [original Italian ed. 1966]); Julian Goodare, 'The cult of the seely wights in Scotland', *Folklore*, 123 (2012), 198–219.
9 Wilby, *Visions of Isobel Gowdie*; Wilby, *Cunning Folk and Familiar Spirits*.
10 Larry G. Peters and Douglass Price-Williams, 'Towards an experiential analysis of shamanism', *American Ethnologist*, 7 (1980), 397–418, at p. 397.
11 Louise Yeoman, '"Away with the fairies"', in Lizanne Henderson (ed.), *Fantastical Imaginations: The Supernatural in Scottish History and Culture* (Edinburgh: John Donald, 2009), pp. 29–46, at p. 38; see also Margo Todd, *The Culture of Protestantism in Early Modern Scotland* (New Haven, CT: Yale University Press, 2002), pp. 393–400.
12 Michael Wasser, 'The mechanical world-view and the decline of witch-beliefs in Scotland', in Julian Goodare, Lauren Martin and Joyce Miller (eds), *Witchcraft and Belief in Early Modern Scotland* (Basingstoke: Palgrave Macmillan, 2008), pp. 206–26. For more on Second Sight, see Domhnall Uilleam Stiùbhart, 'The invention of Highland Second Sight', Chapter 11 this volume.
13 Rebecca Seligman and Laurence J. Kirmayer, 'Dissociative experience and cultural neuroscience: narrative, metaphor and mechanism', *Culture, Medicine and Psychiatry*, 32 (2008), 31–64, at pp. 32, 35; American Psychiatric Association, *Diagnostic and Statistical Manual of Mental Disorders*, 5th ed. (Arlington, VA: American Psychiatric Association, 2013), pp. 291–307 (hereafter 'DSM-5').
14 DSM-5, p. 302; Johnna Medina, '"Other specified" and "unspecified" dissociative disorders' (2018), *PsychCentral*, https://psychcentral.com/disorders/other-specifiedunspecified-dissociative-disorder (accessed 21 November 2018).

15 DSM-5, p. 291; Rochelle M. Kinson, Aaron Ang Lye Poh and Helen Chen, 'Possession trance, epilepsy, and primary psychosis: the challenges in diagnosis and management', *Journal of Neuropsychiatry*, 26 (2014), E26–7; Julio Fernando Peres, Alexander Moreira-Almedia, Leonardo Caixeta, Frederico Leao and Andrew Newburg, 'Neuroimaging during trance state: a contribution to the study of dissociation', *PLoS One*, 7 (2012), e49360; Lisa D. Butler, 'Normative dissociation', *Psychiatric Clinics of North America*, 29 (2006), 45–62.

16 Lisa D. Butler and Oxana Palesh, 'Spellbound: dissociation in the movies', *Journal of Trauma and Dissociation*, 5 (2004), 63–88. When in the state of 'highway hypnosis', people can drive between locations on 'autopilot', retaining no memory of the journey.

17 Richard J. Castillo, 'Trance, functional psychosis, and culture', *Psychiatry: Interpersonal and Biological Processes*, 66 (2003), 9–21, at p. 13.

18 Erika Bourguignon, 'Introduction: a framework for the comparative study of altered states of consciousness', in Erika Bourguignon (ed.), *Religion, Altered States of Consciousness, and Social Change* (Columbus: Ohio State University Press, 1973), pp. 3–35, at pp. 9–11.

19 Sheryl C. Wilson and Theodore X. Barber, 'The fantasy-prone personality: implications for understanding imagery, hypnosis, and parapsychological phenomena', in Anees A. Sheikh (ed.), *Imagery: Current Theory, Research and Application* (New York: Wiley, 1983), pp. 340–87, at pp. 340, 353.

20 Tanya M. Luhrmann, *When God Talks Back: Understanding the American Evangelical Relationship with God* (New York: Knopf, 2012).

21 *DOST*, s.v. Trance, n.

22 Wilby, *Visions of Isobel Gowdie*, pp. 248–9.

23 Seligman and Kirmayer, 'Dissociative experience and cultural neuroscience', p. 50.

24 William Dunbar, *Poems*, ed. James Kinsley (Oxford: Clarendon, 1979), 'Fasternis evin in Hell', p. 150, lines 1–4.

25 NLS, Wod.Qu.LXXII, 'The exercise of Grizell Love', fo. 108ᵛ. Cf. Yeoman, '"Away with the fairies"'.

26 John Stuart (ed.), *Selections from the Records of the Kirk Session, Presbytery, and Synod of Aberdeen* (Aberdeen: Spalding Club, 1846), p. 306.

27 Robert Pitcairn (ed.), *Ancient Criminal Trials in Scotland*, 3 vols (Edinburgh: Bannatyne Club, 1833), III, p. 510.

28 John Hunter (ed.), *The Diocese and Presbytery of Dunkeld, 1660–1689*, 2 vols (London: Hodder & Stoughton, 1918), I, p. 266.

29 Pitcairn, *Trials*, I, part ii, pp. 209–13.

30 Trial of Isobel Elliot, quoted in John G. Dalyell, *The Darker Superstitions of Scotland* (Edinburgh: Waugh & Innes, 1834), p. 590; Pitcairn, *Trials*, III, p. 604; Bessie Henderson's confession quoted in Goodare, 'The cult of the seely wights', p. 208. For more on the experience of flight, see Julian Goodare, 'Flying witches in Scotland', in Goodare, *Scottish Witches and Witch-Hunters*, pp. 159–76.

31 Dalyell, *Darker Superstitions*, p. 591; Pitcairn, *Trials*, III, p. 604.

32 Wilby, *Visions of Isobel Gowdie*, pp. 295–7.

70   *The supernatural in early modern Scotland*

33 James VI, *Daemonologie*, in his *King James VI and I: Selected Writings*, ed. Neil Rhodes, Jennifer Richards and Joseph Marshall (Aldershot: Ashgate, 2003), pp. 149–97, at p. 193 (bk 3, ch. 5).
34 Pitcairn, *Trials*, I, part ii, pp. 50–1.
35 *Ibid.*, p. 52.
36 *Spalding Misc.*, I, pp. 119–25; *Maitland Misc.*, II, pp. 187–91; Pitcairn, *Trials*, I, part ii, pp. 161–5; NRS, JC26/1/67, indictment of Janet Boyman, 1572. I would like to thank Professor Julian Goodare for allowing me to consult his draft transcript of this document. It is due to be published in Julian Goodare and Liv Helene Willumsen (eds), *Scottish Witchcraft Trials* (Woodbridge: SHS, forthcoming). For more on these and other visionaries' relationships with the other-worldly beings that they encountered, see Julian Goodare, 'Emotional relationships with spirit-guides in early modern Scotland', Chapter 3 this volume.
37 Pitcairn, *Trials*, I, part ii, pp. 54, 162; *Maitland Misc.*, II, pp. 187–91; *Spalding Misc.*, I, p. 121.
38 Stanley Krippner, 'Trance and the trickster: hypnosis as a liminal phenomenon', *International Journal of Clinical and Experimental Hypnosis*, 53 (2005), 97–118, at p. 112; Austin quoted in Bever, *The Realities of Witchcraft*, p. 197.
39 A. Roger Ekirch, 'Sleep we have lost: pre-industrial slumber in the British Isles', *American Historical Review*, 106 (2001), 343–86, at p. 364.
40 Quoted *ibid.*, p. 368.
41 Paraphrased *ibid.*, p. 368.
42 Julian Goodare, 'Boundaries of the fairy realm in Scotland', in Karin E. Olsen and Jan R. Veenstra (eds), *Airy Nothings: Imagining the Otherworld of Faerie from the Middle Ages to the Age of Reason: Essays in Honour of Alasdair A. MacDonald* (Leiden: Brill, 2014), pp. 139–69, at p. 159.
43 Wilson and Barber, 'The fantasy-prone personality', pp. 376, 353.
44 Pitcairn, *Trials*, III, pp. 610, 612–13.
45 Wilson and Barber, 'The fantasy-prone personality', p. 353.
46 *Ibid.*, p. 348.
47 *Spalding Misc.*, I, pp. 121–2.
48 Pitcairn, *Trials*, I, part ii, p. 162; William Cramond (ed.), *The Records of Elgin, 1234–1800*, 2 vols (Aberdeen: New Spalding Club, 1908), II, p. 357.
49 Christian Guilleminault, D. Poyares, Falak Abat and L. Palombini, 'Sleep and wakefulness in somnambulism: a spectral analysis study', *Journal of Psychosomatic Research*, 51 (2001), 411–16.
50 Antonio Zadra, Alex Desautels, Dominique Petit and Jacques Montplaisir, 'Somnambulism: clinical aspects and pathophysiological hypotheses', *Lancet Neurology*, 12 (2013), 285–94.
51 Hunter, *Occult Laboratory*, p. 194.
52 *Ibid.*, p. 86.
53 *Ibid.*, p. 91.
54 Castillo, 'Trance, functional psychosis, and culture', pp. 12–13.
55 Hunter, *Occult Laboratory*, p. 92.
56 Goodare, 'The cult of the seely wights'; Julian Goodare, 'Seely wights, fairies and nature spirits in Scotland', in Éva Pócs (ed.), *Body, Soul, Spirits and*

Supernatural Communication (Newcastle: Cambridge Scholars Press, 2019), pp. 218–37.
57 Goodare, 'The cult of the seely wights', p. 206.
58 NRS, JC26/1/67.
59 Peters and Price-Williams, 'Towards an experiential analysis of shamanism', p. 399.
60 Goodare, 'Seely wights, fairies and nature spirits in Scotland'; NRS, JC26/1/67.
61 *Spalding Misc.*, I, pp. 120, 124.
62 NRS, JC26/1/67.
63 *Ibid.*; *Spalding Misc.*, I, pp. 119, 124.
64 Wilson and Barber, 'The fantasy-prone personality', pp. 346–7.
65 *Spalding Misc.*, I, p. 119.
66 Pitcairn, *Trials*, I, part ii, p. 162. For more detail on this aspect of Pearson's experience, see Goodare, 'Emotional relationships with spirit-guides', Chapter 3 this volume.
67 Seligman and Kirmayer, 'Dissociative experience and cultural neuroscience', p. 50.
68 *Ibid.*, p. 51.
69 Tanya M. Luhrmann, Howard Nusbaum and Ronald Thisted, '"Lord teach us to pray": prayer practice affects cognitive processing', *Journal of Cognition and Culture*, 13 (2013), 159–77, at p. 172.
70 *Spalding Misc.*, I, pp. 120–1.
71 Pitcairn, *Trials*, I, part ii, p. 162.
72 *Ibid.*, pp. 162–3.
73 Castillo, 'Trance, functional psychosis, and culture', pp. 13–14.
74 Hunter, *Occult Laboratory*, p. 150.
75 *Ibid.*, p. 88.
76 Martin Martin, *A Description of the Western Islands of Scotland* (London, 1703), p. 302.
77 Hunter, *Occult Laboratory*, p. 91.
78 Pitcairn, *Trials*, III, p. 510; Hunter, *Diocese and Presbytery of Dunkeld*, I, p. 266; Pitcairn, *Trials*, I, part ii, pp. 212–13.
79 Pitcairn, *Trials*, I, part ii, p. 53.

5

The ninety-nine dancers of Moaness: Orkney women between the visible and invisible

Liv Helene Willumsen

Ninety-nine beings – fourscore and nineteen – danced in the fields of Moaness in the Orkney island of Hoy some years before 1643. Or so said Barbara Bowndie, who confessed to having been one of these dancers during her investigation for witchcraft. But it is not entirely clear that the other dancers were human. This chapter subjects her striking tale to detailed analysis.

The number of dancers draws attention to magic numbers in folk belief, while the dance itself is part of the lore – learned or popular – of witches' meetings. During Barbara's interrogation, several other learned ideas about witches and the Devil were introduced through leading questions from the interrogators. However, it is likely that the story of the Dancers of Moaness had been circulating in the local community for many years, and that Barbara knew it through oral transmission before her interrogation began.

The questions will then arise how learned ideas about human beings' relations with the Devil interacted with the ideas of the common people, and to what extent this interaction influenced the development of witchcraft trials. The Orkney women, who frequently struggled to maintain daily existence, were realistic in many senses. However, their beliefs also displayed an invisible and unrealistic thread, which the image of the Dancers of Moaness brings to the fore. This chapter explores the tension between the down-to-earth attitude of early modern Orkney women and the much more dangerous, but still obviously popular, dance with what seem to have been invisible spirits. I will approach the court records of Barbara's case by close reading, trying to understand how Barbara and her female associates in Orkney looked upon supernatural powers as these emerged in a narrative spanning visible and invisible worlds.

Barbara Bowndie lived in Kirkwall in Orkney. She was accused of witchcraft in November 1643, having been denounced by another woman during some linked witchcraft trials, where names of accused persons were connected through denunciations. This was the worst year of witchcraft persecution in Orkney. The origins of Barbara's case involved Elspeth Culsetter, who had been tried for witchcraft and burned in 1642, and Marjorie Paplay, denounced by Elspeth, tried and acquitted in 1642, but still under suspicion of witchcraft when Barbara was accused. Barbara was asked several times to denounce Marjorie as a witch.[1]

Barbara's formal interrogation took place before the presbytery in November 1643. Two ministers were ordained to question her with the moderator, and it appears that any of the other ministers could also question her if they wished. Before this, and five days after her imprisonment, Barbara had been examined 'in private' by two brethren – one minister and one ruling elder – though no written record was made of this at the time.[2] It later emerged that, during this informal questioning, Barbara had been offered strong ale in order to induce her to confess. What she had confessed during this informal questioning was then used against her during the formal interrogation – but, as we shall see, Barbara's answers in the second episode were very different from those in the first.

During Barbara's formal interrogation before the presbytery, she was accused upon nine points, all of them related to the Devil, use of demonic witchcraft or witches' meetings. But even if demonological notions were emphasised during Barbara's interrogation, folkloric beliefs came to the fore in her answers. The interweaving between these two spheres of ideas is the focus of this chapter, with particular attention to ideas about witches' meetings and dances.

Barbara's investigation came to a standstill when she retracted her previous informal confessions during the formal interrogation. The presbytery decided to request a warrant from the privy council to use torture. Two brethren asked the sheriff to retain Barbara in prison until the privy council's answer arrived, and he agreed. Her name was next mentioned in the presbytery minutes on 3 April 1644, stating that the presbytery would wait for more information about her from Shetland. The sheriff once again promised to retain her in prison until this information arrived. After this point there is nothing more to be found in the records about Barbara, and her ultimate fate is unknown.[3] But her remarkable ideas remain for us to analyse.

The discourse unfolding during Barbara's nine-point formal interrogation gives interesting information about the questions put to her, and her answers.[4] However, it also leaves out some pieces of information. The idea of a witches' meeting, the dance, will be central to my analysis. This issue comes in as point eight of the interrogation. However, I would first like to mention the appearance of the Devil in some earlier points of Barbara's interrogation, as it is clear that the interrogators brought this figure on stage from the beginning.

In point one, the interrogators asked Barbara about something she had said about the Devil during her earlier informal questioning: 'concerning her saying, that the Devill told her that if she should be put to death, the whole cornes should be blown in the ayre by him'.[5] Barbara now answered that she had said this 'for weaknesses of her owne flesh, and for the feare of her [life]'.[6] She was not accused specifically of having confessed to a pact with the Devil, but she knew that it was imperative to deny any relation to the Devil.

Barbara was next asked, in point two, 'if she upon occasion of necessitie in Zetland, did condescend to serve the Devill'. She gave an indirect answer, saying, 'that being travelling with ane unhoven childe four yeers [i.e. an unbaptised child aged four] and being fainted by the way she became speechless, and so remained for the space of 24 hours, and was sore tormented'. Here the interrogators were again trying to obtain a confession of the demonic pact, but she avoided this. The interrogators then reminded her that she had previously explained this experience of being 'tormented' by saying that 'people said, that she had been with the Farie'. But Barbara now answered that she 'saw no Farie'. She did not want to have her accident in Shetland connected with the fairies, and when she was asked about the Devil, she chose a strategy of trying to lead the interrogation in another direction.

The interrogators continued to circle around the Devil. In point four, Barbara was asked 'in particular, concerning the Devill his apparitions in diverse shapes upon the Ball-Ley, and his having carnall copulation with Marjorie Paplay at that tyme, as a man hes adoe with a woman'. Here, the Devil is linked to sexual intercourse with a woman at the Ball-Ley, a sports field for ball games. Barbara avoided confirming her earlier statement by claiming that she had been brought strong ale 'which made her speake these wordes'. It is clear that she had described the Devil's various likenesses during the informal questioning, as well as mentioning the names of other women including Marjorie Paplay.

Point five repeats the same question as point four, as Barbara was asked

> whither she knew it to be of veritie, that she had seen the Devill ly with Marjorie Paplay on the Ball-Ley? Replyed that she knew nothing of it, but such as she was tryed upon, And being asked what that meant to be tryed upon? Replyed that the young co[m]missar John Aitkin had said to her, tell mee about Marjorie Paplay what ane woman she is, and thou shall never want they [thy] Life.

Thus it was one of the interrogators who had introduced this theme, promising her that she would not be executed. However, Barbara now said that she 'spake more then enough of the said Marjorie at that tyme, and of sundrie other honest women whom she had named', adding that 'she never knew no ill to these women'. Points one, two, four and five show the interrogators' focus on the Devil and their pressure for denunciations.

Then in the last point of the recorded interrogation, point nine, the focus returned to Marjorie Paplay, the suspect of most concern to the interrogators: 'Being asked what questions John Aitkin spired [i.e. asked] concerning Marjorie Paplay? *Answ*: he spired about the hand of the dead man, that lay above her bed head and stired about her aill; But spired not, if the Devill lay with her upon the Ball Lay; neither yet spired he about any of her sisters, nor of Elspeth Baikie.' Clearly, the main intention here was denunciation of other women. However, the Devil was still connected to the events at the Ball-Ley.

Point eight of Barbara's interrogation is the crucial one for the present analysis. In it, the interrogators returned to the witches' meeting, the dance in 'Munes' (Moaness). Barbara was asked

> to tell if she was one of the fourscore and nynteen that danced on the Links of Munes in Hoy? At first denyed, but therafter confessed that she said it, which being conferred [i.e. compared] with her first words in saying that it was but sixe yeers, since the Devill deceived her, is found to varie in her speeches, for it is elleven yeers, or thereby, since the dancers in Munes were first spoken of.

The interrogators were thus still circling around witches' meetings. Clearly, Barbara had described the dance at Moaness during the informal questioning, and had said that she was one of the dancers. However, the interrogators perceived a contradiction in her story, and felt it important to clarify their view. Indeed we ourselves need to understand the 'fourscore and nynteen that danced on the Links of Munes in Hoy' (Figure 5.1).

Figure 5.1 Looking over the Bay of Creekland (foreground) to the outjutting headland of Moaness, Hoy, Orkney.

What is Barbara's contribution to the information about the dancers rendered in the minutes and what are the interrogators' contributions? The core element was that 'fourscore and nineteen people danced on the Links of Moaness'. This is all we are told explicitly, but there was presumably more in the full version of the story. It seems likely that the dance had been said to have happened on a single occasion. A date was probably given, as the interrogators often asked about dates. Probably the reason for the dance would have been given – something to do with magic, as this is what would lead the presbytery to assume that the dance was a witches' sabbat. We do not know, from the records, the magical elements that might have been in question, except the number ninety-nine. Presumably the original story would have said more about who the dancers were. We do not know whether all the dancers were humans, even if some of them were said to be women. The rest might have included fairies or other nature spirits.

The story about these dancers seems to have been told in the local community during the past eleven years. The information about this is fragmentary but highly suggestive. It is recorded that it was around eleven years 'since the dancers in Munes were first spoken of'. The phrase 'were first spoken of' shows that the first speaking about the dance was not done by Barbara and that the interrogators had previously heard about the dance from other sources; it probably also shows that they had heard about it more than once. In 1642 the presbytery had noted that a previous 'deposition' by 'Elspeth Culsetter the witch' had been given in June 1633, and that there had been an accusation against Marjorie Paplay in March 1632.[7] At the time of Barbara's interrogation in November 1643, these events were indeed 'elleven yeers, or thereby, since', and it may well have been from Elspeth or Marjorie that the presbytery first heard about the Dancers of Moaness. During the informal questioning Barbara was presumably asked about witches' meetings, to which she answered that she was one of the fourscore and nineteen who danced on the Links of Moaness in Hoy. Whether Barbara herself was prompted by the interrogators matters less once we recognise that the story of the dancers arose in the community.

The presbytery believed that the dance of the fourscore and nineteen was a witches' sabbat, but they themselves were making this connection between the dance and the Devil. Having done so, they compared the time span of eleven years with another date given by Barbara, namely that it was six years 'since the Devil deceived her'. By combining these two periods of time in one sentence, the interrogators connected the occasion when the Devil deceived Barbara to the story of the dancers in Moaness. Their reasoning was: she said that she was one of the fourscore and nineteen dancers, but she also said that she made a pact with the Devil six years ago. So there was a contradiction, because Barbara was not yet a witch eleven years ago, when the dance was said to have taken place. The dance thus became related to demonological ideas, but the contradictory dates were impossible.

We, however, can see that Barbara had inserted herself into a pre-existing story about the Moaness dance, simply by confessing that she herself had taken part in it. During the preliminary questioning, she told about these dancers, that she participated in the dance, that the Devil deceived her, that Marjorie Paplay had carnal copulation with the Devil on the Ball-Ley, and that four other named women took part in the dance. The interrogators pressed for confirmation of answers to questions of demonological nature. The narrative about the Dancers of Moaness is an instance of the demonisation of folkloric beliefs during witchcraft interrogations.[8]

One further possibility should be discussed. When John Aitkin asked about Marjorie Paplay having intercourse with the Devil at the Ball-Ley, he may have posed this question because this theme had been part of the original story of the dancers. It is clear that during the informal questioning Barbara had said that this carnal copulation had taken place at the Ball-Ley. However, it is not known whether the link between the Ball-Ley and Moaness was established during that narration. Moreover, the Ball-Ley was a separate place from Moaness, as we see when Barbara later confessed 'that the Farie appeared unto her beside the Ball-Ley coming out of Essinquoy', which is in St Andrews parish, east of Kirkwall. Unfortunately the records do not give us enough information about the original story of the dancers, the story the peasants would have known. My interpretation is that the story of Moaness and the story of the Ball-Ley most likely were combined only during the interrogation itself.

The image of the ninety-nine dancers in Hoy is a complex one. Here we find beauty in language expressed in the most serious situation a woman could find herself in at this time – as an accused person in a witchcraft investigation. The image is connected to the supernatural in the sense that the narrative about the dancers contains marked unrealistic features – in which we may catch a glimpse of the beliefs of common people in an ordinary Orkney village in the middle of the seventeenth century. The story of the Dancers of Moaness is a meeting place between visible and invisible elements. The islands, the shores and the sea formed a backdrop that all people in Orkney knew. The outward and visible frame was all ready for a pastoral celebration. The invisible element had to come from within, from fantasy, oral telling, the range of ideas that had reached the island and formed the imagination of people living there, a melting pot of old and new notions and beliefs.

Barbara's confession about witches' meetings is a poetic one. Such an image, as it is told in a confession in a witchcraft interrogation, is one out of many examples I have seen in witchcraft confessions in court records from many countries, which draws attention to an astonishing and wonderful world. When such imagery is included in a discourse that may ultimately serve to seal the confessing person's own death sentence, it serves a purpose that is far from poetic. The beautiful image becomes an omen of death. Demonological ideas have entered the field of oral discourse in a local community and have been retold before the presbytery in a witchcraft interrogation.

Moaness is on the island of Hoy, near a crossing point from the mainland. The word 'Links' denotes a sandy and grassy area by the coast. Laura Paterson writes that the question of boundaries seems to have been in the awareness of early modern people's belief in fairies as well as their belief in witchcraft:

> In the minds of the confessing Scottish witches there seems to have been little to differentiate between the boundaries that separated mortals from fairies and those that separated mortals from witches. It was believed the liminal space that was marked by boundaries, which were often represented by remote wilderness or even physical boundaries like gates, separated the known world from the dangerous unknown world ... The confessing witches appear to believe that witches inhabited the very same supernatural landscape as supernatural beings, and, as such, were almost inseparable from fairies in this respect. It is, therefore, unsurprising that many of the accused witches believed it would be appropriate to hold their secret witches' gatherings on the boundaries of this supernatural landscape.[9]

Barbara could have seen the dance of Moaness as occurring in such a supernatural landscape. She had been to Shetland, and it had been told locally that she had been with the fairies there. Maybe Moaness could be seen as such a boundary connection, a landscape that on one hand was inviting and beautiful, so the story could depict an idyllic pastoral scenario. Yet, on the other hand, it was placed in a marginal area, where an encounter between mortals and supernatural powers was possible.

Relationships with nature are an essential feature in witchcraft trials. Judicial authorities insist on the women confessing their pacts with the Devil, for by means of their alliance with evil forces, women are able to manipulate the universal ruler and through him also elements of nature. In the seventeenth century, people had a perspective of nature and of their own capacity to influence natural processes that is alien to modern-day society. Julio Caro Baroja stresses the existence of an outlook where the dividing line between physical reality and the imagined mythical world was more obscure than it tends to be today. 'Between what physically exists and what man imagines, or has in the past imagined to exist, there lies a region in which the evidently real and the imaginary seem to overlap.'[10] This was the setting for witches' activities. Why did people believe in allegations about what was physically impossible? By directing our attention to a relationship with nature that was prevalent in the seventeenth century, we might find an answer.

In his book *The Idea of Nature*, R. G. Collingwood presents three different kinds of relationship between man and nature in the Western world: that of the Greeks, of the Renaissance and of our time. In his view, the transition between Greek and Renaissance perspectives, each of which is relevant for my source material, takes place sometime in the sixteenth century.[11]

The Greek perspective of nature is organic, based on an analogy between man and nature. Man is microcosm, nature is macrocosm. Nature is alive and in constant motion and, since it is an intelligent organism, organised. Nature is permeated by a spirit that is an integral part of it, not a separate entity. Such an outlook evokes the likelihood that we can manipulate nature by means of magic. Man's spirit may in theory control that of nature. The sixteenth- and seventeenth-century interest in magic and astrology demonstrates that an organic outlook lingers even when a more mechanistic and naturalistic outlook has started to supplant it.[12] Witchcraft confessions serve as examples of this.

Judicial authorities reflect views that coincide with a Renaissance perspective on nature. Body and soul are separate entities. This applies equally to man and to nature. A central precept of the sixteenth- and seventeenth-century cosmological movement is that laws of nature reflect an intelligence that is detached from nature: that of the holy creator and lord. Since witches defy God and ally themselves with the Devil, disasters descend upon the world to punish us, through God's will. This transition from one perspective of nature to another is a prerequisite for the new academic concept of witchcraft. Seventeenth-century officialdom has implicitly accepted the new outlook, whereas the common people still retain their old relationship to nature. This point of view is supported by my study *Trollkvinne i nord*.[13] It is likewise supported by the Norwegian folklorist and witchcraft scholar Bente Alver.[14]

What first draws the attention to magic in this story is the number ninety-nine. It has its outset in the number three, which is the first odd-numbered prime number, frequently used in fairy tales and other traditional tales. The number three times three, giving nine, is also frequently found in traditional tales, for instance that the hero should be whipped three nights in a row by three trolls.[15] Joyce Miller finds in her study of numbers in Scottish folk magic that nine was a reinforced number, being three times three. The use was always positive. However, nine was not very common, and she did not find any instances of ninety-nine.[16] In these ways of thinking, ninety-nine may be a reinforced nine. In his history of mathematics, David Smith states: 'The beginning of an appreciation of the wonders of mathematics is closely connected with the beginning of religious mysticism'.[17] Man wondered at the peculiarity of geometric forms 'and at the strange properties of such numbers as three and seven, the two primes within his limited number realm that were not connected with his common scales of counting'.[18] We cannot be sure that a number expressed as 'fourscore and nineteen' was recognised as 'ninety-nine', but it was certainly one less than a hundred and thus still an unusual and perhaps magical number.

How could this image fit in with the lives of ordinary women in a small rural community? What role could ideas of magical power play as part of daily rural life? The story about the Dancers of Moaness has many down-to-earth and realistic features. The visible in the story of the Dancers of Moaness is the landscape that we still see before our eyes, the hill, the closeness to the sea. This might be what the women living on Hoy, or looking across to Hoy from the larger island of Mainland, saw every day. However, it could also be related to the boundaries where land and sea meet and where you never can catch the line of the horizon – it lies beyond what is possible to reach. The lives of Scottish women have been examined in a witchcraft context by Lauren Martin and Emma Wilby, among others.[19] It was a hard life, with hard work and uncertainty with regard to necessities like clothes and food. These features are reduced in the story about the Dancers of Moaness, and we get a range of invisible elements coming up – invisible in that they cannot be seen, like the landscape, they cannot be proved, they can only be entangled in a tale.

As I interpret the narrative of the Dancers of Moaness, the visible elements are taken care of by Barbara. She and other Orkney women are the ones who know about an inviting landscape in Moaness, where such a dance might have taken place. But she and the other women are also the tellers of the tale, the ones who know how to insert features of an invisible kind into a story, features appealing to hidden and illegal deeds, appealing to that part of human life that could only live in a tale: temptations, danger, break with an accepted moral code. It may be an escape from harsh daily life, but it may also be an escape from restrictions on human feelings imposed by regulations and admonitions. For those who are the tellers of the story, the story might have been a sign of a desire for freedom and free space. However, the records show us that tales of this type ought to be kept among the women themselves. They care for each other. From point five in the minutes of Barbara's interrogation, it seems that the misery she might cause for other women has become problematic for her. She refuses to denounce Marjorie Paplay and other women. We know that other women came to Barbara in prison, begging her that she should not name any names. When Barbara concludes her answers, underlining these women's innocence, it comes as a sigh from the heart.

The invisible features in a narrative like that of the Dancers of Moaness were regarded as far from innocent when interpreted in contexts that were not the women's own. And it is in this context, the minutes from the presbytery interrogation, that we as readers encounter the story of the dancers today.

Common people in the seventeenth century lived in oral communities. Only a few people could read and write. An oral discourse differs in many ways from a written one and leads to the development of certain structural features in the remembrance and retelling of stories.[20] This has also put a stamp on court records of witchcraft trials.[21]

Witchcraft confessions are in a particular position between oral and written domains of expression, as has been pointed out by Elisabeth S. Cohen.[22] They are oral utterances, yet still written texts. Cohen writes:

> Sharing an intermediate textual zone that has attracted increasing scholarly attention in early modern cultural studies, these several sorts of non-literary sources invite a comparative analysis and double modes of reading. On the one hand, they are 'documents' to be read as straightforward descriptions of the world; on the other, they are constructed texts conceived strategically to represent their speakers and negotiate more complex meanings.[23]

These reflections invite us to undertake a type of close reading of witchcraft records in which we pay close attention to the personal voices of the actors participating in the court proceedings. Cohen argues that it is possible to distinguish between individual persons' voices in court records.[24] This means that interpretation of court records must take account of the plurality of voices that make themselves heard in the documents. By using linguistic methods of discourse analysis, it is possible to listen out for the voice of the accused person. This method of reading witchcraft documents, pointed out by Marion Gibson two decades ago, makes it possible during analysis of witchcraft documents to concentrate precisely on the interaction between learned ideas and the ideas of the common people and in fact find fruitful answers in the sources.[25] It also makes it possible to argue, as Malcolm Gaskill has done among others, that distinct voices heard in courtrooms during witchcraft trials may give us a glimpse of the mentality of the time.[26]

The narrative about the Dancers of Moaness has been transmitted among the populace in Orkney within an oral sphere. The oral accent is strong in the records. There are clear features of orality in the discourse rendered, for instance its closeness to spoken language, a factor mentioned by Walter J. Ong as an orality marker.[27] There are several instances of insertions of direct discourse in passages otherwise given in indirect discourse, either uttered by Barbara or by a commissary. We see this in Barbara's uttering, 'God forgive you that beares over much with them'. An oral accent also comes through in her double negative, 'she never knew no ill to these women'. Other orality markers pointed out by Ong are additive sentence structures, aggregative language elements, redundancy, closeness to the human life world and an agonistic (confrontational) tone.[28] Closeness to the human world is heard in this sentence, which points to the actual remedies that have been offered her: 'In respect that offer had been made unto her by a Ledder of a tow to hang her selfe, or of a knyfe to stick her selfe, quhilk would be ane easier death for her, then to be burnt.'[29] An agonistic tone, striving for effect, as well as a strong oral accent is heard in the phrase 'thou shall never want thy Life'. Several of these features are documented in the minutes of Bowndie's case. Point five in the formal interrogation also has marked features of orality. An additive sentence structure is clear, an attempt is made to draw a timeline, which has importance for the main argument about drinking ale, and direct discourse in the present tense is inserted into the narrative.

In point eight in the formal interrogation, it emerges that oral narratives with demonological content had been told by peasants in the area for many years. It is said that the story about a witches' gathering, the Dancers of Moaness, had started to be told in the area eleven years ago. Looking at Barbara's answers, it is clear that she knows the contents of the story of the Dancers of Moaness from years back. We hear a story that has been told and retold.

Much of this chapter has been about folk interaction with the natural environment. We have the survival of animistic conceptions of the landscape, and the notion that there could be threatening forces lurking at the sites of dances or ball games. These threatening forces might be understood as fairies or nature spirits, or even as the Devil or demons. When Barbara was pressed to denounce Marjorie Paplay, she had no difficulty in telling a story of sex with the Devil set in one of these magical locations.

The type of story we hear told about the dancers falls into a category that in Norway is called 'sagn' (a traditional tale dealing with inexplicable events) and that claims to have happened in reality. It is a genre, often with dark and frightening contents, where the credibility of the story is enhanced by facts – dates, personal and topographical names and descriptions of landscape and events; in the story about the Dancers of Moaness, the factual strand, so to speak, is the landscape, the grass fields – all the visible elements that tie the story to the ground on which the dance has taken place. Then there is the dark part of the narrative, the copulation with the Devil in such a place nearby, the Ball-Ley.

Barbara's interrogation is a meeting place between ideas related to traditional folk belief and learned ideas of demonology. When a group of women tell the story of the Dancers of Moaness among themselves, it might have been entertaining, but Marjorie Paplay's alleged copulation on the Ball-Ley is a shocking and frightening story.

For readers today, the way the story is presented in the presbytery minutes is important. Stuart Clark cites Julio Caro Baroja's idea that the problem of witchcraft was ultimately a conceptual one: 'His solution was to concentrate not on what witches did, but on what they were *said* to do; the reality of witchcraft was a consequence of beliefs and embodied in language.'[30] Caro Baroja concluded that there was a radical dissimilarity between the alleged witches' idea of reality and ours. He argued that

> the beliefs of those who experienced witchcraft ought to be given priority in any attempt to understand its role in their lives. Beliefs about 'reality', likewise, did not exhaust what witchcraft meant to these people; but again, we can agree that their attitude to it must have developed largely on what they felt to be possible and impossible in the real world.

Clark maintained in 2001 that Caro Baroja's advice had been largely forgotten in witchcraft research: 'It is almost as if the experiences of those immediately involved became the last things to consider, not the first – their "point of view" the least significant component, not the most.'[31]

Seen in this light, I believe that Barbara Bowndie's story about the dancers in Moaness gives us a significant glimpse of what Caro Baroja emphasised, namely, in Barbara's words, contemporary beliefs embodied in language. Using the approach of Caro Baroja and Clark, the reality of witchcraft as a possible experience there and then, Barbara's acceptance of the dance taking place within the well-known surroundings of Hoy, makes sense. What for Barbara seemed possible in the real world, is echoed in the story in the description of visible elements, the dance in the landscape.

Still, it remains to be explained how Barbara depicted what was impossible in the real world, namely the beliefs that had to do with the hidden, with wild forces, possibly with sentiments in her own body. Barbara's experience of mutism in Shetland might possibly be interpreted as a visionary experience, a signal that she herself believed that she had experienced encounters with spirits.[32] Such spirits could be evil and threatening powers. These experiences belong to the unreachable in real life; they can only find their place and their embodiment in the language of the story. However, Barbara's attitude towards the tale demonstrates her belief in it, as there is no distancing device to be found. Her attitude is serious, and the story has been told in the community as if it might in fact have happened. Laura Paterson argues that when witchcraft suspects were questioned, it 'gave the accused witches the opportunity to weave their own beliefs and traditions into the framework dictated by their elite interrogators'.[33] Barbara Bowndie's belief in her own 'reality' is something that it is only possible for us to grasp through her words rendered in the minutes. This makes her story valuable for scholars today struggling to understand the mentality of people in days long past.

Notes

1 Liv Helene Willumsen, 'Seventeenth-Century Witchcraft Trials in Scotland and Northern Norway' (PhD thesis, University of Edinburgh, 2008), pp. 165–6.
2 *Ibid.*, pp. 166–7.
3 Liv Helene Willumsen, *Witches of the North: Scotland and Finnmark* (Leiden: Brill, 2013), pp. 189–90.
4 *Ibid.*, pp. 178–90.
5 Orkney Library and Archive, Kirkwall, CH2/1082/1, Orkney presbytery minutes, 1639–46, p. 254. Subsequent quotations concerning Barbara are all from pp. 254–7 of this document. I would like to thank Diane Baptie for help with the transcription.
6 The manuscript is damaged, but 'life' is likely here.
7 Orkney Library and Archive, CH2/1082/1, p. 203. Minutes are not extant before 1639.
8 On this, see Lizanne Henderson and Edward J. Cowan, *Scottish Fairy Belief: A History* (East Linton: Tuckwell, 2001), pp. 106–17.
9 Laura Paterson, 'The witches' sabbath in Scotland', *Proceedings of the Society of Antiquaries of Scotland*, 142 (2012), 371–412, at p. 393.
10 Julio Caro Baroja, *The World of the Witches*, trans. Nigel Glendinning (London: Weidenfeld & Nicolson, 1964), p. 13.
11 R. G. Collingwood, *The Idea of Nature* (Oxford: Clarendon, 1965).
12 For changing attitudes to astrology, see Jane Ridder-Patrick, 'Astrology and supernatural power in early modern Scotland', Chapter 8 this volume.
13 Liv Helene Willumsen, *Trollkvinne i nord* [Witch in the north] (Tromsø: Høgskolen i Tromsø, Avdeling for lærerutdanning, 1994), pp. 68–9.
14 Bente Alver, *Mellem mennesker og magter* [Between human beings and forces] (Bergen: Scandinavian Academic Press, 2008), pp. 265–73.
15 Ørnulf Hodne, *Det norske folkeeventyret: Fra folkediktning til nasjonalkultur* [The Norwegian folk-tale: from popular poetry to national culture] (Oslo: Cappelen, 1998), pp. 43, 63, 75, 172, 169, 188.
16 Joyce Miller, 'Cantrips and Carlins: Magic, Medicine and Society in the Presbyteries of Haddington and Stirling, 1600–1688' (PhD thesis, University of Stirling, 1999), pp. 283–6.
17 David E. Smith, *History of Mathematics*, 2 vols (1923; repr. New York: Dover Publications, 1952), I, p. 16.
18 *Ibid.*
19 Lauren Martin, 'The witch, the household and the community: Isobel Young in East Barns, 1580–1629', in Julian Goodare (ed.), *Scottish Witches and Witch-Hunters* (Basingstoke: Palgrave Macmillan, 2013), pp. 67–84; Emma Wilby, *Cunning Folk and Familiar Spirits: Shamanistic Visionary Traditions in Early Modern British Witchcraft and Magic* (Brighton: Sussex Academic Press, 2005), pp. 8–17.
20 Walter J. Ong, *Orality and Literacy: The Technologizing of the Word* (London: Methuen, 1982), p. 11.
21 Willumsen, 'Seventeenth-Century Witchcraft Trials', p. 19.
22 Elisabeth S. Cohen, 'Between oral and written culture: the social meaning of an illustrated love letter', in Barbara B. Diefendorf and Carla Hesse (eds),

Culture and Identity in Early Modern Europe (1500–1800): Essays in Honor of Natalie Zemon Davis (Ann Arbor: University of Michigan Press, 1993), pp. 181–201.
23 Elisabeth S. Cohen, 'Back talk: two prostitutes' voices from Rome, *c*.1600', *Early Modern Women: An Interdisciplinary Journal*, 2 (2007), 95–126, at p. 95.
24 Liv Helene Willumsen, 'Oral transfer of ideas about witchcraft in seventeenth-century Norway', in Thomas Cohen and Lesley Twomey (eds), *Spoken Word and Social Practice: Orality in Europe (1400–1700)* (Leiden: Brill, 2015), pp. 47–83, at p. 57.
25 Marion Gibson, *Reading Witchcraft: Stories of Early English Witches* (London: Routledge, 1999).
26 Malcolm Gaskill, 'Witches and witnesses in Old and New England', in Stuart Clark (ed.), *Languages of Witchcraft: Narrative, Ideology and Meaning in Early Modern Culture* (Basingstoke: Macmillan, 2001), pp. 55–80, at pp. 56, 60, 71–2.
27 Ong, *Orality and Literacy*, pp. 37–45.
28 *Ibid.*, p. 36.
29 'Ledder' is probably 'ladder', while 'tow' is rope. However, it is strange that the preposition 'of' is used between these words. If the expression denotes means for someone to hang themselves, one should expect an offer of a ladder *and* a rope.
30 Stuart Clark, 'Introduction', in Clark, *Languages of Witchcraft*, pp. 1–18, at p. 2.
31 *Ibid.*, p. 3.
32 For more on visionary experience, see Julian Goodare, 'Emotional relationships with spirit-guides in early modern Scotland', Chapter 3 this volume; and Georgie Blears, 'Experiencing the invisible polity: trance in early modern Scotland', Chapter 4 this volume.
33 Paterson, 'The witches' sabbath in Scotland', p. 380. The following article appeared too late to be used in the present chapter, but its discussion of Marjorie Paplay provides important context for the case of Barbara Bowndie: Peter Marshall, 'The ministers, the merchant and his mother: politics and protest in a 17th century witchcraft complaint', *New Orkney Antiquarian Journal*, 9 (2020), 56–70.

6

Angels in early modern Scotland

Martha McGill

An Ascending Angel, by the Edinburgh-born Richard Cooper (1740–c.1814), is a drawing from the late eighteenth or the early nineteenth century (Figure 6.1). It shows a winged female angel rising in a mass of billowing robes above a half-sketched landscape. The angel is tilted backwards, arms outstretched, breasts bare. Her pose is vulnerable, and she looks rather alarmed by her own ascent. This was a conception of angelic forces that emphasised softness and femininity. Robert Burns (1759–96) probably had a similar vision in mind in 1787 when he termed his sweetheart Peggy Thomson an angel.[1] Numerous less-gifted songsters also employed the metaphor; the following example dates from 1798:

> FAIR modest flower, of matchless worth
> Thou sweet, enticing, bonnie gem,
> Blest is the soil that gave thee birth,
> And blest thine honour'd parent stem.
>
> But doubly blest, shall be the youth
> To whom thy heaving bosom warms;
> Possest of beauty, love, and truth,
> He'll clasp an ANGEL in his arms.[2]

This concept of the angel – beautiful, loving, a model for young women – became even more popular during the Victorian period, and remains recognisable today. Angels in the Christian tradition are embodiments of goodness, just as demons are symbols of evil. However, for most of the early modern period, this goodness came in guises quite unlike these gentle, yielding angelic figures. Early modern angels were noble, but they were not necessarily nice.

Laura Sangha provides a thorough survey of ways of thinking about angels in early modern England. In a discussion of the 'people's angel', she suggests that the most common way of understanding angels between

Figure 6.1 Richard Cooper, *An Ascending Angel*, c.1800. A female angel in classical robes. This style of depiction was common in Italian Renaissance art, but was not generally seen in Scotland before the late eighteenth century.

1550 and 1700 was as guardians of humankind.[3] Darren Oldridge similarly stresses the protective role of early modern angels, concluding that stories of angels must have been 'deeply comforting'.[4] Certainly, songs and visual imagery underlined the idea of the angel as a protector, and stories circulated of angels defending human beings. However, angels were also punishers; they stood ready to avenge humanity's sins at the Last Judgement. Moreover, angels served as God's messengers. In early modern stories, this meant that they most commonly appeared to foretell death and destruction. In Scotland, sentimentalised visions of guardian angels became prominent in the eighteenth century. For most of the early modern period, though, angels were every bit as terrible as they were beautiful.

In medieval European culture, the nature and capability of angels provoked convoluted theological debates. The famous example is the argument about how many angels could fit on a pinhead.[5] Protestant theologians were less interested in metaphysical speculation, but even after the Reformation, early modern Scottish ministers and philosophers engaged in theoretical discussions on angelology. I have discussed these debates elsewhere, and they are not my focus here.[6] Instead, this chapter aims to identify the angelic archetypes that would have been familiar to most early modern Scottish men and women. The chapter has a broadly chronological structure, and considers both continuities and changes over the course of the early modern period.

Angels had an important role in Catholic culture. Archbishop John Hamilton's 1552 catechism stressed that while angels could be called 'potent and mychty', only God was 'omnipotent' and 'almychty'. However, Hamilton also underlined the role of angels as keepers of humankind, who would protect Christians 'fra all perellis' (from all perils). He explained, too, that Christians should pray to angels, as 'ane blissit Angel kennis our prayar, takis it, offeris & presentis it to the presence of goddis majestie'.[7] Formal religious education about the significance of angels was reinforced by community celebrations. Around the mid-fifteenth century, Dundee ordered six pairs of angel wings for a pageant; in 1554, Edinburgh ordered one pair of angel wings and two sets of angel's hair.[8] In Perth in 1518 and 1553, the burgh's hammermen performed a play about the Creation and the Fall that featured both an 'angell' and a 'litill angell'.[9] At royal entries, the keys of the town were often symbolically presented by children or young adults in the guise of angels. In Edinburgh in 1503, Margaret Tudor was handed these keys by an angel leaning through a painted window. In St Andrews in 1538, Mary of Guise was given the keys by 'ane fair lady most lyke an angell' who descended from a mechanised cloud.[10]

Angels also had a visual presence in the pre-Reformation landscape. Images of angels decorated stone slabs and crosses, abbeys, tombs, sacrament houses, prayer books and books of hours, and church or castle walls.[11] Particularly common were angels playing string and wind instruments, often to celebrate Christ's birth, or to evoke the joys of Heaven. There are well-known examples of musician angels carved in stone at Rosslyn Chapel and Melrose Abbey, while the late fifteenth-century Trinity Altarpiece, painted for the Collegiate Chapel of the Holy Trinity in Edinburgh by the Flemish artist Hugo van der Goes, features angels as church organists. Another prominent motif was the angel accompanying and protecting a heraldic device. In the 1430s, James I added a coat of arms to the original entrance of Linlithgow Palace, complete with the Archangel Michael as guardian.[12] Sacrament houses, or receptacles for the consecrated host, often depicted angels bearing a monstrance (Figure 6.2).[13] Finally, there were images of angels superintending humans' bodies after death. Luke 16:22 records that after the beggar Lazarus died, his soul was 'carried by the angels'.[14] The year 1503 saw the publication of *The Art of Good Lywyng & Good Deyng*, translated from French by the Aberdonian Thomas Lewington; it included images of angels waiting at the deathbed.[15] Depictions of angels bearing dead souls appear in Robert Arbuthnott's prayer book (*c*.1482–83), the early sixteenth-century *Book of Hours* of James IV and Margaret Tudor, and wall paintings at the fifteenth-century Fowlis Easter Church near Dundee.[16]

Most of the above examples cast angels in protective roles. However, there were also numerous representations of the Annunciation, and depictions of angels blowing trumpets or sorting the dead at the Last

Figure 6.2 Detail from a sacrament house at Deskford Church, Moray, 1551. Angels bearing a monstrance, which held the consecrated Eucharistic host.

Judgement. Figure 6.3 is from the 1528 tomb of Alexander Macleod at St Clement's Church, Rodel, Harris. It shows an angel weighing souls, while a demon tries to intervene. Other art forms also recognised this angelic role. David Lindsay colourfully illustrated the terrors of the Last Day in *Ane Dialog betwix Experience and ane Courteour* (1554):

> Thare sall ane Angell blawe a blast
> Quhilk sall mak all the warld agast,
> With hydous voce, and vehement
> Ryse, dede folk, cum to Jugement ...
> Conjunit with Saull, Flesche, Blude, & Bonis.   [*conjoined*
> That terribyll Trumpat, I heir tell,
> Beis hard in Hevin, in erth, and hell.[17]

Another work of Lindsay's, *The Satire of the Three Estates*, was first performed in public in 1552, and remained popular throughout the period. It included the character of Divyne Correctioun, who arrived to pass judgement on men and restore order. He was generally portrayed as a formidable sword-wielding angel.[18]

We might also consider an account of an angelic visitation. In the spring of 1588, John, eighth Lord Maxwell, made an abortive attempt to raise a Catholic rebellion against James VI. He was captured and held in Edinburgh Castle, where he remained until September 1589.[19] The following account

Figure 6.3 Detail from Alexander Macleod's tomb at St Clement's Church, Rodel, Harris, 1528. An angel with a sword and scales weighs souls, while a demon causes disruption.

probably refers to the period of Maxwell's imprisonment, although the record – from the Spanish state papers – is unclear. As the story goes, Maxwell was considering securing his liberty by signing the Protestant Confession of Faith. One day at noon (traditionally a magical time), he was visited by an angel. This angel urged him not to sign the papers, adding that if he did he would lose his right hand and die 'a shameful death'. Maxwell was convinced, and refastened a golden crucifix about his neck in a fresh avowal of his devotion to Catholicism. However, within a few years of his release his resolve had wavered. He signed the offending articles of faith in 1590 and 1591. In 1593, a feud with the Johnstones of Annandale erupted into violence. Maxwell was killed and his body dismembered, fulfilling – indeed, rather exceeding – the angel's prophecy.

This angel came to Maxwell at a time of need, but offered no promises of succour. It gave him instructions and upheld them with threats; the focus was on divine punishment, rather than protection. Angels in Catholic culture could doubtless be comforting, but angels also reminded men and women of their religious duties – and, by extension, admonished them for their religious failings.

After the 1560 Reformation, Protestants scaled back the role of angels. Sermons underlined that people should not pray to angels or worship them, and that angels could not perform sacraments.[20] The minister James Durham (1622–58) cautioned against trying to depict angels. He explained that it was impossible to represent a spirit, and that the pictures could encourage idolatry.[21] Iconoclasm in Scotland was severe. Much medieval artwork was destroyed, though a few Catholic representations of angels survived.

Moreover, new images of angels persistently appeared – on gravestones and church walls, in private homes and as decoration in printed works. Angels were depicted on shop signs: between 1638 and 1642, the Edinburgh printer James Bryson sold his wares 'a little above the Kirk Style at the signe of the Golden Angel'.[22] They also made continued appearances in pageants and celebrations. In the royal entry of Mary Queen of Scots to Edinburgh in 1561, the keys of the town were delivered by a child who came from a cloud 'as it had bene an angell'; a similar performance saluted Anne of Denmark in 1590.[23] Michaelmas, also known as the feast of St Michael and All Angels, was well known after the Reformation because it remained a legal term date. In remote areas there persisted what were likely pre-Reformation celebrations. Martin Martin reported in 1703 that the islanders of Skye celebrated the festival with a cake dedicated to the Archangel Michael. Thomas Pennant in the 1770s found that the people of Iona rode around the Hill of Angels, a promontory on which St Columba was said to have met with angels.[24]

Protestant theologians also placed limitations on the protective functions of angels. John Calvin refused to affirm that individuals had their own guardian angels.[25] In his 1597 *Daemonologie*, James VI declared that since biblical times, angels had ceased to make any appearances on earth.[26] Nevertheless, the idea of angelic protectors persisted. In 1602, the sailors' gallery in Burntisland Parish Church was adorned with a solicitous angel, along with the inscription 'Though God's power be sufficient to govern us, yet for man's infirmity he appointeth his angels to watch over us'.[27] Writing in 1656, the minister William Guild rejected the idea that each believer had his or her own angel, but added that angels 'can and do help the godlie ... They are Ministring spirits sent forth for the good of the Elect'.[28] A version of Psalm 91, recorded in 1578, explained:

> His Angellis [God] sall give ane charge,
> That thay on the[e] sall take the cure.   [*care*
> In all thy wayis to be ane targe,   [*shield*
> To keip the[e] from misaventure.[29]

The version in the 1650 *Scottish Metrical Psalter* retained the overarching message:

> No plague shall near thy dwelling come;
> no ill shall thee befall:
> For thee to keep in all thy ways
> his angels charge he shall.[30]

When it came to angelic guardianship of dead souls, theologians were careful to clarify that God did not *need* the service of angels. Robert Rollock (c.1555–99) stated that 'all the Angels in Heaven is not able to raise up a bodie to Heaven', since that power rested only with God. However, sermons continued to reference the notion that angels would carry the body after death.[31] A hymn recorded in 1599 declared:

> The angels sall with singing thee convoy,
> Throw aire and fire up to the heavens sa bright.[32]

Peter Marshall has demonstrated how the theme of angels attending the deathbed remained important in England following the Reformation.[33] The evidence from Scotland is sparser, but early modern gravestones did occasionally depict angels at the deathbed.[34]

Thus, the protective angel remained a prominent theme within Scottish culture. There also remained representations of angels as figures of judgement. As a caution to congregations, sermons quoted 2 Thessalonians 1:7–8, proclaiming that Christ would be 'revealed from heaven with his mighty angels, In flaming fire taking vengeance on them that know not God'.[35] Imagery of angels at the Last Day persisted: the seventeenth-century painted ceiling of St Mary's Chapel, Grandtully, shows angels blowing trumpets as the dead rise from their graves (Figure 6.4). Gravestones

Angels in early modern Scotland 93

Figure 6.4 Detail from the painted ceiling of St Mary's Chapel, Grandtully, Perthshire, *c.*1636. Angels blow trumpets as the dead rise.

also depicted angels weighing the souls of the departed, or heralding the Judgement (Figure 6.5).[36]

Furthermore, there persisted an idea that angels might appear to deliver messages to humans. This angelic role was particularly uncomfortable for Protestant theologians. Calvin emphasised that humans should resist prying into divine mysteries.[37] Rollock similarly lectured that 'we have nothing adoe to be curious in questions, in searching out the secret will of God'. Angels themselves, he added, were kept in the dark about many of God's workings.[38] Accounts of meetings with angels largely disappeared from educated society until the late seventeenth century, but thereafter there was something of a revival of stories of angels, with the angelic messenger as the most prominent archetype.

Throughout the early modern period, folk culture recognised the possibility of angelic apparitions. In searching for these, we should note that fairies, rather than angels, were the most common denizens of the invisible world. In ballads, fairies make frequent appearances, but angels are conspicuously absent.[39] However, fairies themselves could be ontologically ambiguous. There was a belief, traceable back to Plato and Pythagoras, that souls might transmigrate – move from one vessel to another. The souls of fallen angels, for example, might come to inhabit animals.[40] This idea that fallen angels

Figure 6.5 Gravestone in Greyfriars Kirkyard, Edinburgh, 1614. Angels wearing classical robes blow trumpets. The unfurling banners read 'Arise ye dead, unto judgement'.

had become a part of the natural world survived in various forms over the centuries. James VI criticised those 'wretches' who believed that 'at the fall of *Lucifer*, some Spirites fell in the aire, some in the fire, some in the water, some in the lande: In which Elementes they still remaine'.[41] Alexander Carmichael, investigating nineteenth-century folk tradition, recorded a Shetland man's explanation: 'when the angels fell, some fell on the land, some on the sea. The former are fairies [the latter were perhaps seals].'[42]

For the most part, however, fairies and angels retained separate identities. Several scholars have demonstrated the influence of fairy beliefs in moulding evidence presented in the witch trials.[43] Angels were a lesser, but still an identifiable, influence. Accused witch Isobel Watson (Perthshire; summoned by the presbytery of Stirling, 1590) recounted that Satan appeared to her in the form of an angel.[44] Several others reported being visited by apparitions clad all in white (fairies more usually wore green).[45] Jonet Trall (Perthshire, 1623) described a 'bonny white man' – although he also appeared to Trall in green. The same phrasing was used to describe a stranger, thought to be an angel, who saved the covenanting minister Samuel Rutherford when he fell into a well as a child.[46] Also notable is the testimony of John Fian (Haddington, 1590). The Devil appeared to Fian in 'white raiment'. On his second appearance Fian was in bed, and was 'strukin in grit extasies and transis, lyand be the space of twa or thre houris deid, his spreit tane; and sufferit him selff to be careit and transportit to mony montanes, as thocht throw all the warld'.[47] This recalls beliefs about how angels would transport the soul after death.

The most interesting case, however, is that of Andrew Man, who was tried in Aberdeen in 1598.[48] Man testified that he had an angelic adviser, Christsonday. He explained that Christsonday was God's godson, but the two had fallen out and Christsonday was instead associating with the fairy queen. Man could raise Christsonday by speaking the word *Benedicite*. Christsonday wore white clothing, but sometimes appeared in the form of a 'staig', a young horse. Man stated that on the Day of Judgement Christsonday would serve as notary 'to accuse everie man', but would subsequently be 'cassin in the fyre becaus he dissavis wardlingis men' (cast in the fire because he deceives worldly men). Christsonday was described as Man's master, but there is no indication that he provided protection or that Man looked to him for succour. Chiefly, Christsonday seems to have acted as an instructor. As well as foretelling the events of the Last Day, Man discussed methods for ensuring a good harvest and the breeding pattern of crows.[49] Christsonday was also mentioned by Christian Reid and Marion Grant, who were accused as part of the same set of trials, although they did not explicitly identify him as an angel. In the case of Grant, Christsonday appeared in silk, carrying a white candle, and taught her how to charm a sword.[50]

The name 'Christsonday' is an interesting one.[51] Thomas Leys, another accused witch from the same set of trials, used the term 'Christsonday' to indicate a calendar date: 'the said bairne suld be borne upoun ane Chryistsonday sa mony oulkis efter Martimes' (the child should be born on a Christsonday so many weeks after Martinmas).[52] In a tract from 1640, the minister Robert Baillie used 'Christs Sunday' to refer to the Sabbath.[53] An angel called 'Sabbath' is not unreasonable. Edward Lhuyd, in his late seventeenth-century notes on Highland belief, recorded that 'they think the Lords Day is consecrat to ane Angel called Domhin'.[54] Again we have a Sabbath angel, and the name – Domhin – may derive from the Gaelic *Domhnach*, meaning Sunday.

Another possibility is that 'Christsonday' was a term for Christmas Day. There is a Christmas fricassee called 'All Sons of Adam', added to the Wode Psalter probably in the 1620s, and included in John Forbes's 1666 edition of songs from Aberdeenshire. It includes the lines:

> There comes a ship far sailing then,
> Saint Michel was the stieres-man: Saint John sate in the horn:
> Our Lord harped, our Lady sang,
> And all the bells of heaven they rang,
> On Christs Sunday at morn, On Christs Sonday at morn.[55]

Later versions of 'All Sons of Adam' morph into 'I Saw Three Ships', and give either 'Christ's Sunday' or 'Christmas Day'.[56] After the Reformation, church feasts were transferred to the nearest Sunday, so Christmas Day might feasibly become 'Christ's Sunday', or 'Christsonday'.[57] The 'Christmas' definition, however, does not fit as well with Leys's evidence; had it been clear that he was referencing Christmas Day, there would have been no need for the 'so many oulkis efter Martimes'. But by either of these definitions, the term wove the angel Christsonday into the religious calendar. This reinforces the idea that he was understood as something separate from fairies, something bound more explicitly within the Christian framework.

In other respects, too, Christsonday was identifiably angelic. He wore white, and the silk and candle connote holiness, albeit with a Catholic tinge. Christsonday also had an important role at the Last Judgement. However, he failed in the most fundamental qualification. God's angels were supposed to be good; this was the key factor differentiating them from demons. Christsonday was damned to hellfire for deceiving men. Did Andrew Man understand him as a fallen angel? Certainly, the method of raising him (by speaking *Benedicite*) parallels demonology. However, 'angel' was not normally used to refer to a devil without qualification. Man's interrogators identified Christsonday as the Devil, but added that Man believed him to be an angel; the contrast implies that they understood Man to be talking about a good angel.[58] Probably Man did not draw a perfectly clean division between good and evil. Fairies might be classed as evil: it was traditionally held that a proportion of them were swept away to Hell each year.[59] However, they were not averse to occasionally helping humans, and rewarded cleanliness and propriety. Of course, moral ambiguity is also a human quality. Christsonday certainly seems more human than angelic in emotional terms, having a 'thraw' by God (being angry with him). The enigmatic Christsonday demonstrates how far popular understandings of angels might deviate from the familiar model of the serene, virtuous guardian.

As the seventeenth century progressed, accounts of angelic appearances became more common, with visitations reported by both educated and uneducated individuals. Episcopalianism was reinstated after the 1660 Restoration, leading to a protracted dispute between the authorities and the swathes of Presbyterians who refused to conform. Stories circulated of angels rescuing godly Presbyterians from dangerous situations, while visionaries described angelic lectures.[60] A Paisley woman called Grizell Love wrote of angelic encounters from the 1660s. The angels wore long white robes, carried harps, and had eyes 'beautifull and sparkling as Diamonds'. They discoursed on the state of the church, and noted that God was engaged in 'the trying of the faith of his people'.[61] The ten-year-old daughter of Donald McGreiger from Perthshire had numerous visions of angels in 1683 and 1684.[62] These angels generally took the form of beautiful children, who 'had sometimes white feathers in there hands like wings'. They told her to 'read the Bible & pray so oft every day', and also detailed Christ's anger at people's lying, charming, Sabbath breaking and swearing.[63] They later took her on a journey to Heaven, where she received assurance of Christ's support for the Presbyterians. Jonet Fraser, the daughter of a Nithsdale weaver, had similar experiences.[64] In the 1680s, she was visited by three men in white who circled her 'the way the sun goeth', quoting Scripture – including, on one visit, Luke 1:19: 'I am Gabriel that stands in the presence of God & am sent to speak unto the[e]'.[65] During prayer, she heard voices foretelling the deliverance of the church and the punishment of sinners.[66]

Unlike Christsonday, who provided practical assistance, these angels offered spiritual guidance. Love, Fraser and McGreiger's daughter also encountered dark, threatening devils or witches; there was a clear delineation when it came to the Scripture-quoting angels.[67] Of course, these visionaries chose to tell their stories, and others chose to record them, in defence of a certain religious cause. There was reason to keep the accounts as orthodox as possible. The testimony of Man, and other accused witches, was extracted by interrogators who were deliberately looking for signs of contact with the Devil. The differences between the accounts are therefore to be expected, but their similarities are potentially instructive. Like Christsonday, the angels visiting the visionaries acted as instructors, in defiance of post-Reformation orthodoxy. And although they were not morally ambiguous, they were sometimes intimidating, with their majestic appearances and warnings of terror and destruction. At one point, Love saw an angel bearing a sword. She then found herself recalling Psalm 149:6: 'let a two edged sword be in their hand to execute the vengeance upon the heathen'.[68]

After the 1689 re-establishment of Presbyterianism, there were efforts to clamp down on unorthodox visionary activities. In a meeting with the Dumfries presbytery in 1691, Fraser recanted her account, declaring that she 'had sinned greatly in being deluded by Satan'.[69] However, angels continued to proffer alarming judgements on the state of the land. One account, related by the Presbyterian minister James Cowan in 1710, concerned John Duncan, an Edinburgh merchant and town councillor. About five years previously, during a trip to an unspecified English spa town, Duncan had seen a pair of angels flying in the air, bearing a large white sheet. They landed on the ground and trailed the sheet over the grass, which was wet with dew. Once the sheet was soaked, they began to wring it out. The water flowed down, and Duncan heard a voice declaring 'so shall God wring out his judgments on this land'. The angels then vanished, and Duncan was struck blind and mute. His friends called for physicians, but he refused their aid, writing on a piece of paper *Nox dabit consilium* (the night will bring a plan). Sure enough, he presently recovered unaided.[70] Nevertheless, this was an angelic appearance that was awe-inspiring to the point of being actively debilitating for the percipient.

Within cheap pamphlet literature, angels also appeared with threatening religious messages. A 1719 pamphlet told of a farmer from Duns called William Rutherfoord, who met with a 'Young Youth cled in bright Rayiment, his face appearing as the Sun'. Rutherfoord, on seeing him, thought that Judgement Day had arrived. However, the angel was only come to warn about the *potential* of imminent destruction. The angel declared that 'the Land is full of Heatred', with family members and neighbours taking arms against one another; this was likely a critique of the recent Jacobite uprisings. The angel proceeded to foretell the famines, fires, thunderbolts, plagues and earthquakes that would punish the people of Scotland should they fail to repent.[71] In a 1734 pamphlet, a blind visionary from Kintyre described being visited by a young man in white clothing, thronged by 'visional Light'. The apparition proclaimed God's anger with Scotland for 'a broken Covenant, Profanation of the Gospel, and innocent Blood, shed'.[72]

At the same time, however, a gentler vision of the angel was growing in popularity. Robert Kirk, the Episcopalian minister of Aberfoyle, speculated in 1691 that the spirits his parishioners termed fairies were 'of a midle nature betwixt man and Angell'. This race of quasi-angels maintained a correspondence with humans in a 'courteous' attempt to demonstrate the reality of the world of spirits.[73] Kirk's notion of intermediate spirits was exceptional, but more familiar visions of protective angels were also becoming increasingly prominent. Peter Marshall has demonstrated that while English Protestants were initially suspicious of guardian angels, they were worked into Protestantism from the mid-seventeenth century.[74] Similarly in Scotland, educated people gradually softened towards the concept.

In sermons published posthumously in 1703, the Kilmarnock minister Alexander Wedderburn wrote that glorified angels made journeys from Heaven to earth as 'messengers for the good of the Elect'.[75] In 1726, the *Caledonian Mercury* reprinted an article that began: 'The Belief of Guardian Angels is not a whimsical or upstart Notion, but may be plainly proved'.[76] In the late 1720s, the East Lothian minister William Ogilvie suggested that all important towns and families had guardian angels. From 1751 his account circulated as a hugely popular chapbook, *The Laird of Cool's Ghost*.[77] Guardian angels also became a common presence in poetry and songs. Sometimes they were presented as spiritual guides. 'To a Guardian Angel' began:

> Sweet angel, to whose pious care,
> Kind Providence did me assign,
> Defend me from each latent snare,
> And watch o'er this pupil of thine.[78]

Perhaps the best known example was 'Rule Britannia'. The song first appeared in the 1740 play *Alfred: A Masque*, by the Scots James Thomson and David Mallet. It later circulated in chapbooks and on broadsides. According to the first verse, the famous refrain was sung by 'guardian angels'.[79]

The eighteenth century also saw an increase in poetic comparisons between angels and people. Sangha notes the persistent comparisons between people and angels in England between 1550 and 1700.[80] In Scotland there are also examples: William Drummond wrote in 1616 of how 'Angells Gleames shine on her fairest Face', while a 1625 poem by Alexander Garden termed virgins 'Angell-like, and Glorious'.[81] Such poetic productions became more common, and probably circulated more widely, in the eighteenth century. Allan Ramsay's *Tea-Table Miscellany* (1724) recorded many examples, and the 1740 edition includes a poem called 'The Angel Woman', in which a woman's beauty appears

> All bright as an *Angel*
> New dropt from the sky.[82]

By the late eighteenth century there were numerous examples to be found in songbooks, including the one quoted in the introduction to this chapter. In this context, angels were softened and feminised; the emphasis was on beauty and serenity, rather than vengefulness or judgement.

Ministers continued to describe the formidable angels that would usher in the Last Judgement, and trumpeting angels still appeared on monuments and gravestones.[83] In the early nineteenth century, the folklorists Anne MacVicar Grant and Hugh Miller wrote of a Highland belief in a beautiful green-clad woman, the embodiment of smallpox. While the green clothing indicates the influence of fairy folklore, there were also flavours of the destructive angel, who came to take the victims away to God and his judgement.[84] However, with the rise of sentimentalised poetic and artistic depictions of angels, and the re-establishment of the guardian angel, a shift had begun. In the second half of the eighteenth century, angels were less inclined to appear on earth to offer advice or pass judgements; the distant protector was becoming more dominant as an archetype. This was also a period when ministers and philosophers were moving away from rigid Calvinism and placing more emphasis on God's love and benevolence.[85] Guardian angels complemented this more sympathetic vision of the divine.

Thus, both before and after the Reformation, angels had a visual presence in the early modern Scottish landscape, and stories circulated of angels appearing on earth. The angelic protector was a well-established archetype. However, we should hesitate to assume that early modern angels were necessarily comforting figures. There was an emphasis on the role of angels as adjudicators, bearing rods of discipline and ushering in the flames of the Last Day. The angel as an instructor was likewise a prominent motif, particularly in stories of angelic encounters. These angels might offer guardianship in some form, but they also had frightening elements: Andrew Man met with an angel who deceived mortals; visionaries saw angels who spoke of imminent divine punishment; John Maxwell was warned of his own dismemberment; and John Duncan was temporarily deprived of the power to see or speak.

Stories of angels were, most frequently, calls to action, and it is no surprise that they proliferated in response to religious conflict. Within both Catholic and Protestant culture, angels encouraged men and women to remember and to engage with the supernatural world, on pain of divine punishment. They also required submission. Images of trumpeting angels called for resignation in the face of death. Christsonday came to Andrew Man as a master; Maxwell and the late seventeenth-century visionaries received religious commands. Early modern Scots could gain insight and protection from the realm of the supernatural, but owed obedience in return.

As the eighteenth century progressed, there was a change in the emphasis of discourses on angels. Angels of death and judgement survived, but guardian angels became more prominent. Poetry, songs and artwork stressed the role of angels as compassionate protectors, and presented angels in softened, feminised forms. In the nineteenth century, the persistent likening of women and children to angels would further humanise the angelic character. A shift was also under way in the power dynamics between humans and angels. One popular song, which appeared both in pricier songbooks and inexpensive chapbooks from the mid-eighteenth century, made the following plea:

> Guardian Angels, now protect me,
> Send to me the swain I love.[86]

Instead of humans bowing in submission to angels, angels were invoked to answer human concerns – in this case, a decidedly unspiritual concern.

In the nineteenth century, spiritualist communities called on angels to provide instruction. In this context, there was scope for humans to make demands of the supernatural world. In the early modern period, however, it was necessary to tread very carefully when it came to interaction with supernatural forces. Angels represented a supernatural world that was radiant, joyful, full of music and celebration of God. However, it was also a world in which every sin was catalogued, and terrible punishments might rain down on the disobedient.

Notes

1 Autobiographical letter to John Moore, printed in *The Life and Works of Robert Burns*, ed. Robert Chambers, rev. William Wallace, 4 vols (New York: Longmans, Green & Co., 1896), I, pp. 9–21, at p. 16.
2 W. R., 'Song: to a beautiful young lady from the country, whose parents are held in universal estimation', in *Poetry: Original and Selected*, 4 vols (Glasgow, 1798), IV, sec. 23, no. 61.
3 Laura Sangha, *Angels and Belief in England, 1480–1700* (London: Pickering & Chatto, 2012), p. 148.
4 Darren Oldridge, *The Supernatural in Tudor and Stuart England* (Abingdon: Routledge, 2016), p. 104. For a broader view of the functions of English angels, see Alexandra Walsham, 'Invisible helpers: angelic intervention in post-Reformation England', *Past and Present*, 208 (Aug. 2010), 77–130.
5 See David Keck, *Angels and Angelology in the Middle Ages* (Oxford: Oxford University Press, 1998), esp. part ii.
6 Martha McGill, 'Angels, devils, and discernment in early modern Scotland', in Michelle D. Brock, Richard Raiswell and David R. Winter (eds), *Knowing Demons, Knowing Spirits in the Early Modern Period* (Basingstoke: Palgrave Macmillan, 2018), pp. 239–63.
7 John Hamilton, *The Catechisme: That Is to Say, Ane Comone and Catholik Instructioun of the Christin People* (St Andrews, 1552), pp. 98, 198.

8 Anna Jean Mill, *Mediaeval Plays in Scotland* (Edinburgh: St Andrews University Publications, 1927), pp. 172, 173n4, 182.
9 Anna Jean Mill, 'The Perth hammermen's play: a Scottish Garden of Eden', *SHR*, 49 (1970), 146–53, at p. 147.
10 Mill, *Mediaeval Plays*, pp. 190, 287.
11 On stone slabs, see J. Romilly Allen and Joseph Anderson, *The Early Christian Monuments of Scotland*, 2 vols (Edinburgh: Neill & Co. for the Society of Antiquaries of Scotland, 1903); on monuments and church architecture, see David MacGibbon and Thomas Ross, *The Ecclesiastical Architecture of Scotland: From the Earliest Christian Times to the Seventeenth Century*, 3 vols (Edinburgh: David Douglas, 1896–97); on painted ceilings, see Michael Bath, *Renaissance Decorative Painting in Scotland* (Edinburgh: National Museums of Scotland, 2003); on sacrament houses, see Stephen Mark Holmes, *Sacred Signs in Reformation Scotland: Interpreting Worship, 1488–1590* (Oxford: Oxford University Press, 2015), pp. 125–43. On images of angels in sixteenth- and seventeenth-century England, see Alexandra Walsham, 'Angels and idols in England's long Reformation', in Peter Marshall and Alexandra Walsham (eds), *Angels in the Early Modern World* (Cambridge: Cambridge University Press, 2006), pp. 134–67.
12 Jamie Reid-Baxter, 'James IV and Robert Carver: music for the armed man', in Kate Buchanan, Lucinda H. S. Dean and Michael Penman (eds), *Medieval and Early Modern Representations of Authority in Scotland and the British Isles* (Abingdon: Routledge, 2016), pp. 235–52, at p. 245.
13 Holmes, *Sacred Signs in Reformation Scotland*, p. 131.
14 Biblical quotations are from the King James version unless otherwise specified.
15 Audrey-Beth Fitch, *The Search for Salvation: Lay Faith in Scotland, 1480–1560*, ed. Elizabeth Ewan (Edinburgh: John Donald, 2009), p. 26.
16 *Ibid.*, pp. 23, 24, 124.
17 Sir David Lindsay of the Mount, *Works*, ed. Douglas Hamer, 4 vols (Edinburgh: STS, 1931–36), I, p. 364, lines 5586–95.
18 See Douglas Hamer, 'Notes: Ane Satyre of the Thrie Estaitis', in Lindsay, *Works*, IV, p. 153.
19 [Walter Lindsay], 'September 1591: the present state of the Catholic religion in Scotland', in *Calendar of State Papers, Spain (Simancas), Volume 4, 1587–1603*, ed. Martin A. S. Hume (London: HMSO, 1899), pp. 587–92. There is another version in William Forbes-Leith (ed.), *Narratives of Scottish Catholics under Mary Stuart and James VI* (Edinburgh: William Paterson, 1885), pp. 351–60, at pp. 357–8. I am grateful to Professor Julian Goodare for bringing this material to my attention.
20 For example, Robert Bruce, *Sermons Upon the Sacrament of the Lords Supper* (Edinburgh, 1591), sigs K–K^v; William Perkins, *An Exposition of the Lords Praier in the Way of Catechisme* (Edinburgh, 1593), pp. 7–8; Patrick Simson, *A Short Compend of the Historie of the First Ten Persecutions Moved against Christians*, 3 vols (Edinburgh, 1613–16), II, pp. 92–8; William Guild, *The Noveltie of Poperie* (Aberdeen, 1656), ch. 12; Alexander Pitcairn, *The Spiritual Sacrifice* (Edinburgh, 1664), ch. 6, sec. 2.
21 James Durham, *The Law Unsealed: Or, A Practical Exposition of the Ten Commandments*, 2nd ed. (Glasgow, 1676), p. 36.

22 'Bryson (James)', in Henry R. Plomer, *A Dictionary of the Booksellers and Printers Who Were at Work in England, Scotland and Ireland from 1641 to 1667* (London: Bibliographical Society, 1907), p. 37.

23 Mill, *Mediaeval Plays*, p. 190; 'The receiving of King James the Sixt and his Queene, at Lyeth, May 1, 1590', in J. T. Gibson Craig (ed.), *Papers Relative to the Marriage of King James the Sixth of Scotland, with the Princess Anna of Denmark* (Edinburgh: Bannatyne Club, 1828), pp. 35–42, at p. 40.

24 Martin Martin, *A Description of the Western Islands of Scotland* (London, 1703), p. 213; Thomas Pennant, *A Tour in Scotland, and Voyage to the Hebrides 1772*, 2 vols (Chester, 1774), I, p. 297.

25 John Calvin, *Institutes of the Christian Religion*, ed. John T. McNeill, trans. Ford Lewis Battles, 2 vols (Philadelphia, PA: Westminster Press, 1960), I, p. 167 (bk 1, ch. 14:7).

26 James VI, *Daemonologie*, in his *King James VI and I: Selected Writings*, ed. Neil Rhodes, Jennifer Richards and Joseph Marshall (Aldershot: Ashgate, 2003), pp. 149–97, p. 188 (bk 2, ch. 7).

27 Margo Todd, *The Culture of Protestantism in Early Modern Scotland* (New Haven, CT: Yale University Press, 2002), p. 210.

28 William Guild, *An Answer to a Popish Pamphlet Called The Touch-Stone of the Reformed Gospell* (Aberdeen, 1656), pp. 214–15, 221.

29 John Wedderburn (ed.), *Ane Compendious Buik of Godlie Psalmes and Spirituall Sangis* (Edinburgh, 1578), p. 94.

30 *Scottish Metrical Psalter: Psalms of David in Metre* (Washington, DC: Eremitical Press, 2007), p. 165.

31 For example, Ninian Campbell, *A Treatise Upon Death* (Edinburgh, 1635), sig. E7^v; William Annand, *Pater Noster, Our Father* (Edinburgh, 1670), p. 67.

32 Alexander Hume (ed.), *Hymnes, or Sacred Songs* (Edinburgh, 1599), p. 22.

33 Peter Marshall, 'Angels around the deathbed: variations on a theme in the English art of dying', in Marshall and Walsham, *Angels in the Early Modern World*, pp. 83–103.

34 Hamish Brown, *The Scottish Graveyard Miscellany: The Folk Art of Scotland's Graves* (Edinburgh: Birlinn, 2008), pp. 93–4; Dane Love, *Scottish Kirkyards*, new ed. (Stroud: Amberley, 2010), p. 75.

35 For example, Rollock, *Lectures*, p. 222; James Durham, *Christ Crucified, or, the Marrow of the Gospel* (Edinburgh, 1683), p. 12.

36 Brown, *The Scottish Graveyard Miscellany*, pp. 91–3; MacGibbon and Ross, *The Ecclesiastical Architecture of Scotland*, III, pp. 369–70.

37 Calvin, *Institutes*, I, pp. 167–9 (bk 1, ch. 14:7).

38 Robert Rollock, *Five and Twentie Lectures, Upon the Last Sermon and Conference of Our Lord Jesus Christ* (Edinburgh, 1619), p. 65.

39 On fairies, see Lizanne Henderson, 'The road to Elfland: fairy belief in the child ballads', in Edward J. Cowan (ed.), *The Ballad in Scottish History* (East Linton: Tuckwell, 2000), pp. 54–72.

40 See Benjamin P. Blosser, *Become Like the Angels: Origen's Doctrine of the Soul* (Washington, DC: Catholic University of America Press, 2012), ch. 7.

41 James VI, *Daemonologie*, p. 163 (bk 1, ch. 6).

42 Quoted in Lizanne Henderson and Edward J. Cowan, *Scottish Fairy Belief: A History* (East Linton: Tuckwell, 2001), p. 23.

43 For example, Henderson and Cowan, *Scottish Fairy Belief*, esp. pp. 118–41; Alaric Hall, 'Getting shot of elves: healing, witchcraft and fairies in the Scottish witchcraft trials', *Folklore*, 116 (2005), 19–36; Julian Goodare, 'Boundaries of the fairy realm in Scotland', in Karin E. Olsen and Jan R. Veenstra (eds), *Airy Nothings: Imagining the Otherworld of Faerie from the Middle Ages to the Age of Reason: Essays in Honour of Alasdair A. MacDonald* (Leiden: Brill, 2014), pp. 139–69; Ronald Hutton, *The Witch: A History of Fear, from Ancient Times to the Present* (New Haven, CT: Yale University Press, 2017), ch. 8.
44 NRS, CH2/722/2/25, Stirling Presbytery Records, May 1590.
45 See the cases of Ellen Gray (Aberdeenshire, 1597) and Jonet Rendall (Orkney, 1629) in Julian Goodare et al., *The Survey of Scottish Witchcraft* (Edinburgh: University of Edinburgh, 2003), www.shca.ed.ac.uk/Research/witches/ (accessed 8 August 2017).
46 Henderson and Cowan, *Scottish Fairy Belief*, pp. 57–8; Robert Wodrow, *Analecta: Or Materials for a History of Remarkable Providences*, ed. Matthew Leishman, 4 vols (Edinburgh: Maitland Club, 1842–43), I, p. 57, III, pp. 88–9.
47 Robert Pitcairn (ed.), *Ancient Criminal Trials in Scotland*, 3 vols (Edinburgh: Bannatyne Club, 1833), I, part ii, p. 210.
48 See also the discussions in Goodare, 'Boundaries of the fairy realm', pp. 144–5; and Edward J. Cowan, 'Witch persecution and folk belief in Lowland Scotland: the Devil's decade', in Julian Goodare, Lauren Martin and Joyce Miller (eds), *Witchcraft and Belief in Early Modern Scotland* (Basingstoke: Palgrave Macmillan, 2008), pp. 71–94, at pp. 83–5.
49 *Spalding Misc.*, I, p. 121.
50 *Spalding Misc.*, I, pp. 119–25 (Andrew Man), pp. 170–2 (Marion Grant), pp. 172–4 (Christian Reid).
51 Margaret Murray proposed that it was a corruption of 'Christus Filius Dei' or 'Son Dei' (Christ, son of God), but this mixture of languages seems unlikely. Margaret A. Murray, *The God of the Witches* (New York: Oxford University Press, 1970 [1933]), p. 40.
52 *Spalding Misc.*, I, p. 98.
53 Robert Baillie, *Ladensium Autokatakrisis, the Canterburians Self-Conviction* (n.p., 1640), p. 87.
54 Michael Hunter (ed.), *The Occult Laboratory: Magic, Science, and Second Sight in Late Seventeenth-Century Scotland* (Woodbridge: Boydell, 2001), p. 72. Hunter notes that this line was crossed out in the original manuscript (n46).
55 BL, Add MS 33933, Thomas Wode (ed.), *Wode Psalter*, contra-tenor partbook, pp. 210–12; EUL, MS Dk.5.15, Thomas Wode (ed.), *Wode Psalter*, bass partbook, pp. 205–7; John Forbes (ed.), *Cantus, Songs and Fancies* (Aberdeen, 1666), K^v–K2^v.
56 See, for example, John Drinkwater (ed.), *The Way of Poetry: An Anthology for Younger Readers* (Boston, MA: Riverside Press, 1922), p. 75.
57 I am grateful to Professor Alasdair A. MacDonald for this point.
58 *Spalding Misc.*, I, p. 120.
59 Henderson and Cowan, *Scottish Fairy Belief*, pp. 80–1.
60 See Louise Yeoman, '"Away with the fairies,"' in Lizanne Henderson (ed.), *Fantastical Imaginations: The Supernatural in Scottish History and Culture* (Edinburgh: Birlinn, 2009), pp. 29–46.

61 NLS, Wod.Qu.LXXII, 'The exercise of Grizell Love', fos 109–109^v.
62 EUL, Dc.8.110, account of Donald McGreiger's daughter in *Admiranda et Notanda*, pp. 1–25^v.
63 *Ibid.*, pp. 2^v, 8^v, 14.
64 In EUL, Dc.8.110, account of Jonet Fraser in *Admiranda et Notanda*, pp. 3–45.
65 *Ibid.*, pp. 10, 12.
66 *Ibid.*, for example pp. 34–9.
67 *Ibid.*, p. 4; account of McGreiger's daughter in *Admiranda et Notanda*, pp. 3–4^v; 'The exercise of Grizell Love', fo. 108^v.
68 'The exercise of Grizell Love', fos 120^v–121, version as given by Love.
69 Yeoman, '"Away with the fairies"', p. 40.
70 NLS, Wod.Lett.Qu.II, letter from James Cowan to Robert Wodrow, 1710, fo. 143. See Martha McGill (ed.), 'Angels, ghosts and journeys to the afterlife: the "very rare and memorable" stories of James Cowan (1707–10)', in *Miscellany of the Scottish History Society,* Volume 16 (Woodbridge: SHS, 2020), pp. 159–94.
71 *A Wonderful Vision or Prophesie, which was Revealed to William Rutherfoord* ([Edinburgh?], [1719?]), pp. 4–7.
72 *An Account of Some Strange Apparitions Had by a Godly Man in Kintyre* ([Edinburgh?], 1734 [1730]), p. 3.
73 Hunter, *Occult Laboratory*, pp. 79, 96. See Julian Goodare, 'Between humans and angels: scientific uses for fairies in early modern Scotland', in Michael Ostling (ed.), *Fairies, Demons, and Nature Spirits: 'Small Gods' at the Margins of Christendom* (London: Palgrave Macmillan, 2018), pp. 169–90.
74 Peter Marshall, 'The guardian angel in Protestant England', in Joad Raymond (ed.), *Conversations with Angels: Essays Towards a History of Spiritual Communication, 1100–1700* (Basingstoke: Palgrave Macmillan, 2011), pp. 295–316.
75 Alexander Wedderburn, *Heaven Upon Earth* (Edinburgh, 1703), p. 159.
76 'From Mist's Weekly Journal, Sept. 3', *Caledonian Mercury*, 12 September 1726, pp. 6111–12.
77 William Ogilvie, *The Laird o' Coul's Ghost*, ed. J. F. S. Gordon (London: Elliot Stock, 1892), p. 33. See Martha McGill, *Ghosts in Enlightenment Scotland* (Woodbridge: Boydell, 2018), pp. 72–7.
78 *A Collection of Spiritual Songs* (Aberdeen, 1791), p. 108.
79 James Thomson and David Mallet, *Alfred: A Masque* (Dublin, 1740), Act II, Scene V, p. 33.
80 Sangha, *Angels and Belief in England*, p. 164.
81 *Poems: By William Drummond, of Hawthorne-Denne* (Edinburgh, 1616), 'Upon That Same [a Portrait]', sig. P4^v; Alexander Garden, *Characters and Essayes* (Aberdeen, 1625), 'A Virgine', p. 43.
82 Allan Ramsay (ed.), *The Tea-Table Miscellany*, 4 vols, 10th ed. (London, 1740), I, p. 370.
83 For example, *Sermons By Mr. Joseph Foord* (Edinburgh, 1719), p. 43; James Browning, *Jesus Christ the True God: A Sermon* (Edinburgh, 1792), p. 42; Archibald Bruce, *Corruptions in the Church to be Eradicated* ([Edinburgh?], [1797?]), p. 55.

84 Hugh Miller, *Scenes and Legends of the North of Scotland* (Edinburgh: Adam & Charles Black, 1835), p. 15; Anne MacVicar Grant, *Essays on the Superstitions of the Highlanders of Scotland*, 2 vols (London: Longman, Hurst, Rees, Orme & Brown, 1811), II, pp. 169–70.
85 See Jeffrey M. Suderman, 'Religion and philosophy', in Aaron Garrett and James A. Harris (eds), *Scottish Philosophy in the Eighteenth Century: Volume 1: Morals, Politics, Art, Religion* (Oxford: Oxford University Press, 2015), pp. 196–238.
86 Appeared in numerous English and Scottish songbooks; the quoted version is from *British Songs, Sacred to Love and Virtue* (Edinburgh, 1756), p. 18. For a chapbook version, see *The Blythsome Bridal, Bonnie Katherine Ogie, Guardian Angels, Britannia Rule the Waves, The Flower of Yarrow* ([Glasgow?], 1799).

7

Scottish political prophecies and the crowns of Britain, 1500–1840

Michael B. Riordan

Early modern Europeans believed that God endowed certain men and women with the power to reveal the future – or, at least, had done so in the past. Prophecies were frequently political, designed to get people to accept an outcome, or modify behaviour, because God had foreseen it.[1] Three distinct types of prophecy were used politically. All Christians accepted that the prophets of ancient Israel enjoyed contemporary authority. Claims to divine inspiration made by living people carried less weight, and accordingly their political pronouncements proved more controversial. This chapter is concerned with a third type of prophecy: sayings attributed to figures from Europe's past, enlisted to make claims about Europe's future. Most scholars have reserved the term 'political prophecy' for these pronouncements, following Rupert Taylor in his 1911 catalogue of them.[2] Several collections of these prophecies circulated in early modern Britain. Attributed to seers like Robert Nixon and Mother Shipton, they exhorted people to embrace political causes.[3]

Scotland had the most famous compilation. Constructed in the sixteenth century, *The Whole Prophesie* initially circulated in manuscript at court. It presented the Union of Crowns as divinely sanctioned, using prophets from England, Wales and Scotland to show that the Scottish Stewarts were legitimate heirs to England's Tudors, and restorers of an ancient Britannic monarchy. The collection gathered prophecies ascribed to real and legendary figures from British history. The Yorkshire friar John of Bridlington rubbed shoulders with the tenth-century abbot of Melrose, St Waltheof, while Merlin sat alongside William Banastre, who reputedly predicted the death of Edward in 1307.[4] The leading prophet was the thirteenth-century borders laird Thomas Rimour of Erceldoune, sometimes known, from his surname, as 'Thomas Rhymer', and sometimes by his abode, 'Thomas of Erceldoune' (now Earlston). Erceldoune's name became almost synonymous with Scottish prophecy.[5] The Union of Crowns was justified by the number of prophets that God had sent to predict it.

Some scholars believe that these prophecies were remnants of a non-Christian world view in oral circulation among the people. Elites appropriated this tradition to appeal to the masses.[6] Others contend that only the elite could make sense of the genre's political allusions. Victoria Flood has argued that Erceldoune's prophecies were first used by fourteenth-century English border lords to elicit royal assistance defending the northern border.[7] Edward J. Cowan, Karen Moranski and Alasdair MacDonald all believe that *The Whole Prophesie* was elite discourse.[8] Tim Thornton takes the middle ground: political prophecy functioned as a language shared by nobles and people.[9] These studies highlight the 'political' over the prophetic. Political prophets embraced prophecy because it justified their politics. This chapter attempts to inject the supernatural back into the study of political prophecy, using *The Whole Prophesie* to measure prophecy belief over time.

The Whole Prophesie was the widest-circulating prophecy collection in early modern Britain. First printed in 1603, it achieved thirty-three editions to 1833.[10] It can, therefore, be used to track shifting attitudes towards prophecy throughout the early modern period. People circulated prophecies because they believed them. If their audiences tried to fulfil the predictions of ancient prophets, it shows that they also believed in the power of prophecy. Accordingly, by tracing the circulation of political prophecy, we can test belief in prophecy's power.

Why might early modern Christians trust ancient prophets? To answer this we must examine a neglected aspect of Christianity's history: its veneration of the Roman Sibyls, whom European monarchs appropriated to make assertions about their territorial rights. The Sibyls laid the foundations for the discourse of political prophecy.

Supporters of English Tudor and Scottish Stewart monarchs used Sibylline prophecies to make dynastic claims.[11] Christians could legitimately use these apparently pagan sources because the Sibyls were believed to have predicted Christ's coming. Second-century Christians had used Sibylline riddles to undermine pagan polytheism, putting prophecies of the Messiah into the Sibyls' mouths. Some writers, like Lactantius, made more references to Sibylline pronouncements than Old Testament prophecies. This pattern persisted until the eighteenth century, when Sibylline and biblical prophecies frequently circulated together.[12]

For early modern monarchs, the Sibyls' utility lay in their prophecy of the messianic reign of the Last World Emperor, 'Constans', true successor to the first Christian emperor. The prophecy foretold Constans's reign over an era of peace when Christianity would triumph over Jews and Gentiles. Constans would travel to Jerusalem, abdicating his power to God. Antichrist would reign under God's watch until Christ appeared to destroy him and sit in judgement.[13] Supporters of both English Tudors and Scottish Stewarts presented them as second Constantines.[14]

When they did so, they were drawing on a version of the prophecy developed by the twelfth-century chronicler Geoffrey of Monmouth, foretelling that the Last World Emperor would be British. The prophecy was ascribed to the Queen of Sheba, whose meeting with Solomon was recorded in 1 Kings. Many believed that the queen had gained knowledge of Christ's crucifixion by worshipping the wood of the Cross. She revealed its location to Helena, Constantine's mother, who went on pilgrimage and recovered fragments from Calvary. Relics of the Holy Rood were captured in 1187 during the siege of Jerusalem. Building on the 'Constans' prophecy, crusaders aimed to return the relics to Rome. Helena's story was popular in Britain, thanks to Geoffrey, who claimed that she had been born in Britain.[15] When they compared their monarchs to Constantine, political writers in sixteenth-century Scotland and England were asserting their monarchs' rights, as Helena's heirs, to recover the Cross and be proclaimed Last World Emperors.

Geoffrey's *History of the Kings of Britain* (*c*.1136) placed the emperor at the culmination of a British apocalyptic drama, in which early modern monarchs wanted to perform. The British people once ruled the island. But 'pride brought retribution' upon them. Before their decline in the seventh century, the northern Welsh king, Cadwaladr, received an angelic vision predicting that 'the British people' would one day 'regain the island'. Elsewhere, Merlin predicted that a sixth king, Sextus, would 'undermine the walls of Ireland', restoring 'the traditional seats of the blessed throughout the land'. The Normans would 'lose the island and be deprived of [their] former dignity ... The native citizens shall return to the island; for the downfall of the foreigners shall commence'. Cadwaladr would lead an army to unite the original inhabitants of Britain against English expansionism. England destroyed, Sextus would restore the holy place of the saints.[16] Supporters of both Henry Tudor in 1485, and James Stewart in 1603, presented their leaders as King Sextus, descendants of the original inhabitants of Britain, who would reunite Britain and defeat the Turk in Jerusalem, fulfilling Merlin's prophecy.[17]

One striking adaptation of Geoffrey's text was the English romance, *Thomas of Erceldoune*, dating from the 1380s or 1390s.[18] Thomas meets a beautiful woman whom he initially mistakes for the Virgin Mary.[19] He begs her for sex, pledging undying loyalty.[20] But the woman transforms into a monstrous shape. She takes Thomas to her castle in another country, where Thomas dwells until the woman tells him that he must leave. Thomas protests that he has been there only three days, but the woman replies that it has been three years. He must leave to escape the Devil, who is coming to collect his fee.[21] Thomas pleads for a token, and she gives him a tongue incapable of lies.[22] Thomas asks when the

Anglo-Scottish wars will end. The woman's prophecies all predict English victories presaging a time of suffering. An English royal 'bastard' will destroy the Scots at Sandyford and unify Britain, bringing peace to both nations. He will go on crusade and die in Jerusalem.

These anti-Scottish prophecies were popular in England in the 1520s, when the Cheshire landowner Humphrey Newton reported a local minstrel singing 'a song of Thomas Ersholedon & the quene of ffeiree'. The fairy had predicted Henry VIII's victory over James IV at Flodden in 1513.[23] These prophecies continued to influence English opinion. Protestant opponents of Mary Tudor used them to predict the resurrection of their last Protestant king, Edward VI.[24] As late as 1652, the romance was published to justify Oliver Cromwell's invasion of Scotland.[25]

By the sixteenth century, then, there was an established tradition of English engagement with ancient prophets. The most famous was Thomas of Erceldoune, who predicted an end to wars with Scotland. This was a Christian tradition. Once the English conquered Scotland, a British king would lead a crusade to the Holy Land to be crowned Last World Emperor, as ancient Sibyls had predicted.

Sixteenth-century Scottish monarchs, meanwhile, appropriated political prophecies to claim that they, not the English, would be Last World Emperors. Developments in Scottish political prophecy followed moments of English dynastic crisis, when Stewarts sought to parade their claims. *The Whole Prophesie* contains prophecies written for monarchs from James IV to James VI. This section traces how this tradition emerged.

James IV's marriage to Henry VII's daughter, Margaret Tudor, brought prospects of a dynastic union that would give a Stewart control over Great Britain. The Stewarts were dynastically more secure than the early Tudors. James's marriage made it possible that he or his successors would inherit the English crown. James saw himself as a unifier, of Scotland, Britain and Christendom. He attempted to bring Gaeldom under royal control and sought to persuade European monarchs to launch a crusade against the Ottomans. As he prepared for union with England, James appropriated ideas from Geoffrey of Monmouth.[26]

The *Whole Prophesie* provides evidence that some courtiers believed that James IV was the Emperor Constans. The text printed in 1603 invokes Sheba's prophecy of the Last World Emperor, to present 'the sixte King of the name of Steward', James IV, as Constantine's heir. Elaborating on Constantine's British birth, it recasts the emperor as a crusading Scottish prince who converted heathens abroad and united his people at home. Constantine was forced to divide the island of Britain, to 'give [up] the thirde parte of his Realm, to have the forth parte [England] in peace'. The 'Wolfe the Dragon with the Lyon, shall divide the Realm' of Britain. After many wars, the kingdoms of the Wolfe (Wales), Dragon (England) and Lyon

(Scotland), would 'long lay in their den[s]' and live at peace. Sheba ends by warning the 'Stalwart and the Storke' – the kings of the world and the Muslim infidel – that Constans will spread Christianity across the world.[27] It makes sense to date this to after the Anglo-Scots alliance collapsed in March 1513. It may have been intended to win around the queen's party, who were reluctant to go to war with her brother, Henry VIII.[28]

We have substantial evidence for the tradition of political prophecy during the regime of the Duke of Albany, who twice acted as regent to James's successor, James V. Albany's policy was directed by the French crown.[29] In 1517, the English heard reports that James was preparing to invade with French support. In 1518, the artist and author Bremond Domat dedicated a 'prognostication of the prince, John Duke of Albany' to Albany's wife, Anne de la Tour d'Auvergne. It made Albany's imperial aspirations clear. He

> will by sea conquer,
> Scotland also England,
> and put them into subjection,
> by strength of arms and of war,
> he will take possession of them.[30]

A version appeared in *The Whole Prophesie*:

> Yet shall there come a keene Knight over the salt sea,
> a keene man of courage, and bolde man of armes,
> A Dukes sonne doubled, a borne man in France,
> That shal our mirthes amend, and mend all our harms,
> After the date of our Lord 1513. & thrice three after
> Which shal brooke all the braid Ile to him selfe.
> Betwixt xiii. and thrice three, the threip shal be ended,　　[*conflict*
> the Saxons shal never recover after,
> He shal be crowned in the kith, in the Castle of Dover,　　[*his native country*
> Which weares the golden Garland of Julius Caesar.[31]

This prophecy is one of several in the collection that refer to events during Albany's regency. It suggests that Erceldoune's prophecy of peace will be fulfilled in 1522, '1513 & thrice three after', when Albany, 'a borne man of France', will rule all Britain. Albany's threat was taken seriously in the early 1520s, when Henry heard rumours that he intended to marry Margaret Tudor, thus becoming Henry's heir.[32]

Albany's vision of Scottish dominion found further expression in prophecies modelled on the Erceldoune tradition, but ascribed to Thomas and two fellow prophets, Merlin and the ecclesiastical historian Bede. A version survives in an early sixteenth-century manuscript connected to the Welsh landowner Rhys ap Gruffydd, executed in 1531 for conspiring against Henry VIII. Rhys was accused of spreading 'ancient prophecies' predicting the conquest of England by a Scoto-Welsh alliance under James V's command.[33] Thomas's original prophecies had been pro-English: 'a [royal] bastard' would be born 'in south England'. Gruffydd's text, however, stated that the king would come over 'the Salwey Sandes', from Scotland, not England. This 'child with a chaplett' would summon parliament and appoint a protector to 'reign both even and morne / And falsehood shall banished be'. The pope would send the child to Jerusalem to reclaim the Cross. After 'seven mortall battelles' with the Turks, he would return the Cross to Rome, dying 'wythout batell' in the Valley of Jehosophat – which the Sibylline tradition identified as the site of the Last Judgement[34] – and be glorified among the saints. His protector would rule a united island where Protestant 'falsehoode be banished for aye / And [Catholic] truth shall reade be'. The prophecy ends with a date – 1531 – for the child's return to Rome, which shows that some people expected imminent Scottish victories over English and Turk.[35]

James V shared his predecessors' crusading aspirations. In 1530, Pope Clement asked him to confer with European monarchs about defeating the Ottomans, who had taken Hungary. James sent Albany to Rome for the conference and solicited French assistance.[36]

We can date the first Scottish text of *The Whole Prophesie* to James's majority. Its closing prophecy provides the evidence:

> A frenche wyf sall beir the sone
> Sall weild all Bartaine to the sey   [*sea*
> th[ai]r of the Brucis blude sall com   [*that*; *Bruce's*
> Als neir as the nynt degre.[37]

James V was in the ninth degree of descent from Robert Bruce, and married into French royalty twice: first to Madeleine of Valois (1537), who died less than two months into their marriage, and then to Mary of Guise (1538). Either queen could be the 'frenche wyf' destined to bear the son who would unite Britain. The prophecies are contained within Cotton Vespasian E.VIII, a heraldic manuscript depicting the arms of the Scottish and English nobility and royalty, which was intended for the king's eyes (see Figure 7.1).

The Sibylline prophecies of James IV, the 'prognostication of Albany' and the 'frenche wyff' prophecies, were all aimed at Scottish courtiers. At the court, prophecy could be controlled. But away from it, prophecy could cause diplomatic problems.

English Catholics used Erceldoune's prophecies to suggest that James V would march on London and reverse Henry VIII's reforms. Rumours of Scottish conquest circulated in the early 1530s, when Elizabeth Amadas prophesied that Henry was cursed and that James would soon conquer England.[38] In 1537, the Scottish Erceldoune prophecies circulated in Yorkshire.[39] In 1538, Henry's government heard that Scots were peddling

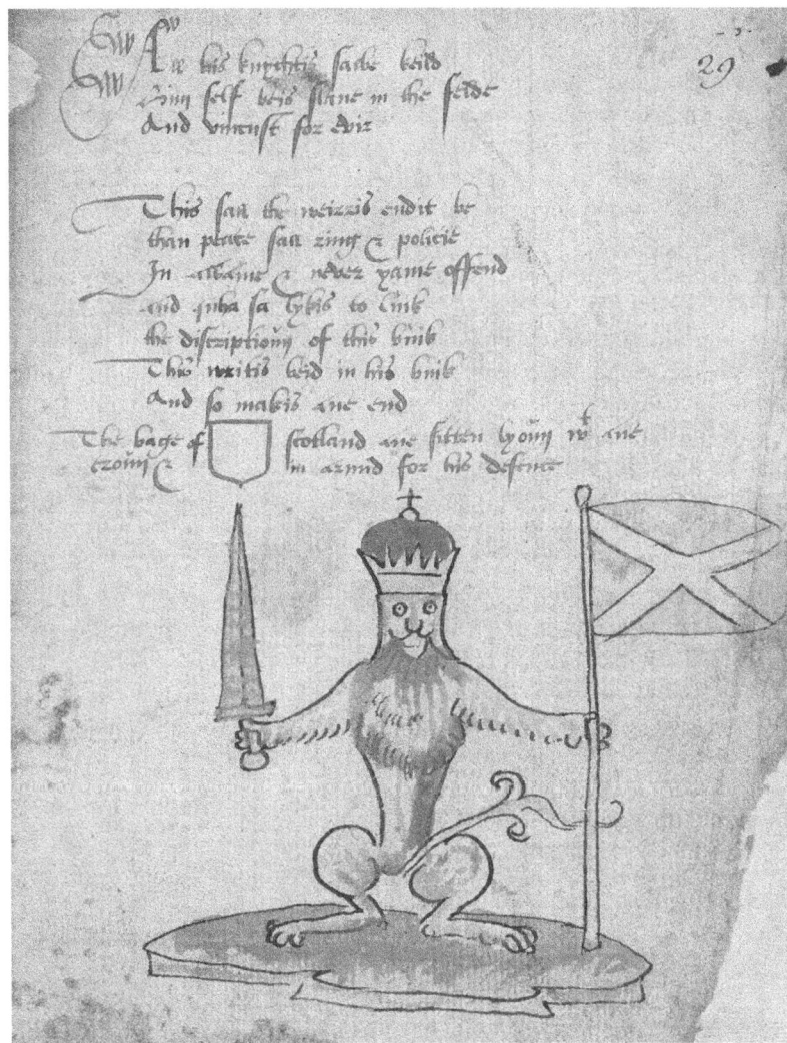

Figure 7.1 Prophecies with the badge of Scotland.

prophecies at Chester-le-Street, county Durham. They predicted that 'their King should be crowned king of England in London before Midsummer day three years or a month after'.[40] Further investigations revealed that the culprit was not a Scot, but John Borobie, prior of the White Friars in Scarborough, who was distributing Merlin's and Thomas's prophecies.[41] The dangers became evident in May, when James returned from France with his new wife, Madeleine. The king's party landed near Scarborough to replenish supplies. Locals implored James 'to come in as they were oppressed and slain'. Afterwards, 'a gentleman of the county' requested an interview, but the king sailed north to Whitburn, where some of his party disembarked. The local priest railed against Henry's government, adding that, if the Scots invaded, the locals would carry James in triumph to London, as Merlin and Erceldoune had predicted.[42]

English fears of a Scottish threat explain why the English parliament banned the printing, writing, speaking or singing of prophecies in 1542.[43] But Scottish prophecies did not necessarily represent court opinion. In early 1539, James V wrote to Henry VIII, dismissing the 'dispitfull and sclandarus ballattis' as 'wane and fantastik prophecyis'. True to his word, James ordered the destruction of all prophecies in circulation. James's protestations suggest that he did not believe in the power of prophecy himself. He reassured Henry that he 'nevir tuk, ne sall tak, regard to thame', because they were 'thingis proceding without fundament and aganis the gude cristin faith'.[44] The circulation of prophecies at his court may have been intended to win over credulous courtiers, but this did not mean that James believed them. When they went against his political interests, he was prepared to distance himself.

After James's death in 1542, royal Stewarts resumed using prophecies to promote their claim on the English crown. The French printed prophecies to mark Mary's 1558 marriage to the Dauphin Francis, heir to the French throne.[45] Mary's return to Scotland was celebrated at the Palace of Seton in 1562 with a performance of Alexander Scott's 'New Year's Gift', which transferred the 'frenche wyffe' prophecy to her heir:

> quhat berne shold bruke all Bretene be the see?   [*child; possess*]
> The prophecie expresslie doth conclude
> 'The frencsh wife of the Brucis blode suld be'   [*the Bruce's*]
> Thow art be lyne, fra him the nynte degree   [*in line from*
> And was king fraances pairty, maik and pair;
> So be discente, the same sowld spring of the[e].[46]

According to the last line, it was not Mary, but her offspring, who would reign over a united Britain.[47]

Following Mary's execution in 1587, securing the English succession became the cornerstone of her offspring's policy. Defenders of James VI brought the prophetic traditions of the Stewart court into print. Prophecies circulated in English, Welsh, Irish and Latin across Britain and Europe. The French Wife prophecy was known on the Continent thanks to the jurist Thomas Craig, who wrote a poem in 1603 celebrating James's coronation. This revelled in 'the songs of the poets' prophesying that 'beautiful Britannia will subject herself' to 'a man, born from a French wife, [who] would come from the bloodline of the Bruce'.[48]

The Whole Prophesie took shape in this context. The day James left Scotland to assume the English throne, an Edinburgh burgess,

Robert Birrel, recorded that 'all the haill comons of Scotland that had red [reason] or understanding, wer daylie speiking and exponeing of Thomas Rymer hes [his] prophesie, and of uth[e]r prophesies q[uhi]lk wer prophesied in auld tymes'.⁴⁹ There were at least four separate versions, as Figure 7.2 shows. The surviving copies were printed in London.⁵⁰ These translated a Scottish edition that has not survived, which contained a prophecy referring to James, 'Frae Hempe is begun, God give it long to last: Frae Hempe begun, England may take rest'.⁵¹ H, E, M, P and E denoted the preceding monarchs to rule England: Henry VIII, Edward VI, Mary, her husband Philip, and Elizabeth. And England's 'rest' marked the dawn of a new nation, Great Britain. This prophecy survives from the 1615 edition (Figure 7.3).⁵² We also have evidence for a shorter Scots text, which survives in a manuscript in the

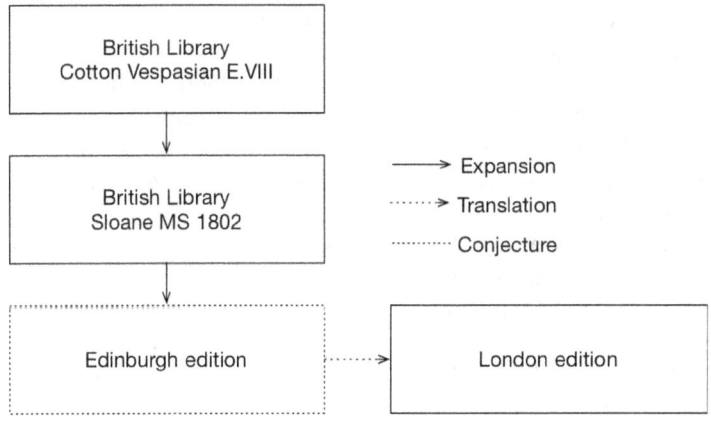

Figure 7.2 Reconstruction of the evolution of the texts of *The Whole Prophesie*.

When **HEMPE** is come and alſo gone,
SCOTLAND & **ENGLAND** ſhall be all one.

K	K	Q	K	Q
HENRY	EDWARD	MARIE	PHILIP	ELIZABETH
the 8.	the 6.		of Spain M. huſb.	
H	**E**	**M**	**P**	**E**

Praiſed be God alon, for HEMPE is cum & gon
And left vs old *Albion,* by peace joyned in one.

Figure 7.3 The HEMPE prophecy.

British Library, Sloane MS 1802 – a much expanded, and reorganised, version of the manuscript compiled for James V.

This manuscript was collected for James's English accession by the antiquarian Robert Cotton, a keen advocate of union.[53] The HEMPE prophecy was supplied to him by Elizabeth's godson, John Harington, who had heard it when growing up in London.[54] Harington and Cotton were among a larger group of scholars who believed that the Union could be defended using prophecy.

This group hoped to convince James VI that prophecy could win the support of those Catholics who posed a threat to his rule. In *Daemonologie*, certainly, James dismissed non-biblical prophecies as the Devil's work.[55] In *Basilikon Doron*, he argued that they had ceased at Christ's resurrection.[56] Yet Harington's group suspected that James was more sympathetic to prophecies than this.[57] Harington reported that James 'did much remarke of' the gift of Second Sight, and 'saide he had soughte out of certaine books a sure waie to attaine knowledge of future chances'.[58] In a tract addressed to the king, Harington argued that prophecy could convince Catholics, who were more touched by prophecy than 'either Protestantes or Puritans, especiallie the vulgar and unlearned sorte'.[59] The 'vulgar and unlearned' were less likely to be persuaded by prophecy than the learned, because only the learned had the resources to interpret political prophecies.

Welsh scholars argued that James was the sixth king predicted by Geoffrey, who would restore Cadwaladr's lost kingdoms. In his *Prophecy of Cadwallader* (1604), William Herbert wrote that Henry VIII's Laws of Wales Acts had fulfilled half of Cadwaladr's prophecy. Union of England and Scotland would fulfil the other half.[60] William Maurice of Clenennau recited an old Welsh prophecy to England's 1604 parliament:

> A king of British blood in cradle crown
> with lion marke shall joyne all British ground
> Restorne the crosse, & make the Ile renowned.

Prophets since Cadwaladr had foretold one 'out of the Brytishe line' that 'sholde Restore the kingdoome of brittane to the pristine estate'. Privately, Clenennau revealed that his support for James rested 'uppon the maxime of all our prophesyes'.[61]

Prophetic jockeying was the full-time job of James Maxwell.[62] Like Harington, Maxwell was a royal godchild, in his case to Mary, Queen of Scots. All of his works were published with royal permission.[63] Also like Harington, Maxwell thought that Catholics were more convinced by prophecy. But, where Harington's attitude to prophecy was utilitarian – it was useful to gain Catholic support – Maxwell believed in prophetic power, devoting six years to scouring European libraries for prophecies.[64]

His diligence was motivated by desire for peace. His *Admirable and Notable Prophesies* (1614) called Roman Catholics to convert to the true Catholic Church. Union of Christendom would encourage 'Jewes and Gentiles' to convert. 'No longer scandalized by our dissensions and divisions', they would see 'Peace and Unity flourishing amongst us'.[65] The *Prophesies* appeals to the seven kings of Christendom to extend God's kingdom 'from sea to sea'.[66] But it was originally addressed to James alone. 'The prince of peace', Maxwell wrote, 'hath inabled your princlie and peaceable Spirit, far above all your Brethren the kings of the Earth, to be an especiall advancer and furtherer of such a Designe'. The Union of Crowns was just the start. The Devil, the 'Spirite of Division', had been 'cast out of the British body of this occean-walled world', but was now 'wandring through the wildernesse'. 'The breaches and desolations of Gods house' had to be 'redressed, and the much despised concorde restored at last unto Christendome'.[67]

The bulk of Maxwell's work was taken up with prophecies, attributed to twenty-four Catholic writers, including twelve saints. Many of his authorities had earlier appeared in *The Whole Prophesie*, from which he may have drawn inspiration.[68] Maxwell's work shows why James's supporters thought that prophecies were useful. The fall of the Roman Catholic Church had 'beene seene, yea forseene and foretolde, by divers of her owne followers'.[69] The combined weight of their inspiration proved that the Union of Christendom under James's leadership was now not only desirable, but an inevitable consequence of God's plan, already revealed through his prophets. The sheer number of divine authorities who had predicted it would convince Catholics that it was an inevitable part of this plan, which deserved their support.

James VI, then, was the Scottish king who would come 'over the Salwey Sands', lead a crusade against the Turks and recover the Holy Rood for Holyrood. Visions like this proved useful to Stuart kings and their Jacobite heirs until 1746, when the last Jacobite uprising was defeated. Royalist editions of *The Whole Prophecies* appeared in 1639, 1644, 1680 and 1683.[70] The 1639 edition was designed to rally royalists in the Bishops' Wars.[71] During the Interregnum, exiled Scottish royalists used prophecies to predict a Stuart restoration. In 1657, the statesman Robert Moray wrote to the Earl of Kincardine about a prophecy ascribed to Thomas of Erceldoune, which predicted that Cromwell would die 'when [the] fifth year of his protectorate is ended and the sixt beginning', paving the way for a Stuart restoration. Kincardine shared his faith in the prophecy.[72] This faith was vindicated when Cromwell died in September 1658, five years into his protectorate.

The Restoration regime continued to buttress its authority with prophecy. After it became known in 1673 that James, Duke of York, had converted to Catholicism, the English parliament moved legislation to exclude him from the succession. In 1678, Titus Oates and Israel Tonge concocted a plot alleging a Catholic conspiracy to assassinate Charles II. James took up residence in Scotland, where he faced less opposition.[73] To mark the occasion, the king's Scottish printer published another edition of *The Whole Prophecies*.[74] Ironically, justification was provided by Tonge's own *Northern Star* (1680), which gave Charles what Maxwell had provided for James VI. Tonge used Maxwell's prophecies to prove that Charles and his successors were 'founders of the northern, last, fourth and most happy monarchy'. The work endeavoured to proclaim Charles's title by mixing 'Expedition from Prophetick Stars, Prodigies' and 'prodigious Dreams and Visions'.[75]

After the deposition of James II and VII in 1688–89, prophecies proclaiming divine backing for the 'Sacred and August Monarch James, King of Great Britain' and his heirs gained new relevance for the emerging Jacobite movement. *The Whole Prophecies* was reprinted before the Battle of the Boyne in July 1690. This edition was mainly a shoddy reprint of royalist editions, but one new emendation shows how the text was now understood. In previous editions Sibylla had prophesied 'the sixth King of the Name of Stewart of Scotland, the which *is* our most noble King'. The 1690 edition recognised the new reality by changing the tense: 'the sixth King of the Name of Stuart of Scotland, the which *was* our most noble King'.[76] Jacobites in 1715 and 1745 made other textual changes. A telling example was a verse written into a copy of the 1745 edition, which referred to Maria Clementina Sobieska, Polish consort of James, the Old Pretender:

> The Heroe comes for Thy relief,
> And boldy makes a staind;
> A Polish Lady Fair and Sheen,
> Come Tripping in his Hand.[77]

The Whole Prophecies circulated among troops before and during Jacobite rebellions. In 1714, prophets proclaiming James's imminent return mobilised Jacobite resistance. The Jacobite victory at Prestonpans became known as 'Gladesmoor' in deference to Thomas of Erceldoune's prophecy that 'in Gladys moor shall the battle be'. In 1745, Lord Lovat rallied his men by claiming that Thomas had predicted Jacobite victory.[78]

Evidence for how Jacobites understood the prophecies survives from the Edinburgh printer, John Reid, who printed two editions of *The Whole Prophecies*. His 1714 edition supplemented a more interesting tract, *A Strange and Wounderfull Yet True Relation of the Assembling of the Crows of England Scotlad* [sic] *and Ireland*, distributed to would-be Jacobite soldiers in north-east England. To prove that its prophecies could be trusted, the *Relation* outlines 'Matters of Fact', occurrences that 'presage' recent events. God sent these providences whose 'meaning and signification shall be fully manifested' in time. The text then turns to disaffected Jacobites – 'crows' in the prophecies – throughout Ireland, Scotland and England. They must unite to ensure victory over government forces. Thomas predicts a great battle between loyalists and Jacobites 'in the latter end of this Year or the beginning of next', where the 'fat ones' of the kingdom will all die.[79]

Their contemporary opponents claimed that Jacobites were particularly prone to 'superstitious' belief in supernatural powers.[80] But Whigs had prophecies, too. The best-known were ascribed to an ancient prophet from north-east England, Robert Nixon. In 1713, John Oldmixon published Nixon's prophecies predicting Jacobite failure.[81] The earliest surviving Scottish edition appeared in 1737. Nixon foretold that 'George the son of George will put an end to all ill'.[82] Whigs adapted Scottish prophecies, too. In 1745, *The Young Pretender's Destiny Unfolded* rallied loyalists against 'the present rebellions' by retailing the predictions of John Fergesson, a second-sighted Highlander.[83]

The Stuarts' opponents also appropriated the Stuart prophetic tradition. Attempts to fashion an alternative Erceldoune tradition had started in 1652, when the original anti-Scottish romance was published. As we have seen, the romance predicted English victories against the Scots. Its appearance, during negotiations for union between England and Scotland, implied that where Scottish kings had failed, Cromwell would unite the island.[84]

Late eighteenth-century editors similarly adapted *The Whole Prophesie* to British interests. In a series of *Explanations* of the text published between the 1770s and the 1800s, Thomas predicted Stuart failure at Hanoverian hands. These *Explanations* glorified Prince Charles Edward Stuart's defeat at Culloden by the forces of George II, 'a wise prince of the Hanoverian race and family'.[85] The HEMPE prophecy was rewritten in an edition published in 1794. 'Prophecies concerning Hempe' were 'fulfilled in the late King William who came out of Holland, which in old times was vulgarly called the land of Hempe' and 'the joining of the two unions together, signifies the Union'.[86] Holland was known for its production of hemp. This interpretation implied that William had 'come and gone' in the Revolution of 1688, and 'Old Albion by peace' had been 'joined in one' in 1707, not 1603.[87] The 1798 *Prophesies of Thomas the Rymer* recast 'An old Scottish prophecy' to emphasise Scotland's subservient status within Great Britain:

> Scotland be sad now and lament
> For honours thou hast lost
> But yet rejoice in better times
> That now repay the cost.

Scotland was to be sad because it had lost not just a prince, but 'honours' in the Jacobite risings. But union and defeat of the Jacobites would 'now repay the cost'. Saved from slavery under their 'enemies' the Stuarts, Scotland would find new liberty under British laws:

> Tho' into thraldom you should be
> brought by your enemies,
> You shall have freedom from them all,
> And enjoy your liberties.[88]

The Whole Prophesie had got the whole thing wrong: Thomas was not a prophet of Stuart glory, but of Scottish failure. The *Explanations* recounted his role in the Scottish chronicles, where Thomas had predicted many disasters for the Scots on the back of Alexander III's death: 'no peace, but wars in Scotland.'[89] Both the 1652 edition and the late eighteenth-century editions thus used historical scholarship to challenge the dominant Stuart interpretation. In both cases, that interpretation was replaced by alternative readings, prophesying union under Cromwell or glorying in the prophecies' fulfilment in the Act of Union and Hanoverian monarchy.

Antiquarian critique acted differently, however. Antiquaries thought that prophecy was nonsense, and sought to challenge ancient prophets' supernatural authority by showing that they were not ancient. From the 1770s, the *Whole Prophesie* was central in these debates.[90] In his 1773 *Remarks on the History of Scotland*, David Dalrymple, Lord Hailes, distinguished true history from the 'silly fables' told by previous generations. A key passage of *The Whole Prophesie*, which the Stuarts used to make their dynastic claims, did not match the rhyme scheme and therefore, Hailes claimed, had been added later. The verses, he suggested, were propaganda for the Duke of Albany and referenced either Albany or his mother, Anne de la Tour. But it didn't matter who was intended, because the prophecies were 'political artifice, to prepossess the vulgar with an extravagant idea of the glories of the Duke of Albany's administration.'[91]

Hailes's critique was popularised in the early nineteenth century by Sir Walter Scott. Scott was fascinated by Thomas. He extended his Abbotsford estate in 1816 and in 1822 to encompass sites associated with the Rhymer.[92] Scott credited him with authorship of the metrical romance, *Sir Tristrem*, which he published in 1804.[93] But Scott was keen to distance the poet Thomas from his prophecies. The 'anecdotes concerning Thomas the Rhymer are partly historical and partly preserved by tradition'. Thomas was 'a man of considerable rank … honoured with the acquaintance of the great and gallant'. The prophecies ascribed to him, however, were remnants of 'pagan' superstition, which had been deployed by the 'adherents of the house of Stuart' for political propaganda.[94]

The prophecies had thus lost their literal credibility. After the 1840s, no more editions of the prophecies appeared. They became a cultural relic. The publication of a scholarly facsimile of the 1603 edition by the Bannatyne Club, overseen by Scott, finally stripped Thomas of his supernatural powers.[95] An edition of his prophecies alongside *The Comical Story of Thrummy Cap and the Ghaist* in the 1840s illustrates the reduction in his status. Thrummy was an elf described in Northumbrian folk tales, who had first appeared in a 1796 ghost story by John Burness that became a chapbook classic. As his companion between the covers, Thomas was shorn of his prophetic role and became a character of fiction.[96]

For Sir Walter Scott, political prophecy was the language of the superstitious masses derived from 'pagan' traditions. Stewart monarchs used it, he thought, to convince the backward multitude of their cause. Modern scholars have broadly accepted this view by suggesting that prophecy had more to do with political expediency than genuine belief. It was promulgated to appeal to the people with their folklore, rather than to scholars with Christian theological training.

As the widest-circulating collection of prophecies in late medieval and early modern Scotland, *The Whole Prophesie* allows us to test the truth of this. It began, we have seen, not in local tradition, but at court, intended to convince elite courtiers to support political factions, like Albany's, or causes, like the Union of Crowns. It achieved this through a learned engagement with Sibylline traditions of ancient Rome.

The *Whole Prophesie* shows how elite political argument made supernatural claims. These claims were not 'superstitious', but invoked rationally argued theology. The learned defenders of the Stewart monarchy used Sibylline and other post-biblical prophets because they believed that Britain's prophets received their power from God.

Until the modern era, it was normal to find elites relying on ancient prophets to justify themselves to the political nation, regardless of whether they held power or sought it. When prophecy escaped from the court, it acquired new interpretations, often running counter to elite interests, such as Prior Borobie's anti-Tudor reading, and Jacobite interpretations that arose after the downfall of the Stuart dynasty.

The *Whole Prophesie* persisted through the eighteenth century, often promoted by opponents of the Hanoverian dynasty. But there was nothing backward about Jacobite prophecy, and it was not only romantic supporters of the Stuarts' cause who used it. Defenders of the established order relied on prophecy to get across the importance of loyalism. The *Whole Prophesie* did not die because people became less superstitious, but because antiquarians like Scott challenged the historical authenticity of ancient prophets such as Thomas of Erceldoune. Until then, political publicists of all parties used prophecies of victory to champion their cause, attesting to the continuing power of the supernatural in the age of Enlightenment.

Notes

1. Arthur H. Williamson, *Apocalypse Then: Prophecy and the Making of the Modern World* (Westport, CT: Praeger, 2008).
2. Rupert Taylor, *The Political Prophecy in England* (New York: Columbia University Press, 1911).
3. Keith Thomas, *Religion and the Decline of Magic: Studies in Popular Beliefs in Sixteenth and Seventeenth Century England* (London: Weidenfeld & Nicolson, 1971), ch. 13; Tim Thornton, *Prophecy, Politics and the People in Early Modern England* (Woodbridge: Boydell, 2006).
4. Michael B. Riordan, 'Mysticism and Prophecy in Scotland in the Long Eighteenth Century' (PhD thesis, University of Cambridge, 2015), pp. 34–5.
5. BL, Add MS 28640, fo. 101^v; Cyril Edwards, 'Thomas of Erceldoune [called Thomas the Rhymer] (fl. late 13th cent.)', *ODNB*.
6. Emily B. Lyle, *Fairies and Folk: Approaches to the Scottish Ballad Tradition* (Trier: Wissenschaftlicher Verlag, 2007), pp. 5–60; Kylie Murray, 'Rhyme(r) and reason: Thomas the Rhymer, prophecy, and Anglo-Scottish identity', in J. Derrick McClure, Karoline Szatek-Tudor and Rosa E. Penna (eds), *'What Country's This? And Whither Are We Gone?': Papers from the Twelfth International Conference on the Literature of Region and Nation* (Newcastle: Cambridge Scholars, 2011), pp. 322–39.
7. Victoria Flood, *Prophecy, Politics and Place in Medieval England: From Geoffrey of Monmouth to Thomas of Erceldoune* (Cambridge: D. S. Brewer, 2016), ch. 3.
8. Edward J. Cowan, 'The discovery of the future: prophecy and second sight in Scottish history', in Lizanne Henderson (ed.), *Fantastical Imaginations: The Supernatural in Scottish History and Culture* (Edinburgh: John Donald, 2009), pp. 1–28; Karen R. Moranski, 'The son who rules "all Bretaine to the sey": *The Whole Prophesie* and the Union of the Crowns', in E. L. Risden, Karen Moranski and Stephen Yandell (eds), *Prophet Margins: The Medieval Vatic Impulse and Social Stability* (Bern: Peter Lang, 2004), pp. 167–84; Alasdair A. MacDonald, 'Poetry, propaganda and political culture: *The Whole Prophesie of Scotland* (1603)', in David J. Parkinson (ed.), *James VI and I, Literature and Scotland: Tides of Change, 1567–1625* (Leuven: Peeters, 2013), pp. 209–31.
9. Thornton, *Prophecy, Politics and the People*.
10. All editions are cited as 'WP' and date. Full references can be found at www.michaelriordan.co.uk/wholeprophesie (accessed 28 November 2018). The full title of the first edition, in 1603, was: *The whole prophesie of Scotland, England, & some-part of France, and Denmark, prophesied bee meruellous Merling, Beid, Bertlingtoun, Thomas Rymour, Waldhaue, Eltraine, Banester, and Sibbilla, all according in one. Containing many strange and meruelous things.*

11 Jessica L. Malay, *Prophecy and Sibylline Imagery in the Renaissance: Shakespeare's Sibyls* (Abingdon: Routledge, 2010), ch. 3; Mary Pryor, 'The Sibyls as signifiers: from prophetesses in antiquity to cultural and religious icons in seventeenth-century Scotland', in Nicholas C. J. Pappas (ed.), *Antiquity and Modernity: First International Conference on European History* (Athens: Atiner, 2004), pp. 141–8.
12 Malay, *Prophecy and Sibylline Imagery*, pp. 151–2; Anke Holdenreid, *The Sibyl and Her Scribes: Manuscripts and the Interpretation of the Latin Sibylla Tiburtina Tradition* (Aldershot: Ashgate, 2006), pp. xix–xxi.
13 Marjorie Reeves, *The Influence of Prophecy in the Middle Ages: A Study in Joachinism* (Oxford: Clarendon, 1969), pp. 299–301.
14 Frances Yates, *Astraea: The Imperial Theme in the Sixteenth Century* (London: Routledge and Kegan Paul, 1975), pp. 38–47.
15 Antonina Harbus, *Helena of Britain in Medieval Legend* (Cambridge: D. S. Brewer, 2002); Barbara Baert, 'The wood, the water, and the foot, or how the Queen of Sheba met up with the True Cross', *Mitteilungen für Anthropologie und Religionsgeschichte*, 16 (2004), 217–78.
16 Geoffrey of Monmouth, *History of the Kings of Britain*, trans. Michael A. Faletra (Peterborough, ON: Broadview, 2008), pp. 43, 134–5.
17 For Henry, see Sydney Anglo, 'The *British History* in early Tudor propaganda', *Bulletin of the John Rylands Library*, 44 (1962), 17–48; David Starkey, 'King Henry and King Arthur', in James P. Carley and Felicity Riddy (eds), *Arthurian Literature*, 16 (1988), 171–96; Antonia Gransden, 'Antiquarian studies in fifteenth-century England', *Antiquaries Journal*, 60 (1980), 75–97. Prophecies relating to James and 1603 are discussed later in the present chapter.
18 Ingeborg Nixon (ed.), *Thomas of Erceldoune* (Copenhagen: Akadamisk Forlag, 1980) I follow Flood's dating: *Prophecy, Politics and Place*, ch. 3.
19 Nixon, *Thomas of Erceldoune*, I, pp. 32–3, lines 87–96.
20 *Ibid.*, pp. 32–3, lines 99–109.
21 *Ibid.*, pp. 46–9, lines 278–92.
22 *Ibid.*, pp. 50–1, lines 311–12.
23 Bodleian Library, Oxford, MS Lat. Misc. c. 66, fo. 104, col. 2.
24 Sharon L. Jansen-Jaech, 'British Library MS Sloane 2578 and popular unrest in England, 1554–1556', *Manuscripta*, 29 (1985), 30–41.
25 William P. Albrecht, *The Loathly Lady in Thomas of Erceldoune* (Albuquerque: University of New Mexico Press, 1954), pp. 71–115.
26 Katie Stevenson, 'Chivalry, British sovereignty and dynastic politics: undercurrents of antagonism in Tudor-Stewart relations, *c*.1490–*c*.1513', *Historical Research*, 86 (2013), 601–61.
27 WP, 1603, sigs Cviii^v–Dii^v.
28 Norman Macdougall, *James IV* (Edinburgh: John Donald, 1989), pp. 263–4.
29 Bryony Coombs, 'The artistic patronage of John Stuart, Duke of Albany 1518–19: the "discovery" of the artist and author, Bremond Domat', *Proceedings of the Society of Antiquaries of Scotland*, 144 (2014), 277–309.
30 *Ibid.*, p. 292.
31 WP, 1603, sig. A8^v.
32 *The Letters of James V*, ed. Robert Kerr Hannay and Denys Hay (Edinburgh: HMSO, 1954), p. 86.

33 Sharon L. Jansen and Kathleen H. Jordan (eds), *Welles Anthology: MS Rawlinson 813: A Critical Edition* (Binghamton: Medieval & Renaissance Texts & Studies, 1991), pp. 7–8, 10–11; Victoria Flood, 'Political prophecy and the trial of Rhys ap Gruffydd, 1530–31', *Studia Celtica*, 50 (2016), 133–50.
34 Sylvia Slein, *Gateway to the Heavenly City: Crusader Jerusalem and the Catholic West (1089–1187)* (Aldershot: Ashgate, 2005), pp. 152–3.
35 Jansen and Jordan, *Welles Anthology*, pp. 85–7, 89–90, lines 442, 478–9, 514–15, 593–5, 609–10.
36 *Letters of James V*, pp. 180–2, 188, 223–4, 329.
37 BL, Cotton Vespasian E.VIII, fo. 28ᵛ. I am grateful to Dr Jamie Reid-Baxter for producing a transcription of the prophecies in this manuscript.
38 *L&P Henry VIII*, VI, p. 399 (entry 923); Thornton, *Prophecy, Politics and the People*, pp. 30–1.
39 Thornton, *Prophecy, Politics and the People*, pp. 35–41.
40 *L&P Henry VIII*, XII (II), p. 28 (entry 80).
41 *Ibid.*, p. 426 (entry 1212).
42 *L&P Henry VIII*, XII (I), p. 586 (entry 1286); XII (II), p. 171 (entry 422 (ii)).
43 *The Statutes of the Realm*, 11 vols (London: Dawsons, 1963), III, p. 850.
44 James V to Bishop of Llandaff, Edinburgh, 5 February 1538/39, in *Letters of James V*, p. 365.
45 National Library of Wales, Peniarth MS 414, fo. 83.
46 Alexander Scott, *Poems*, ed. Alexander Karley Donald (London: Kegan Paul, 1902), 'Ane new yeir gift to the Queen Mary', p. 8.
47 Theo van Heijnsbergen, 'Advice to a princess: the literary articulation of a religious, political and cultural programme for Mary Queen of Scots, 1562', in Julian Goodare and Alasdair A. MacDonald (eds), *Sixteenth-Century Scotland: Essays in Honour of Michael Lynch* (Leiden: Brill, 2008), pp. 99–122, at pp. 115–16.
48 Thomas Craig, *Serenissimi et Invictissimi Principis Iacobi Britanniarum et Galliarum Regis Στεφανοφόρια*, trans. David McOmish and Steven J. Reid, www.dps.gla.ac.uk/delitiae/display/?pid=d1_CraT_004 (accessed 28 November 2018).
49 'Diary of Robert Birrel', in John Graham Dalyell (ed.), *Fragments of Scotish [sic] History* (Edinburgh, 1798), sig. H2ʳ.
50 WP, 1603.
51 'Diary of Robert Birrel', sig. H2ʳ.
52 WP, 1615, sig. A4ʳ.
53 BL, Cotton Vespasian E.VIII, fos 16ʳ–74ᵛ; David Howarth, 'Sir Robert Cotton and the commemoration of famous men', in C. J. Wright (ed.), *Sir Robert Cotton as Collector: Essays on an Early Stuart Courtier and His Legacy* (London: British Library, 1997), pp. 40–67; Susan Doran, 'Polemic and prejudice: a Scottish king for an English throne', in Paulina Kewes and Susan Doran (eds), *Doubtful and Dangerous: The Question of Succession in Late Elizabethan England* (Manchester: Manchester University Press, 2014), pp. 215–35.
54 Sir John Harington, *A Tract on the Succession to the Crown*, ed. Clements R. Markham (London: Roxburghe Club, 1880), pp. 17–18.
55 James VI, *Daemonologie*, in his *Minor Prose Works*, ed. James Craigie (Edinburgh: STS, 1982), pp. 1–56, at pp. 2 (bk 1, ch. 1), 45 (bk 3, ch. 2).

56 James VI, *Basilikon Doron*, in his *Political Writings*, ed. Johann P. Sommerville (Cambridge: Cambridge University Press, 1994), pp. 1–61, at p. 51 (bk 3).
57 Jason Scott-Warren, *Sir John Harington and the Book as Gift* (Oxford: Oxford University Press, 2001), ch. 6.
58 John Harington, *Letters and Epigrams of Sir John Harington*, ed. Norman Egbert McClure (University Park, PA: University of Pennsylvania Press, 1930), p. 111.
59 Harington, *Tract*, p. 120.
60 [William Herbert], *Prophecy of Cadwallader* (London, 1604).
61 Scott-Warren, *Harington*, p. 172.
62 Reeves, *Influence of Prophecy*, pp. 391, 499–500; Arthur H. Williamson, *Scottish National Consciousness in the Age of James VI* (Edinburgh: John Donald, 1979), pp. 103–26; Arthur H. Williamson, 'Maxwell, James', *ODNB*.
63 BL, Royal MS 18.A.LI, Maxwell's proposed 'Discourse under the name of Britaine's union in love'; BL, Add. MS 72458, Maxwell's 'A preamble to a project of greatest importance'.
64 Williamson, 'Maxwell'.
65 James Maxwell, *Admirable and Notable Prophesies* (London, 1615), p. 160. Only the title page of the 1614 edition survives.
66 *Ibid.*, p. 155.
67 BL, Royal MS 18.A.LI, fos 3^{r-v}, 5^v.
68 Maxwell, *Prophesies*, sigs B2^r, C2^v.
69 *Ibid.*, p. 153.
70 Most editions printed after 1644 carry a title in the plural (*Whole Prophecies*).
71 WP, 1639.
72 *Letters of Sir Robert Moray to the Earl of Kincardine, 1657–73*, ed. David Stevenson (Aldershot: Ashgate, 2007), pp. 93–4, 105.
73 Alastair Mann, *James VII: Duke and King of Scots* (Edinburgh: John Donald, 2014), ch. 4.
74 WP, 1680.
75 Israel Tonge, *The Northern Star* (London, 1680), sigs A1^r, B1^r.
76 WP, 1680, sig. D2^v; WP, 1690, sig. D1^v.
77 WP, Edinburgh, 1745, viii: NLS, L.C.628(7).
78 Daniel Szechi, *1715: The Great Jacobite Rebellion* (New Haven, CT: Yale University Press, 2006), pp. 62–5, 73, 256; *Memoirs of John Clerk of Penicuik*, ed. John M. Gray (London: Roxburghe Club, 1895), p. 186; Andrew Henderson, *History of the Rebellion, 1745 and 1746* (Edinburgh, 1748), p. 119.
79 *A Strange and Wounderfull Yet True Relation* (Edinburgh, 1714), pp. 2, 7.
80 Juliet Fiebel, 'Highland histories: Jacobitism and second sight', *Clio*, 30 (2000), 51–77; William E. Burns, *An Age of Wonders: Prodigies, Politics and Providence in England, 1657–1727* (Manchester: Manchester University Press, 2002), ch. 5; Vladimir Jankovic, 'The politics of sky battles in early Hanoverian Britain', *Journal of British Studies*, 41 (2002), 429–59.
81 Thornton, *Prophecy, Politics and the People*, ch. 3.
82 *A Wonderful Prophecy by One Called Nixon* (Edinburgh, 1737), p. 8.
83 *The Young Pretender's Destiny Unfolded* (London, 1745), sig. A1^r.
84 Albrecht, *Loathly Lady*, p. 71; G. E. B. Eyre (ed.), *A Transcript of the Registers of the Worshipful Company of Stationers, from 1640–1708 AD*, 3 vols (London: privately printed, 1913–14), I, p. 397.

85 Allan Boyd, *The Whole Explanation of Thomas the Rymer's Prophecies* (n.p., 1778; NLS, 5.3021(26)), p. 2.
86 Allan Boyd, *The Prophecies of Thomas Rymer* (n.p., 1794; ESTC T176986), p. 9.
87 *Ibid.*, p. 8.
88 WP, 1798, p. 10.
89 Boyd, *Explanation*, p. 2.
90 Riordan, 'Mysticism and Prophecy', pp. 68–75.
91 Sir David Dalrymple, *Remarks on the History of Scotland* (Edinburgh, 1773), pp. 1, 89–110, at p. 107.
92 Lyle, *Fairies and Folk*, p. 14; Iain Gordon Brown, 'Scott, literature and Abbotsford', in Iain Gordon Brown (ed.), *Abbotsford and Sir Walter Scott* (Edinburgh: Society of Antiquaries of Scotland, 2003), pp. 4–36, at p. 18.
93 Walter Scott (ed.), *Sir Tristrem: A Metrical Romance of the Thirteenth Century* (Edinburgh: Archibald Constable, 1811).
94 *Ibid.*, pp. xi, xv–xvi, xxi.
95 *Collection of Ancient Scottish Prophecies, in Alliterative Verse: Reprinted from Waldegrave's Edition, 1603*, ed. David Laing (Edinburgh: Bannatyne Club, 1833).
96 *The Prophecies of Thomas the Rhymer, and the Comical Story of Thrummy Cap & the Ghaist* (Glasgow, n.d.); David Buchan and James Moreira (eds), *The Glenbuchat Ballads* (Jackson, MS: University of Mississippi Press, 2007), p. lv.

8

Astrology and supernatural power in early modern Scotland

Jane Ridder-Patrick

During the early modern period in Scotland, as in Europe and beyond, the concepts and symbolism of astrology were tightly woven into the prevailing world view. Astrology can be defined as any theory, practice or belief that draws inferences from, or parallels between, events and patterns in the sky and events and circumstances on earth. Its use of the sky – the 'heavens' in contemporary parlance – meant that it linked the supernatural and natural worlds.

There was scarcely an aspect of contemporary life that astrology did not inform. Its imagery was found in literature of all sorts, and discourses of both practical and speculative matters borrowed heavily from its perspective. It was taught at universities to the educated elite, and read in the popular almanacs by all sectors of society. Astrology provided a supernatural framework and a language to account for the triumphs and reverses in individual destinies, the cycles and calamities of the natural world, and political and religious upheavals.

Yet despite such ubiquity, attitudes towards the activity were polarised. Astrology had immense power as it appeared to offer hidden knowledge, often highly detailed, which could not be obtained by any other means. Some regarded it with suspicion, as an activity to be strictly controlled, while others were determined to defend its legitimacy and its use. Claims and counterclaims about the relationship between astrology and power – natural, supernatural, preternatural and superstitious – lay at the core of this dispute. In this chapter, the course of the dispute is examined between the Reformation of 1560 and the early eighteenth century.

The central concept of astrology is that the patterns in the sky *mean* something. Its danger lay in its power – in the influence that interpretations of this meaning could have on people's beliefs and behaviour. As subjective judgement was required to decipher the heavens, the conclusions drawn depended on the intelligence, education, allegiances and motivations of the individual making that judgement. In the wrong hands it could cause serious trouble, especially if strong emotions were aroused in the populace or the meaning elicited was contrary to the interests of those in authority.

The humanist, poet and historian George Buchanan showed himself keenly aware of this danger in his pedagogic poem on astronomy, *De Sphaera*, written between the 1550s and 1570s. He railed against the astrologer who, when eclipses occur, 'makes use of the stupidity of the mob and of their easily-led credulity. He threatens great and horrible things: maddening hunger, pestilence decimating the cities, wars, and whatever the insane bloodshed of wars brings on, and the gods in wrath against the affairs of men'.[1]

Some way had to be found, therefore, of distinguishing between the sanctioned and useful practices of astrology and the potentially dangerous ones. Astrology was customarily divided into two kinds, 'natural' and 'judicial', by medieval and Renaissance theologians; this provided some useful demarcation lines. Natural astrology dealt with anything considered to be within the sphere of natural philosophy or its practical applications, such as weather, agriculture and medicine. It was generally endorsed. Judicial astrology offered more dangerous knowledge and was often condemned as blasphemous and demonic.

Judicial astrology itself could be divided into four branches: nativities, questions, elections and predictions. Nativities dealt with 'not onely the nature and complexion of men: but also al their fortunes as they call them, yea and all that they shal either do or suffer in ther life'.[2] Questions, also known as horary questions or interrogations, attempted to provide answers and information to help individuals make decisions and solve problems of every kind. In elections the practitioner sought out future celestial configurations in order to select the most propitious date and time for an intended purpose. Finally, there was the area of predictions, which concerned 'the whole estate of the world'.[3]

In the universities another division of astrology was also used. The main astrological teaching text was Ptolemy's *Tetrabiblos*, written in the third century, which split astrology not into the 'natural' and 'judicial' divisions of later theologians, but into 'universal' and 'genethlialogical' prognostications. Universals covered wars, famines, pestilences and weather, while genethlialogical or natal astrology concerned the affairs of individuals. This distinction, however, lacked the judgemental heft of the natural and judicial divide and was seldom, if ever, found in the debate about astrology's legitimacy.

In his *Admonicion Against Astrology Iudiciall*, first published in 1549, John Calvin praised natural astrology while venting a passionate polemic against the judicial variety, thus highlighting the fracture line that ran through contemporary views of astrology. He spelled out what the study of the heavens could offer: 'the starres be signes unto us to shewe us times to sow or plant, to let bloode or to minister Phisike and to cut wood ... I know that to knowe the course of the starres, their vertue, ... is not onely very profitable to men: but also doth styre them up to magnifie the name of God in his wonderfull wisedom which he sheweth there.'[4] He elaborated: 'the influence of heaven doth often times cause tempest whirle windes and chaunge of weather, and continuall raines: so consequently it bringeth barrennes and pestilences weather, and continual rains.'[5] Further, he claimed that through astrology the effects on earth 'are advertised before they come ... which ... geveth also some conjectures for the tyme to come'.[6] He even attested that the planets might play a part in shaping and influencing human bodies and personalities: 'We must needes confesse that there is a certain convenience betwyxte the starres or planets and the disposition of mans body ... [and] that a man is of a more choleric than phlegmatic complexion or contrariwise'.[7] He saw an 'order and as it were a knot and tying together of the things which are above with things that are beneath [and was] not against but that one may seek in the heavenly creatures the beginning and cause of the accidents which are seen here in the earth', but 'not as the first and principal cause, but as an inferior means of God's will ... to accomplish his work'.[8] None of these passages can be read other than as an endorsement of natural astrology. His condemnation was reserved for the 'shameless deceivers' who called themselves mathematicians and 'counterfeited' another kind of astrology, which they called judicial.[9] There was, then, no contradiction between Calvin's Protestant vision and the central astrological concept of correlation between celestial events and earthly affairs, nor any condemnation of the practice of natural philosophical astrology, with one proviso: that God be acknowledged as the first cause of any power it might have. As Calvin put it in his influential textbook of the Protestant faith, *Institutes of the Christian Religion*:

> If the government of God ... extends to all his works, it is a childish cavil to confine it to natural influx. Those moreover who confine the providence of God within narrow limits, as if he allowed all things to be borne along freely according to a perpetual law of nature, do not more defraud God of his glory than themselves of a most useful doctrine.[10]

King James VI's principal royal physician, Gilbert Skeyne, claimed even greater power for God. He suggested that, as well as having created the natural cycles of the heavens, God could and did intervene preternaturally to use his power over the stars to punish sinners and warn them of his anger. In 1568, the year of a great plague in Edinburgh, Skeyne published *Ane Breve Descriptioun of the Pest*. It was the first medical book to be written in Scots instead of Latin; Skeyne wanted to help 'the common vulgar people', as well as the learned. The 'first and principal cause' of the plague, he wrote, was 'ane scurge and punischment of the maist just God, without quhais dispositioun in all thingis, utheris secund causis wirkis no thing'.[11] God achieved this scourge through 'the Heavine', his 'admirable instrument, as quhan the maist nocent [i.e. harmful] Sterres to man kynd convenis, quhilkis be Astrologis ar callit infortunat'.[12] The second sign too came from Heaven: 'quhan the Eclypsis of the Sone are greit and frequent, quhan Cometis or fyrie flammatiounis, or as Starris falland of the Heavin are sene'.[13] Skeyne claimed that these celestial movements influenced and impregnated the air. When mixed with corruptions from the inferior elements of earth, like 'stink and corruption & filth', the air became the carrier of the contagion of epidemics.[14]

Skeyne claimed that God had sent the plague because people had become full of hatred towards each other, especially the rich who looked down on the poor as if they were not created equal to them, but instead lacked soul or spirit and were like degenerate beasts rather than humans.[15] It followed then logically that the 'principal preservative cure … is to returne to God' and implore Him to pacify his wrath and take away his punishment.[16] This was not only considered an individual act of humility and contrition, it was also required for the healing of the whole community.[17] Skeyne's interpretation of astrology sought to channel the fears of the populace towards civic and ecclesiastic obedience rather than the unrest and criminal behaviour that some feared could be incited by astrologers. This may be why his book was 'acceptable and allowit' by the Edinburgh magistrates.[18]

Not everyone, however, was convinced about preternatural influence over the heavenly bodies. Let us return to George Buchanan and his *Sphaera*. Buchanan argued that ignorance of the true causes of natural phenomena led to superstitious practices and beliefs, such as the idea that eclipses could be caused by witches' magic chants and dispelled by striking gongs. Not only were the common people stricken with fear, their leaders too 'dreaded the eclipse of the sun and the pallor of the moon in darkness'.[19] He cited the Athenian leader, previously victorious, who after a lunar eclipse lost courage and fearing to lead his fleet into battle 'against the will of heaven' thereby lost his ships, his men and his life. Perseus of Macedonia too, he related, came to a similar end through ignorance. Buchanan urged his pupil Timoléon de Cossé, to whom *De Sphaera* was dedicated, to pay close attention to his tutor's descriptions of the natural causes of solar and lunar eclipses and the phases of the moon.

All of this appears to be a flat contradiction of, or at least scepticism about, the conviction articulated by Calvin and Skeyne that God manipulated heavenly events at will. For Buchanan, celestial movements were natural phenomena that could be explained rationally. The real 'pestilence' was the astrologers themselves, whose wild speculations incited the superstitious and gullible mob. He declared that their predictions were a licence to plan and commit every sort of crime and encourage the foolishness of kings while absolving the criminal of all responsibility and blaming it on the innocent stars.[20]

Buchanan was tutor to James VI from 1570 until 1578. Book Five of *De Sphaera*, which contains his criticism of astrologers, was written during 1576 to 1579, after Timoleon's death. James Naiden has advanced a compelling suggestion that Buchanan, aware from history of the evil influence of astrology upon princes, and having a king under his care, may have felt responsible for protecting his impressionable young charge from the predictions of soothsayers.[21]

Buchanan's scepticism seems to have been well absorbed by James VI, but the king's views developed further when he had a personal encounter with the supernatural in 1590. The North Berwick witches confessed to having raised storms against James and his new wife as they sailed from Copenhagen to Leith. According to the partly fictionalised pamphlet account, *Newes from Scotland*, James dismissed the accused as 'extreme liars' until one of their number, Agnes Sampson, took him aside and whispered in his ear the very words that had passed between him and his bride on their wedding night.[22] James's fears may have been intensified by the fact that the Earl of Bothwell, himself embroiled in the North Berwick panic, also practised judicial astrology.[23]

In 1597 James published *Daemonologie*, the first section of which discussed magic and necromancy – and the lawful and unlawful uses of astrology. The book throws light on James's attitude to astrology and its relationship to the supernatural powers of magic and witchcraft. The story of the conversation with Agnes Sampson may have influenced his passage about Satan being able 'to reveale to them [i.e. witches] the secretes of anie persons, so being they bee once spoken, for the thought none knowes but GOD'.[24] He reviewed the merits of astronomy and natural astrology:

> *Astronomia* ... is one of the members of the *Mathematicques*, & not onlie lawful, but most necessarie and commendable. *Astrologia* ... [is] the word, and preaching of the starres ... [it] is divided into two partes: The first, by knowing thereby the powers of simples [i.e. medicines], and sickenesses, the course of the seasons and the weather, being ruled by their influence; which part depending upon the former, although it be not of it selfe a part of *Mathematicques:* yet it is not unlawful, being moderately used, suppose not so necessarie and commendable as the former.[25]

It may have been Buchanan's schooling that persuaded James that astronomy was superior to natural astrology, granting only a grudging and qualified approval to the latter. Astrology, however, was deemed 'utterlie unlawful to be trusted in' when used in its judicial form to fore-tell what common-weales shall florish or decay ... what side shall winne in any battell: what man shall obtaine victorie at singular combate: what way, and what age shall men die: what horse shall winne at matche-running; and diverse such like incredible things, wherein *Cardanus, Cornelius Agrippa*, and diverse others have more curiously than profitably written at large ... this last part of *Astrologie* ... now is utterlie unlawful to be trusted in, or practized amongst christians, as leaning to no ground of natural reason: & it is in this part which I called before the devils schole.[26]

James also maintained that there were 'certaine seasons, dayes and houres' that conjurers observed in raising apparitions. This indicates that he considered that magicians used elections, a branch of judicial astrology, for timing their rituals.[27]

Much of the polarisation of opinion about astrology was supported by the selective choice and interpretation of biblical passages. At the Reformation the Bible, as the Word of God, became the prime source of authority for the Scottish church. The Geneva Bible, translated by a group of English-speaking religious exiles that included John Knox, came into use in churches soon after its publication in 1560. In 1579 it became the first bible to be printed in Scotland, and was dedicated to James VI.[28] The Geneva translators added to the Holy Scriptures 'most profitable annotations upon all the hard places'.[29] These marginal notes discussed witchcraft, idolatry and demonic possession and linked astrology directly with these enemies of God.

In *Daemonologie*, James used the Geneva Bible, and its annotations, to shore up his arguments against astrology. He wrote that 'in the Scriptures in the Prophet *Ieremie* it is plainelie forbidden, to beleeve or harken unto them that Prophecies and fore-speaks by the course of the Planets & Starres'.[30] James here cited Jeremiah 10, and, in the Geneva translation, Jeremiah 10:2 reads: 'Thus saith the Lorde, Learne not the way of the heathen, and be not afraide for the signes of heaven, though the heathen be afraid of such.' A command not to fear it is hardly a serious indictment of astrology, but the accompanying annotation in the Geneva Bible most certainly is:

> God forbiddeth his people to give credit or fear the constellations of stares, and planets which have no power of themselves, but are governed by him, and their secret motions and influences are not knowen to man and therefore there can be no certaine judgement thereof, Deut. 18, 9b meaning not onely in the observation of the starrs but their Lawes and ceremonies whereby they confirm their idolatorie which is forbidden.

This marginal note in turn cites Deuteronomy, which commands: 'Let none be found among you ... that useth divination, or [is a] regarder of the times ... or a charmer, or that counselleth with spirits, or a soothsayer, or that asketh counsel at the dead. For all that do such things are abomination unto the Lord, and because of these abominations the Lord thy God doth cast them out before thee.'[31] James was concerned by the dangers associated with astrology, but, rather than putting this down to ignorance and superstition as Buchanan had done, he blamed the vanity and curiosity of the educated, which led them into the Devil's clutches:

> The learned have their curiositie wakened up; and fedde by that which I call his [i.e. the Devil's] schoole: This is the *Astrologie* judiciar. For divers men having attained to a great perfection in learning ... assaie to vendicate unto them a greater name, by not only knowing the course of things heavenly, but likewise to clim[b] to the knowledge of things to come thereby.[32]

At first, astrology seemed lawful to these learned men, as such knowledge appeared to be grounded only in natural causes. But later, finding their practice 'prove true in sundrie things', they 'studie to know the cause thereof: and so mounting from degree to degree, upon the slipperie and uncertain scale of curiositie; they are at last entised, that where lawfull artes or sciences failes, to satisfie their restles mindes, even to seeke to that black and unlawfull science of *Magie*.'[33] They would then become involved in casting spells and raising spirits to answer questions. At first 'they blindlie glorie of themselves', but then find they have become 'bond-slaves to their mortall enemie' and receive 'the horrors of Hell for punishment thereof.'[34]

Declaring judicial astrology unlawful, and linking it with the diabolical, implied more than a stern rebuke to its practitioners. Shortly after the Reformation, in 1563, the Scottish Witchcraft Act was passed. Julian Goodare has pointed out that the 'vane superstitioun' mentioned in the Act was not false and ignorant belief, but false and dangerous belief. Without God's authorisation, any practices were superstitions – but, if any effect arose from them, then the power for this must come from the Devil, not God.[35] The Witchcraft Act ordered that 'na persoun seik ony help, response or consultatioun at ony sic usaris or abusaris foirsaidis of Witchcraftis, Sorsareis or Necromancie, under the pane of deid, alsweill to be execute aganis the usar, abusar, as the seikar of the response or consultatioun'.[36] The word 'response' in the Act may also have been intended as a caution to those who claimed to practise the interrogations branch of judicial astrology, as well as their clients. In this transaction, clients came to the astrologer with a question and the astrologer would give a response based on a horoscope that he would draw up for the time and place at which the query reached him.

This understanding of the Witchcraft Act can be found later in the journal of Sir John Lauder of Fountainhall, one of Scotland's leading judges. In 1685 he expressed outrage at a broadsheet that James Cathcart, 'a pretended mathematician or astrologer', had issued in Edinburgh. Cathcart's advertisement 'cited some texts of Scripture allowing ane influence to the stars', and invited people to come to him for resolutions of any difficult questions they had, such as 'anent ther death, ther marriage, what husbands or wives they would get, and if they would prosper and succeed in such projects as love or journeyes, &c'. He also professed skill to cure the French pox (syphilis) and other diseases. Lauder wrote that it was 'a great impudence in a Christian Commonwealth to avow such ane art, for if he had it by magick he was a sorcerer, if not he was an impostor and abuser of the people, which even is death by our 73 Act Parliament 1563' (the Witchcraft Act).[37]

While the Act was certainly enforced against many accused of witchcraft, there is little evidence to show that astrologers were charged under it. Nor are there records of prosecutions under the 1575 Poor Law Act, which aimed to suppress idle beggars and mandated punishment for anyone claiming 'knawlege in physnomie, palmestre or utheris abused sciencis, quhairby thay perswade the people that thay can tell thair weardis [i.e. fates] deathis and fortunes and sic uther fantasticall ymaginationis', which might be expected to include astrology.[38] According to P. G. Maxwell-Stuart, 'specific mention of astrology in Scottish ecclesiastical records is most uncommon'.[39]

One case, however, was recorded in 1669. It concerned James Hog in Humbie, who went to a man called Seal in Newbattle to ask who had stolen corn and cloth from his house. Seal 'was under ane promise to the presbiterie of Dalkeith not to medle w[i]t[h] in any thing in that kinde', but he gave Hog a letter of introduction to a person in Edinburgh who would tell him who the thief was. Hog sent his man John Wood to the astrologer, David Ewart, with money and Seal's letter. Ewart sent back a paper describing the thief in detail, writing that he 'dwelt southward from the place that he was of sandie coloured hair, blew watering eyes with a big brow having a scar in his hedd on whierr there is no hair, and that he was ane old souldier or smith'.[40] On 25 April 1669, Hog and Wood appeared before Humbie kirk session and confessed to consulting Ewart: 'Whereupon the said James Hog and Johne Wood were sharplie rebuked for their sin in going to consult with one whom they supposed ane magician or wizard, their sin being laid out wnto them, they were exhorted to mourne for the same. But what their censure should be the session thought fit to referre that to the presbiterie.' On 16 May the session reported that the presbytery had ordained that the men should 'publicklie be rebuked', and on 30 May it was recorded that 'James Hog and Johne Wood did acknowledge th[ai]r sorrow for th[ai]r heinous sin of consulting with David Ewart ane supposed sorcerer anent th[ai]r stollen goods'.[41]

No matter how humiliating a public rebuke might be, Hog and Wood got off lightly for their offence of consulting someone variously described

Astrology and supernatural power 135

as a magician, wizard and sorcerer. This, along with the scarcity of such astrological misdemeanours in kirk records, suggests that judicial astrology as it was practised at the folk level for obtaining personal information was treated more as a superstitious folly to be contained and censured, rather than as a substantial danger.

Some learned men, however, did practise judicial astrology and used it in association with their other intellectual pursuits. Three examples of such men may be given, one each for the three pursuits of natural philosophy, chronology and mathematics.

Writing his memoirs in the years after 1603, the courtier Sir James Melville recalled a conversation that his brother Robert had had in 1562 with James Bassantin or Bassendyne (d. 1568), a Glasgow-educated academic who had been a professor of mathematics at Paris.[42] Bassantin had predicted that Queen Mary, in whose interest Robert Melville was then working, would suffer 'captyvite and utter wrak' at the hands of Queen Elizabeth. Melville retorted that he 'lyked not to heir of sic develisch newes, nor yet wald he credit them in any sort'; such things were 'false ungodly and unlawfull for Christians to medle them with'.[43] Bassantin, however, justified his use of astrology by declaring that 'Philip Melanthon, who was a godly theologue, has declaired and wreten anent the naturell scyences, that ar laufull and daily red in dyvers Christien universites'.[44]

Bassantin seemed to make no distinction between natural and judicial astrology, and clearly considered the latter to be just as permissible theologically as the former. To add legitimacy to his art, he characterised his own aptitude for prescience as God-given. He enlarged on his predictions to Melville, despite the latter's protests, explaining that 'as in all uther artis, God geves to some les, to some mair and clearer knawlege then till [i.e. than to] uthers; be the quhilk knawlege I have also that at lenth, that the kingdome of England sall of rycht fall to the crown of Scotland, and that there are some born at this instant that sall bruk landis and heritages in England'.[45] It may well be that Sir James Melville had been burnishing Bassantin's predictions over the years, since his account was written after 1603 by which time they had come true.

For the use of astrology in the intellectual study of chronology we turn to Robert Pont. Pont was a prominent minister, one of the founding fathers of the Scottish Reformation and six times moderator of the general assembly of the Church of Scotland. In October 1599, scarcely two years after the publication of *Daemonologie*, he published *A Newe Treatise*.[46] Pont's ambitious work, involving astrology, numerology, chronology and apocalyptic foreboding, was an attempt to calculate the age of the world and the time of its imminent end, and to counter the Catholic claim that 1600 was a Jubilee year. It also robustly defended his views on astrology – views that were largely contrary to

James's. The work could even have been a rebuke from Pont, an 'aged Pastour in the Kirk of Scotland', to the much younger king, whom he knew well.[47] Pont wrote:

> I would informe them to amend their errour also, that deny the heavenly influences to be effectual, because the predictions of such as commonly set out the vulgare Prognostications oft-times, take not effect: I say, these men declare them selves very ignorant in naturall Philosophie, and are convict by experience and ensample of such things, as daily fal out, by vertue of the heavenly influences.[48]

Pont drew a distinction between these vulgar practitioners and men learned in the art: 'many evident signes are founde in the motiones, configurations, and interchangeings of the courses of the heavenly light, where by men, who are expert in divine science of Astrology, may gather and conjecture, many things to fall out, not only in the aire, but also in the naturall inclination of earthly creatures.'[49] Having used astrology and proved to his own satisfaction that there was value in it, it is unsurprising that he regarded it as a divine science and therefore a priori lawful. He argued that 'birds and animals have been given the ability to sense coming changes in the weather so then how should we altogether deny fore-knowledge to be graunted to men, to conjecture of these accidents, having reason, judgement, and experience to lead them thereunto?'[50]

To support his viewpoint Pont, like James, marshalled his own preferred verses of Scripture, here from Genesis 1:14, declaring: 'For that cause, the eternall God appoynted them in the beginning, not onely to shine and shew lights unto the world, but also to be for signs of things to come: as it is testified in Genesis … to give light unto the Earth … to distinguish times, dayes, and yeares … to forewarne men of many things profitable for this life.'[51] Pont was profoundly affected by the millennialism that was sweeping Europe. He was convinced, like his friend John Napier, inventor of logarithms and writer on the book of Revelation, that the world would end soon after 1600. He cited several astrological portents that backed up his calculations, such as the solar eclipse of 1598, followed by the extraordinary number of eclipses to come. Using sensational language that Buchanan would surely have found regrettable, he expressed a particular concern about 'that fearefull Eclipse of the 1605 yeare, wherein the Sun shall be allutterlie darkned at Noone-daie, whereof the effectes shall continue certain yeares thereafter; pretende great mutations and perturbationes to ensue in those few yeares following; As warres, seditiones, pestilences, famine, with many other grievous calamities.'[52] Pont also used his astrology to support his passionate and often vindictive theology, crusading against the corruption and 'pompose superstition' of the Church of Rome. He saw divers apparitions in the heaven, namely, that most notable star or comete, which appeared in the yeare of our Lord 1572. Most cleare, without any spowting haires or beames from it, the which the most learned did take for a signe of the approching of the Lord to judgemente against the bloudy tyrants of the earth, & namely, that Herode of France.[53]

Pont's linking of future predictable astronomical phenomena with God's punishment for sinners and the end of days suggests that he believed that these events were preordained and that the chronology of the future could be calculated by learned men with the help of astrology.

Colin Campbell of Achnaba (1644–1726) was another Church of Scotland minister who investigated astrology in depth. Campbell was an esteemed mathematician and metaphysician who kept up an extensive correspondence with fellow mathematicians in Scotland and beyond. Letters to Campbell show that he almost certainly learned judicial astrology from the almanac-maker James Corss. In his 1663 Edinburgh almanac, Corss advertised his services in teaching of the 'mathematical ... Arts and sciences' including 'showing how to resolve all manner of questions' and how to 'erect Celestial Schems or Figures for any time assigned'.[54] Corss, in a letter dated 23 April 1664, gave an extraordinarily detailed and confident response to a question that Campbell had asked about a child's paternity, writing that the child was legitimate but would not live long:

> I thinke the paren[ts] have had severall jarrs and discontents. Yet I am sure the child is his owne. It will not live long for when Venus comes (by direction) to the body of Saturn, lord of the 4th, it will then expire ... The childs mother would willingly aggre with, and does greatly love her husband but he is possessd with jealousie and fury and the woman viz. his wife is most falsly calumniate and slandred. I perceave they are but poor & have no great wealth. It will be a difficult bussines to reconcile them.[55]

Campbell's interest in the topic persisted and deepened. A letter to him in 1701 suggests that he had been making an ambitious attempt to integrate mathematics, astrology, Newtonian physics and theology into a unified system.

> You have with great accuracy considered the matter not only mathematically & in the way of judicial astrology, but also have given excellent phylosophical & theological reflections on the same ... You have intertwined several most curious observations which I scarce heard of before as the calculation of the varieties of one system from Newton and that which you call a primary law of nature; the mutual tendency of all particles of matter to one another in a duplicate reciprocal proportion.[56]

His correspondent added that the Earl of Tullibardine and his son 'were very much taken with' Campbell's reflections, and that 'his l[ord]s[hi]p kept it ever since until lately upon my earnest request he returned it. Several other ingenious gentlemen are curious to have a double of it.' At this late date there were apparently educated and influential men who still took an interest in what judicial astrology might have to offer in helping them understand their world.

The ever-present threat, however, of being accused of dealing with the Devil had many treading warily throughout the period. Mindful that they could be under suspicion, astrologers were ever ready to proclaim their allegiance to God. In 1562 James Bassantin (discussed earlier in the chapter) was keen to absolve himself of the charge of involving himself in the Devil's work; as he protested to Robert Melville, 'I am a Christien of your religion, and feares God, and purposes never to cast my self in any of the unlawfull artis that ye mean of.'[57]

Some of the pious were keen to dissociate themselves from astrology altogether. One couple, in the mid-seventeenth century, felt so strongly about its illicit nature that they had their opinion carved in stone on the front wall of Lauriston Castle near Edinburgh. The castle had formerly been the home of the judge Sir Alexander Napier, later Lord Lauriston (1572–1629), half-brother of John Napier. According to the Napier family biographer, Alexander 'read his session-papers in the stars, and wrote his interlocutors in the twelve houses of the heaven, being a most learned judicial astrologer.'[58] After he inherited the castle in 1604 he had a stone engraved with his own horoscope placed above his front door. Sometime in the 1650s the castle was acquired by another lawyer, Robert Dalglish, and his wife Jean Douglas. They removed the horoscope and replaced it with a Latin-inscribed slab that firmly refuted astrology.[59] It reads: 'Astra nec vitae moderatores nec bonorum meorum causas agnosco haec quae possideo Dei benignitati accepta fero ejus fidei juranda voluntati disponenda committo ab eo gratiam omnibus pro ipso utendi expeto et expecto.' (I acknowledge the stars neither as moderators of my life nor the causes of my wealth. These things I possess I consider as witness of God's goodness, and I commit the same to God's faith to be disposed of by his will. I ask for and expect from Him the grace to use these things for His sake.[60]) Even as late as 1695, the astrologer John Stobo, who offered his surgical services in 'amputations, cancers and hairlips etc', still felt he had to justify himself and his predictions to the public and the Kirk. In his lurid broadsheet the *Scottish Mercury*, he assured readers: 'This I write with a publick Spirit, only for Caution to such as it may concern, well understanding God rules all eternally by Providence, having left to man but a Glimpse of Prescience.' He resolved 'to build my tabernacle upon the Reformed Church of Scotland and will conform my life accordingly.'[61]

Yet, as evidenced by student notebooks, astrology was taught as part of the natural philosophy syllabus at all of the Scottish universities until the final quarter of the seventeenth century. The First Book of Discipline (1561) recommended astrology's inclusion in the syllabus.[62] As church and state, and in Edinburgh the Town Council, took a watchful interest in university matters, there can be no doubt that astrology was accepted as part of the scholastic curriculum by these authorities.[63] Students were instructed in the foundational principles of astrological theory that would have allowed them to interpret a horoscope, for both natural and judicial astrology. One reason that some learned men made little distinction between natural and judicial astrology may have lain in the fact that Ptolemy's category of universal astrology straddled the territories of the later-imposed divisions of natural and judicial astrology. As the *Tetrabiblos* was a core scholastic text, it would have made speculation on such matters legitimate for educated men.

In 1672 at King's College, Aberdeen, the regent Robert Forbes taught that judicial astrologers used the positions of the planets in houses, along with good and bad aspects, to make their judgements. He gave some explanatory notes and maxims about this, then used the nativity of Charles II to teach his students how to draw up a horoscope describing the different areas of life that the planets could influence.[64] At Edinburgh University in 1673, the regent James Pillans, after giving details of the relative strengths of planets in different signs, taught his students that it was not only judicial astrologers who gave consideration to this. Moderate, learned and experienced men did so too, he explained, and used the information with diligence in judging their advice, plans and deliberations.[65]

Forbes and Pillans were, however, remnants of a dying order. By the early 1680s Descartes had supplanted Aristotle and Ptolemy in the natural philosophy syllabus at Scottish universities. Newton's *Principia Mathematica*, too, was introduced shortly after its publication in 1687.[66] Jacques Rohault's *Tractatus Physicus* was the most prominent teaching manual of physics in the universities and it contained a chapter deriding judicial astrology as lacking in any foundation, firm and unquestioned principles or basis in experience and puncturing the false reasoning used to defend it. In 1683 the influential David Gregory became professor of mathematics at Edinburgh University and, pouring scorn on astrology, insisted that it had no place in physics and the education of magistrands. He also harboured a bitter political grudge against astrologers for the damage that the predictions they had invented had done to the Stuart monarchs.[67]

Previously astronomy and astrology had been taught together, the former as the theoretical branch of the subject and the latter as its practical division. Astrology was now divorced from the coupling and by 1700 the idea that celestial events had meaning had largely been discarded in academia. Stripped of that connection, astrology lost its potency; it could now be dismissed, especially by those interested in the new science, as a baseless superstition.

The temperature of the theological debate about astrology's connection with magic and the diabolical, though still significant, had also cooled somewhat. Some were coming to doubt that sorcerers existed, and this included the physician David Abercromby. Writing in 1685 that he could 'conceive no worse use of *Wit*, than to be busie about acquiring too much insight in Judiciary Astrology', he added: 'Tis not only in my Judgement Sin which we should chiefly fear, to consult with Magicians and Witches, *if there be any*, concerning contingent effects and contingencies.'[68]

In popular culture by the early eighteenth century, the connection between astrology and the Devil was being treated as more a matter for mirth than for belief or prosecution. A verse broadsheet purporting to announce the demise of James Cathcart, the itinerant quack and judicial astrologer of Edinburgh who thirty-five years earlier had incurred Sir John Lauder's ire, made speculative fun of the notion:

> Tho' some alleadg'd he was nae chancie,
> A Practiser of Nicromancie,
> Yet others say that's a fool Fancie,
> And boldy dars,
> To Swear he shines for ought they can see
> Amo' the Star's.
> Others do confidently tell,
> That Orpheus like he went to Hell,
> And in black Art and Magick Spell
> Such Knowledge got,
> As to out-wit Auld Nick himsell,
> Like Mitchell Scot.[69]

Even in the annual almanacs, the weather forecasting that had traditionally been based on astrology was being mocked.[70] This verse appeared in Edinburgh's New Almanack for 1713:

> The Weather here we cannot want,
> Least we Displease the Ignorant;
> Who thinks that Mortals have a Notion,
> Of Weather by the Planets Motion.[71]

With astrology's loss of institutional status came a loss of credibility among the educated and those aspiring to respectability. Celestial events in the universities were now firmly regarded as part of the natural order, acknowledged as created by God but with no inherent meaning. Preternatural explanations no longer featured in students' notebooks.

The information given by the new natural philosophy based on mathematics had a powerful advantage with which astrology could not compete. It gave practical, economic benefits in a wide range of fields such as navigation, surveying and map-making and these were now being taught at Edinburgh University. Astrology had become largely a thing of the past as the fashion and appetite for mathematics grew. Colin Maclaurin, who took up the post of professor of mathematics in 1725 at Edinburgh University, complained that he sometimes had as many as 126 students in his class.[72]

The supernatural power of astrology – divine according to its proponents, diabolical according to its critics – was thus fading away. The fiercely defended polarities between licit and illicit and natural and supernatural categorisation that divided attitudes to astrology in earlier years were becoming irrelevant. Educated opinion tipped to the consensus that astrology was a superstition practised and believed in by the vulgar. Although a lingering miasma of suspicion about the diabolical still hung about astrology, this too had largely become a laughing matter. Yet diminished though it was in establishment regard, astrology did not die; it found sub-mainstream channels to carry it forward, and its history moved on to a fresh chapter.

Notes

1 James R. Naiden, *The Sphera of George Buchanan* (Philadelphia, PA: privately printed, 1952), p. 139.
2 Jean Calvin, *An Admonicion Against Astrology Judiciall* (London, 1561), [p. 15]. This was first published in French as *Advertissement Contre L'astrologie Judiciaire* in Geneva in 1549. Square brackets are used to note pages, counted from the initial page, in this and other unpaginated books.
3 *Ibid.*, [p. 15].
4 *Ibid.*, [pp. 47–8].
5 *Ibid.*, [p. 32].
6 *Ibid.*, [p. 13].
7 *Ibid.*, [pp. 14–15].
8 *Ibid.*, [p. 32].
9 *Ibid.*, [p. 15].
10 John Calvin, *Institutes of the Christian Religion*, trans. Henry Beveridge, 3 vols (Peabody, MA: Hendrickson, 2008), I, p. 116 (bk 1, ch. 16:3). For more on providence, see Martha McGill and Alasdair Raffe, 'The uses of providence in early modern Scotland', Chapter 10 this volume.
11 Gilbert Skeyne, *Ane Breve Descriptioun of the Pest* (Edinburgh, 1568), [p. 3].
12 *Ibid.*, [p. 3]. Mars and Saturn were known as the lesser and greater malefic respectively. They come into a significant aspect every six months.
13 *Ibid.*, [p. 6].
14 *Ibid.*, [p. 4].
15 *Ibid.*, [p. 43].
16 *Ibid.*, [p. 15].

17 *Ibid.*, [p. 43].
18 *Ibid.*, [p. 2].
19 Naiden, *Sphera*, p. 139.
20 *Ibid.*
21 *Ibid.*, p. 26.
22 Lawrence Normand and Gareth Roberts (eds), *Witchcraft in Early Modern Scotland: James VI's* Demonology *and the North Berwick Witches* (Exeter: University of Exeter Press, 2000), p. 316.
23 Mark Napier, *Memoirs of John Napier of Merchiston* (Edinburgh: William Blackwood, 1834), p. 217.
24 James VI, *Daemonologie*, in his *Minor Prose Works*, ed. James Craigie (Edinburgh: STS, 1982), pp. 1–56, at p. 15 (bk 1, ch. 6). This edition of *Daemonologie* is used throughout.
25 *Ibid.*, p. 9 (bk 1, ch. 4).
26 *Ibid.*, pp. 9–10 (bk 1, ch. 4).
27 *Ibid.*, p. 12 (bk 1, ch. 5).
28 William T. Dobson, *History of the Bassandyne Bible, the First Printed in Scotland* (Edinburgh: William Blackwood, 1887), pp. 120–1.
29 1560 Geneva Bible, title page.
30 James VI, *Daemonologie*, p. 10 (bk 1, ch. 4).
31 1599 Geneva Bible, Deuteronomy 18:9–12.
32 James VI, *Daemonologie*, p. 7 (bk 1, ch. 3).
33 *Ibid.*
34 *Ibid.*
35 Julian Goodare, 'The Scottish witchcraft act', *Church History*, 74 (2005), 39–67, at pp. 51–2.
36 Quoted *ibid.*, p. 39.
37 Sir John Lauder of Fountainhall, *Historical Observes of Memorable Occurrents in Church and State, 1680–1686*, ed. Adam Urquhart and David Laing (Edinburgh: Bannatyne Club, 1840), p. 145.
38 *RPS*, A1575/3/5. In the revised 1579 re-enactment, this phrase became 'knawlege of prophecie, charmeing or utheris abusit sciences': 1579/10/27.
39 P. G. Maxwell-Stuart, *An Abundance of Witches: The Great Scottish Witch-Hunt* (Stroud: Tempus, 2005), p. 163.
40 NRS, CH2/389/1, Humbie kirk session minutes, 1643–77.
41 *Ibid.*
42 A. J. Turner, 'Bassantin [Bassendyne], James (d. 1568)', *ODNB*.
43 Sir James Melville of Halhill, *Memoirs of His Own Life*, ed. Thomas Thomson (Edinburgh: Bannatyne Club, 1827), p. 203.
44 *Ibid.*
45 *Ibid.*, p. 204. For more on such political prophecies, see Michael B. Riordan, 'Scottish political prophecies and the crowns of Britain, 1500–1840', Chapter 7 this volume.
46 Robert Pont, *A Newe Treatise* (Edinburgh, 1599).
47 *Ibid.*, title page. Cf. Arthur H. Williamson, 'Number and national consciousness: the Edinburgh mathematicians and Scottish political culture at the Union of the Crowns', in Roger A. Mason (ed.), *Scots and Britons: Scottish Political Thought and the Union of 1603* (Cambridge: Cambridge University Press, 1994), pp. 187–212, at pp. 193–7.

48 Pont, *Treatise*, p. 44.
49 *Ibid.*, p. 45.
50 *Ibid.*, p. 46.
51 *Ibid.*, p. 45. He also referred to Job 38:31.
52 *Ibid.*, p. 87.
53 *Ibid.*, p. 82. The 'Herod of France' was King Charles IX, who was considered to have been responsible for the Massacre of St Bartholomew in 1572.
54 James Corss, *Mercurius Coelicus* (Edinburgh, 1663), [p. 14].
55 EUL, MS.3099.9.
56 EUL, M. Murray to Colin Campbell, 1701, MS.3097.8, fo. 27.
57 Melville, *Memoirs*, p. 203.
58 Napier, *Memoirs*, p. 320.
59 John Philip Wood, *Antient and Modern State of the Parish of Cramond* (Edinburgh, 1794), pp. 40–1.
60 The translation is my own.
61 John Stobo, *Mercurius Scotus* (Edinburgh, 1694), p. 2.
62 John Knox, *The History of the Reformation of Religion in Scotland*, ed. William M'Gavin (Glasgow: Blackie & Son, 1841), p. 500.
63 Jane Ridder-Patrick, 'Astrology in Early Modern Scotland' (PhD thesis, University of Edinburgh, 2012), p. 32.
64 NLS, MS Acc.4975.
65 EUL, MS.Dc.6.5, James Pillans, 'Philosophia peripetetica'.
66 Jane Ridder-Patrick, 'The marginalisation of astrology in early modern Scotland', *Early Science and Medicine*, 22 (2017), 464–86.
67 NLS, MS.2075, lectures of Herbert Kennedy transcribed by Edward Lewis, 1685; EUL, Dc.8.118, lectures of Herbert Kennedy transcribed by Robert Kello, 1693; EUL, La.III.570, lectures of David Gregory transcribed by Francis Pringle, 1690.
68 David Abercromby, *A Discourse of Wit* (London, 1685), pp. 141–2. Emphasis added.
69 NLS, Ry.III.c.36 (153), Anon., 'An account of his strange life and wonderful actions, &c' (c.1720). Michael (or Mitchell) Scot was a medieval scholar, rumoured to have been a wizard. See Piero Morpurgo, 'Scot [Scott], Michael (d. in or after 1235)', *ODNB*.
70 For astrology and Scottish almanacs, see George M. Brunsden, 'Seventeenth- and eighteenth-century astrology, and the Scottish popular almanac', in Lizanne Henderson (ed.), *Fantastical Imaginations: The Supernatural in Scottish History and Culture* (Edinburgh: John Donald, 2009), pp. 47–69; Ridder-Patrick, 'Astrology in Early Modern Scotland', pp. 101–38.
71 John Thomson, *Edinburgh's New Almanack* (Edinburgh, 1713), [p. 16].
72 Paul Wood, 'Science in the Scottish Enlightenment', in Malcolm Oster (ed.), *Science in Europe, 1500–1800* (Basingstoke: Palgrave, 2002), pp. 194–211, at pp. 194–5.

9

Fallen spirits and divine grace: sermons and the supernatural in post-Reformation Scotland

Michelle D. Brock

On 11 May 1655, a 'solemn Day of Humiliation', the minister Francis Aird delivered a stirring sermon at Carluke, Lanarkshire. His text was Hosea 9:12, and his remarks centred on the reasons why an angry God might depart from his people, leaving them bereft of the divine presence and faced with a range of worldly evils:

> When the Lord departs, the Devill come in his room. The Lord save us from this Judgement: for it is not long since the Devilles and Brownies, throosh the Barnes [threshed the corn in the barns], & danced up and down the Land, before the light of the Gospell grew clear: and its ominous-like, that Devill is yet coming in some houses speaking, disputing; and if it be thus, it appears he has taken the musell off his mouth again; And o but this is a sad matter; for ye may read when the Lord departed from Saul, The Devill entered into him.[1]

This sermon, though remarkable in some respects, typifies the ways in which we find Scottish ministers incorporating the supernatural into their sermons. Throughout, the true source of power, supernatural or otherwise, is God, who is both bearer of judgement and deliverer from evil. The Devil, devious and unleashed, looms ready to capitalise on innate human corruption. These themes – divine sovereignty, human depravity and demonic alacrity – appear as theological pillars in many sermons in the post-Reformation era.

What is extremely unusual is Aird's mention of 'Devilles and Brownies'. These belonged, in his mind, to a bygone, pre-Protestant world full of dark beings and deeds. The 'supernatural' power of God and evil of Satan were to be expected as part of the landscape of godly life. The presence of 'Brownies' in tandem with various other 'Devilles', however, was a vestige of an ungodly past, part of a supernatural realm that should find no place in a land illuminated by 'the light of the Gospel'. At the same time, by referencing non-human beings like brownies – ambiguous spiritual creatures that inhabited the same natural realm as fairies – Aird evoked the popular memory, and perhaps continued belief, of his audience a century after the Reformation.[2] This chapter surveys how Scottish ministers defined, described and used the 'supernatural' in their sermons during the century and a half following the Reformation.

Scholars have generally treated the 'supernatural' as the realm of beliefs and folklore that the Scottish Kirk sought to sideline, demonise or eradicate during the early modern period. God and the divinity of Christ are not usually categorised as 'supernatural' by modern scholars, even though they are inexplicable by the laws of nature. This is, of course, because of their normativity and orthodoxy in the pre-modern world and, for many, today; few explicitly challenged these core principles of faith until the mid-eighteenth century.[3] In this chapter, I primarily use the term 'supernatural' to describe the powers, actions and natures of God, Satan, angels and a range of other beings that operated outside ordinary natural explanation. It might be argued that doing so ignores the category of 'preternatural', to which all such 'other-worldly' beings other than God technically belonged. However, as early modern ministers rarely used the term 'preternatural', this category will be collapsed into the 'supernatural' here.[4]

Supernatural and preternatural beings like fairies, and traditions like Second Sight, found little place in post-Reformation theology and faced constant onslaughts by the Kirk.[5] It is perhaps unsurprising, then, that as sources for understanding the supernatural, sermons have been largely overlooked. And yet, as Aird's fast sermon suggests, even in the dichotomous world of the Reformed Kirk, sermons set the parameters for how Scots should understand and engage with the supernatural.

This chapter examines how early modern Scottish ministers evoked and circumscribed the supernatural in their sermons, both through explicit mention of the term and implicit discussion of supernatural beings and forces. The supernatural as framed in these sermons was a broad category that might include God, the Devil, divine power and knowledge, the occasional angel, or evil more generally, depending on audience, author and intent. I suggest that sermons shaped expectations for consistent engagement with the supernatural in three mutually constitutive ways: they cultivated hope for access to the wisdom and grace of God and Christ, they emphasised the personal presence of Satan in human lives, and they attempted to limit the roster of supernatural beings in the mental worlds of the godly.

Reformed ministers rarely attempted to explicitly define 'supernatural' as a precise category of beings or abilities. When ministers used the term 'supernatural' in sermons, they almost always did so in the context of describing the power of God, Christ or the divine presence more broadly construed. In a fast sermon delivered in the summer of 1697, minister James Webster explained the true meaning and efficacy of repentance. 'Its supernatural', he observed, for 'it takes all the power of an exalted [Christ] to give repentance to one soul'.[6] James Clark, preaching to the parishioners of Athelstaneford in 1700, decried the 'Rapide Propensions and Agitations of mind' displayed by the Quakers and Anabaptists, and described, in contrast, the genuinely 'supernatural work' of Christ's spirit.[7] He went on to clarify that Christ does not operate against 'the will of a Rationall Creature', but rather 'works agreeably to our Nature, altho by a Supernatural Efficacie ... whereby of Naturallie unwilling, he makes Supernaturallie willing in a way of his Power'. Only supernatural persuasion could convert human hearts and attract otherwise fallen men to 'that which is truely Good'.[8] Ministers did not characterise the supernatural as unnatural or even opposed to nature, except insofar as it alone could redirect those on an evil course – quite an inclusive category in Reformed theology – back towards righteousness.

If the supernatural was defined at all in early modern sermons, it was as a body of divine truths and forces that lay beyond the terrestrial comprehension of 'natural' – i.e., post-lapsarian and of the flesh – men and women. As Alexander Wedderburn pointed out when preaching on Acts 26:28, 'the contents of the Gospel are supernatural, so must they be supernaturally discerned' with the aid of 'illumination from the Spirit'.[9] In a collection of sermons on 1 Corinthians, Edinburgh's Robert Rollock explained that, even in an age of reformation, 'there was never a naturall man that could comprehend the wisdome of this Gospell. For why? [the Gospell] is spirituall, supernaturall, and above nature, and therefore the naturall wit could never bee able to comprehend her'.[10] In another sermon he wrote that

> as for the subject of this wisdom, thy naturall eye never saw it, thy naturall care never heard it, and it never entered into thy naturall heart: and therfore whosoever wil see these things, he must seek an eye that is more than natural, that is supernaturall, that is spirituall: seeke an eare that is supernaturall and spirituall. Goe to the heart, content not thy selfe with a naturall heart: seeke an heart that is spirituall and supernaturall.[11]

For Rollock and his fellow Reformed ministers who fundamentally distrusted corrupted human minds, true wisdom did not come from empirical inquiry or observation, but from seeking the supernatural knowledge of God.

This definition was echoed repeatedly in William Colvill's 1673 collection of sermons on Isaiah 11, most of which revolved around the nature of truth and post-lapsarian man's struggle to understand the will and ways of God. Colvill, minister and principal of the University of

Edinburgh, implored his audience to seek supernatural knowledge as a remedy to spiritual malaise. 'Art thou dull in understanding', he asked, 'and hath little or no sharpness of wit to understand and discern spiritual and supernatural truths, no more then a blind man has sight to discern colours? Go to the Lord Jesus Christ, in whom was and is the spirit of understanding'.[12] Here, Colvill argued that supernatural truths existed not beyond the reach of man altogether, but only beyond man's reach alone. In another sermon from the same collection, he instructed his readers that they 'must be frequent in prayer to God', for 'without the concourse and strong influence of the special help of supernatural Grace', humans remained trapped in the depravity of their natural state.[13]

Colvill's sermon on Isaiah 11:6 dealt with the question of evidence, and the terrestrial challenges of understanding the mysteries of the world and of Holy Scripture. He warned that in seeking 'the natural knowledge and science of these divine truths', humans might be prone, in their 'infirmity and ignorance', to interpret the wonders worked by God as 'contrary to Natural and Philosophical verity'.[14] Colvill insisted, however, that 'Supernatural verities are not contrary to Natural truths; because God, the prime verity, is the Author of all real verity'. He concluded this portion of his sermon with the suggestion that the godly 'submit our faith to divine revelation in the Word, and not oppose the barkings of humane reasonings against revealed truths'.[15] This was not, therefore, a sermon about defining the supernatural or identifying which beliefs belonged within, as Colin Kidd puts it, the 'officially approved supernaturalism' of the Kirk.[16] Rather, Colvill hoped to convince an educated audience, some of whom may have been university students engaged in intense philosophical and scientific study, to recognise the limitations of their own intellectual capacity to comprehend supernatural truths and phenomena. For many Reformed Scots, trusting the Scriptures, rather than observing the natural world, was the key to godly belief and behaviour.

Unsurprisingly, ministers also discussed the supernatural to emphasise the depravity and spiritual impotence of mankind in their 'natural' states. In one late seventeenth-century sermon, an anonymous minster explained that while 'a man in his natural state can do nothing that is spiritually or supernaturally good', this should not impede individuals from striving to live virtuous lives.[17] More bluntly, in a sermon on Psalm 130:7 George Hutcheson told his audience that because 'defection, declining, and departing from God, is the sinful byass of our hearts', whenever they moved to do right, 'that motion is preternatural, or rather supernatural; we are naturally inclined to go a whoring from God'.[18] James Durham, minister of St Mungo's in Glasgow, used the idea of the supernatural to characterise the nature of grace and underline human depravity in the face of demonic temptations. When the godly are confronted by the Devil, the Lord 'may quicken his own People, to more lively exercise of their Grace, when they know that there is such an enemy in their bosom'.[19] Such divine intervention was essential, for there was nothing 'in any man naturally to engadge him, or to help him to fight against Self' but the 'supernatural speciall Grace' freely given by God.[20] On this point Aberdeen Doctor James Sibbald agreed, explaining in stark terms in a sermon on John 6:43 why divine aid was essential for men and women to be and do good: 'Our *minds* are full of *blindnes, vanity* and *forgetfulnes:* our *wills* are *perverse* and bent to *evil* and our spirituall *enemies* are mighty, Yea beside that, these *actions* whereby we must follow GOD are *sublime, heavenly* and *supernaturall*, which nature of it self can never reach unto.' Human virtuousness itself, therefore, was imbued with a supernatural quality, for it, like salvation, was entirely impossible without 'the speciall Assistance of GOD'.[21]

Other ministers suggested that, if prior to the Fall men and women had some access to supernatural good through their resemblance to God, it had been permanently blocked through the transgression of original sin. In the mid-seventeenth century, the minister Hugh Binning noted that to discern the 'excellency of God shinning in the word', true Christians must rely upon a 'supernaturall eye' that the Lord had created in their souls in the beginning. Supernatural sight was necessary to comprehend supernatural glory, and both of these were gifts of a supreme God.[22] However, as Binning explained in another sermon from the same collection, the gift of a 'supernaturall eye', which had 'formed man for communion with God', had been ruined by the Fall and the machinations of Satan who 'hath spoyled us of our rich treasure, that glorious image of holiness'.[23] The chasm between humanity and the divine was thus wider than ever, and only supernatural aid from the creator could bridge it.

This usage of 'supernatural' to highlight the spiritual infirmity of 'natural man' and reiterate the necessity of reliance on divine aid reinforced the broader corpus of Reformed theology and practice in early modern Scotland. Indeed, post-Reformation ministers consistently foregrounded their descriptions of the Devil and humankind alike in an affirmation of the sovereignty of God. Divine supremacy governed Reformed thinking about the terrestrial world, so we should be unsurprised that it did so for events, beings and forces that existed beyond nature. It is equally fitting that ministers felt no need to define explicitly a category that, until the eighteenth century and well beyond, was assumed by all levels of society to exist. Even as the Kirk sought to eradicate or recategorise beliefs in 'grey-zone' beings like fairies and ghosts, few in Scotland would have denied that they lived in a world populated by demons, angels, witches and, of course, God.[24] During the early Enlightenment, when some rationalists attempted to exclude most supernatural phenomena from the realm of the possible, most learned Scots were primarily concerned with defending organised religion from the perceived threat of atheism.[25]

Yet ministers did employ the label of 'supernatural' to identify forces and truths that the godly should not only believe in, but aspire to. As James Sibbald put it, 'God giveth us Faith to be a spirituall eye, so he giveth us supernaturall Love and Hope, to be the feet of our soule whereby we may move and runne after Christ in the way of the obedience of these commandements'.[26] Knowledge and pursuit of the supernatural, when circumscribed by the Kirk and confirmed by the Scriptures, were even presented as markers of election. In a fast sermon preached before the House of Commons in 1644, Samuel Rutherford spoke of the elect – a group in which he confidently included himself – as having obtained, through grace, a 'supernatural sense' or instinct that allowed them to discern, if not wholly know, truths otherwise inaccessible to ordinary men and women.[27] It was only when early modern Scots showed credence in beings and forces that fell outside these approved categories of beliefs that the supernatural quickly became superstition in the minds of ministers.[28]

Of course, Scottish ministers wrote and preached about the supernatural constantly, without naming it as such. God featured as the primary wielder of the supernatural in their sermons. Beyond the references to supernatural knowledge discussed above, ministers frequently spoke of divine power in order to awe, warn and edify their audiences. During a fast sermon delivered at Dalserf in 1655, James Nesmith explained to his congregation that 'it is the Believers best practice to be seeking light from the Lord whereby he may understand such great misteries, hid up by the Lord from his eyes: for sometimes he lets out Threatnings to terrifie, and sometimes promises to allure his people'.[29] The language of 'mystery' to portray God's power and practices supplemented the sermonic characterisation of divine knowledge as supernatural. Here, Nesmith attempted to persuade his flock that the only type of knowledge necessary to godly life was the knowledge of God and trust in his will. The supernatural was, then, fundamentally inaccessible to man but also constantly encountered, out of reach but unavoidable. Ministers viewed supernatural knowledge and power as part of the broader package of divine supremacy, something that could never be fully understood but was nonetheless the ordering principle of human life and salvation.

Above all, ministers emphasised that God used his supernatural abilities to punish and correct the sinful actions of men and women. Preaching on Amos 3:2, Rob Mcquare told his Glasgow congregation in 1661 that they were part of a 'corrupt generation' that had 'done abominable iniquities'.[30] 'There are feu or none among us', he observed, that 'doeth good', for 'all flesh hath corrupted their ways & god sees tho we observe it not that our wickedness is great upon the earth'.[31] Divine power was inherently supernatural, but it also needed to be so in order to counter the overwhelming iniquities committed in the natural realm, which itself was under the sway of Satan. Similarly, Binning, in an unpublished sermon on Isaiah 32:1, discussed how all the children of Adam, condemned by their perpetual sins, ought to prepare themselves for a 'whirlwind of god's anger'.[32] In 1700, preaching after a fire had raged near parliamentary buildings in Edinburgh, James Webster described the wrath God had wrought with supernatural flourish: 'There he sat upon his throne, his flaming throne, and gave forth the sentence and called out his fire and his wind, these two terrible devouring elements and he said go to the houses and burn them, go and scatter so many families, and never stop until you have executed your commission and I call you back again.'[33] This image of God controlling the elements and wielding the sword of justice would have inspired both wonder and fear in Webster's hearers. Divine power was terrifying, but it was also fundamentally terrestrial, made manifest as earthly judgement upon a deserving populace. Indeed, this was a constant theme in discussions of the supernatural in Scottish sermons; references to God and the Devil were universal, but made almost exclusively in relation to human lives. Very rarely was there any sustained conversation of the supernatural in the broader cosmos; the 'super' was only that in comparison to the mundane world of the flesh.

Signs and portents of impending judgements also featured prominently in Scottish sermons. John Baird implored his congregation on 24 June 1683 to look within and without for the signs of the impending wrath invited by their sins: 'Do not all the threatenings of the word sound this alarm in our ears? Do not also the aspects of providence and dispensations look this way, as the tendencie of things seem to prognostick such events, but especially our illness of temper, the fullness of our cupe, the maturity of our sin declaring us to be ripe for judgement?'[34] Supernatural signs usually portended future punishments, but they could also be more positive. As Andrew Ramsay explained in 1638, 'becaus of the love and cair he hath of his elect allwayies', God sends both 'glaiding signes' and 'griving signes' of his impending judgements in order to warn and prepare the godly.[35] Divine signs, both worrying and reassuring, anticipated displays of supernatural power and illustrated God's care for his people.

Along with and usually in opposition to God, the Devil loomed large from the pulpit and on the page. Indeed, from sermons we know as much, if not more, about what early modern ministers – and perhaps their audiences – believed about the nature of Satan as they did about God. The demonic imagery in sermons served three primary purposes: to capture audience attention by invoking a potent and familiar figure, to educate hearers and readers about core Reformed ideas on human nature and divine sovereignty and to inspire Scots of all sorts to believe and behave in ways befitting a godly community.[36] While God's supernatural power could manifest in a myriad of invisible ways – through grace, goodness and knowledge – as well as the manipulation of external forces like weather and fire, ministers construed the Devil as a primarily internal force, though this did not negate physical consequences of demonic interactions.[37]

Ministers tailored their discussions of Satan to match specific audiences and political contexts, but all agreed on a number of scripturally inspired fundamentals about the nature of the great enemy. Above all, they depicted the Devil as immensely cunning and deceptive. John Welsh, famed son-in-law of John Knox, described Satan as 'that subtle serpent that deceives all the world; he is that seven-headed dragon that has such wit and wisdom that no wisdom can come about it but only the wisdom of God.'[38] This power was made manifest in Genesis, when, according to common interpretation, the Devil so easily beguiled Eve and prompted the Fall of Man. One minister explained to his flock that 'it is a very wylie sin, at first forged solely and subtilly in our first Parents, by the father of lieers, the Devill himself ... for he [Satan] having thus poisoned the root purposes also to poyson the branches'.[39] John Brown warned his audience around 1660 that, given the dual threat of human corruption and demonic deceits, they must not give heed 'to the lying Injections and temptations of Satan: It is not safe to entertain discourse with such an enemy ... He is too great a Sophist and Disputer for us.'[40]

Ministers coupled their exhortations on the threat of demonic temptations with lamentations of the depraved natures of humankind. The two were sides of the same coin, one enabling the other, a dangerous pairing for godly men and women hoping for closer communion with God. As Robert Bruce described in a sermon in 1591, Satan 'insinuates himself in our affections by reason of the corruption that is in us'.[41] Perhaps the most evocative description of the relationship between human corruption and demonic wiles came from a mid-seventeenth-century minister who explained to his parishioners that post-lapsarian men and women were perpetually inclined to evil, for their 'Corrupt Nature the Devill's Agent, leading us like as many dogs in a Leish to provock the Lord.'[42] As fundamentally fallen individuals, even the elect were unable to overcome the Devil's temptations on their own. As such, they must constantly rely upon divine strength for relief. In the words of Robert Baillie, addressed to the presbytery of Irvine, men must 'pray to God for our cause and Church: God will help us against all, men and devilis: No man is to be trusted; the best is naturallie false.'[43] Here again, only supernatural good could bring delivery from natural evil.

In emphasising the strength and cunning of Satan, who preyed upon the spiritual frailty of all men and women, ministers also took pains to emphasise his constant, even ubiquitous presence in human lives. Their audiences should expect to be perpetually affronted by the evil one, for, as 1 Peter 5:8 evocatively explained, 'the devil, a roaring lion, walketh about, seeking whom he may devour.'[44] Alexander Henderson explicitly suggested that the Devil, though a liar, had insight into true and hidden desires of men and women: 'The devil, he knows every man's disposition, how it is set; if he see him to be a voluptuous man; if he be one whom he sees to be ambitious; or if he be one whom he sees to be covetous. And he knows also the complexion and constitution of man's body ... and he has temptations fitted for all these.'[45] As another late seventeenth-century minister put it, 'when Satan gets one thought, he will get another thought, and then the man is all blown up with filthy lusts.'[46]

Some Reformed ministers took this a step further by suggesting that the Devil – or at least a demonic presence – resided inside the hearts and minds of all mankind. In a 1589 sermon, Robert Bruce told his audience they must always strive to overcome their own natures, 'for we have to do with principalities and powers, with spiritual wickedness, which are above us and within us also. For he is not that has corruption within him, but Sathan is in him; So we cannot be half walkrife [wakeful], ever studying to cast out the devill, to renounce our selfs, and to submit to the obedience of Christ.'[47] Also drawing on the language of informal possession, Andrew Gray lamented in 1628 that 'many of us may be afraid that the devil dwels and keeps possession in many of our hearts, and alace! He is like to be a possessor of some of them perpetually.'[48] As I have argued elsewhere, these ministers did not mean a physical demonic possession, but rather a spiritually innate one, grounded in the Reformed idea that all human beings, thanks to their inherent wickedness, were perpetually possessed by Satan.[49]

Satan's entire *raison d'être* was – with divine instruction – to attempt the subversion and inversion of what was good and godly. Ministers clearly hoped that the hearers and readers of their sermons would grasp the full extent of demonic presence and prowess and turn, accordingly, to Scripture and the Kirk for guidance and relief. One mid-seventeenth-century minister anticipated that someone, upon hearing about connections between human depravity and the Devil, might claim in despair that 'I can no sooner have a good motion in my heart but Satan is ready to steal it out, and my own corruption extinguishes it before I can get it brought forth to action.'[50] The good minister, named in an anonymous sermon notebook as 'Mr Hill', explained in response that the godly must 'study to practice these rules which by Gods grace may help thee to cherish good motions, and further them out to practice in thy life and conversation'. Moreover, as Christian life was at its core spiritual warfare, the godly must constantly bring 'good motions weapons and arguments against our corruption and satan's temptations.'[51] The Devil was no paltry enemy; all men and women should expect his constant presence within their own lives and should shield themselves accordingly against sin and Satan.

Lest their parishioners be overwhelmed in contemplating demonic strength and cunning, ministers stressed that the elect would ultimately be wrested from Satan's grasp by the supreme power of God.[52] Though the Devil was mighty, he could only operate under divine direction. As John Welsh explained, 'when it is said that he [the Devil] is powerful, it is true, but his power is limited and bounded, and there are marches and bounds set unto him, that he dare not pass over'.[53] In the face of the 'enemies of god and of his kirk', another minister reassured his audience in 1624 that the 'Godly man' will always find 'the lords gratious and favorable assistance, in his dangers and distresses, in his troubles and tentations, in his afflictions and perfections'.[54] As Michael Bruce, himself no stranger to earthly afflictions, put it, 'tribulation is a piece of the paved way to the kingdom of God … our Master can borrow the Devils wind to guarantee his ship sail the better to the Harbour; Tribulation shall blow us to the kingdom, and shall not blow us by it'.[55] Discussions of Satan thus allowed ministers to accomplish two crucial and related pastoral goals: to educate audiences about the dual doctrines of divine supremacy and human depravity, and to encourage godly behaviour through resistance to demonic temptation and reliance on God and the Kirk.

The Devil, practically omnipresent in Scottish sermons, was the sole supernatural being other than God consistently discussed from the early modern pulpit. In sermons Satan was only occasionally attended by his servile demons, which ministers generally referred to as 'devils'. Exhorting his parishioners, as Ephesians 6:11 instructed, to put on the whole armour of God, Welsh explained that the godly must ready themselves for onslaughts by 'legions of devils'.[56] In a discussion of the glories of everlasting life that awaited the elect, John Brown described Heaven as a place where there would be 'No Devils, nor Instruments of Devils there, to molest or tempt us'.[57] By contrast, another minister warned his congregation in the late seventeenth century that God would not hesitate to send the reprobate to 'the pit below among the devils & damned spirits in that lake that burns with fire & brimstone'.[58] Devils were not only depicted as earthly nemeses and companions in Hell; ministers also commonly spoke of 'men and devills' as a pair, highlighting their shared degeneracy.[59] As with sermonic invocations of Satan, the image of devils could be used to convince hearers of their own internal iniquities. In an evocative sermon by Hugh Binning, he told his audience than all post-lapsarian men were 'wholly defiled and depraved by sin, our Souls are become the habitation of Devils, and a Cage of every unclean and hateful Bird'.[60]

Only rarely does one find substantive descriptions of these lesser devils and their nature. In a sermon delivered in the chaotic early 1640s, Samuel Rutherford described the blackness of devils, a colour caused by their 'being fallen in a smokey Hell, and kept under the Power and Chains of Darkness, they are but Lumps of black Hell and Darkness, whereas they was created fair Angels'.[61] In general, though, Reformed ministers followed the precedent set by John Calvin by remaining largely uninterested in the material mechanics of Satan, and even less so in his servile devils.⁶² After all, their presence on earth had been proven by the words of Scripture and the challenges of human life. A minister's priority, then, was not to ruminate on the physical natures of the Devil and his minions, but to ready his flock to resist a life of perpetual internal and external corruptions.

Angels, whose existence was likewise scripturally confirmed, also made cameo appearances in Scottish sermons, but they did so far less often than their demonic counterparts. When discussed at all, angels tended to appear amid the recounting of a Bible story connected to a sermon's text. Binning, who seems to have invoked angels in his sermons more frequently than many of his contemporaries, did so in a sermon on Romans 8:3 to emphasise the great mercy of God in sacrificing Jesus: 'Had he sent an Angel, it had been wonderful, one of these *ministering Spirits* about the Throne, being far more glorious then man. But *God so loved the world, that he sent his Son*.'⁶³ Preaching in 1702 on Colossians 3:4, James Webster described in detail how on the day of judgement, Christ would be attended by the 'Glory of all his holy Angels'.⁶⁴ Occasionally, ministers described Satan as 'the destroying Angell' or quoted 2 Corinthians 11:14 – 'And no marvel; for Satan himself is transformed into an angel of light' – to highlight the deceptiveness of the Devil and the susceptibility of humans to demonic wiles.⁶⁵ Seldom, though, did ministers discuss angels in isolation or at length in their sermons. Moreover, unlike God and the Devil, these heavenly hosts rarely featured in the portion of sermons dedicated to the application of Scripture to daily life.⁶⁶

Beings like fairies, brownies and elves are almost entirely absent from the early modern sermons I have examined. Francis Aird's sermon, quoted at the beginning of this chapter, is an exception to this rule. Though one could argue that Aird's mention of brownies implicitly confirmed their existence, he simultaneously relegated the beings to a distant, pre-Reformation past. Moreover, his pairing of 'Devills and brownies' suggests that he viewed brownies as a subset of demons, rather than as nature spirits that were neither wholly good nor wholly evil. It is impossible to say with certainty whether his audience, men and women living in South Lanarkshire and abutting the heart of Covenanter country, would have thought differently.⁶⁷ The general absence of brownies and their fellow nature spirits in Scottish sermons is a telling omission, one that reveals even more about didactic, theological norms than we learn from the rare appearances of such beings.

Scottish ministers often policed the boundaries of belief tightly. So what accounts for the sparsely populated supernatural landscape of their sermons? Certainly, it would be inaccurate to view sermons as merely responding to popular belief here. The work of Lizanne Henderson, Edward J. Cowan, Julian Goodare and others has shown that fairies and other such beings continued to flourish in a supernatural grey zone among much of the populace.⁶⁸ Moreover, as Martha McGill has noted, the lack of sermonic attention to angels stands in contrast to the treatises and lecture notes of theologians and philosophers that contain detailed considerations of the nature and capabilities of angels.⁶⁹ Moreover, as Louise Yeoman has shown, even the religious lives of committed Calvinists could remain full of dreams, prophetic visions and visits from other-worldly beings reminiscent of much older views.⁷⁰

Excluding fairies and their ilk from sermons, and relegating angels and devils to supporting roles, was thus a purposeful choice on the part of Scottish ministers. In part, this reflects a black and white theological world view, one that held that the age of miracles had ended and that all creatures not of God were demonic. This was also a didactic move intended to focus all attention and energy on God (and, by extension, Christ), Satan and human depravity – three pillars of godly belief. Above all, ministers stressed that genuine supernatural power and truth remained confined to God alone. In the first generation after the Reformation, Robert Rollock wrote that all creatures have within them 'searching' spirits that would constantly seek knowledge for edification and gain: 'the spirite of an Angell, of the devill, of a man, search but the creatures: As for the Creator, no spirit is able to search in Him but His owne Spirit, yea, they knowe nothing in Him, but so much as He will reveale unto them'.⁷¹ Here Rollock articulated what was to become the guiding principle of the supernatural in Scottish sermons for the next century: the world remained as enchanted as ever, but all that was truly mystical, unknowable and good belonged only to God.

More often than not, then, the supernatural in Scottish sermons was surprisingly quotidian. Explanations of the divine and warnings about the evil one reinforced theological norms and served to categorise knowledge and depict the probable or desired landscape of godly life. On the rare occasions that ministers evoked spiritual entities that fell outside the God–Devil dichotomy, they did so not to denounce beliefs in such beings themselves, but to attack – and arguably to caricature – the pre-Protestant world in which they thought that such beings were found.

Sermons were crucial vehicles for conveying ideas about what constituted what we might call the 'godly supernatural' and suggesting which beliefs deviated from the prescribed orthodoxy of the Kirk. Often, it seems that supernatural beings considered aberrant were not identified by name, but rather rejected by omission. In regularly preaching about God and Satan and occasionally speaking of devils and angels, ministers lent credence to the existence of those beings. Indeed, the words of a parish minister conditioned communal expectations for what one might encounter upon the landscape of godly life. But the brownies, fairies and other spirits that had flourished in the pre-Reformation era are almost entirely absent in extant sermons. As Henderson and Cowan have argued, by 'reinventing a world where there could be only the forces of good, upheld by God, and the forces of evil, controlled by the Devil', Calvinist Reformers 'destroyed the grey area once inhabited by fairies, ghosts, and witches, and relegated them all to the dominion of Satan, whose power appeared to be growing ever stronger'.[72]

The sermons of the late sixteenth and seventeenth centuries suggest that, while the supernatural realm held as much power and mystique as ever, a dichotomous consolidation of the mystical and inexplicable had indeed taken place, at least in theory. As the records of kirk sessions and presbyteries from across Scotland attest, the elimination of a range of spirits and other-worldly beings from sermons did not eradicate them from popular belief. The limited supernatural roster of sermons – usually populated by only two entities, an all-powerful God and an ever-menacing Satan – instead shaped godly expectations for a life of constant reliance on divine aid and inescapable battle with the twin enemies of innate corruption and demonic temptation.

Notes

1. NLS, MS 5769, fo. 151.
2. On brownies, see Julian Goodare, 'Boundaries of the fairy realm in Scotland', in Karin E. Olsen and Jan R. Veenstra (eds), *Airy Nothings: Imagining the Otherworld of Faerie from the Middle Ages to the Age of Reason* (Leiden: Brill, 2014), pp. 139–69, at p. 150. As Goodare points out, James VI similarly characterised brownies in his 1597 *Daemonologie* as a remnant of a time of 'papistrie and blindnesse'.
3. For the origins of genuine challenges to belief in God, see Michael Hunter and David Wooton (eds), *Atheism from the Reformation to the Enlightenment* (Oxford: Oxford University Press, 1992).
4. See Julian Goodare and Martha McGill, 'Exploring the supernatural in early modern Scotland', Chapter 1 this volume, for further discussion of the concept of the 'preternatural' and its relationship to the 'supernatural'.
5. Much of the literature on the supernatural in early modern Scotland has focused on folk belief in fairies and attempts by the Kirk to categorise fairies as demons. See Lizanne Henderson and Edward J. Cowan, *Scottish Fairy Belief: A History* (East Linton: Tuckwell, 2001).
6. NRS, GD18/4001/2.
7. James Clark, *Christs Impressions Strong, Sweet, and Sensible on the Hearts of Believers* (Edinburgh: John Reid, 1700), p. 5.
8. *Ibid.*, pp. 12–13, 6.
9. Alexander Wedderburn, *Believers Priviledges and Duties and the Exercise of Communicants* (Edinburgh, 1682), p. 163.
10. Robert Rollock, *Certaine Sermons, Upon Severall Texts of Scripture* (Edinburgh, 1616), p. 112.
11. *Ibid.*, pp. 115–16.
12. William Colvill, *The Righteous Branch Growing out of the Root of Jesse* (Edinburgh, 1673), p. 16.

13 *Ibid.*, p. 119.
14 *Ibid.*, pp. 135–6.
15 *Ibid.*
16 Colin Kidd, 'The Scottish Enlightenment and the supernatural', in Lizanne Henderson (ed.), *Fantastical Imaginations: The Supernatural in Scottish History and Culture* (Edinburgh: John Donald, 2009), pp. 91–109, at p. 91.
17 EUL, La.III.85, fo. 55.
18 George Hutcheson, *Forty-Five Sermons Upon the CXXX Psalm* (Edinburgh, 1691), p. 456.
19 James Durham, *The Great Corruption of Subtile Self* (Edinburgh, 1686), p. 33.
20 *Ibid.*
21 James Sibbald, *Diverse Select Sermons upon Severall Texts of Holy Scripture* (Aberdeen, 1618), pp. 154–5 (original emphasis).
22 Hugh Binning, *The Common Principles of Christian Religion* (Glasgow, 1667), p. 35.
23 *Ibid.*, p. 219.
24 As Brian P. Levack has pointed out, 'there were few countries in Europe in which a philosophical or intellectual opposition to witch-hunting had a weaker voice or commanded less widespread support than in Scotland'. See Levack, 'The decline and end of Scottish witch-hunting', in Julian Goodare (ed.), *The Scottish Witch-Hunt in Context* (Manchester: Manchester University Press, 2002), pp. 166–81, at p. 168. Certainly, sceptical texts about the actions of demons and witches in the world circulated in Scotland, such as Englishman Reginald Scot's *Discoverie of Witchcraft* (1584), but even this work did not deny the existence or power of Satan and the possibility that witchcraft might exist. The dearth of scepticism about witches and demons also extended, of course, to scepticism about God. As Alasdair Raffe has pointed out, in late seventeenth-century Scotland, as in England and France, 'there is much more evidence that orthodox churchmen worried about irreligious ideas, than that people expounded them'. Alasdair Raffe, *The Culture of Controversy: Religious Arguments in Scotland, 1660–1714* (Woodbridge: Boydell, 2012), p. 58.
25 Kidd, 'The Scottish Enlightenment and the supernatural'. On the anxiety over irreligion and atheism in early Enlightenment Scotland, see Michael F. Graham, *The Blasphemies of Thomas Aikenhead: Boundaries of Belief on the Eve of the Enlightenment* (Edinburgh: Edinburgh University Press, 2008), esp. pp. 46–8.
26 Sibbald, *Diverse Select Sermons*, p. 155.
27 Samuel Rutherford, *A Sermon Preached to the Honourable House of Commons at their Late Solemne Fast* (Edinburgh, 1644), pp. 35, 63.
28 On the category of superstition in early modern Europe, see Euan Cameron, *Enchanted Europe: Superstition, Reason, and Religion, 1250–1750* (Oxford: Oxford University Press, 2010).
29 NLS, MS 5769, fos 95–6.
30 NLS, Wod.Oct.XXIX, fo. 22^v.
31 *Ibid.*
32 EUL, La.III.87, fos 11–12.
33 NLS, MS 2206, fos 19–20.
34 EUL, La.III.102, fo. 398.

35 NRS, GD1/395/1, page marked 'folio B'.
36 For a more thorough treatment of the role of the Devil in Scottish sermons, see Michelle D. Brock, *Satan and the Scots: The Devil in Post-Reformation Scotland* (London: Routledge, 2016), ch. 2.
37 On Satan as a primarily internal force in Reformed theology, see Nathan Johnstone, 'The Protestant Devil: the experience of temptation in early modern England', *Journal of British Studies*, 43 (2004), 173–205.
38 John Welsh, *Forty-Eight Select Sermons* (Edinburgh, 1744), p. 165.
39 NLS, MS 5769, fo.133. This particular sermon is undated, though many of the others in the sermon notebook are from 1655.
40 John Brown, *Christ in Believers the Hope of Glory Being the Substance of Several Sermons* (Edinburgh, 1694).
41 Robert Bruce, *Sermons*, ed. William Cunningham (Edinburgh: Wodrow Society, 1843), p. 389.
42 NLS, MS 5769, fo. 133.
43 Robert Baillie, *Letters and Journals, 1637–1662*, ed. David Laing, 3 vols (Edinburgh: Bannatyne Club, 1841), I, p. 350.
44 For examples of sermons that reference 1 Peter 5:8, see David Fergusson, *Ane Answer to ane Epistle Written by Renat Benedict the Frenche Doctor* (Edinburgh, 1563); NLS, Adv. MS 5.2.6; NLS, MS 2206; Welsh, *Forty-Eight Select Sermons*.
45 Henderson, *Sermons*, 477.
46 NLS, MS 5770, fo. 69.
47 Bruce, *Sermons*, pp. 23–4.
48 Andrew Gray, *Directions and Instigations to the Duty of Prayer* (Glasgow, 1669), p. 106.
49 Michelle D. Brock, 'Internalizing the demonic: Satan and the self in early modern Scottish piety', *Journal of British Studies*, 54 (2015), 23–43, esp. pp. 33–4.
50 NLS, MS 5769, fos 12–13.
51 *Ibid*.
52 On attempts by ministers to reassure their congregations of the inevitability of divine victory in the face of demonic struggles, see Brock, *Satan and the Scots*, pp. 71–4.
53 Welsh, *Forty-Eight Select Sermons*, p. 166. Ephesians 6:11 was a common theme of sermons. See, for example, NLS, Adv. MS 5.2.6 and Alexander Henderson, *Sermons, Prayers and Pulpit Addresses of Alexander Henderson*, ed. Thomas R. Martin (Edinburgh: John Maclaren, 1867). On the biblical armour of God and references to Ephesians in Protestant British sermons, see Alec Ryrie, *Being Protestant in Reformation Britain* (Oxford: Oxford University Press, 2013), pp. 243–5.
54 EUL, Dc.4.79, fo. 4^r.
55 Michael Bruce, *Soul-Confirmation, or a Sermon Preached in the Parish of Cambusnethen in Clyds-dail* ([Edinburgh?], 1709), pp. 2–3.
56 Welsh, *Forty-Eight Select Sermons*, p. 114.
57 Brown, *Christ in Believers*, p. 10.
58 EUL, La.III.85, fo. 15. Similar discussions of devils to illustrate the tortures of Hell and estrangement from God are fairly common and can be found, among other places, in Robert Bruce, *Sermons Upon the Sacrament of the Lords Supper* (Edinburgh, 1591), fos 3^v–4^r; James Durham, *The Blessednesse*

of the Death of These That Die in the Lord (Edinburgh, 1681), p. 34; and James Canaries, *A Sermon Preached at Edinburgh* (Edinburgh, 1689), p. 14.

59 See, for example, Robert Baillie, *Satan the Leader in Chief to All Who Resist the Reparation of Sion* (Edinburgh, 1643), p. 3; Samuel Rutherford, *The Trial and Triumph of Faith* (Edinburgh, 1645), p. 38; and Michael Bruce, *A Sermon Preached by Master Michael Bruice, in the Tolbooth of Edinburgh* (Edinburgh, 1668), p. 10.

60 Hugh Binning, *Heart-Humiliation, or, Miscellany Sermons Preached Upon Some Choice Texts at Several Solemn Occasions* (Edinburgh, 1676), p. 219.

61 Rutherford, *Trial and Triumph of Faith*, p. 40.

62 On Calvin's writings on the Devil and demons and their influence on the Scottish clergy, see Brock, *Satan and the Scots*, ch. 1.

63 Hugh Binning, *The Sinners Sanctuary* (Edinburgh, 1670), p. 89 (original emphasis).

64 EUL, La.III.93. This sermon notebook, probably consisting of assorted auditors' notes, is not paginated, but this passage on angels comes at the end of sermon 45 in the collection.

65 See, for example, NLS, MS 5770, fo. 110; James Durham, *Christ Crucified, or, the Marrow of the Gospel, Evidently Holden Forth in LXXII Sermons* (Edinburgh, 1683), p. 300; Andrew Gray, *The Mystery of Faith Opened Up* (Edinburgh, 1668), p. 44.

66 For the structure of sermons, see Margo Todd, *The Culture of Protestantism in Early Modern Scotland* (New Haven, CT: Yale University Press, 2002), p. 49; and Brock, *Satan and the Scots*, pp. 5–6.

67 On the idea of the 'radical south-west' during the mid-seventeenth century, see Sharon Adams, 'A Regional Road to Revolution: Religion, Politics and Society in South-West Scotland, 1600–50' (PhD thesis, University of Edinburgh, 2002). See also Walter Makey, *The Church of the Covenant, 1637– 1651: Revolution and Social Change in Scotland* (Edinburgh: John Donald, 1979), esp. pp. 165–78.

68 See Henderson and Cowan, *Scottish Fairy Belief*; Goodare, 'Boundaries of the fairy realm'.

69 See Martha McGill, 'Angels, devils, and discernment in early modern Scotland', in Michelle D. Brock, Richard Raiswell and David R. Winter (eds), *Knowing Demons, Knowing Spirits in the Early Modern Period* (Basingstoke: Palgrave Macmillan, 2018), pp. 239–63.

70 Louise Yeoman, '"Away with the fairies"', in Henderson, *Fantastical Imaginations*, pp. 29–46.

71 Rollock, *Certaine Sermons*, p. 129.

72 Henderson and Cowan, *Scottish Fairy Belief*, p. 116.

10

The uses of providence in early modern Scotland

Martha McGill and Alasdair Raffe

For early modern Scots, the doctrine of providence – the claim that God actively governed his Creation – expressed basic truths about the universe. God was both creator and maintainer, legislator and executive. He defined the goal or end of human existence, while intervening in the daily lives of his creatures. He oversaw the affairs of princes and armies, and was also responsible for the most mundane of occurrences. As Scottish preachers reminded their congregations, Matthew's gospel taught that even the most insignificant sparrow 'shall not fall on the ground without your Father' (Matt. 10:29).[1] Providing ways for Christians of all complexions to comprehend divine activity in the world, providence enlaced the natural and supernatural realms.

For all the ubiquity of providence in early modern thought, Scottish historians have not systematically investigated how the doctrine was used. This is in spite of a rich literature on early modern English understandings of the subject.[2] Perhaps one reason for this neglect is that providence was not an especially controversial idea. Most Protestants and Catholics shared a similar conception of providence, and the Reformation did not bring significant changes. Unlike church government, ideas of salvation or theories of resistance to political authority, providence was rarely a source of conflict in Scottish society. But this does not mean that theologians and laypeople – even those preoccupied by these divisive subjects – overlooked providence in their treatises, sermons, diaries and letters. Not only do their widespread discussions call for historical analysis, but in turning our attention to providence, we can map part of the extensive ideological terrain that constituted shared ground for Scottish Christians.

This chapter surveys some of the ways in which Scots wrote about providence after the Reformation. It is necessarily selective and hopes to inspire more detailed research. It begins by introducing the doctrine, as found in confessions of faith, catechisms, sermons and didactic writings. The chapter then examines how Scots used providence to ascribe meaning to their experiences and a context to their lives. 'General providence' was God's design for the universe as a whole, while 'special providences' – in the plural – were acts of spontaneous intervention on the part of the deity. By thinking about special providences, individuals could understand their relationship with God. Next, the chapter assesses the ways in which Scots related special providences to the plan of general providence so as to contemplate the affairs of nations. Finally, we consider how Enlightenment discourses perpetuated the belief in providence, while also encouraging a shift away from the sixteenth- and seventeenth-century emphasis on apocalypticism and towards a new celebration of humankind's progress.

The doctrine of providence was inherited from the medieval church, but it was given new prominence in the confessions of faith and catechisms of the early modern Church of Scotland. These documents defined providence, taught Scots how to understand it and pointed to some of the theological difficulties in doing so. According to the Scots Confession of Faith (1560), 'all thingis in hevin and eird' had 'bene creatit, to be retenit in thair being and to be rewlit and gydit' by God's 'inscrutabil providence'. This providential government served the ends appointed by God in his 'eternall wisdome, guidnes and justice' and was 'to the manifestatioun of his awin glorie'.[3] The Westminster Confession of Faith of 1646 offered a similar, if more elaborate, definition. 'God the great Creator ... doth uphold, direct, dispose, and govern all creatures, actions, and things', the Confession stated. Providence operated according to God's 'infallible fore-knowledge, and the free and immutable counsel of His own will'. It inspired praise of the divine 'wisdom, power, justice, goodness, and mercy'.[4]

As these definitions imply, providence was one aspect of a wider theological understanding of God's decrees and actions. For the minister Alexander Hume, in 1594, providence was a framework within which Christians should comprehend Creation, because God had designed everything in the world for his glory or humanity's use.[5] The Westminster Confession, in its third chapter, 'Of God's eternal decree', taught that God had 'unchangeably' ordained 'whatsoever comes to pass'. As part of this decree, God had predestined the elect to salvation and the reprobate to damnation.[6] God executed his decree, the Westminster Assembly's shorter catechism (1648) explained, by means of 'the works of creation and providence'.[7] God's initial Creation and subsequent providential government were two means by which he realised his cosmic plan. The divine actions that brought the world into being and thereafter directed the course of history were complementary. As the Presbyterian minister Thomas Blackwell argued in 1710, Creation 'gloriously manifested the Divine *Wisdom, Power* and *Goodness*, yet there remained some other great Perfections in the Deity ... not as yet displayed'. Through providence, God continued to exhibit his divine sovereignty, justice and mercy.[8]

The doctrine of providence prevailing in Scotland thus assumed that God was active in the world. He preserved and upheld life, and he governed events. In a 'special act of providence', he had covenanted with Adam, offering eternal life in exchange for perfect obedience. If God's providence had particular significance for humanity, it also extended to the smallest creatures and the most trivial episodes.[9] In *Pater Noster* (1670), William Annand, Episcopalian minister of the Tolbooth parish, Edinburgh, warned that fallible humans were tempted to ignore or misconstrue God's providence. 'Let not thy Age, Poverty, Family, question his Providence, for, but for that, how oft hadst thou been choaked in thy Drink', he asked.[10] Hugh Binning, an intellectual heavyweight among the hard-line Protester party of Presbyterians in the 1650s, insisted that God was 'not shut up in Heaven'; he 'immediately cares for, governs, and disposes all things in the World'.[11] David Dickson, Binning's more moderate Presbyterian contemporary, concurred, attributing doubts about this truth to the modern heterodoxies of Socinianism and Arminianism and the recently revived ancient philosophy of Epicurus. The Reformed understanding of providence had to be defended from these sources of error. But Dickson's cursory treatment of the subject, and the similarity of views between the Episcopalian Annand and the Protester Binning, suggest that, in Scotland at least, there was little real controversy about the doctrine of providence.[12]

Nevertheless, Protestants distinguished their doctrine carefully from the conception of fate held by the ancient Stoics. According to Calvin, the Stoics thought that all occurrences were determined necessarily, by the perpetual chain of causes in nature. Such a view obscured God's government of worldly affairs, Calvin asserted.[13] Stoicism also called into question human free will, seeming to deny that men and women were responsible for their actions. To resolve the difficulty, theologians tended to distinguish between the contrasting perspectives of God and humanity. '[I]n relation to the fore-knowledge and decree of God', the Westminster Confession put it, 'all things come to pass immutably'. But considered in terms of natural or secondary causes, the vantage point of humans, events might appear to happen contingently.[14] Thus the doctrine of providence was compatible with free will. George Mackenzie, the Episcopalian lawyer and future lord advocate, was more sympathetic than Calvin to Stoicism and sought to reconcile the ancient philosophy with Christianity. Each of God's creatures resembles a watch, he argued, which 'goes by its own Springs and Wheels', without its maker's 'continual assistance'. But when 'its motion becomes irregular, or when the owner finds it fit', he could adjust it 'at his pleasure'.[15]

Another fallacy, likewise relating to free will, was to hold that God's active direction of all earthly events made him responsible for human sin. All Christian traditions denied that God was the author of sin, but avoiding this fallacy was a particular challenge for the Reformed Protestants of Scotland. Providence gave order and direction to the 'first fall, and all other sins of angels and men', the Westminster Confession claimed. Whereas Catholics, Lutherans, Arminians and Socinians allegedly held that God allowed for sin 'by a bare permission', Reformed theologians gave God a more active role in employing sin to execute his decree. As Dickson pointed out, the Bible repeatedly claimed that God hardens the hearts or blinds the eyes of particular sinful men. But, Dickson continued, it was a libertine error to conclude that God was himself the author of sin. The blame for sins rested with humanity.[16]

Did God's providential intervention take the form of miracles? Whereas Catholics wrote of medieval and contemporary miracles, most Protestant theologians argued that God had not performed miracles since biblical times – an orthodoxy reiterated by James VI in his 1597 *Daemonologie*.[17] Special providences were instead classed as 'wonders'.[18] Miracles were supernatural: they directly violated the order of nature. Wonders, on the other hand, were preternatural: God acted by manipulating secondary causes. Writing in 1686, the Episcopalian minister John Cockburn explained this distinction:

> Though neither *privat Persons* nor *publick States*, are now to expect to be maintained & supported by Miracles and *extraordinary manifestations* of the *Divine Power*, so much and so frequently as the *Children of Israel* were of old, yet *particular Providences* must not be denied ... [N]ow as much as formerly, [God] still shews a special care of his own, and when *ordinary means* and *methods* fail, and prove ineffectual for compassing their good; He interposeth himself by Wayes and Means extraordinary.[19]

Most Scottish theologians were similarly careful to distinguish between 'supernatural' and 'preternatural', and 'miracles' and 'providences'. However, there were exceptions. Robert Fleming, a renowned Presbyterian who published several theological tracts between the 1660s and the 1690s, described providential occurrences as 'supernatural' and referred to contemporary cases that were 'so wonderful ... as might truely be called miracles'.[20] It could be argued that the distinction was, in practice, unimportant; even when providences were not recognised as supernatural, their status as 'wonders' encouraged the idea that God was regularly intervening in the world.

For all its complexity, providence had considerable value in apologetic works, those defending the Christian religion against unbelievers. Alexander Hume, as we saw above, stressed the connection between Creation and providence. By observing the world around us, he argued, we become aware of God's Creation and providential work. The fitness of human physiology, for example, proves 'the Creator to be a singular artificer', and should prompt us to 'admire the wisedome and providence of the most high.'[21] Sir William Anstruther of Anstruther, a senator of the college of justice, made the argument more explicitly in 1701, a time of growing concern about the perceived spread of atheism. 'All thoughtful Men must acknowledge a *Superlative Energy* and *Wisdom* in the wonderful unexpected events of Providence', Anstruther asserted. This clearly proved the existence of God.[22] And while many complained about 'the *Apparent Inequality of Providence*', the frequency with which the wicked prospered while the virtuous suffered setbacks, this merely proved humans' ignorance of the perspective of God and our inability to follow what Anstruther called the 'Meandrous Labyrinths' of the deity's 'hidden ways'.[23] If the glory of God was evident, his goals remained shrouded in mystery.

Nevertheless, according to the conversion-centred piety of Scottish Presbyterianism, the reborn Christian might obtain greater understanding of God's purposes. One way in which this could be achieved was through close observation of special providences. As the believer's 'understanding is renewed' by the Holy Spirit, William Guthrie explained, he or she sees 'the Heavens declaring' God's 'Glory and Power, and somewhat of God in providence and dispensations that fall out'.[24] The seventeenth century witnessed a burgeoning trend of individuals recording and analysing providential occurrences. Cataloguing these occurrences was an act of worship. Alexander Hume explained to his readers that 'the memory … of these things, shal kindle and inflame thy spirit to be fervent in praier, & zealous in the service of thy Creator'.[25] Men and women were also encouraged by the notion that providences might hint at God's will. The mid-seventeenth-century Glasgow minister James Durham declared that everybody was obliged to note 'daily occurring providences', 'in the careful marking and suitable improving whereof, there lyeth a special piece of spiritual wisdom'.[26]

Interest in providences became particularly pronounced following the restoration of episcopacy in 1661–2. For the Presbyterian ministers who lost their parishes for refusing to conform to the re-established church, there was fresh motivation to identify marks of divine favour, and several authors produced collections of providences.[27] This practice persisted even after the reinstatement of Presbyterianism in 1690. The minister Robert Wodrow recorded providences from 1701 until his death in 1734. The radical Patrick Walker chronicled the providential experiences of the dissenting ministers of the Restoration period in the late 1720s and early 1730s.[28]

Special providences came in a wide range of forms. There were accounts of ministers prophesying and healing the sick. A particularly remarkable example concerned the minister John Welsh of Ayr: after a gentleman died in his house in the early seventeenth century, Welsh postponed burial and 'cried to the Lord with all his might', upon which the dead man revived.[29] On the fringes of Presbyterian culture, visionaries claimed to have travelled to Heaven and held conferences with Christ.[30] Others reported apparitions in the air, such as battles waged between ghostly armies, which usually foreshadowed earthly battles.[31] Alexander Stirling, a 'solid, serious, zealous Christian' from Stirlingshire, saw a group singing a psalm, accompanied by a 'milk-white horse' with a 'blood-red saddle'. He concluded that the white horse was the gospel, oppressed by the saddle of persecution.[32] The minister Archibald Gillespie saw the sun in the form of a woman. She was then attacked by two pointed clouds; her dress tore and blood rained down.[33] This vision likely warned of divine wrath. Comets, shooting stars and deformed (or 'monstrous') births similarly suggested God's displeasure. Some prodigies offered particularly explicit reminders of the need for religious obedience: one case concerned a Dutch boy with 'Deus meus' inscribed around his eyeballs.[34]

These phenomena were out of the ordinary. However, the doctrine of providence also attributed significance to everyday events. It thus became deeply embedded in the lives of pious Scots. The judge and statesman Archibald Johnston of Wariston took a particularly keen interest in discerning the divine will. He made routine decisions by casting lots, appointing providence as his guide. In diary entries from the 1650s he gratefully acknowledged God's assistance in matters such as letter writing, public speaking and curtailing his arguments with his wife.[35]

Providence offered comfort in the face of adversity. Wariston declared that God had given him 'out of his loving, indulgent, bountiful, merciful providence ane extraordinar great measure both of inward and outward consolations'.[36] The seventeenth-century spiritual diarist Katharine Collace was left with a 'constant wound in her heart' when one of her children died (she had twelve in total, all of whom predeceased her). She nevertheless thanked God for 'discovering to me his love in all providences, even in these that appear to be most sharp'.[37] Yet attributing everything to God's providence could also be emotionally taxing. Wariston interpreted the death of his first wife as a punishment for his sins. His diary entries on the topic make for harrowing reading:

> I had never feared nor dreamed on the desolation quhil [until] on a sudainte it overquhelmed quhen I sau al comfort depairting from the heaven and the earth ... it was my old Comforter quho nou was terrifiing my mynd with the sight of my sinnes and his wrayth, tormenting my body and troubling my estaite and drouning my saule in bitternes, filling it with gal and wormewood ... by taking her away [the Lord] had maid me ane visible to the world, and sensible to myselth, object of his wrayth, displeasure, and indignation.[38]

Godly men and women were often thrown into confusion by apparent manifestations of divine anger. The diarist Marion Veitch expressed a prevalent sentiment when she lamented that God's 'outward dispensations seem to contradict his promises.'[39]

In response, ministers and devotional writers counselled that the elect had to be tried, tested and prepared by God's 'shaking providences'.[40] In posthumously published sermons, the seventeenth-century minister Alexander Wedderburn asserted that 'God trysts Christians with cross Providences, purposly to make them rely on the Covenant.'[41] James Durham suggested that the mixed dispensations of providence mirrored the blend of grace and corruption within human beings. He also extolled the value of suffering: 'the Flesh and Unregenerate part' of man requires 'crosses to whip it up, and drive it forward; and the Spirit and Regenerate part [calls] for them also, to keep it awake and on its guard.'[42] Preaching in the late eighteenth century, the Leith minister John Logan expressed this principle particularly clearly: 'When under the afflicting hand of Heaven ... you are standing a candidate for immortality; you are singled out by Providence to exert the part of a Christian, and you are called forth to exhibit to the world a pattern of the suffering virtues.'[43] Above all, ministers stressed that God's long-term plan allowed for no injustices, and that Christians in need of assurance should turn to their bibles. Wedderburn taught his congregation that 'if ye would know a Providence, if it be an Act of Mercy, or an Act of Wrath, ye are to try it by the Word, ye are not to try the Promises by the Providences.'[44]

Overall, providences offered relatively little insight into the divine will. The faithful chroniclers of God's dispensations were often confused as much as comforted, and theologians were compelled to reiterate that Scripture was a Christian's surest guidebook. As the eighteenth century progressed, the habit of observing daily providences seemed to decline. It did not disappear, however, and both conservative and moderate Presbyterians continued to defend the practice. Writing in 1756, George Anderson, a former schoolmaster and opponent of David Hume, devoted a chapter to explaining and defending the doctrine of particular providences.[45] The more liberal John Logan taught his flock that 'the arm of the Almighty reaching from heaven to earth, is continually employed. All things are full of God.'[46] This idea that things were *full of God* had a significant and enduring influence on pious Scots. Providences may have confounded human reason, but there was substantial emotive power in a doctrine that infused everyday events with supernatural resonances.

Providence was also a tool for interpreting occurrences of national or international significance, from military victories to natural disasters. Just as God guided the life of each of his creatures, so he had plans for all kingdoms and peoples. The role of providence in national events, as in individuals' daily experiences, was ambiguous. Nevertheless, early modern writers used providence to vindicate political decisions and to reflect historically on the experiences of the Scottish people.

Beginning in the 1560s, the church courts responded to the country's challenges and setbacks by appointing national fasts. These were occasions of special worship, with topical prayers and sermons encouraging Scots to reflect on the providential meaning of recent developments.[47] *The Ordour and Doctrine of the Generall Fast* (1566), written by a committee of the general assembly in advance of the first national fast days in February and March 1566, described fasting as a means of repenting publicly and beseeching God's future blessings. Given the people's 'great abuse of his former benefites', they were obliged to 'prostrat them selves before their God, craving of him pardone and mercy.'[48] This fast, like many of the others called in the first decades of the Reformation, reacted to perceived threats to the Kirk in its existential struggle against Catholicism. Protestants understood the battle between the true religion and the Roman Antichrist as part of God's plan to bring about the end of the world. When used to interpret the progress of the national church, then, the doctrine of providence was explicitly concerned with the forthcoming apocalypse.[49]

Early modern fast orders emphasised what we might call the human's-eye view on the works of providence. As we saw above, theologians asserted God's ordination of all events, while attempting to preserve human free will and culpability. Those participating in national fasts were expected to remember that God's decrees were immutable, but they nevertheless hoped to see their prayers answered and their circumstances improved. This wish was apparent in the royal proclamation appointing a national fast in July 1675, after a period of drought and food shortages. In 'his most Wise and Righteous Providence', the proclamation maintained, God was manifesting his justified anger at sinful humans, 'particularly by the sad and pinching dearth'. This natural calamity demanded a response from the Scottish population in the form of fasting and humble repentance. But it was to be expected, the proclamation continued, that the fast itself could lead to relief from the drought. On witnessing Scots' 'serious Mourning for' their sins, God 'may graciously pardon them and repent Him of the evil seemingly determined by Him, and most righteously deserved by us', by granting rain and a satisfactory harvest.[50]

Scots responded to signs of divine displeasure through collective repentance, and they organised similar occasions of special worship to give thanks for God's blessings. In perhaps the earliest post-Reformation case, the magistrates of Edinburgh, at James VI's command, appointed a service to thank God for the birth of the king's son Henry in February 1594.[51] In 1600, after James survived an alleged attempt on his life by Alexander Ruthven and his brother John, third Earl of Gowrie, parliament instituted an annual thanksgiving day on 5 August, the anniversary of the event. The occasion was intended to acknowledge the 'singular benefite, grace and favour of God' bestowed in 'his miraculous and extraordinar delyverie' of the king from danger.[52] This thanksgiving day set a precedent for other annual observances, most obviously that marking the anniversary of James's delivery from the Gunpowder Plot on 5 November 1605, which was celebrated at royal command.[53] These occasions of special worship taught Scots to trace God's guidance of their own recent history.

Though most contemporaries could agree that the drought of 1675 warranted humiliation and that the king's escape from assassination called for thanks, other episodes divided opinion. For many Scots, the revolution of 1688–90 was a major providential blessing. According to the convention of estates in 1689, William of Orange's successful invasion constituted a 'great delyverance' from the 'danger of popery and arbitrary power', for which God was to be thanked.[54] From a Jacobite point of view, however, the revolution was the calamitous manifestation of God's anger against a sinful people. During the rising of 1715, the Jacobite army observed a fast day for the success of their campaign. The order appointing this worship described the revolution as one of a series of 'National judgments & plagues' provoked by the 'great Corruption of all Ranks & Degrees'.[55]

Political writers seized upon apparent signs of God's favour or design to promote particular policies. This was true of the campaigns in support of Anglo-Scottish union, both after James VI's accession to the English throne in 1603 and prior to the parliamentary Union of 1707. John Russell, who wrote in favour of further integration under James, considered the regal union one of the 'great and infinit benifittis bestouit' by 'the providence of the eternall God upon the ile of Britanie'. This blessing should, he argued, inspire a still greater unity between Scots and English 'in heartis and myndis'.[56] In 1707, the advocate Sir Francis Grant published *The Patriot Resolved*, in which he argued in favour of accepting the Treaty of Union. Among other considerations, Grant explained that a 'chain of providences' seemed to point to incorporating union. Whereas previously it had been impossible for the crown and the parliaments to agree on a new Anglo-Scottish relationship, there was now a consensus in support of the treaty and other options had failed.[57]

Competing political programmes inspired rival interpretations of providence. God's plans were difficult to comprehend, and any group's claim to enjoy divine backing could easily be portrayed by its opponents as a self-serving delusion. In July 1650, as the Scottish political elite reconciled itself to the young Charles II, the English parliament attempted to neutralise the threat that this posed to their new republic by making war on the Scots. The senior officers of the English army adopted a declaration explaining their decision to invade Scotland. The English were confident of the righteousness of their case, the declaration announced, looking on their previous successes as 'the eminent actings of the Providence and Power of God'.[58] On the Scottish side, the general assembly published a response, which admitted that their opponents had been 'blest' by 'many providences'. But apparent success could not 'justifie evil doers, nor be a rule for any man to walk by'. Christians were not to improvise their conduct on the basis of uncertain readings of providence. Instead, they were to look to 'the writen Word of God, wherein he hath taught every man his dutie'.[59] Writing some years afterwards, the Presbyterian minister Alexander Pitcairn reiterated the point. While the 'brutish multitude' might be impressed by a 'continued series and succession of favourable Providences' benefiting one party – 'As in the late case while [the English] Sectaries did prosper for so long a time' – providence could not prove the justice of a cause. It demonstrated God's glory and power, but providence 'cannot discover our duty', Pitcairn wrote.[60]

If providence was an unreliable guide to action in the present, it nevertheless helped Scots to interpret their past.[61] Indeed, providence was perhaps the most obvious framework within which to understand history. According to Alexander Skene, the Restoration chronicler of the affairs of Aberdeen, 'there is nothing more ordinarie amongst all *Nations*, then to set down what hath been the most remarkable *Providences of GOD* to their *Countries* and *Places* of their *Nativity*'.[62] In 1641, the University of Glasgow received a bequest to fund an annual payment to a theology student, who would make a book of 'the most rare and remarkable passagis of Gods providence which have fallen furth ... in the Kingdome of Scotland'.[63] As these statements suggest, providence could serve in the writing of explicitly national histories, in which God's particular favours to Scotland would be memorialised.

It was thus particularly appropriate for ecclesiastical historians, concerned with the propagation of true religion, to illustrate the ways in which God had guided his church in Scotland. John Knox's *History of the Reformation in Scotland* depicted the progress of Protestantism in providential terms. God preserved true believers in their conflicts with the Catholic authorities, through to the triumph of the Reformation and beyond. God's relationship with Scottish Protestants recalled his special treatment of ancient Israel. The achievement of a singularly pure Protestantism in Scotland was a crucial element in his plan for the world, and in the apocalyptic confrontation between the forces of God and Satan.[64]

A century and a half later, Robert Wodrow built on similar assumptions in his *History of the Sufferings of the Church of Scotland from the Restoration to the Revolution* (1721–22). The revolution of 1688–90 was preceded by a time 'when our Reformation from Popery, with all the religious and civil interests of Europe, were in utmost danger'. Scots were in the vanguard of the global struggle against popery. In his dedication of the work to King George I, Wodrow quoted Psalm 126:3: 'Then the Lord did great things for us, whereof we were glad.'[65] The emancipation of Presbyterian Scotland was accomplished by God.

The mid-eighteenth-century historian William Robertson similarly invoked providence to explain the course of events.⁶⁶ Preaching to the Society in Scotland for Propagating Christian Knowledge (SSPCK) in 1755, Robertson argued that sacred history offered the most transparent evidence of God's direction of events. Though the task of interpreting providence was more difficult for 'civil' historians, 'Careful observers' could nevertheless 'form probable conjectures with regard to the plan of God's providence'.⁶⁷ In his *History of Scotland, During the Reigns of Queen Mary and of King James VI* (1759), Robertson dwelt primarily on the human causes of political developments. But at crucial points in his narrative, he turned to providence as an explanatory factor. He noted that Scots welcomed the death in 1560 of King Francis II, husband of Mary Queen of Scots, in the belief that the loss of a French monarch would improve the security of the Reformed religion in Scotland. It was 'no wonder', Robertson continued, that contemporary historians (he cited Knox) should attribute the death 'to the immediate care of Providence, which, by unforeseen expedients, can secure the peace and happiness of kingdoms, in those situations, where human prudence and invention would utterly despair'. When he recounted the scattering of the Spanish Armada in 1588, Robertson invoked 'the blessing of Providence, which watched with remarkable care over the Protestant Religion, and the liberties of Britain'.⁶⁸ Like Wodrow, Robertson believed that God had protected, and would continue to support, Protestant Scotland.

In two respects, however, Robertson's conception of providence marked a departure from that of Wodrow, indicating a widespread change of emphasis in the eighteenth century. Robertson lacked his predecessor's enthusiasm for special providences. And his understanding of general providence was bound up with the Enlightenment notion of stadial social development. In his sermon to the SSPCK, Robertson detailed how the 'progressive plan of Providence' guided humankind on a course from primitivism to civilisation. Providence, he implied, was driving the SSPCK's endeavour to convert the Scottish Highlanders into 'good Christians and useful subjects'.⁶⁹

Other eighteenth-century thinkers similarly envisaged providence as a divine mechanism enforcing social progression. William Cleghorn, professor of moral philosophy at Edinburgh from 1745, wrote that the 'general Appearance of Progression thro' Nature is a great proof of Providence. Nature is ever active & full of Variety. Everything is shifting itself to a more perfect form … In this world all things tend to Perfection in a constant Order.'⁷⁰ Adam Ferguson adopted a comparable vision of providential progress. God had designed nature to be in a continual state of change. The 'progress of intelligent being … must receive continual increments of knowledge and thought'; provided that people had a drive to learn, each generation would necessarily advance further than the generation before.⁷¹ Adam Smith argued that humans instinctively improved their societies: 'by acting according to the dictates of our moral faculties, we necessarily pursue the most effectual means for promoting the happiness of mankind, and may therefore be said ... to advance as far as in our power the plan of Providence.'[72] Whereas sixteenth- and seventeenth-century discussions of providence generally evoked the themes of sin, repentance and the oncoming apocalypse, Enlightenment discourses offered a more optimistic view of humankind's advancement.

Admittedly, a Scottish jeremiad tradition persisted in the eighteenth century. Significant upheavals, such as the Jacobite risings and the French Revolution, provoked flurries of sermons calling for nationwide repentance.[73] But while Moderate clergymen might prophesy calamity from the pulpit, they nevertheless emphasised providential order. Preaching in the late 1770s, the Edinburgh minister and rhetorician Hugh Blair noted that 'when wars and commotions shake the earth ... Providence seems, at first view, to have abandoned public affairs to the misrule of human passions'. However, 'from the midst of this confusion, order is often made to spring'. Violent upheavals roused nations from 'dangerous lethargy', drew forth 'public spirit', and inspired 'larger views of national happiness'.[74] Eighteenth-century preachers continued to warn of divine wrath, but they communicated a new sense that peace and harmony were achievable on earth.

Enlightenment discourses about providence had an enduring influence in social and economic thought. The emphasis on a divinely ordered universe encouraged the idea that established hierarchies were sanctioned by God. Ferguson used providence to justify inequality, writing that 'it has pleased Providence, for wise purposes, to place men in different stations, and to bestow upon them different degrees of wealth ... Every person does good, and promotes the happiness of society, by living agreeable to the rank in which Providence has placed him.'[75] In the expanded sixth edition of the *Theory of Moral Sentiments* (1790), Smith argued that the 'peace and order of society', as 'wisely judged' by nature, was 'of more importance than even the relief of the miserable.'[76] This line of thinking remained prominent in the nineteenth century.[77]

Similarly persistent was the use of providence to justify imperialist ventures. Just as Robertson suggested that providence was guiding the SSPCK's missions in the Highlands, nineteenth-century politicians and philosophers drew on the idea of divinely ordained social progression to glorify European empire-building.[78] While providence was used here to defend economic intervention, it could also serve the reverse purpose: in suggesting that an invisible hand guided the operation of markets, Smith provided the theoretical underpinning for laissez-faire policies.[79] Providence had long offered a framework for understanding the past and present. During the Enlightenment, it was increasingly employed to advance a vision of social evolution in the future.

Early modern Scots used the doctrine of providence in various ways. It was a means to assert God's glory, sovereignty and interest in the affairs of individuals and nations. Ministers referred to acts of providence to remind parishioners of their devotional duties, or to refute the imagined arguments of atheists. Providence offered comfort in the face of hardship. And it served as an explanatory model in which historical events, or passages in an individual's life, could demonstrate God's support for particular causes. Sixteenth- and seventeenth-century accounts of providence frequently emphasised the religious conflict prefiguring the apocalypse, and called on Scots to repent of their sins. Ideas of general providence persisted into the eighteenth century and beyond, but influential philosophers and ministers began to use providence to articulate an optimistic conception of social progress.

The doctrine of providence encouraged Christians to identify and enjoy God's blessings. But it also highlighted his judgements and punishments, provoking anguished soul-searching in men and women who struggled to find divine justice in personal tragedies. Moreover, interpretations of God's support for political causes drew on selective evidence, provoking refutations from opponents. Theologians reiterated that God's ways were obscure; Christians could learn more by reading Scripture than by scrutinising the passages of their lives. The usefulness of providence, therefore, had limits. But the greatest effect of the doctrine lay not so much in making supernatural power comprehensible, as in making it continually present. By turning everyday events into manifestations of the divine will, providence broke down the barriers between natural and supernatural and gave early modern Scots a deeply personal sense of God's governance.

Notes

1 For example, Peter Hewat, *Three Excellent Points of Christian Doctrine* (Edinburgh, 1621), sig. G2ᵛ; Ninian Campbell, *A Treatise Upon Death First Publickly Delivered in a Funerall Sermon, Anno Dom. 1630* (Edinburgh, 1635), sig. C4ᵛ; Hugh Binning, *The Common Principles of Christian Religion. Clearly Proved, and Singlarly Improved: Or, a Practical Catechism* ([Edinburgh?], 1660), pp. 220–8.

2 Important discussions include Keith Thomas, *Religion and the Decline of Magic: Studies in Popular Beliefs in Sixteenth- and Seventeenth-Century England* (London: Weidenfeld & Nicolson, 1971), ch. 4; Boyd Hilton, *The Age of Atonement: The Influence of Evangelicalism on Social and Economic Thought, 1785–1865* (Oxford: Clarendon, 1986); Alexandra Walsham, *Providence in Early Modern England* (Oxford: Oxford University Press, 1999); William E. Burns, *An Age of Wonders: Prodigies, Politics and Providence in England, 1657–1727* (Manchester: Manchester University Press, 2002).

3 *RPS*, A1567/12/3.

4 *The Confession of Faith of the Assembly of Divines at Westminster*, ed. S. W. Carruthers (Glasgow: Free Presbyterian Publications, 1978), p. 7 (ch. 5, art. 1).

5 A[lexander] H[ume], *Foure Discourses of Praise Unto God. To Wit, 1 In Praise of the Mercie and Goodnesse of God. 2 In Praise of His Justice. 3 In Praise of His Power. 4 In Praise of his Providence* (Edinburgh, 1594), pp. 38–44.
6 *Confession of Faith*, p. 6 (ch. 3, arts 1, 3).
7 Thomas F. Torrance, *The School of Faith: The Catechisms of the Reformed Church* (London: James Clarke, 1959), p. 263.
8 Thomas Blackwell, *Schema Sacrum, or, a Sacred Scheme of Natural and Revealed Religion* (Edinburgh, 1710), pp. 60–1 (original emphasis).
9 Torrance, *School of Faith*, p. 264; Thomas Vincent, *An Explicatory Catechism: Or, an Explanation of the Assemblies Shorter Catechism* (Glasgow, 1674), pp. 35–7.
10 William Annand, *Pater Noster, Our Father: Or, the Lord's Prayer Explained* (Edinburgh, 1670), p. 30.
11 Binning, *The Common Principles of Christian Religion*, p. 163.
12 [David Dickson], *Truths Victory Over Error: Or, an Abbreviation of the Chief Controversies in Religion*, trans. George Sinclair (Edinburgh, 1684), pp. 42–4.
13 John Calvin, *Institutes of the Christian Religion*, ed. John T. McNeill, trans. Ford Lewis Battles, 2 vols (Philadelphia, PA: Westminster Press, 1960), I, p. 207 (bk 1, ch. 16:8).
14 *Confession of Faith*, p. 7 (ch. 5, art. 2).
15 [George Mackenzie], *Religio Stoici* (Edinburgh, 1663), second pagination sequence, pp. 35–6, at p. 35. For Stoic themes in Mackenzie's work, see David Allan, *Philosophy and Politics in Later Stuart Scotland: Neo-Stoicism, Culture and Ideology in an Age of Crisis, 1540–1690* (East Linton: Tuckwell, 2000), pp. 190–200.
16 *Confession of Faith*, p. 8 (ch. 5, art. 4); [Dickson], *Truths Victory Over Error*, pp. 43–4.
17 James VI, *Daemonologie*, in his *King James VI and I: Selected Writings*, ed. Neil Rhodes, Jennifer Richards and Joseph Marshall (Aldershot: Ashgate, 2003), pp. 149–97, at p. 188 (bk 2, ch. 7).
18 See Walsham, *Providence in Early Modern England*, pp. 226–32.
19 John Cockburn, *Jacob's Vow, or, Man's Felicity and Duty* (Edinburgh, 1686), pp. 45–6 (i.e. sig. H^{r-v}) (original emphasis).
20 Robert Fleming, *The Fulfilling of the Scripture, or, an Essay Shewing the Exact Accomplishment of the Word of God in His Works of Providence, Performed & to Be Performed* ([Rotterdam], 1669), pp. 269–71, at p. 269; Robert Fleming, *A Discourse of Earthquakes: As They Are Supernatural and Premonitory Signs to a Nation* (London, 1693), esp. p. 6.
21 H[ume], *Foure Discourses of Praise Unto God*, p. 46.
22 William Anstruther, *Essays, Moral and Divine: In Five Discourses* (Edinburgh, 1701), pp. 1, 5 (original emphasis).
23 *Ibid.*, pp. 39, 48.
24 William Guthrie, *The Christians Great Interest: Or a Short Treatise*, 4th ed. (London, 1667 [1659]), p. 60.
25 A[lexander] Hume, *Ane Treatise of Conscience, Quhairin Divers Secrets Concerning That Subiect, Are Discovered* (Edinburgh, 1594), pp. 73–4.
26 James Durham, *The Law Unsealed: Or, a Practical Exposition of the Ten Commandments*, 2nd ed. (Glasgow, 1676), p. 112.

27 For example, John Livingstone, *Memorable Characteristics, and Remarkable Passages of Divine Providence*, in W. K. Tweedie (ed.), *Select Biographies*, 2 vols (Edinburgh: Wodrow Society, 1845–47), I, pp. 293–348; Robert Law, *Memorialls: Or the Memorable Things That Fell Out Within This Island of Brittain from 1638 to 1684*, ed. Charles Kirkpatrick Sharpe (Edinburgh: Archibald Constable, 1818); Fleming, *The Fulfilling of the Scripture*.

28 Robert Wodrow, *Analecta: Or Materials for a History of Remarkable Providences Mostly Relating to Scotch Ministers and Christians*, ed. Matthew Leishman, 4 vols (Edinburgh: Maitland Club, 1842–43); Patrick Walker, *Six Saints of the Covenant: Peden; Semple; Welwood; Cameron; Cargill; Smith*, ed. David Hay Fleming, 2 vols (London: Hodder & Stoughton, 1901).

29 Margo Todd, *The Culture of Protestantism in Early Modern Scotland* (New Haven, CT: Yale University Press, 2002), pp. 394–9, at p. 397.

30 Louise Yeoman, '"Away with the fairies"', in Lizanne Henderson (ed.), *Fantastical Imaginations: The Supernatural in Scottish History and Culture* (Edinburgh: John Donald, 2009), pp. 29–46.

31 For example, Law, *Memorialls*, pp. xc, 128, 179; Wodrow, *Analecta*, IV, pp. 90–1; Walker, *Six Saints of the Covenant*, I, pp. 36–7.

32 Walker, *Six Saints of the Covenant*, I, p. 35.

33 Robert Wodrow, *The Correspondence of the Rev. Robert Wodrow*, ed. Thomas M'Crie, 3 vols (Edinburgh: Wodrow Society, 1842–43), I, pp. 561–2.

34 Wodrow, *Analecta*, I, p. 4; see Burns, *An Age of Wonders*, pp. 79–80.

35 Archibald Johnston, *Diary of Sir Archibald Johnston of Wariston, Volume II: 1650–1654*, ed. David Hay Fleming (Edinburgh: SHS, 1919), pp. 124–7; Louise Yeoman, 'Archie's invisible worlds discovered: spirituality, madness and Johnston of Wariston's family', *Records of the Scottish Church History Society*, 27 (1997), 156–86.

36 Archibald Johnston, *Diary of Sir Archibald Johnston of Wariston, 1632–1639*, ed. George Morison Paul (Edinburgh: SHS, 1911), p. 76.

37 'Katharine Collace, Mistress Ross: *Memoirs or Spiritual Exercises of Mistress Ross. Written with Her Own Hand*', in David George Mullan (ed.), *Women's Life Writing in Early Modern Scotland: Writing the Evangelical Self c.1670–c.1730* (Aldershot: Ashgate, 2003), pp. 39–94, at p. 82; L. A. Yeoman, 'Ross [née Collace], Katherine (*c*.1635–1697)', *ODNB*.

38 Johnston, *Diary, 1632–1639*, pp. 14–15, 16.

39 David George Mullan, *Narratives of the Religious Self in Early-Modern Scotland* (Farnham: Ashgate, 2010), pp. 294–5.

40 John Welwood to Elizabeth Collace, 25 February 1676, in David George Mullan (ed.), *Protestant Piety in Early-Modern Scotland: Letters, Lives and Covenants, 1650–1712* (Edinburgh: SHS, 2008), p. 128.

41 Alexander Wedderburn, *David's Testament Opened Up in Fourty Sermons* (Edinburgh, 1691), p. 367.

42 Durham, *Law Unsealed*, sig. *2ʳ.

43 John Logan, *Sermons by the Late Reverend John Logan*, 2 vols (Edinburgh, 1790–91), I, p. 162.

44 Wedderburn, *David's Testament*, p. 398.

45 G[eorge] Anderson, *A Remonstrance Against Lord Viscount Bolingbroke's Philosophical Religion* (Edinburgh, 1756), ch. 10.
46 Logan, *Sermons*, I, p. 155.
47 On the topic, see esp. the 'Introduction', in Natalie Mears *et al.* (eds), *National Prayers: Special Worship Since the Reformation: Volume 1: Special Prayers, Fasts and Thanksgivings in the British Isles, 1533–1688* (Woodbridge: Boydell/ Church of England Record Society, 2013), pp. xlvii–cvi; W. Ian P. Hazlett, 'Playing God's card: Knox and fasting, 1565–66', in Roger A. Mason (ed.), *John Knox and the British Reformations* (Aldershot: Ashgate, 1998), pp. 176–98.
48 Mears *et al.*, *National Prayers*, pp. 91–2.
49 For various perspectives on this theme, see Arthur H. Williamson, *Scottish National Consciousness in the Age of James VI: The Apocalypse, the Union and the Shaping of Scotland's Public Culture* (Edinburgh: John Donald, 1979); S. A. Burrell, 'The apocalyptic vision of the early Covenanters', *SHR*, 43 (1964), 1–24; Crawford Gribben, 'The Church of Scotland and the English apocalyptic imagination, 1630 to 1650', *SHR*, 88 (2009), 34–56.
50 Mears *et al.*, *National Prayers*, pp. 703–4.
51 *Ibid.*, p. 206.
52 *RPS*, 1600/11/12. See also [William Alexander], *A Short Discourse of the Good Ends of the Higher Providence, in the Late Attemptat Against His Maiesties Person* (Edinburgh, 1600).
53 *RPC*, 2nd ser., II, pp. 473–4, 3rd ser., I, pp. 62–3, 616.
54 *RPS*, 1689/3/180.
55 NRS, CH12/20/49, Jacobite form of prayer for a fast to be observed on 23 Nov. 1715, p. 1.
56 John Russell, 'A treatise of the happie and blissed Unioun', in Bruce R. Galloway and Brian P. Levack (eds), *The Jacobean Union: Six Tracts of 1604* (Edinburgh: SHS, 1985), pp. 75–142, at p. 78. See also Bruce Galloway, *The Union of England and Scotland, 1603–1608* (Edinburgh: John Donald, 1986), pp. 33–4.
57 [Francis Grant], *The Patriot Resolved: In a Letter to an Addresser, from His Friend* ([Edinburgh?], 1707), pp. 5–7, at p. 5.
58 *A Declaration of the Army of England Upon Their March into Scotland* (Edinburgh, 1650), p. 9.
59 *A Short Reply Unto a Declaration Intituled, The Declaration of the Army of England Upon Their March into Scotland* ([Edinburgh?], 1650), p. 7.
60 Alexander Pitcairn, *The Spiritual Sacrifice: Or, a Treatise, Wherein Several Weighty Questions and Cases, Concerning the Saints Communion with God in Prayer, Are Propounded, and Practically Improved* (Edinburgh, 1664), pp. 158–63, at pp. 161, 162.
61 David Allan has argued that the importance of providence in Scottish historical writing increased during the seventeenth century. David Allan, *Virtue, Learning and the Scottish Enlightenment: Ideas of Scholarship in Early Modern History* (Edinburgh: Edinburgh University Press, 1993), pp. 108–28.
62 Philopoliteius [Alexander Skene], *Memorialls for the Government of the Royal-Burghs in Scotland* (Aberdeen, 1685), p. 206 (emphasis in original).
63 NRS, GD172/2482, 'Copy mortification by Mr David Dickson, preacher at Glasgow and John Stewart, late provost of Ayr, of 2,500 merks bestowed by

Margaret Graham relict of John Boyd of Kirkdyke in Kilmarnock', 28 April 1641. We are not aware of any evidence that this book was in fact produced.

64 Richard Kyle, 'John Knox's concept of divine providence and its influence on his thought', *Albion*, 18 (1986), 395–410, at pp. 403–6; Richard Kyle, 'John Knox's concept of history: a focus on the providential and apocalyptic aspects of his religious faith', *Fides et Historia*, 18 (1986), 5–19; Allan, *Virtue, Learning and the Scottish Enlightenment*, pp. 119–21; Jane Dawson, *John Knox* (New Haven, CT: Yale University Press, 2015), pp. 251–7.

65 Robert Wodrow, *The History of the Sufferings of the Church of Scotland from the Restoration to the Revolution*, ed. Robert Burns, 4 vols (Glasgow: Blackie, Fullarton & co., 1828–30), I, pp. xxxviii, xxxiii.

66 See Allan, *Virtue, Learning and the Scottish Enlightenment*, pp. 208–11; Nicholas Phillipson, 'Providence and progress: an introduction to the historical thought of William Robertson', in Stewart J. Brown (ed.), *William Robertson and the Expansion of Empire* (Cambridge: Cambridge University Press, 1997), pp. 55–73.

67 William Robertson, *The Situation of the World at the Time of Christ's Appearance, and Its Connexion with the Success of His Religion, Considered* (Edinburgh, 1755), pp. 3–4.

68 William Robertson, *The History of Scotland, During the Reigns of Queen Mary and of King James VI*, 2 vols (London, 1759), I, p. 212, II, p. 166.

69 Robertson, *Situation of the World at the Time of Christ's Appearance*, pp. 7, 39.

70 Jeng-Guo S. Chen, 'Providence and progress: the religious dimension in Ferguson's discussion of civil society', in Eugene Heath and Vincenzo Merolle (eds), *Adam Ferguson: History, Progress and Human Nature* (London: Pickering & Chatto, 2008), pp. 171–86, at p. 178.

71 Adam Ferguson, *Principles of Moral and Political Science*, 2 vols (Edinburgh, 1792), I, pp. 172–80, 189–95, at p. 192. See also Chen, 'Providence and progress', pp. 176–80.

72 Adam Smith, *The Theory of Moral Sentiments* (London, 1759), part iii, p. 284. On Smith and providence, see Paul Oslington, 'Divine action, providence and Adam Smith's invisible hand', in Paul Oslington (ed.), *Adam Smith as Theologian* (Abingdon: Routledge, 2011), pp. 61–74.

73 Richard B. Sher, 'Witherspoon's *Dominion of Providence* and the Scottish jeremiad tradition', in Richard B. Sher and Jeffrey R. Smitten (eds), *Scotland and America in the Age of Enlightenment* (Edinburgh: Edinburgh University Press, 1990), pp. 46–64; Richard B. Sher, *Church and University in the Scottish Enlightenment: The Moderate Literati of Edinburgh* (Princeton, NJ: Princeton University Press, 1985), pp. 206–11; Emma Vincent, 'The responses of Scottish churchmen to the French Revolution, 1789–1802', *SHR*, 73 (1994), 191–215.

74 Quoted in Sher, *Church and University in the Scottish Enlightenment*, p. 208.

75 Adam Ferguson, *The Morality of Stage-Plays Seriously Considered* (Edinburgh, 1757), p. 24. On this theme, see Jacob Viner, *The Role of Providence in the Social Order: An Essay in Intellectual History* (Philadelphia, PA: American Philosophical Society, 1972), ch. 4.

76 Adam Smith, *The Theory of Moral Sentiments*, ed. Knud Haakonssen (Cambridge: Cambridge University Press, 2002), pp. 265–6.

77 F. David Roberts, *The Social Conscience of the Early Victorians* (Palo Alto, CA: Stanford University Press, 2002), pp. 127–30.
78 David Fergusson, 'Divine providence', in Nicholas Adams, George Pattison and Graham Ward (eds), *The Oxford Handbook of Theology and Modern European Thought* (Oxford: Oxford University Press, 2013), pp. 655–73, at pp. 660–6; Stewart J. Brown, *Providence and Empire: Religion, Politics and Society in the United Kingdom, 1815–1914* (Harlow: Pearson Education, 2008).
79 Roberts, *The Social Conscience of the Early Victorians*, pp. 123–38; Fergusson, 'Divine providence', pp. 666–70.

11

The invention of Highland Second Sight

Domhnall Uilleam Stiùbhart[*]

This chapter examines and reassesses some accounts from early modern Scotland referring to a constellation of diverse supernatural abilities, primarily relating to premonition and clairvoyance, often described in English as Second Sight, and in Scottish Gaelic as *an dà shealladh* or *taibhsearachd*. It is indebted to the scholarship of numerous historians of early modern thought, religion and popular belief, in particular the work of Michael Hunter, whose annotated sourcebook *The Occult Laboratory* offers an essential and accessible introduction to the earliest narratives specifically devoted to Highland Second Sight: a series of interrelated late seventeenth-century texts ranging from concise observations on the subject to more extended analyses, stimulated in the first place by the curiosity of the Anglo-Irish natural philosopher Robert Boyle (1627–91).[1]

Although the chapter opens with a brief excursus on Martin Martin's influential account concerning the Second Sight in his *Description of the Western Isles of Scotland* (1703), I shall, for the time being, forgo detailed inquiry into the canonical texts edited by Hunter: the Rev. Robert Kirk's 'Secret Commonwealth'; correspondence to Samuel Pepys, and to John Aubrey; the Rev. John Fraser's *Deuteroskopia* (1707); and the anonymous manuscript 'Highland Rites & Customes'. Instead, I shall consider what appear to be the earliest references to the phenomenon in Scotland, in two contrasting witchcraft confessions from 1595 and 1616, before turning to a sequence of references to Second Sight in the late 1670s in the covenanting heartlands of Renfrewshire and Ayrshire. These Lowland narratives represent an unexpected inspiration for the detailed accounts of Highland Second Sight assembled in *The Occult Laboratory*.

In modern English-language scholarship and popular discourse alike, Second Sight tends to be regarded as distinctive to the people of the Scottish Highlands: a primal, hereditary phenomenon involving involuntary visions of future events. Close analysis of the earliest Scottish references, however, taken together with evidence from elsewhere in

Europe, suggests that current notions of Second Sight may in fact differ markedly from the various supernatural phenomena associated with the expression in the past. The concept itself clearly derives from theological discourse; I shall suggest that its adaptation into popular belief may represent a pragmatic, creative response to increasing anxieties in interpreting supposed visions of and encounters with a supernatural other world, first in an era of growing clerical hegemony actively hostile to lay attempts to engage with occult powers and ever more concerned about the dangers of Satanic paction, then, subsequently, at a time of growing disbelief and derision concerning the very existence of such unearthly spirits.

This may indicate that Second Sight follows a common trajectory to other early modern 'superstitions', from being a cause of clerical concern to an object of learned scepticism and enquiry.[2] At the same time, drawing upon work by Moshe Sluhovsky, we might construe Second Sight, considered as a direct personal encounter with the supernatural, as resembling spirit possession. In an era when the development and spread of mystic religious practices heightened already existing concerns about the reliability, sincerity and moral significance of visionary experiences, Second Sight, along with spirit possession, supernatural apparitions, portents and dreams, shifted from being a relatively mundane phenomenon to one attracting interest and scrutiny among the learned.[3]

As to why the theological concept of Second Sight was adapted into popular belief in Scotland rather than elsewhere, we might first invoke the extensive propagation of Reformed doctrine, particularly but not exclusively in the Lowlands, before tentatively observing how the prominence of Second Sight may have been reinforced by the appropriation of the term by two other groups in Scotland: speculative Freemasons and Covenanters. Both of these groups, in different ways, emphasised inner personal experience as a path to spiritual illumination. Though relevant evidence is sparse and often obscure, it appears that Second Sight has a history, revealing the indelible mark left by the Reformation upon popular beliefs as well as upon institutional religion.

The most influential early modern depiction of the phenomenon, underpinning most subsequent written accounts on the subject, is the 'Account of the Second Sight, in Irish call'd Taish', purveyed by the Skye traveller and author Martin Martin (*c*.1665–1718) in his *Description of the Western Islands of Scotland*.[4] Martin introduces his subject as: 'a singular Faculty of Seeing, an otherwise invisible Object, without any previous Means us'd by the Person that sees it for that end; the Vision makes such a lively impression upon the Seer, that they neither see nor think of any thing else, except the Vision, as long as it continues'.[5] This ability characteristically involves the perception of likenesses of absent living individuals. The seer may see images of future spouses or unanticipated visitors; primarily, however, Second Sight prefigures death in the neighbourhood:

> When a Shroud is perceiv'd about one, it is a sure Prognostick of Death, the time is judged according to the height of it about the Person ...
> Some find themselves as it were in a croud of People, having a Corpse which they carry along with them, and after such Visions the Seers come in sweating, and describe the People that appear'd; if there be any of their Acquaintance among 'em, they give an account of their Names, as also of the Bearers, but they know nothing concerning the Corps.[6]

Although frequently perplexing, the imagery can be deciphered methodically by accomplished interpreters within the community: 'Every vision that is seen comes exactly to pass, according to the true Rules of Observation, tho' Novices and heedless Persons do not always judge by those Rules'.[7]

Subsequent examples recorded by Martin as illustrations of Second Sight suggest an altogether more disparate bundle of phenomena, extending the range of his initial assertions. Seers can observe not only people, but forthcoming 'Houses, Gardens and Trees, in places void of all three', as well as corn-drying kilns going up in flames.[8] The faculty involves not only visual likenesses, but symbols such as 'a spark of fire ... a forerunner of a dead Child', as well as other sensory phenomena, such as the death-cry known as '*Taisk*' (*tàsg* or *tathasg*), or even the smell of the seldom eaten foods 'Fish or Flesh'.[9] Moreover, rather than being visions passively perceived, at least a couple of Martin's examples demonstrate an alarming corporeality. The likeness of an 'ill natur'd Woman' threatened 'with her head and hands' a man in a neighbouring village who had disappointed her, until he 'dropt from his Seat backward, and then fell a Vomiting'. An importunate spirit 'appearing in all Points' like the seer, after the latter was advised 'to cast a live Coal' in its face, 'appear'd to him in the Fields, and beat him severely, so as to oblige him to keep his Bed for the space of fourteen days after'.[10] Towards the end of his account, Martin recounts an anecdote involving a seer being diverted by the comical play-acting of a household familiar, 'the Spirit call'd *Browny* in Humane Shape'. In conclusion, he briefly alludes to 'Spirits also that appear'd in the Shape of Women, Horses, Swine, Cats, and some like fiery Balls, which would follow Men in the Fields', as well as to various other supernatural phenomena:

> Sounds in the Air, resembling those of a Harp, Pipe, Crowing of a Cock, and of the grinding of Querns; and sometimes they have heard Voices in the Air by Night, singing Irish [i.e. Gaelic] Songs; the words of which Songs some of my Acquaintance still retain. One of 'em resembled the Voice of a Woman who had died some time before, and the Song related to her State in the other World.[11]

Martin's anecdotes thus digress markedly from his initial programmatic depiction of Second Sight as an abstracted, spontaneous spiritual perception.

Earlier references in Martin's writings are similarly problematical. In his 1698 account of St Kilda, Martin describes the island cult leader, Roderick the Impostor, as 'endued with that rare Faculty of enjoying the *Second Sight*, which makes it the more probable that he was haunted by a familiar Spirit.'[12] Martin's phrase 'familiar spirit' evokes the biblical Witch of Endor (1 Samuel 28:7), an allusion suggesting questionable, even demonic practices.

Again, having completed his research expeditions in the Hebrides, Martin writes to his London patron Hans Sloane: 'If you had been endued with that rare faculty of the second sight, you could no more avoid seing of me frequently, than the Islanders do in the like caice. for in the whol course of my late travels, when any thing that was remarkable fell under my observation, I presently directed my thoughts towards your Society.'[13] In other words, he depicts himself as so taken up with contemplating his sponsors in the Royal Society that, if they were gifted with Second Sight, they would see his spirit double.

Martin Martin thus begins his excursus on Second Sight by delineating a set of phenomena familiar in later accounts of the phenomenon: involuntary, mainly visual premonitions associated with a limited range of generic events, principally concerning impending death. Certain of his anecdotes concerning Second Sight, however, seem to indicate a more variegated set of popular beliefs. Some of these beliefs ascribe to *taibhsearan* or seers a learnt capacity for intentional perception of, and even communication with, invisible, capricious, supernatural personal beings capable of physical action as well as of imparting occult knowledge and power inaccessible or opaque to other mortals. These notions are clearly grounded in popular conceptions across Europe of an invisible world: 'liberally and abundantly populated with creatures who did not fit into the Christian-Aristotelian-Thomist categories of God, people, angels and demons. These creatures could interact with people in a range of ways, sometimes as friends or helpers, sometimes as sources of threats or mischief.'[14] The fluid and diffuse range of beliefs and practices associated with such a world view clearly not only derived from indigenous ideas, whatever these might have been, but were shaped and informed by understandings, concepts and rituals drawn from folklorised Christianity, as well as from scholarly disciplines, particularly theology, demonology, astrology and learned magic. Certain recurrent themes and motifs can indeed be identified, but assumptions regarding what was perceived, how observations might be interpreted, and, above all, the nature of the 'gift' itself and how it might be acquired, varied not only from place to place, but also according to individual predilections among seers, their audiences, and the narrators of the resulting anecdotes.

Martin's assertions in the *Description* might thus be read as an attempt to quarantine uncanny phenomena, setting them apart from broader concepts of occult communication with supernatural beings. Two reasons might be suggested for this manoeuvre. It may be that such beliefs were perceived as being increasingly hazardous in the Highlands during the 1690s, when the imposition of Presbyterian authority across the region, not to mention growing social dislocation and exceptional mortality in the wake of war, dearth and famine, heightened community tensions, with accompanying accusations of witchcraft.[15] Then again, to many of Martin's interlocutors in London, the idea of active conversation with spirits was not so much dangerous as credulous, ludicrous and hopelessly rustic. Martin failed in his endeavour to present Second Sight as a valid subject for philosophical investigation, decoupled from superstitious beliefs in witches or demons; his subsequent reputation suffered grievously as a result.[16]

An examination of earlier references to Second Sight, however, suggests that Martin's dilemma was far from a new one. Meagre though these references are, they suggest that from the late sixteenth century onwards, due to a combination of intellectual, theological, political and cultural circumstances, a category of intuitive premonitions came to be separated off from a wider spectrum of popular supernatural beliefs. This mysterious visionary faculty came to be conceived of as somehow emblematic of the Scottish Highlands: the invention of Highland Second Sight. Before examining this process in greater detail, however, it may be useful to situate the beliefs characteristic of Second Sight within a wider thematic and geographical context, as part of a broad European repertoire of vernacular prophecy and divination.

Martin Martin was writing at the end of a century marked by revelatory, often eschatological prophecies alluding to regional or national upheavals, or even global apocalypse: a genre of particular import in Europe during the troubled post-Reformation era.[17] In popular Gaelic culture this broad category of supernatural visions, often referred to as *fiosachd*, tended to draw upon indigenous mythic paradigms rather than scriptural exegesis. Retailed in suitably allegorical, poetic language, these prophecies were generally ascribed to historical characters, themselves semi-mythical, whose fame travelled well beyond their own districts. Indeed, the most renowned prophet across much of the early modern Highlands, just as in the Lowlands, was Tòmas Reumhair: Thomas the Rhymer, the thirteenth-century Thomas of Erceldoune.[18] 'High-status' predictions, whether 'ancient' or biblical in character, may usefully be contrasted with more mundane, parochial visions arising out of and playing a part in everyday life, in particular the involuntary premonitions, mostly associated with impending death within the community, which have come largely to epitomise Second Sight today.

As with *fiosachd*, other Highland beliefs regarding the prediction of future events can also best be understood within a wider European context. This is particularly evident in the case of those involving distinctive ritual observation techniques, which were widespread across Europe. *Slinneineachd* or scapulimancy, for example, was a divinatory technique employing a sheep's shoulder blade – a relatively low-grade, short-term method for allaying household anxieties. *Manadaireachd*, or the *frìth*, referred to auspices taken before commencing a momentous undertaking.[19] A number of crystal amulets preserved in Highland families, ostensibly for healing, may also have been employed for divination by scrying.[20] Even the ill-reputed *taghairm*, by which the aspirant seer summoned demons by means of running water, a cowhide or cat roasting, may partake of recognisable European parallels.[21]

Second Sight follows a similar pattern. Far from being an archetypally Highland phenomenon, it too can best be interpreted within a European framework. Narratives about the class of premonitions nowadays seen as characteristic of Second Sight demonstrate striking similarities to a constellation of related belief legends – even, to use the folkloristic idiom, a commonly held *Erzählkultur* or tale culture – that was prevalent until comparatively recently among peoples of the North Sea region and, perhaps, Scandinavia and the Baltic coasts.[22]

Like Second Sight, expressions such as north-western Low German *Vorspok*, Dutch *voorloop* or Danish *forvarsel* refer to an extrasensory perceptive ability possessed by certain humans and animals alike. Like Second Sight, this faculty was the subject of local belief legends concerning involuntary premonitions, usually visions but occasionally heard phenomena, or even those perceived with other senses, foretelling death or disaster within the community. Again, the same narrow range of tale types constantly recurs, with particular prominence given to phantom funerals. Premonitions often include seemingly incongruous, perplexing details that, on being fulfilled, confirm their veracity to a previously sceptical audience. The ability itself is reckoned a curse, not a gift.[23]

Such striking similarities between tales of Highland Second Sight publicised by romantic-era authors on the one hand, and long-standing traditions of folk premonitions in their own cultures on the other, led nineteenth-century folklorists in north-west Germany and the Netherlands to adopt the expression into their own languages to describe phenomena hitherto locally designated by a plethora of dialectal terms.[24] Nevertheless, we should not overlook the regional variations and inflections to be observed in the phenomena they regarded as 'Second Sight' – *das zweite Gesicht* or *het tweede gezicht* – arising from socio-economic, religious and environmental circumstances quite distinct from those in the Scottish Gàidhealtachd. A significant factor in this respect may be the ready availability of wood in these regions compared with the Highlands. Thus premonitions of death on the Continent historically tended to focus upon wooden coffins, rather than apparitions shrouded in winding sheets. Again, conflagrations of wooden houses serve as a perennial subject for Continental premonitions, much more than the occasional kiln-burning foretold in Gaelic traditions.[25]

Discourses regarding Second Sight elsewhere were influenced and modified by other beliefs and practices concerning divination and premonitions, whether in regional or Continental contexts. In the Highlands, as in practices of occult perception elsewhere in Europe, it was believed that the gift could be acquired through bodily contact with a seer – canonically, foot on his foot and hand on his shoulder – or else by looking through a hole, for example a knothole in a board of wood. The capability, in common with other occult faculties, was often ascribed to people born on specific holy days in the Catholic ritual year, to those possessing particular physical features, or else to those born with a caul or amniotic sac. Again, comparable premonitory abilities were believed to be effective only during particular times of the year set apart for divination, for example the Twelve Days of Christmas in Scandinavia, when a seer might visit the local graveyard at midnight in order to foretell the number of funerals in the community during the coming year.

It is striking that even the early modern examples of the phenomenon recorded by Continental scholars appear to foreshadow later instances: intuitive, spontaneous, mysterious in origin, apprehended either as morally neutral curiosities or else as illustrating divine providence. One might argue, however, that we have here a retrospective imposition of a later taxonomy, that such examples attracted folklorists' attention because of their clear-cut resemblance to the paradigm of Second Sight as understood in their own era: a term, as stated above, that was adapted into German and Dutch from English in the first half of the nineteenth century, drawing upon romantic Highlandism.[26]

A more extensive analysis of early modern sources, corroborated by more recent instances from Scandinavia where the modern term 'Second Sight' does not appear to have gained a hold in folklore scholarship let alone vernacular discourse, suggests an altogether more complex and ambiguous picture. Some older accounts of Second Sight certainly emphasise its supposedly abstract, innocuous nature. Other evidence, however, associates the faculty with more dangerous powers involving direct communication with occult other-world entities, be they spirits, fairies or *Doppelgänger* of the living.[27] Early modern sources for Second Sight in Scotland afford both these perspectives: they demonstrate that Second Sight as we know it today is not necessarily how it was understood historically by the people of the Scottish Gàidhealtachd. Moreover, they suggest that the very category of Second Sight derives from early modern theological discourse and may have been created with the intention of dividing off this particular subcategory of supernatural experience from a wider spectrum of occult interactions, in an attempt to render it innocuous and inoffensive.

The expression 'Second Sight' derives from learned European epistemological hierarchies of perception, developed from late classical neoplatonic traditions and primarily mediated through St Augustine's *De Genesi ad litteram*. Crudely put, the first sight is physical (*visio corporalis*); the second, spiritual (*visio spiritalis*); the third and highest, intellectual, avisual and mystical (*visio intellectualis*). This theory came to play a lasting and significant role in the classifying and interpretation of visionary experiences.[28]

As stated above, as a term designating perceptions involving divination and clairvoyance, 'Second Sight' stands apart from indigenous vernacular expressions used to classify analogous phenomena elsewhere in northern Europe. An abstruse category apparently originating in learned culture, it refers to the visionary faculty itself, rather than to the specific subjects of visions – funerals, conflagrations, ghosts or apparitions – referred to in vernacular terminologies. Ostensibly denoting intuitive powers of premonition and clairvoyance, 'Second Sight' not only passes over any inductive techniques by which the cognitive faculty might be acquired; it does not indicate what is seen either. A fundamental question, then, is how and why this apparently uncharacteristic designation came to be adopted in Scotland, particularly in the Scottish Gàidhealtachd, rather than in other European cultures?

Alluding to perception, the referential imprecision of 'Second Sight' allows for ambiguity and flexibility. This gives it a capacity to sidestep potentially dangerous questions regarding what is seen, how it is seen and how it might be put to the test. The first traceable reference to the expression that appears to be associated with its later vernacular connotation is in a confession made on 5 October 1595 relating to events following the murder of John Campbell of Cawdor or Calder, one of the guardians of the young Archibald Campbell, seventh Earl of Argyll, on the night of 4 February 1592 at Knipoch on the south side of Loch Feochan, Argyllshire.[29] The confession was made by Margaret Campbell, widow of Iain Òg Campbell of Cabrachan who had been one of those most closely involved in the conspiracy of discontented Campbell nobility first to assassinate Cawdor, then to dispatch the young Earl of Argyll himself. Margaret recounted how, the summer after Cawdor's killing, their cousin, John Campbell of Ardkinglas, being suspected of the murder, summoned her from her lands on the Island of Lismore. Ardkinglas conferred with her regarding how she and other witches in Lorn – they being 'wiser nor the women in Argyll' – might win him back the favour of the Earl of Argyll.

Margaret's account suggests that at least four consultations took place, involving witches from Lismore and beyond. They attempted to discern the conspirators' eventual fates; to protect them from weapons; and, most significantly, to deflect their opponents' hostility by bewitching them. Some elements of purposive ritual were clearly involved. Ardkinglas made his initial request when 'the first begining of the harvest quarter approtches', having been told 'all witchcraft is to be practised in the beginning of every quharter'.[30] The witches 'namit God in thair words': that is, they recited incantations derived from liturgical prayers and blessings.[31] Margaret also required honest, full disclosure of what Ardkinglas knew of the conspiracy, without which 'sche culd doe him na gude': this implies, over and beyond a prudent concern to appreciate just what she was getting into, that the witches would undertake, as it were, a systematic appraisal of all circumstances involved.[32]

Margaret Campbell was clearly anxious not to incriminate her servant and messenger: 'ane woman of Lismore callit Mary voir Nicvolvoire vic Coil vic Neil' (*Màiri Mhòr nic Mhaol-Mhoire mhic Dhomhnaill mhic Nèill*) who, according to Margaret, 'is not ane witch but sche will see things to cum be sum second sicht'.[33] Màiri Mhòr's ability – occult, but involuntary and mysterious ('*sum* second sicht') – is thus deliberately contrasted with the active, purposeful witchcraft practised by other women enumerated by her mistress. In fact, Margaret Campbell's account, though judiciously devoid of specific detail concerning the rituals they employed, suggests an accepted hierarchy of ability among witches in the region. As already seen, those in Lorn were reckoned more skilled than those in Argyll. Some could not only see the future, but were able to alter future events; 'the twa Nicricherts' even claimed to be able to ensure their MacDougall chief's release from prison, and to protect him from harm even 'geif my Lord Argyll, Caddel, and thair haill friends and forces wald cum in Lorne with displayit banners'.[34]

In addition, religious circumstances were changing. After the Reformation, there were no longer the Catholic clergy from whose liturgy prayers and blessings had been adapted for everyday use: Margaret stated that it was 'Auld Mackellar of Cruachan that lernit hir his charmis and that the said McEllar lernit them at the pryoris of Icolmkill [the prioress of Iona]'.[35] Claims were also being made for altogether different diabolic sources of supernatural power: according to Margaret, Ardkinglas eventually abandoned the witches in favour of the Rev. Patrick MacQueen, 'a far better inshanter nor any of thame' who could 'invokate upon seven divils quhilks waitit on him' and was 'sae skillet in his craft' that he could build a castle between sunrise and sunset.[36] In contrast to such assertions, spontaneous visions of events of local significance were of minor import.[37]

The meticulous research of Diarmid Campbell into the MacConnochie Campbells of Inverawe, Margaret's kindred, reveals an unexpected twist in the tale. Margaret Campbell, accomplished in witchcraft, the first person associated with the use of the term 'Second Sight' in its vernacular connotation, appears to be none other than the widow of John Carswell (*c.*1522–72), Bishop of Argyll.[38] Carswell is an outstanding figure in the early modern Gaelic world. His magnum opus, a translation of John Knox's 1564 version of the Book of Common Order into classical Gaelic as *Foirm na n-Urrnuidheadh* (1567), combines traditional learning with contemporary Renaissance humanism: 'an astonishing achievement', encompassing 'in one sweep, the Gaelic vocabulary for the worship and ministry of the Protestant church on Knox's model'.[39] It would be hardly less remarkable if one of the wives of John Knox himself was revealed to posterity as an adept in the occult arts.

The episode may be more striking still. At the beginning of the transcription, the scribe states that the three witnesses were 'exponeris of the said Margaret's language to me'.[40] In other words, the confession was delivered in her native Gaelic, and translated – and possibly reworked – into English. Two possibilities present themselves. The first, more speculative, is that in her original confession Margaret used a direct Gaelic equivalent of the term 'Second Sight', say *'an dà shealladh'*; the second is that a possibly more diffuse Gaelic description of Màiri Mhòr's supernatural capability was condensed by her cross-examiners into English 'Second Sight'.

If the former, it may be that we see here Margaret and her contemporaries adapting into their own interpretative framework a theological expression that had come to be specifically associated with visions and premonitions and that had acquired renewed significance in contemporary ecclesiastical debate: carrying out, as it were, an epistemic transfer from one branch of understanding to another. This expression and others like it – such as the *'súile sbioratálta'* used by Carswell to convey Knox's 'eyes spiritual' in the baptismal section of *Foirm na n-Urrnuidheadh* expounding the Creed – formed part of a long-established Christian vocabulary concerning modes of mystical perception and experience then being translated and adapted for Protestant worship and ministry in the post-Reformation Gàidhealtachd.[41] If this is so, it may be that in creating a new, durable lexicon for Highland worship – as Donald Meek puts it, Carswell 'translated the Reformation itself, into Gaelic terms'[42] – the bishop, along with his university-educated clerical collaborators, also, possibly unwittingly, supplied a concept, or conceptual framework, out of which developed an expression that would come to be emblematic of Highland supernatural belief.

Even if 'Second Sight' was an English interpretation by her translators, rather than coming directly from Margaret herself, we still see a theological expression being used to describe – and perhaps even to define – a category of vernacular belief. In this case, the prime suspect for its use is likely to be the principal questioner Neil Campbell (d. *c*.1613), himself Bishop of Argyll, who enjoyed a bookish reputation among his contemporaries.[43] Campbell's presence supervising Margaret's confession in the Castle of Carnasserie – built by her first husband, occupied by her stepson, the building where her second husband, who loved her 'verie weil', had recently been tortured and executed[44] – helps to account for her unexpected candour: the bishop was either her son- or stepson-in-law.

One subsequent reference to Second Sight in the context of Scottish witch trials might suggest that the carefully drawn distinction between spontaneous visions and ritual witchcraft did not necessarily always hold. On 12 March 1616 there was brought to trial in Kirkwall Elspeth Reoch, the daughter of the late Donald Reoch, piper to the Earl of Caithness (*riabhach*, brindled or swarthy, is an ill-omened hue associated with the Devil).[45] According to her account – evidently spoken in English rather than translated from Gaelic[46] – when aged around twelve, Elspeth had spent eight weeks in Lochaber with her aunt, wife of 'Allane McEldowie', 'quho duelt with hir husband in a Loch'. That is, she stayed with Allan Cameron (*Ailean, Mac Dhomhnaill Duibh*), chief of the clan, and his wife, a daughter of John Stewart, fifth of the Stewarts of Appin, in the chief's stronghold of Eilean nan Craobh in Loch Eil.[47] What appears to have been an uncomfortable encounter between the suggestible young girl and two joshing older men, one in 'grein tartane', the other 'cled in blak', set in train a series of traumatic, alienating events.[48] It should be mentioned in passing that two major late sixteenth-century figures associated with the Camerons, individuals well-known throughout the Gàidhealtachd, were credited with supernatural powers. Elspeth's dark-apparelled fairy man is reminiscent of the near contemporary clan hero Tàillear Dubh na Tuaighe ('the Black Tailor of the Axe'), to whom some traditions give fairy ancestry.[49] Again, during her stay in Lochaber, Elspeth would certainly have heard of, and maybe even met, Gormshuil Mhòr na Maighe, reputedly the most powerful witch in the Highlands of her time.[50]

In a subsequent meeting in Murthlie in Strathspey – most likely Elspeth's home parish – the 'blak man', then calling himself 'ane farie man quha was sumtyme her kinsman', importuned her, now mother of an illegitimate child, and eventually 'semeit to ly with her'.[51] She apparently lost her power of speech and subsequently led a marginal life as an indigent fortune teller, '[s]ynding [i.e. making signs] telling and foir shawing [her clients] quhat they had done and quhat they sould do'. Elspeth ended up in Orkney, caught up in a witch-hunt incited by the new political and religious order in an archipelago riven by a recent armed rebellion and suffering the aftermath of disastrous weather conditions the previous year. Unlike Margaret Campbell, Elspeth's Highland gentry connections availed her little; if anything, they made matters worse, with her putative uncle Allan Cameron recently outlawed for rebellion by the Privy Council.[52]

As in Margaret Campbell's account of Màiri Mhòr, Elspeth Reoch's ability was associated with the central western Highlands; both women had connections with Lismore and Appin. Elspeth's prescient ability, however, was described not as 'sum second sicht', but as 'the secund sicht'. In fact, Elspeth's prosecutors seem deliberately to be using her experience as a test case to dismantle the notion of Second Sight as spontaneous and inexplicable, reconfiguring it as the outcome of a Satanic pact deserving the severest penalty. Elspeth's muteness was thus censured as a ruse to avoid answering hard questions about the true, demonic origins of her ability. Her revenant fairy kinsman warned that she was 'to be dum for [his] haveing teacheit hir to sie and ken ony thing she desyrit He said that gif she spake gentlemen wald trouble hir and gar hir give reassounes for hir doings Quhairupoun she mycht be challengeit and hurt'.[53] According to Elspeth's declaration, her clairvoyant and predictive power was granted to her after intercourse with the fairy man, redefined by the court as the Devil, concerning whom she confessed she had subsequently been 'useing, hanting and conversing with'.[54]

Elspeth Reoch was the unlucky victim of a virulent witch-hunt, her confession skewed in order to demonstrate how ostensibly inexplicable divinatory powers were really conferred by diabolical compact. In this respect, it is striking that there is only one apparent reference to Second Sight, in passing, in a subsequent Scottish witch trial. Here, the faculty is specifically distinguished from active witchcraft. Among the charges brought against Janet Cock of Dalkeith in 1661 was the foretelling that a certain William Mitchell should be hanged: Janet's lawyer, however, alleged that 'she might have done that from conjecture, such threatnings being usually made by persons injured, and if any crime could be inferred from this, it is not sorcery, but that which the Lawyers call Deuterscoscopia [sic, i.e. Second Sight], which is not lybelled'.[55] This absence of Second Sight references may be owing to the paucity of witchcraft cases in the Highlands, if the ability was indeed particularly associated with the region. The most significant documented seventeenth-century Highland witch-hunt, that of early 1662 in the Isle of Bute, was taken up with accusations of *maleficium* – shooting elf shot and blasting – rather than the occult divination and clairvoyance that might have invited charges of Second Sight.[56] It may be, however, that two specific causes lie behind the dearth of Second Sight accusations in witch trials. First, local communities may have been unwilling to pursue individuals credited with Second Sight, for the very reason that they were not perceived as harmful witches; rather, they had much in common with the relatively benevolent 'cunning-folk' found elsewhere in Europe.[57] Second, as would be demonstrated in the case of the analogous faculty of 'spectral' or 'special sight' in the 1692 Salem witch trials, in the absence of direct confession of the kind extracted from Elspeth Reoch, spectral testimony on its own was notoriously ambiguous and problematic as evidence in court.[58]

The theological model of a spiritual Second Sight may have not only been adapted into Highland supernatural belief during this period, but into another, perhaps equally unlikely milieu: the establishment and consolidation of speculative Freemasonry. Early Freemasonry was a predominantly Scottish phenomenon that promised its adepts insights into ancient, arcane knowledge allowing them to penetrate outward appearances to esoteric secrets within. Masonic claims concerning a mysteriously acquired 'Second Sight' – a concept most likely adapted from contemporary theological discourse rather than directly from occult Neoplatonism – may have spurred curiosity among initiates and interested parties alike regarding parallel assertions of prescience and clairvoyance among their own countrymen, the more so given that such beliefs appeared distinctively Scottish within an emerging British context.

The expression is used in a well-known excerpt from amusing verses published in 1638 praising Perth, ostensibly in memory of the poet Henry Adamson's friend James Gall. The poet speculates on rebuilding of Perth Bridge:

> Thus *Gall* assured me it would be so,
> And my good *Genius* [spirit] truely doth it know:
> For what we do presage is not in grosse,
> For we be brethren of the *Rosie Crosse*;
> We have the *Mason word*, and second sight,
> Things for to come we can foretell aright.[59]

It is surely significant that the earliest written reference in England to Second Sight recorded by Michael Hunter, in the diarist John Evelyn's commonplace book, directly follows a discussion on the secretive indication of recognition known as the 'Mason Word', both being mysterious phenomena regarded as peculiarly Scottish.[60] This association is also touched on by the Rev. Robert Kirk in his writings on the Second Sight, while in his correspondence with John Aubrey, the Aberdonian scholar Professor James Garden tellingly equates Second Sight with Rosicrucian esoteric knowledge: 'As strang things are reported with you of the 2nd sighted-men in Scotland, so with us here of the Rosicrucians in England.'[61]

During the late seventeenth century, as the Scottish Gàidhealtachd was increasingly integrated with the rest of the country, cultural brokers from both sides of the Highland Line collected, analysed and disseminated knowledge about the region and its people, their society, customs, practices and beliefs. Prominent in such accounts were anecdotes and conjectures regarding Second Sight. Although these reports were concerned with the Highlands, the actual stimulus for investigations into the phenomenon may have arisen in a quite different part of Scotland: the covenanting western Lowlands.

Michael Hunter has identified Robert Boyle as a crucial collector and circulator of 'matters of fact' regarding Second Sight. Motivated by 'curiosity about the natural world and deep religiosity', Boyle considered trustworthy empirical data regarding preternatural occurrences, retailed by credible informants, as a means of verifying the independent existence of an active spirit world and challenging the disturbing growth in reductive secular materialism and sceptical and iconoclastic 'atheism', notably among metropolitan coffee-house wits. Hunter posits that Boyle's interest in Second Sight was encouraged by an interview he conducted with George Mackenzie of Tarbat in 1678, a period when his letters suggest he was suffering a 'sense of crisis', apprehensive that familiar witchcraft and wonder narratives increasingly lacked credibility as proof of a spirit world. For Boyle, the Highlands offered a region 'where the reality of the preternatural could be soberly and scientifically tested'.[62]

One episode, only briefly touched upon by Hunter, suggests that a growing interest in Second Sight was by no means limited to Scottish magnates and London virtuosi, but was preoccupying all levels of society, particularly in the western Lowlands. This is the notorious, widely reported case of Jonet Douglas, the ostensibly mute adolescent girl whose detection of hidden hex dolls and increasingly reckless denunciations led to seven executions for witchcraft and two suicides in Paisley and Dumbarton in three separate trials in early 1677.[63] Douglas's own occult career was probably informed by the example of William Edmonstone, the deaf and dumb laird of Duntreath in Stirlingshire known for his prophetic and clairvoyant abilities, who was active in nearby Paisley at the same time.[64] The two are linked in the covenanting preacher Robert Law's contemporary account:

> Siclyke, in February 1677, did the dumb Laird of Duntraith, at Pasely, make signs to some of great troubles and fightings to be in this land for a few months. These seem to be presages of sad things following, together with the strange revelations made to the foresaid dumb lass [Jonet Douglas], in discovering witches, seems to be a presage of great alterations.[65]

In April 1677, having recovered her speech, Douglas was imprisoned by the clearly apprehensive authorities in order to test the provenance of her powers. According to Law: 'She declared that she knew not from what spirit, only things were suggested to her, but deny'd that she had any correspondence with Sathan. The best construction that can be put on her, as some think, is that she has the second-sight, by a compact of her parents with the devill, and that she may be passive in it.'[66] This stance was echoed by the lawyer Sir John Lauder:

> If hir knowledge be so strange as its reported to be, its just shee tell whence shee hes it; but if it be an unvoluntar possession, or by a spirit's frequenting of hir, or by the second sight without a paction [i.e. demonic pact], it can never be made criminall; its hir misfortune, to be prayed and fasted against, but not hir guilt, no more then ane infant or madman are punished.[67]

These two quotations highlight the ambiguous nature of Second Sight in the period. Both men appear to favour the notion that young Jonet Douglas acquired the faculty involuntarily, hence blamelessly. One, however, ascribes her ability to a mysterious providence; for the other, it retains a taint of evil, possibly arising from a Satanic pact by her parents. Both Law and Lauder, however, accept that in some cases, perhaps particularly those involving older, more experienced suspects, there at least existed the possibility that Second Sight had been acquired actively and deliberately, through a pact with the Devil.

The widespread notoriety of the Jonet Douglas case suggests that, despite the absence of 'Second Sight' in documentary sources during much of the seventeenth century, the term retained its associations with supernatural perception in popular discourse. Indeed, it may have been given a new lease of life in the context of the theology then espoused by militant Scottish Covenanters in the western Lowlands, sectaries whose belief system was marked by deep-rooted providentialism, ecstatic prophecies, spirit possessions, apocalyptic dreams and visions, confrontations with the Devil and converse with angels. Particularly significant in this respect is the centrality to covenanting theology of 'heart-work', the heightened interior spiritual experience related to the 'Second Sight' extolled by the exiled Presbyterian minister the Rev. Robert McWard in his uplifting tract *The Poor Man's Cup of Cold-Water* (1678): 'O noble look! this is that blessed *second sight*, whereby a Saint, in the darkest night of distress, sees that which is soul-supporting: O! the invisible God made visible to the poor persecuted creature, in his omnipotent power, his infinit love, and his unfailing faithfulnesse, makes all visible dangers evanish into an invisibility.'[68] The salience of covenanting perspectives in the late 1670s may not only have habituated people to the notion of Second Sight, whether specifically as an inner spiritual perception, or more generally as a supernatural ability involving prophecy and clairvoyance. As the case of Jonet Douglas suggests, it may also have awakened popular interest in its purported origins and validity. Given that covenanting theology perceived inner spiritual enlightenment as arising from a personal covenant with the deity, was Second Sight, in its occult sense, thus the result of a comparable contract – and, if so, was the pact with God or Satan?

Three additional observations might be made in conclusion. First, that there are links between the two 'second-sighted' figures depicted above and the covenanting movement. Sir George Maxwell of Pollok, in whose household Jonet Douglas had stayed and concerning whose mortal illness she made her allegations, had been an enthusiastic supporter of the cause, as was Archibald, brother and guardian of William Edmonstone, the prophesying deaf-mute laird of Duntreath.[69]

Second, a tentative observation in passing: given the curiosity among some Freemasons regarding the possibility of achieving spiritual insight through their craft, it may be worth remarking upon the apparent takeover during the 1670s of Kilwinning Lodge by non-operatives – that is, non-stonemasons – with covenanting sympathies. As well as being the most prestigious Masonic lodge, Kilwinning was unique in the extent of its sphere of authority, taking in the strongly covenanting areas of north Ayrshire and Renfrewshire: the very region in which claims of Second Sight were to the fore in the late 1670s.[70]

Finally, and most significant for this chapter, is the fact that although the references examined above originated in the western Lowlands, Second Sight itself was seen as a faculty particularly associated with Highlanders. Jonet Douglas was described by Law as coming 'from the north'. Even more persuasive are the reminiscences of James Nisbet concerning the clairvoyant powers of the pillaging 'Highland Host' upon his family farm in Ayrshire during early 1678:

> Such was their thievish disposition, and so well acquaint were they with the second-sight, that let people hide their goods never so well, yet these Athole and Broad-Albians [i.e. Breadalbane] men would go as right to where it was hid, whether beneath or above the ground, as if they had been at the putting of it there, dig it up, and away with it, rejoicing as though it had been their own.[71]

Contemporary accounts from the end of the 1670s draw attention to the febrile atmosphere of Lowland Scotland, susurrating with reports of apparitions and portents of imminent armed uprising. It is not surprising that Second Sight, however understood, appears as at least a passing topic of discussion in the Scottish political circles in 1678, in conversations involving the Duke of Lauderdale, Sir George Mackenzie of Tarbat, the Earl of Seaforth and John Dalrymple of Stair – as well as, in that very year, Boyle's interview with Tarbat.[72] As has been seen, interest in the phenomenon was far from confined to high political circles. Indeed, as demonstrated by a passing reference in Nathaniel Lee's play *The Princess of Cleve*, first performed in 1680, Second Sight was now recognised beyond Scotland:

> *Poltrot*:
> O he's infallible! why what did you never hear of your second-sight men, your Dumb High-landers that tell Fortunes? why you wou'd think the Devil in Hell were in him, he speaks exactly.
>
> *Elianor*:
> I thought you had said he was Dumb?
>
> *Poltrot*:
> Right, but I am his Interpreter, and when the fit comes on him, he blows through me like a Trunk, and strait I become his speaking Trumpet.[73]

Earlier in the play there is an allusion to 'the Dumb Man, the Highlander that made such a noise': presumably a recent arrival in the capital who was familiar to the theatre audience. It is likely that this 'Highlander' and his interpreter were exploiting the recent notoriety of Second Sight in Scotland, and its specific connection with the Highlands, to carve out an arcane niche for themselves in the wider London fortune-telling market.[74] Lee's mocking aside suggests that Highland Second Sight was already a topic of discussion – and scepticism – in metropolitan street culture at a time of heightened awareness and concern regarding portents and prophecy during the Exclusion Crisis of 1679–81.[75]

The notion of Second Sight as involuntary precognition and clairvoyance may have emerged out of a much broader spectrum of popular supernatural beliefs and practices, including communication with otherwise invisible spirits. This is not to say, of course, that supposedly spontaneous, innate experiences allowing access to the supernatural were unknown before the early modern period. Indeed, the concept of involuntary Second Sight is suprisingly reminiscent of 'alternative blame mechanisms' in popular belief. These include spirit possession or Evil Eye, by which *maleficium* might be ascribed to certain individuals in a locality without necessarily invoking active spiteful intent, so alleviating, if not altogether bringing to an end, disruptive community tensions.[76] The innovative step during the post-Reformation era, I suggest, was the grouping together, under the name of Second Sight, of a variety of passive, supposedly innate experiences and observations involving divination and clairvoyance, at least partly framed in order to circumvent the aggressive stance taken against demonically inspired *maleficia* by religious reformers. Second Sight narratives thus allow us unexpected insights into how the Reformation exerted a lasting influence upon popular beliefs.

Fundamental to Second Sight is an emphasis upon direct, unmediated contact with the supernatural world. In this, the phenomenon might fruitfully be compared to the growth of mysticism across western Europe that reached a peak during the late seventeenth century. Through practising the spiritual techniques associated with the movement, aiming at interiorised, passive interactions with the divine, female visionaries in particular could evade the formal authority of the church and speak out in their own voice.[77] In the distinctive context of Protestant Scotland, incidents of Second Sight are reminiscent of the experiences of the devout seventeenth-century covenanting prophetesses investigated by Louise Yeoman. Their intensely felt visions, articulated in times of crisis, achieved a synthesis of older popular beliefs with an orthodox interpretative framework acceptable to educated clergymen.[78] We have seen how, at the end of the 1670s, heightened concern regarding the proliferation of supposed visionary encounters with the supernatural in Lowland covenanting heartlands may have directed attention to similar experiences in the Gàidhealtachd. Across much of that region, however, above all in the north-west, large parishes in which sermons were poorly attended, and the unavailability of cheap religious material in Gaelic, meant that orthodox ecclesiastical perspectives were only weakly acculturated among the people. As a result, accounts of prognostic or clairvoyant phenomena continued to be interpreted according to older, heterogeneous beliefs, rather than being assimilated to narrowly dualistic theological assumptions and treated as numinous examples of divine providence or diabolic temptation. Such stories also remained part of mundane community discourse. This gave the impression to outsiders that instances of Second Sight were experienced more frequently, and multifariously, in the region, and thus were distinctively Highland in nature.

Clearly, the gender dimension of these issues requires much further analysis. We might note that Second Sight beliefs allowed a voice to non-literate, monoglot Gaelic tenants and servants: in early modern accounts, generally male rather than female visionaries. As with mysticism, Second Sight leaves its believers open to charges of excess credulity and irrational 'enthusiasm'. Indeed, although modern concepts of Second Sight eschew any explanatory framework, they are nevertheless susceptible to the same enduring interpretative impasse as other mystical experiences regarding how inner spiritual perceptions might be discerned, assayed and related to outward reality.

The story of Second Sight from the end of the seventeenth century remains to be traced, a drawn-out process by which earlier models of active engagement with a supernatural other world gradually faded away, leaving the modern concept of an innate, involuntary capacity somehow to see events in the future or, less commonly, at a distance.[79] This shift was facilitated and accelerated by the steady spread of religious orthodoxy, the English language, and the acculturation of influential explanatory frameworks, derived from Martin Martin in particular. Second Sight was redefined as characteristically and exceptionally Highland, exoticised, romanticised and reinterpreted according to outside understandings of what prophecy could and should involve. Comparable processes took place in the eastern Netherlands and north-western Germany: out of a previously diverse, geographically widespread spectrum of beliefs, a notion of involuntary visions was identified and ascribed to a specific region. Seers now not only foresaw death or conflagration, but future technologies, transports and wars: a means of coping with change in a fast-transforming world.

Notes

* For their kind advice and assistance, I should like to thank Abigail Burnyeat, Diarmid Campbell, Mark Jardine, Gordon MacGregor, Louise Yeoman and the late John MacInnes; also the staff of Edinburgh University Library Special Collections, National Library of Scotland, the Royal Society, Sabhal Mòr Ostaig Library and the Archives of the School of Scottish Studies. My

especial gratitude to Julian Goodare and Martha McGill for their guidance, generosity and patience; and to my students at Sabhal Mòr Ostaig for many useful suggestions and observations. The initial research for this chapter was enabled by a British Academy Mid-Career Fellowship.

1 Michael Hunter (ed.), *The Occult Laboratory: Magic, Science, and Second Sight in Late Seventeenth-Century Scotland* (Woodbridge: Boydell, 2001); Michael Hunter, 'The discovery of second sight in late 17th-century Scotland', *History Today*, 51:6 (2001), 48–53; Mario M. Rossi, *Il cappellano delle fate* (Naples: Giannini, 1964), pp. 38–77, 118–23, 139–54, 165–98; Alex Sutherland, *The Brahan Seer: The Making of a Legend* (Oxford: Peter Lang, 2009), pp. 91–125.

2 Michael D. Bailey, *Fearful Spirits, Reasoned Follies: The Boundaries of Superstition in Late Medieval Europe* (Ithaca, NY: Cornell University Press, 2013); Fabián Alejandro Campagne, *Homo Catholicus, Homo Superstitiosus: El discurso antisupersticioso en la España de los siglos XV a XVIII* (Buenos Aires: Miño y Dávila, 2002); Lucie Desjardins, 'Archéologie de la superstition (XVIe–XVIIIe siècles). Histoire des croyances ou histoire littéraire?', *Revue d'histoire littéraire de la France*, 111 (2011), 29–43; Jean-Marie Goulemot, 'Démons, merveilles et philosophie à l'âge classique', *Annales. Histoires, Sciences Sociales*, 35 (1980), 1223–50; Girolamo Imbruglia, 'Dalle storie di santi alla storia naturale della religione: L'idea moderna di superstizione', *Rivista storica italiana*, 101 (1989), 35–84.

3 Moshe Sluhovsky, *Believe Not Every Spirit: Possession, Mysticism, and Discernment in Early Modern Catholicism* (Chicago, IL: Chicago University Press, 2007); Moshe Sluhovsky, 'Rationalizing visions in early modern Catholicism', in Yohanan Friedmann and Christoph Markschies (eds), *Rationalization in Religions: Judaism, Christianity and Islam* (Berlin: De Gruyter, 2019), pp. 127–45; also Stuart Clark, *Vanities of the Eye: Vision in Early Modern European Culture* (Oxford: Oxford University Press, 2007), pp. 1–77, 123–60, 204–35, 266–364; Claire Gantet, *Der Traum in der Frühen Neuzeit: Ansätze zu einer kulturellen Wissenschaftgeschichte* (Berlin: De Gruyter, 2010). For parallels between Second Sight and spirit possession, see Martin Martin, *A Description of the Western Islands of Scotland* (London, 1703), pp. 300, 304, 315–17, 334; Hunter, *Occult Laboratory*, pp. 104–5, 146; Cathaldus Giblin (ed.), *Irish Franciscan Mission to Scotland, 1619–1646: Documents from Roman Archives* (Dublin: Assisi Press), pp. 88–9.

4 Martin, *Description*, pp. 300–35.
5 *Ibid.*, p. 300.
6 *Ibid.*, pp. 302, 304.
7 *Ibid.*, p. 310.
8 *Ibid.*, pp. 303, 318–19, 323–4.
9 *Ibid.*, pp. 304, 305–6.
10 *Ibid.*, pp. 316–17; also Hunter, *Occult Laboratory*, pp. 79–80, 82, 84–7, 89–90, 96, 97, 150.
11 Martin, *Description*, pp. 334–5.
12 Martin Martin, *A Late Voyage to St Kilda* (London, 1698), pp. 156–7 (original emphasis); see also Hunter, *Occult Laboratory*, pp. 82, 107.

13 Royal Society Archives, London, EL M.2.17 (Martin to Hans Sloane, 16 January 1700).
14 Euan Cameron, *Enchanted Europe: Superstition, Reason, and Religion, 1250–1750* (Oxford: Oxford University Press, 2010), p. 42.
15 Karen Cullen, *Famine in Scotland: The 'Ill Years' of the 1690s* (Edinburgh: Edinburgh University Press, 2010), pp. 28–9, 48–9, 86–91, 101–4, 132, 135, 145–50.
16 See J. A. I. Champion, 'Enlightened erudition and the politics of reading in John Toland's circle', *Historical Journal*, 49 (2006), 111–41.
17 See, for example, Stuart Clark, *Thinking with Demons: The Idea of Witchcraft in Early Modern Europe* (Oxford: Clarendon, 1997), pp. 335–88; Andrew Cunningham and Ole Peter Grell, *The Four Horsemen of the Apocalypse: Religion, War, Famine and Death in Reformation Europe* (Cambridge: Cambridge University Press, 2000), pp. 1–91; Crawford Gribben, *Evangelical Millennialism in the Transatlantic World, 1500–2000* (Basingstoke: Palgrave Macmillan, 2011), pp. 20–50; Arthur Hübscher, *Die Grosse Weissagung* (Munich: Heimeran, 1952), pp. 123–34, 141–63, 189–92, 203–10; Reinhart Koselleck, *Futures Past: On the Semantics of Historical Time*, trans. Keith Tribe (New York: Columbia University Press), pp. 9–25; Keith Thomas, *Religion and the Decline of Magic: Studies in Popular Beliefs in Sixteenth- and Seventeenth-Century England* (London: Penguin, 1973 [1971]), pp. 155–73, 461–514; also Michael B. Riordan, 'Scottish political prophecies and the crowns of Britain, 1500–1840', Chapter 7 this volume.
18 John Gregorson Campbell, *The Gaelic Otherworld*, ed. Ronald Black (Edinburgh: Birlinn, 2006), pp. 147–51, 398–409; John MacInnes, 'The seer in Gaelic tradition', in Hilda Ellis Davidson (ed.), *The Seer in Celtic and Other Traditions* (Edinburgh: John Donald, 1989), pp. 10–24, at pp. 21–2; Michael Newton, 'Prophecy and cultural conflict in Gaelic tradition', *Scottish Studies*, 35 (2010), 144–73; also Katherine J. Olsen, '"Earth and sky will be ablaze": the apocalypse, Hell, and judgment in pre-modern Ireland, Scotland, Wales, Cornwall, and Brittany', in Michael A. Ryan (ed.), *A Companion to the Premodern Apocalypse* (Leiden: Brill, 2016), pp. 331–51.
19 Campbell, *Gaelic Otherworld*, pp. 138–46, 392–8; Macinnes, 'The seer', pp. 16–18; see also Hunter, *Occult Laboratory*, pp. 59–60, 88; also Charles Burnett, *Magic and Divination in the Middle Ages* (Aldershot: Variorum, 1996), nos. XII–XVI; Richard Kieckhefer (ed.), *Forbidden Rites: A Necromancer's Manual of the Fifteenth Century* (Stroud: Sutton, 1997), pp. 96–126; Thomas, *Religion and the Decline of Magic*, pp. 282–91; Christa Agnes Tuczay, *Kulturgeschichte der mittelalterlichen Wahrsagerei* (Berlin: De Gruyter, 2012), pp. 119–23, 131–4.
20 Hugh Cheape, 'From natural to supernatural: the material culture of charms and amulets', in Lizanne Henderson (ed.), *Fantastical Imaginations: The Supernatural in Scottish History and Culture* (Edinburgh: John Donald, 2009), pp. 70–90, at pp. 75–80.
21 Andrew Wiseman, 'Caterwauling and demon raising: the ancient rite of the taghairm?', *Scottish Studies*, 35 (2010), 174–208; see also Kieckhefer, *Forbidden Rites*, p. 123n18; Edward Muir, *Ritual in Early Modern Europe* (Cambridge: Cambridge University Press, 2005), p. 145.

22 See in particular, Linda Dégh, *Legend and Belief: Dialectics of a Folklore Genre* (Bloomington, IN: Indiana University Press, 2001).
23 Denmark: Evald Tang Kristensen (ed.), *Danske Sagn, som de har Lydt i Folkemunde* (Århus, 6 vols in 7, 1892–1901), II, pp. 397–420, 456–82. German lands: Gerda Grober-Glück, 'Zur Verbreitung und Deutung des Zweiten Gesichts nach den Sammlungen des Atlas der deutschen Volkskunde', *Zeitschrift für Volkskunde*, 55 (1959), 227–58; Gerda Grober-Glück, 'Geistersichtig', in Rolf Wilhelm Brednich et al. (eds), *Enzyklopädie des Märchens*, 15 vols (Berlin: De Gruyter, 1977–2015), V, cols 1939–44; Will-Erich Peuckert, 'Vorgeschichte', in Hanns Bächtold-Staubli (ed.), *Handwörterbuch des deutschen Aberglaubens*, 10 vols (Berlin: De Gruyter, 1987 [1927–42]), VII, cols 1691–727; Gisbert Stotdrees, 'Das „Zweite Gesicht" in Westfalen', in Jan Carstenen and Gefion Apfel (eds), *"Verflixt!" – Geister, Hexen und Dämonen* (Münster: Waxmann, 2013), pp. 33–44; Gisbert Stotdrees, 'Das Zweite Gesicht', in Lena Krull (ed.), *Westfälische Erinnerungsorte: Beiträge zum kollektiven Gedächtnis einer Region* (Paderborn: Ferdinand Schöningh, 2017), pp. 523–36; see also Annette von Droste-Hülshoff, *Gedichte* (Stuttgart: J. G. Cotta'scher Verlag, 1844), pp. 294–8. Netherlands: Henk Krosenbrink, 'Het tweede gezicht: voorgevoelens en andere toekomstaanduidingen', *Volkscultuur*, 4 (1987), 22–31; S. J. van der Molen, 'Het tweede gezicht', *Neerlands Volksleven*, 17 (1967), 5–77; see also S. P. Scheltema, *Over het Voorgevoel bij den Mensch* (Arnhem: Stenfert Kroese, 1844). Sweden: Bengt af Klintberg, *The Types of the Swedish Folk Legend* (Helsinki: Folklore Fellows, 2010), pp. 32–3, 182, 202, 238, 283–4, 352. Cf. John Brand, *Observations on the Popular Antiquities of Great Britain*, ed. Sir Henry Ellis, 3 vols (London: Henry G. Bohn, 1855), III, pp. 155–60, 227–9, 235, 237–8; John Jamieson, *An Etymological Dictionary of the Scottish Language*, 2 vols (Edinburgh: William Creech, Archibald Constable & William Blackwood, 1808), s.v. 'second-sight', 'wraith'.
24 Markus Denkler, 'Das „Zweite Gesicht" in Westfalen', pp. 45–8; Molen, 'Het tweede gezicht', pp. 33–7; Irmgard Simon, 'Spokenkieker – Spökeding – Füerbedriif: Wörter, Zitate, Redewendungen zum Phänomenon „Vorgeschichte" (Zweites Gesicht) und zu andern gespenstischen Erscheinungen', *Niederdeutsches Wort*, 43 (2003), 369–85.
25 Kristiansen, *Danske Sagn*, II, pp. 541–52; Molen, 'Het tweede gezicht', pp. 13, 15–17, 52–55; Stotdrees, 'Das „Zweite Gesicht"', p. 35.
26 Van der Molen, 'Het tweede gezicht', p. 7; Stotdrees, 'Das „Zweite Gesicht"', pp. 33–4, 35, 40.
27 As sourcebooks, see Claude Lecouteux, *Witches, Werewolves and Fairies* (Rochester, VT: Inner Traditions, 2003); Jan de Vries, *Altgermanische Religionsgeschichte*, 2 vols (Berlin: De Gruyter, 1970 [1956]), I, pp. 220–33.
28 Goulven Madec, 'Savoir c'est voir: Les trois sortes de «vues» selon Augustin', in Goulven Madec, *Lectures augustiniennes* (Paris: Institut d'Études Augustiniennes, 2001), pp. 221–39; also Jesse Keskiaho, *Dreams and Visions in the Early Middle Ages: The Reception and Use of Patristic Ideas, 400–900* (Cambridge: Cambridge University Press, 2015), pp. 137–216; Goulven Madec, 'Porphyre et Augustin: Des trois sortes de «visions» au corps de

résurrection', *Revue d' études augustiniennes et patristiques*, 51 (2005), 233–56; Stéphane Toulouse, 'Influences néoplatoniciennes sur l'analyse Augustinienne des visiones', *Archives de philosophie*, 72 (2009), 225–47.

29 J. R. N. MacPhail (ed.), 'Papers relating to the murder of the Laird of Calder', *Highland Papers*, Vol. 1 (Edinburgh: SHS, 1914), pp. 159–75; Donald Gregory, *The History of the Western Highlands and Isles of Scotland*, 2nd ed. (London: Hamilton, Adams & Co., 1881), pp. 244–61; also Alastair Campbell of Airds, *A History of Clan Campbell*, 3 vols (Edinburgh: Edinburgh University Press, 2002), II, pp. 91–117; Alison Cathcart, *Kinship and Clientage: Highland Clanship, 1451–1609* (Leiden: Brill, 2006), pp. 166–200; Edward J. Cowan, 'Clanship, kinship and the Campbell acquisition of Islay', *SHR*, 53 (1979), 133–44; Nicholas Maclean-Bristol, *Murder Under Trust: The Crimes and Death of Sir Lachlan Mor Maclean of Duart, 1558–1598* (East Linton: Tuckwell, 1999), pp. 100–34.

30 MacPhail, 'Papers', p. 165.

31 *Ibid.*, p. 167.

32 *Ibid.*, p. 163.

33 *Ibid.*, pp. 166–7.

34 *Ibid.*, pp. 160, 165, 166, 167.

35 *Ibid.*, p. 166; see Éva Pócs, 'Church benedictions and popular charms in Hungary' and Dániel Bárth, 'Benediction and exorcism in early modern Hungary', both in James Kapaló, Éva Pócs and William Ryan (eds), *The Power of Words: Studies on Charms and Charming in Europe* (Budapest: Central European University Press, 2013), pp. 165–97, 199–210; Sluhovsky, *Believe Not Every Spirit*, pp. 34–9, 61–4, 91; see also Adolph Franz, *Die kirchlichen Benediktionen im Mittelalter*, 2 vols (Graz: Akademische Druck- und Verlagsanstalt, 1960 [1909]). Mackellars: Duncan Beaton, 'The Clan Mackellar: the early history up to the 18th century', *Scottish Genealogist*, 48:2 (June, 2001), 54; Iain G. MacDonald, *Clerics and Clansmen: The Diocese of Argyll between the Twelfth and Sixteenth Centuries* (Leiden: Brill, 2013), p. 159. Cruachan here is not the mountain, but the township on the west side of Loch Awe.

36 MacPhail, 'Papers', pp. 167–8.

37 See Jane Dawson, 'Calvinism and the Gaidhealtachd in Scotland', in Andrew Pettegree, Alastair Duke and Gillian Lewis (eds), *Calvinism in Europe, 1540–1620* (Cambridge: Cambridge University Press, 1994), pp. 231–53, at pp. 250–1.

38 Diarmid Campbell, 'Was Bishop Carswell's widow a witch?', *West Highland Notes & Queries*, series 4, 13 (June 2020), 18–20; see Cosmo Innes (ed.), *Origines Parochiales Scotiæ* (2 vols in 3, Edinburgh: W. H. Lizars, 1851–5), II(1), pp. 165–6.

39 Donald E. Meek, 'The Reformation and Gaelic culture: perspectives on patronage, language and literature in John Carswell's translation of "The Book of Common Order"', in James Kirk (ed.), *The Church in the Highlands* (Edinburgh: Scottish Church History Society, 1998), p. 55; also Domhnall Uilleam Stiùbhart, 'Carswell, John [Séon Carsuel]', *ODNB*.

40 MacPhail, 'Papers', p. 159.

41 R. L. Thomson (ed.), *Foirm na n-Urrnuidheadh* (Edinburgh: Scottish Gaelic Texts Society, 1970), p. 57, line 1977; John Knox, *Works*, ed. David Laing, 6 vols in 7 (Edinburgh: Bannatyne Club, 1846–64), VI, p. 322.
42 Meek, 'Reformation and Gaelic culture', p. 41.
43 MacPhail, 'Papers', p. 180.
44 *Ibid.*, p. 160.
45 *Maitland Misc.*, II, pp. 187–91; Julian Goodare, 'Visionaries and nature spirits in Scotland', in Bela Mosia (ed.), *Book of Scientific Works of the Conference of Belief Narrative Network of ISFNR 1–4 October 2014, Zugdidi* (Zugdidi: Shota Meshkia State Teaching University of Zugdidi, Georgia, 2015), pp. 102–16, at pp. 109–10; Liv Helene Willumsen, *Witches of the North: Scotland and Finnmark* (Leiden: Brill, 2013), pp. 161–3, 165–8.
46 The term 'Priestgone' that 'the farie man' uses to describe Orkney in Elspeth's confession is so idiosyncratic that it may well be directly recorded from her own speech. Indeed, it appears to be a misunderstanding, by Elspeth or the scribe, of an original 'priest-begone' (full of priests or ministers) analogous to 'woebegone' and to sixteenth-century Scots usages such as 'gold begone' and 'bluid begone'. More straightforward evidence that the confession was delivered in English comes from Elspeth's use of 'a[u]nt' rather than the more specific 'father's/mother's sister' that would be expected were it translated from Gaelic. *Maitland Misc.*, II, pp. 190, 188.
47 For the historical, political and religious context to Elspeth's family connections, see Cathcart, *Kinship and Clientage*, pp. 148–50, 192–5, 197–8; Ross Mackenzie Crawford, 'Warfare in the West Highlands and Isles of Scotland, c.1544–1615' (PhD thesis, University of Glasgow, 2016), pp. 193–206; [John Drummond of Balhaldie], *Memoirs of Sir Ewen Cameron of Locheill* (Edinburgh: Maitland Club, 1842), pp. 36–59; Ruth Grant, 'George Gordon, Sixth Earl of Huntly, and the Politics of the Counter-Reformation in Scotland, 1581–1595' (PhD thesis, University of Edinburgh, 2010), pp. 286–335; Ian Grimble, *Chiefs of Mackay* (London: Routledge & Kegan Paul, 1965), pp. 40–63; Gordon MacGregor, *The Red Book of Scotland*, 10 vols (privately published, 2018), II, pp. 102–5; VIII, pp. 193–4; John H. J. Stewart and Lieutenant Colonel Duncan Stewart, *The Stewarts of Appin* (Edinburgh: privately published, 1880), pp. 109–10.
48 The recommendation to Elspeth that to acquire divinatory powers she should 'Tak ane eg and rost it And take the sweit of it thre Sondays' may have been a private joke between the two men, alluding to the notion that water boiled in eggshells gave one supernatural powers over another, for example in love magic. See Campbell, *Gaelic Otherworld*, pp. 108, 126, 139, 364n354; Joe Neil McNeil, *Sgeul gu latha – Tales until Dawn: The World of a Cape Breton Gaelic Story-Teller*, ed. and trans. John Shaw (Kingston: McGill-Queen's University Press, 1987), pp. 386–7 (no. 24).
49 Mary Mackellar, 'History of the Camerons', *Celtic Magazine*, 8 (1883), 269–74; Alexander MacKenzie, *History of the Camerons* (Inverness: A. & W. Mackenzie, 1884), pp. 48–58; Malcolm Campbell Taylor, '"Tàillear Dubh na Tuaighe" – a Cameron warrior', *Celtic Magazine*, 9 (1884), 525–30, 565–71; also 'Sigma' [?Rev. John Sinclair], 'Tragedy of Clach-nan-Ceann', *Celtic Magazine*, 12 (1887), pp. 392–3; 13 (1888), pp. 153–8, 240, 311–18, 376–82, 444–50.

50 Alasdair Camshron, 'Gormshuil Mhòr na Maighe', *An Gàidheal*, 52:3 (March 1957), pp. 27–8; Mary Mackellar, 'Traditions of Lochaber', *Transactions of the Gaelic Society of Inverness*, 16 (1889–90), 272–6; Norman MacLeod, *Reminiscences of a Highland Parish* (London: Strahan, 1871), pp. 247–50.

51 Note 'Donaldus More MacGillereacht' (*MacGilleRiabhaich*) in the list of parishioners espousing the presentation of John Gordon as parish clerk of Mortlach in 1550, vacant after the demission of his uncle, Master William Gordon, treasurer of Caithness. Joseph Robertson (ed.), *Illustrations of the Topography and Antiquities of the Shires of Aberdeen and Banff*, 4 vols (Aberdeen: Spalding Club, 1847–69), p. 261. This Domhnall Mòr ('Big Donald') is the earliest documented member of a Reoch kindred who appears in Mortlach parish marriage and death records throughout the seventeenth and eighteenth centuries. Elspeth's family might be related to a nineteenth-century Atholl family of 'hereditary ear pipers' originating in Appin. See Bridget Mackenzie, *Piping Traditions of Argyll* (Edinburgh: Birlinn, 2004), pp. 221–2; Lt. John MacLennan, 'Notices of pipers', *Piping Times*, 27:6 (March 1975), 29.

52 *Register of the Privy Council of Scotland*, 1st series, X, pp. xxxiv–xxxvi, 183, 184–91, 235, 250, 274n.5, 276–7, 293, 322–3; Grimble, *Chief of Mackay*, pp. 60, 61.

53 *Maitland Misc.*, II, p. 189.

54 See Sierra Dye, '"Devilische Wordis": Speech as Evidence in Scotland's Witch Trials, 1563–1736' (PhD thesis, University of Guelph, 2016), pp. 236–40; Michael Ostling, 'Introduction: Where've all the good people gone?' in Michael Ostling, (ed.), *Fairies, Demons, and Nature Spirits: 'Small Gods' at the Margins of Christendom* (London: Palgrave Macmillan, 2018), pp. 1–53, at p. 16.

55 W. G. Scott-Moncrieff (ed.), *The Records of the Proceedings of the Justiciary Court of Edinburgh, 1661–1678* (Edinburgh: SHS, 1905), p. 16. My thanks to Dr Louise Yeoman for this reference.

56 Lizanne Henderson, 'The witches of Bute', in Anna Ritchie (ed.), *Historic Bute: Land and People* (Edinburgh: Scottish Society for Northern Studies, 2012), pp. 151–61.

57 Owen Davies, *Cunning-Folk: Popular Magic in English History* (London: Hambledon and London, 2003), pp. 1–20, 29–39; Andrew Sneddon, *Witchcraft and Magic in Ireland* (Basingstoke: Palgrave Macmillan, 2015), pp. 27, 35, 38–52; Thomas, *Religion and the Decline of Magic*, pp. 291–7, 301–18.

58 Clark, *Vanities of the Eye*, pp. 123–60; Wendel B. Craker, 'Spectral evidence, non-spectral acts of witchcraft, and confession at Salem in 1692', *Historical Journal*, 40 (1997), 331–58; see Robert Calef, *More Wonders of the Invisible World* (London, 1700), sig. A4^v; Increase Mather, *A Further Account of the New-England Witches* (London, 1693), pp. 9–10, 12–13; also C. S. Watkins, *History and the Supernatural in Medieval England* (Cambridge: Cambridge University Press, 2007), pp. 140–53, 168–9.

59 Henry Adamson, *The Muses Threnodie* (Edinburgh, 1638), p. 32 (original emphasis). Adamson's 'brethren of the *Rosie Crosse*' refers to the recently publicised notion of the Rosicrucians, a mysterious fraternity said to possess ancient esoteric knowledge.

60 Hunter, *Occult Laboratory*, pp. 3–4, 32 99; David Stevenson, *The Origins of Freemasonry* (Cambridge: Cambridge University Press, 1988), pp. 125–35.
61 Hunter, *Occult Laboratory*, p. 151; also p. 83.
62 Hunter, *Occult Laboratory*, pp. 1–21; see also, for example, William E. Burns, *An Age of Wonders: Prodigies, Providence and Politics in England, 1657–1727* (Manchester: Manchester University Press, 2002), pp. 12–19, 39–45, 57–96, 125–38; Clark, *Thinking with Demons*, pp. 294–311; Michael Hunter, 'The decline of magic: challenge and response in early Enlightenment England', *Historical Journal*, 55 (2012), 399–425; Clare Jackson, *Restoration Scotland, 1660–1690* (Woodbridge: Boydell & Brewer, 2003), pp. 186–90; Colin Kidd, 'The Scottish Enlightenment and the supernatural', in Henderson, *Fantastical Imaginations*, pp. 91–109, at pp. 91–100; Martha McGill, *Ghosts in Enlightenment Scotland* (Woodbridge: Boydell & Brewer, 2018), pp. 49–83, 203–4. Note the gendered character of this 'sober, scientific testing': Second Sight narratives were generally associated with male seers.
63 Joseph Glanvill, *Saducismus Triumphatus* (London, 1681), pp. 291–300; Robert Law, *Memorialls: Or the Memorable Things That Fell Out Within This Island of Britain from 1638 to 1684*, ed. Charles Kirkpatrick Sharpe (Edinburgh: Archibald Constable, 1818), pp. lxxiv–lxxvii, 110–11, 120–34; George Sinclair, *Satans Invisible World Discovered* (Edinburgh, 1685), pp. 1–18, 203–7; also Richard L. Harris, 'Janet Douglas and the witches of Pollock: the background of scepticism in Scotland in the 1670s', in Steven R. McKenna (ed.), *Selected Essays on Scottish Language and Literature: A Festschrift in Honor of Allan H. MacLaine* (Lewiston: Edwin Mellen, 1992), pp. 97–124.
64 Law, *Memorialls*, p. 119.
65 *Ibid.*, p. 130.
66 *Ibid.*, pp. 129–30.
67 *Ibid.*, p. 130n.
68 Rev. Robert McWard, *The Poor Man's Cup of Cold-Water* ([Amsterdam], 1678), p. 4 (original emphasis). See also David Dickson, *Therapeutica Sacra* (Edinburgh, 1664 [1656]), pp. 12, 14–15, 95; Samuel Rutherford, *Influences of the Life of Grace* (London, 1659), pp. 165, 180–8, 215–17; Louise Yeoman, 'Heart-Work: Emotion, Empowerment and Authority in Covenanting Times' (PhD thesis, University of St Andrews, 1991), pp. 54–74, 132–229.
69 Sir William Fraser, *Memoirs of the Maxwells of Pollok*, 2 vols (Edinburgh: privately published, 1863), I, pp. 63–76; Sir Archibald Edmonstone of Duntreath, *Genealogical Account of the Family of Edmonstone of Duntreath* (Edinburgh: privately published, 1875), pp. 49–51.
70 Stevenson, *Origins of Freemasonry*, pp. 193, 200–1; David Stevenson, *The First Freemasons: Scotland's Early Lodges and their Members* (Aberdeen: Aberdeen University Press, 1988), pp. 37–9, 63–74.
71 Law, *Memorialls*, p. 110; James Nisbet, *Private Life of the Persecuted* (Edinburgh: William Oliphant, 1827), pp. 50–1 (my thanks to Dr Mark Jardine for this reference); see Hunter, *Occult Laboratory*, p. 101; Davies, *Cunning-Folk*, pp. 93–101, 174–7; Johannes Dillinger, *Magical Treasure Hunting in Europe and North America* (Basingstoke: Palgrave Macmillan, 2012), pp. 15–20, 61–113, 122–41, 153–63, 166–74, 191–208.

72 Hunter, *Occult Laboratory*, pp. 2, 19, 51–3, 173–5, 177–8, 179.
73 Nathaniel Lee, *The Princess of Cleve* (London, 1689), p. 45.
74 See Jennifer Mori, 'Magic and fate in eighteenth-century London: prosecutions for fortune-telling, c.1678–1830', *Folklore*, 129 (2018), 254–77.
75 Burns, *Age of Wonders*, pp. 97–113.
76 Hunter, *Occult Laboratory*, p. 95; R. C. Maclagan, *Evil Eye in the Western Highlands* (London: David Nutt, 1902), pp. 35–6, 40–2, 68–9; Nancy Caciola, 'Spirits seeking bodies: death, possession and communal memory in the Middle Ages', in Bruce Gordon and Peter Marshall (eds), *The Place of the Dead: Death and Remembrance in Late Medieval and Early Modern Europe* (Cambridge: Cambridge University Press, 2000), pp. 66–86, at pp. 85–6; Watkins, *History and the Supernatural*, pp. 228–34.
77 See, for example, Marie-Florine Bruneau, *Women Mystics Confront the Modern World* (Albany: State University of New York Press, 1998), pp. 4–9, 143–81, 221–5; Sluhovsky, *Believe Not Every Spirit*, pp. 97–136. It may be relevant that Professor James Garden who wrote to Aubrey concerning Highland Second Sight was the elder brother of Dr George Garden who translated works by the French mystic and prophetess Antoinette Bourignon, herself a correspondent of Robert Boyle. The brothers, 'one in outlook', were crucial figures in the Episcopalian Quietist movement in north-east Scotland. Sarah Apetrei, 'Gender, mysticism, and enthuiasm in the British post-Reformation', *Reformation and Renaissance Review*, 17 (2005), 116–28; Mirjam de Barr, *'Ik moet spreken': Het spiritueel leiderschap van Antoinette Bourignon (1616–1680)* (Zutphen: Walburg Pers, 2004), pp. 218–19, 300, 525–8; G. D. Henderson, *Mystics of the North-East* (Aberdeen: Third Spalding Club, 1934); Michael B. Riordan, 'The Episcopalians and the promotion of mysticism in north-east Scotland', *Scottish Church History*, 47 (2018), 31–56.
78 Louise Yeoman, '"Away with the fairies"', in Henderson, *Fantastical Imaginations*, pp. 29–46.
79 For the wider context, see A. J. L. Busst, 'Scottish Second Sight: the rise and fall of a European myth', *European Romantic Review*, 5 (1995), 149–77; Elsa Richardson, *Second Sight in the Nineteenth Century: Prophecy, Imagination and Nationhood* (London: Palgrave Macmillan, 2017).

12

The pagan supernatural in the Scottish Enlightenment

*Felicity Loughlin**

Antiquity held an important place in the Scottish Enlightenment. Throughout the eighteenth century, classical languages and literature were deeply embedded in the curricula of Scotland's universities. Printing presses, such as the Foulis Press in Glasgow, responded to the demand for classical texts and competed to produce the finest editions of Greek and Roman masterpieces.[1] Immersion in the classics inspired many of the literati to publish histories of the laws, governments and customs of ancient nations.[2] This chapter explores an important dimension of this widespread Scottish interest in antiquity, one that has been almost entirely forgotten: the fascination with pagan religious beliefs in supernatural beings and phenomena. It takes as its focus the writings of the many educated Scots who delved into the ancient past, seeking to explain the pagans' conceptions of divinatory oracles, divine power and the invisible world of the afterlife.

Their investigations concentrated primarily on Greek and Roman beliefs. The verses of Pindar and Horace, the epics of Homer and Virgil, the philosophy of the Presocratics and Cicero and many other ancient texts informed the Scots' understanding of pagan religion. Yet, to an eighteenth-century European, 'paganism' meant any religious beliefs and practices that were distinct from the Abrahamic traditions of Christianity, Judaism and Islam. Scottish investigations of pagan antiquity thus extended far beyond Greece and Rome. Herodotus, Plutarch and Strabo were consulted for details of Egyptian, Persian and Indian supernaturalism, while reports of modern pagans in non-European lands supplied deficiencies in the ancient records.

The Scottish literati's fascination with the pagan gods was shared by thinkers across Europe.[3] Indeed, eighteenth-century Scots were participating in debates that dated back to the late Roman Empire, when the Church Fathers had fought to secure the triumph of Christianity over the pagan establishment. In the eighteenth century, as in late antiquity, explorations of pagan supernaturalism were by no means the product of disinterested scholarly curiosity. On the contrary, they were propelled by a desire to answer some of the most pressing religious and philosophical questions of the age. Foremost among these problems was where to draw the boundaries between acceptable and reprehensible beliefs in the supernatural. As Colin Kidd has noted, Christianity remained the officially sanctioned form of supernaturalism in Enlightenment Scotland, but the respectability of certain ideas within the Christian tradition – including the existence of ghosts, claims of immediate divine inspiration and the miraculous intervention of God in present-day human affairs – was hotly disputed. Debates over these issues not only separated Christian thinkers from radical freethinkers, deists and sceptics, but also created divisions between Scottish Christians.[4]

Here, I wish to draw attention to the importance of pagan religion in the Scottish literati's attempts to define and defend true supernaturalism. I begin by exploring interpretations of the pagan oracles, which interested many Scottish thinkers in the first half of the eighteenth century. How did they explain the oracular pronouncements? How did these explanations contribute to redefining understandings of the supernatural realm in Scottish intellectual culture? In the remainder of the chapter, I focus on Scottish interpretations of the pagans' beliefs in divine power and the afterlife. Why did these elements of paganism continue to intrigue the literati throughout the century? Why were they deemed important in contemporary religious debates? And how far did Scottish thinkers reach a consensus in their evaluation of pagan supernaturalism?

At the turn of the eighteenth century, the pagan oracles played an important role in Scottish religious apologetics. This was not the first time the oracular prophecies had been called upon to defend the truth of Christianity. In late antiquity, it had been imperative for the early Christians to offer a new explanation of the oracles. How could their prophecies be explained if the gods deemed to inspire them were false? The Church Fathers had taken their lead from pagan philosophers, who had noted the ambiguity of the oracles, debated their efficacy and put forward varying accounts of the oracular prophecies.[5] These explanations included the inspiration of spirits or *daemones*, the effects of natural vapours at Delphi, and priestly imposture. Christians of late antiquity also seized upon pagan reports that the oracles were declining, a phenomenon that they presented as a contingent effect of Christ's appearance in the world.[6]

Lecture notes taken by students of metaphysics at Scottish universities in the late seventeenth and early eighteenth centuries reveal that several of these theories remained influential. Most notably, the pagan oracles were often explained as the work of evil spirits or *daemones*, who were identified as *mali angeli* – wicked angels, understood to be 'demons' in Christian terms.[7] For the Scottish regents (lecturers), the oracles were thus imbued with apologetic significance because they appeared to prove the existence of an immaterial spiritual realm. This fundamental Christian assumption had been controversially attacked by radical materialists of the seventeenth century, most notoriously Thomas Hobbes and Baruch Spinoza.[8] It was in this context therefore that Peter Rae, a student of John Law at Glasgow University, recorded in 1693 that the pagan oracles could scarcely be explained if invisible substances such as angels or demons did not exist.[9] Anonymous notes by a student of 1695 similarly stated that the oracular prophecies had probably been produced by wicked angels.[10] James Craig, a student of John Loudon at Glasgow, recorded in 1700 that the wondrous effects of the pagan oracles had been brought about by evil agents with superhuman powers, which proved the existence of wicked and, by extension, good angels.[11]

Explanations of the pagan oracles were also deployed to combat other erroneous understandings of the supernatural realm. A central target was deism, which posited a non-interventionist deity in place of the Christian god and undermined the authority of the Christian Scriptures. In 1723, the minister of Paisley Abbey, Robert Millar, rejoiced at the 'death and departure of those *Daemons* which presided over the oracles', who had disappeared at the coming of Christ.[12] For Millar, as for the early Christian scholar Eusebius, the flight of these demonic spirits upon Christ's appearance was a 'great argument' against contemporary infidels in favour of 'our Saviour's divinity, and the truth of his doctrine'.[13] For fellow minister James Bell, writing in 1737, the 'pretended miracles' of the pagan oracles served to bring into sharper relief the true miracles of the Christian God. Bell adamantly denied the efficacy of the oracular pronouncements. Those that had proven to be correct had never constituted true prophecies like those contained in the Scriptures. They were either lucky guesses or reports of current affairs communicated in real time by evil spirits. These spirits did not have divinatory powers; they were merely able to carry knowledge of events 'in a moment, from distant places, where the things themselves were a doing'.[14] Bell hoped that arguments of this kind would combat the 'confederacy' of contemporary freethinkers, who aimed to 'destroy the credit and truth of divine revelation' and to make Scots 'lay aside the name and character of christians, for that of good moral pagans'.[15]

Yet by the 1730s, supernatural explanations of the oracles' prophecies as the workings of demonic spirits faced competition: a naturalistic theory now attributed them to human imposture. This theory received its fullest development from Thomas Blackwell, Professor of Greek at Marischal College in Aberdeen, in his *Enquiry into the Life and Writings of Homer* (1735). He argued that the oracles had been invented by wise lawgivers, skilled in the arts of government, who had possessed a wide knowledge of foreign lands that enabled them to appear to make probable prophecies concerning them. For Blackwell, the Cretans, under the rule of King

Minos, were therefore the most likely promulgators of the oracles in Greece, having previously taken the idea from the Egyptians.[16] Indicative of the growing interest in naturalistic explanations of the oracles is the publication of a new edition of Stephen Whatley's English translation of Fontenelle's *Histoire des oracles* (1686) in Glasgow in 1753.[17] Fontenelle, following the Dutch scholar Antonie van Dale, had controversially presented the oracles as the work of deceitful priests who had used secret technologies to assist them in duping the population, including concealed trumpets that distorted and projected the voice of the oracular priestess.[18] The publication of this Glasgow edition suggests that by mid-century the Scottish literati were catching up with earlier European trends.

The conceptual shift in Scottish understandings of the pagan oracles is most apparent in contemporary responses to *The History of Croesus*, published anonymously by the minister Walter Anderson in 1755. Croesus, king of ancient Lydia, had notoriously lost his empire by misinterpreting an ambiguous oracular prediction. Anderson's history began by surveying existing explanations of the pagan oracles in a way that had long been conventional, noting that the 'pens of the learned' had been much employed in debating whether the oracular responses 'are to be altogether regarded as the artful devices of the priests, or as dictated by daemons, and spirits more intelligent than men'.[19] In Anderson's view, few if any of the pagan oracles could be described as truly 'miraculous'.[20] He nevertheless suggested that too much confidence had lately been placed in theories attributing every oracle to the 'craftiness of imposture'.[21] It was important to remember, he argued, that early human societies were 'rude and unexperienced', and *all* their inhabitants were 'certainly as apt to be themselves the dupes of delusion, as to delude others'.[22] Even the priests were initially incapable of abandoning their 'religious fear' and deceiving the rest of the population. For Anderson, the general ignorance of ancient societies suggested that 'daemonism itself' was at least a plausible explanation of the oracles' prophecies.[23]

By 1755, however, consideration of the very possibility that oracular predictions had been produced by demons met with opposition. Anderson's critics regarded it as superfluous to resort to supernatural beings to explain these unusual phenomena; plausible natural explanations could readily be supplied. For one anonymous English reviewer, Anderson's work was patently outdated:

> What could be more unnecessary ... than a detail of reasons for doubting the divinity or daemoniacism of the ancient oracles? Who believes, at this time of day, that they were either inspired by the deity, or influenced by the devil? What can be more superfluous than a minute commentary and investigation of the absurdities in the plea of the priestess, when she was taxed with falsehood and equivocation?[24]

The reviewer took the opportunity not only to discredit Anderson's endeavour, but to take a gibe at two additional targets, the Scots and the Presbyterian establishment:

> But, we must beg our author's pardon; he wrote for readers that dwell beyond the *Tweed*, who have not yet renounced all commerce with those familiar spirits, which are so totally discarded from this part of the island. There is still a race of soothsayers in the *Highlands*, derived if we may believe some curious antiquarians, from the *Druids* and *Bards*, who were set apart for the worship of *Apollo*. The author of the history now before us, may, for ought we know, be one of those venerable seers, tho' we rather take him to be a Presbyterian teacher, who has been used to expound apothegms that needed no explanation.[25]

William Robertson, one of the most prominent clerics in the Moderate Party of the Church of Scotland, did not share the anonymous reviewer's disdain for Presbyterianism, nor his wish to associate all Scots with barbarous Highlanders. Nevertheless, he agreed that Anderson's subject was inappropriate for serious historical study. For Robertson, Anderson's history possessed 'an air and character which will appear uncouth to a modern reader: oracles, dreams, prodigies, miraculous interpositions of the gods, and no less miraculous instances of credulity and folly among men, are the objects perpetually before him'.[26] He regretted that the 'rage of reading novels, which has spread so wonderfully over Britain', might have 'accustomed the public ear to such improbabilities'.[27] Robertson himself took the view that the 'fond desire of prying into futurity' was simply a staple feature of pagan superstition, which had been encouraged by deceitful priests, who 'as the ministers of Heaven, pretend to deliver its oracles to men'.[28]

By the 1750s, therefore, Scottish thinkers increasingly favoured naturalistic accounts of the oracles over supernatural explanations that attributed them to evil spirits. In this case, enquiries into paganism contributed to the declining respectability of explanations of historical change that appealed to the direct intervention of supernatural beings. In the process of disenchantment, the oracles also lost much of their importance in the fight against materialism and deism and attracted far less scholarly attention.

While the oracles largely disappeared from Scottish investigations of pagan supernaturalism, pagan conceptions of divine power and the afterlife remained objects of serious study. For orthodox Presbyterians, these ideas corresponded to the two principles of 'natural religion': the existence and attributes of God and the immortality of the soul. In their view, these fundamental *supernatural* truths were discoverable by the 'light of nature': the *natural* powers of human reason. It was evident, they argued, that the harmonious order displayed in the universe proclaimed to all rational beings the existence of a benevolent, almighty and providential creator.[29] In the same way, reason revealed that spiritual substances such as the soul were immaterial and therefore exempt from the death and decay of material bodies.[30]

Nevertheless, the orthodox asserted that reason could not discover all supernatural truths. Enlightenment of this kind could only stem from knowledge of the divine revelation recorded in the Scriptures. Above all, the orthodox made it clear that natural knowledge of God and the afterlife were insufficient for salvation. It was only through sincere faith in the message of the Bible, with its record of Christ's teachings, miracles and redemptive sacrifice, that individuals could hope to be saved.[31]

In the early decades of the eighteenth century, however, this orthodox position on natural religion was challenged by deist thinkers, including Charles Blount, John Toland, Anthony Collins and Matthew Tindal. The deists did not agree on the precise tenets of natural religion, but they shared the view that only the supernatural truths discernible by the natural powers of reason were necessary for human happiness and salvation.[32] As Wayne Hudson has shown, all deists therefore entertained the possibility that revealed religions such as Christianity were in fact superstitions, which had been perpetuated by deceitful and self-interested clerical classes.[33] Indeed, many deists concluded that the Christian Scriptures were erroneous fables or, at best, surplus to requirements.

Amid the challenge of deism, natural religion became a central point of theological divergence within the Church of Scotland. As Thomas Ahnert has shown, from the 1720s several heterodox ministers within the Kirk expressed doubts over the natural ability of human reason to discover supernatural truths.[34] From the 1750s, the very possibility of natural religion was similarly questioned by the Moderates, who dominated the Kirk until the end of the century. Indeed, as Ahnert has suggested, the Moderates' doubts over the religious powers of human reason brought them closer to the more extreme sceptical philosophy of David Hume, who argued that reason was entirely unable to prove the existence of God and the afterlife.[35]

These disagreements over natural religion imbued ancient paganism with new relevance and importance. As historical examples of human beings who had lacked access to divine revelation, the pagans presented an opportunity to prove the relationship between natural human reason and knowledge of the supernatural realm. To meet the challenge of natural religion, it was vital to understand how the ancient pagans had conceptualised supernatural power and the afterlife.

It was generally agreed that most pagans had been misled by a superstitious, irrational and erroneous polytheism, believing in multiple deities with powers over specific spheres of life. The perceived irrationality of polytheism stemmed from the idea that the regular, general laws that operated in the natural world necessarily favoured a belief in a single, omnipotent deity who created and governed the world. Thus the judge and politician Duncan Forbes of Culloden, writing in 1732, found it striking that 'all the antient nations entered readily into the belief of a *Plurality* of Deities, how contrary soever the opinion might be to *the light of Nature*'.[36] Egyptian polytheism tended to be regarded as the most absurd of all forms of paganism on account of the bestial forms of some of its deities. Robert Millar's *Propagation of Christianity* (1723) argued that although 'the *Egyptians* were reputed the wisest of the Gentiles, yet they appear in their religious worship of beasts, to have acted contrary to common sense', and pointed out that the 'very heathens' of Greece and Rome 'ridiculed this kind of idolatry'.[37] The antiquarian Sir John Clerk of Penicuik similarly regarded the Egyptians' devotion to their bestial gods as 'stupid to the highest degree'.[38]

Scottish writers of the second half of the century were also struck by the irrationality of polytheistic pagan beliefs. Lord Kames, David Hume, William Robertson and Lord Monboddo, among others, equated polytheism with barbarism.[39] They argued that the first polytheistic societies were likely to have been primitive communities, beset by toil and labour, which did not possess the rational abilities required for monotheism.[40] For Robertson, the belief in multiple deities could never proceed from reason or philosophy. Polytheism was the product of 'rude' societies whose inhabitants had 'neither the leisure nor capacity for entering into that path of intricate and refined speculation, which conducts to the knowledge of the principles of rational religion'.[41]

While the polytheism of the pagan masses was generally viewed as an irrational and reprehensible form of supernaturalism, opinion was divided over the theology of the pagan philosophers. How far had the pagan elite, whose philosophical achievements the Scottish literati so admired, attained knowledge of God's existence and attributes? This enquiry had considerable significance in debates over natural religion. If the wise philosophers of antiquity had been unable to discover this fundamental principle through rational enquiry, the possibility of natural religion would appear negligible.

The heterodox minister and professor, Archibald Campbell, tackled this subject in his *Necessity of Revelation* (1739). He demonstrated that most pagan philosophers of Greece and Rome, despite their great wisdom and detailed enquiries into the origin of the world, had never discovered the true God.[42] On the contrary, most had deified the sun, moon and stars. Only Anaxagoras, Socrates and Plato had acknowledged a deity that corresponded to the Christian belief in an eternal, incorporeal God. Yet even these wise philosophers had been unable to give convincing reasons for this belief, and had relied on tradition for their knowledge of this truth.⁴³ In Campbell's view, the philosophers' inability to offer rational proofs of the deity's existence demonstrated that this traditional knowledge must originally have stemmed from supernatural revelation and probably dated back to God's instruction of Noah after the biblical Flood.⁴⁴ The pagan past therefore provided valuable evidence, against both the deists and the orthodox Presbyterians, of the severe limits of the religious powers of human reason and of the absolute necessity of divine revelation in guiding human beings to even the most fundamental supernatural knowledge.

Faced with Campbell's attack on the very possibility of natural religion, the student and future minister John Erskine published a pamphlet reaffirming the orthodox position.⁴⁵ He accepted that Campbell's historical study proved that 'some nations and persons have, notwithstanding their natural reason, been ignorant of the great truths of natural religion', which he welcomed as proof of 'the great benefit the world has received from Christianity'.⁴⁶ Nevertheless, Erskine profoundly disagreed with Campbell's suggestion that reason was incapable of discovering God's existence and key attributes. In Erskine's view, God had 'afforded the Heathen world such advantages' for the discovery of these truths, 'that their ignorance or disbelief of them could be owing to nothing but their own negligence or perverseness'.⁴⁷ After all, the Scriptures themselves testified that the works of Creation were sufficient to lead humankind to knowledge of God's power and providence.⁴⁸ Faced with a lack of written evidence that any Greek or Roman pagan philosopher had deduced the principles of natural religion, Erskine conjectured that some had concealed their knowledge through fear of opposing popular religious prejudices, a course of conduct that he regarded as 'mean and dastardly'.⁴⁹

Despite Erskine's rebuttal, other Scots continued to dispute the ability of even the wisest pagans to attain knowledge of God through reason alone. Thomas Blackwell argued in 1748 that although the Greek philosophers, through their detailed knowledge of natural philosophy, came to believe in some form of supreme divine power, they never had any conception of a creator deity akin to the Christian God.⁵⁰ Like Campbell, Blackwell stressed the necessity of supernatural revelation in leading humanity to the truth of such a deity's existence.⁵¹

While David Hume's religious scepticism set him apart from most of his contemporaries, he shared the view that paganism proved the deficiencies of human reason in discovering the existence and attributes of the deity. His *Natural History of Religion* (1757) asserted that although the Greek and Roman philosophers had enquired into the origins and nature of the world, 'it was pretty late ... before these bethought themselves of having recourse to a mind or supreme intelligence, as the first cause of all'.⁵² On the contrary, most pagan philosophers had accounted for the origin of the world without a deity and still believed in the power of fate over the gods.[53] Indeed, Hume went so far as to claim that the pagan philosophers' conception of divine power was so deficient that 'it is great complaisance, indeed, if we dignify with the name of religion such an imperfect system of theology and put it on a level with latter systems, which are founded on principles more just and more sublime'.[54] That the wise philosophers were unable to reason God's existence from the natural world left little chance that the 'common people' would ever 'push their researches far, or derive from reasoning their systems of religion'.[55] Hume did not yoke his account of pagan religion to a defence of the authority or necessity of divine revelation. On the contrary, his *Natural History of Religion* offered a provocative challenge to the perceived superiority of Christianity over other religious traditions.[56] Yet his assertion of the limits of reason in the discovery or proof of the Christian deity's existence and attributes was corroborated by several of his contemporaries.

Thus, William Robertson regarded the pagan past as providing evidence to doubt the extent to which the natural powers of human reason could discover God.[57] He conceded that rational observation of the general laws that governed the universe could lead individuals to acknowledge the existence of a supreme creator deity. Nevertheless, he emphasised the great struggle involved in arriving at this fundamental truth without the aid of supernatural revelation. His *History of America* asserted that the concept of a divine creator was more complex than many appreciated: 'The idea of Creation is so familiar, wherever the mind is enlarged by science, and illuminated with revelation, that we seldom reflect how profound and abstruse this idea is, or consider what progress man must have made before he could arrive at this elementary principle in religion.'[58] It was only when pagan societies had begun to make advances in science, he suggested, that their philosophers had acquired the rational principles required to become monotheists. He was particularly impressed by the Indian and Greek philosophers, whose observations of 'the wisdom, the foresight, and the goodness displayed in preserving, and governing the world' had led them to 'ideas concerning the perfections of the one Supreme Being, the Creator and Ruler of the universe, as just and rational as have ever been attained by the unassisted powers of the human mind'.[59] Yet he pointed out that even these wise philosophers had erroneously believed that God was a 'vivifying principle' diffused throughout Creation, rather than a distinct divine entity.[60] Such deficiencies in their understanding of God led Robertson to assert that 'so unable are the limited powers of the human mind to form an adequate idea of the perfections and operations of the Supreme Being, that in all the theories concerning them, of the most eminent philosophers in the most enlightened nations, we find a lamentable mixture of ignorance and error'.[61] The literati's investigations into pagan religious history therefore cast considerable doubt on the extent to which reason could lead humanity to knowledge of God's existence and attributes. Many were struck by the absence or deficiencies of these beliefs in the theology of the pagan philosophers. Blackwell and Robertson granted that a few exceptional pagan thinkers had acquired basic knowledge of a supreme deity through rational enquiry. Campbell and Hume were more sceptical and denied that reason had led any pagan philosophers to this belief. Pagan supernaturalism thus set many of the Scottish literati against the orthodox and deistic view of the natural ability of human reason to discover the true God. With the exception of Hume, these thinkers instead regarded the pagan past as proof of the vastly superior supernatural knowledge provided by the divinely inspired Christian Scriptures.

Pagan conceptions of a future state provided further opportunities for Scottish thinkers to test the limits of natural religion.[62] The works of classical antiquity, combined with reports of modern paganism in non-European lands, seemed to prove that most pagans had some conception of an afterlife. The extent to which these beliefs derived from rational enquiry, however, was contested. As we have seen, orthodox Calvinists and many deists were confident that reason could lead humans to knowledge of the soul's immortality. The pagans' beliefs in the afterlife thus had important ramifications on attempts to unravel the religious powers of human nature.

Archibald Campbell argued that although several wise philosophers of Greece and Rome had believed in an afterlife, they did not owe this belief to reason. He began his discussion with Socrates, whom he regarded as 'the most distinguished philosopher that ever was in the world' and the first to attempt to explain the soul's immortality.[63] He argued that Socrates's defence of this teaching was fundamentally flawed. Far from offering a convincing rational demonstration of the soul's immortality, the great Athenian philosopher was 'much like a man, who without all sort of reasoning has somewhere or other picked up a truth, but can give no account of it'.[64] Nor could better explanations be found among other pagan philosophers who believed in the afterlife.[65] Campbell concluded that the pagans' belief in the immortality of the soul, like their knowledge of God, stemmed from dim recollections of the original supernatural revelation granted to Noah.[66] Pagan discussions of the immortality of the soul thus proved that '*over-wise gentlemen*' like the deists had been gravely mistaken in their endeavour to 'zealously condemn all *supernatural revelation* as quite needless'.[67]

John Erskine was unconvinced by Campbell's arguments.[68] In his pamphlet of 1741, he upheld the orthodox line that the incorporeality of the soul had provided philosophers such as Thales, Anaxagoras and Plato with sufficient evidence to deduce its immortality.[69] Though he acknowledged that several pagan philosophers had mistakenly believed in the transmigration of the soul, an error that he regarded as the product of 'a roving imagination', he concluded that their belief in the soul's immortality was nevertheless fundamentally rational.[70]

Campbell was not the only thinker to depart from the orthodox position on reason's ability to discover the true nature of the soul and the existence of an afterlife. Nor was this debate restricted to the Presbyterian clergy. Andrew Ramsay, a Scottish convert to Catholicism, similarly argued that pagan knowledge of the soul's immortality originated in recollections of God's revelation of supernatural truths to Noah after the Flood.[71] Only the shared Noevian origins of the pagans' religious traditions could explain their universal knowledge of this supernatural truth. Yet Ramsay's development of this argument was highly eccentric. He argued that even pagan beliefs in the pre-existence of the soul, which were generally regarded as erroneous, stemmed from the Noevian tradition. Controversially, he asserted that this fact enabled the pagan tradition to shed light on the correct interpretation of the Book of Genesis, which he regarded as an abridged version of an earlier account. In Ramsay's view, the text implied that all human souls had pre-existed in paradise, had sinned alongside Adam and Eve, their common parents, and had been punished for their disobedience by imprisonment in mortal bodies.[72] Following a long period of purgation, all human souls would be purified at the Last Judgement and return to their pre-existent paradisiacal state.

For Ramsay, only this interpretation of the Fall was conformable to our knowledge of the deity's benevolence. He defended this unorthodox teaching by asserting that these divinely revealed ideas had been preserved to varying degrees by all pagan traditions. He therefore cited passages that he perceived as allusions to the pre-existence, corruption and restoration of human souls in recent translations of Chinese and Indian sacred texts, and in a host of works by Greek and Roman philosophers and poets, particularly Pythagoras and Orpheus.[73] Similarly, he argued that the pagan tradition revealed the true fate of the souls of fallen angels, who were traditionally thought to be fated to suffer eternal damnation. According to Ramsay, the Book of Genesis indicated that their souls had been forced to inhabit bestial bodies as punishment for their rebellion against God but would, after a long period of transmigration, be sufficiently purged and readmitted to paradise at the Last Judgement.[74] He justified this reading by appealing to pagan references to the transmigration of the soul, which he similarly presented as dim recollections of divinely revealed truths.[75]

From both Catholic and Protestant perspectives, Ramsay's views on the soul's pre-existence and the transmigration of the souls of fallen angels were highly unorthodox.[76] Yet Ramsay's denial that reason had informed the pagans' knowledge of the human soul and the future state was shared by other Scots. For Thomas Blackwell, the philosophical wisdom of the pagan elite had not led them to discover the soul's immortality. On the contrary, pagan philosophers had only invented stories of divine judgement and the afterlife in order to promote moral conduct among the masses.[77] David Hume similarly doubted the extent to which the pagan philosophers had been persuaded of the soul's immortality, pointing out that Cicero, Seneca and Plato had regarded the eternal terrors of the afterlife as childish fables.[78]

William Robertson also departed from the orthodox position on the ability of reason to discern this fundamental supernatural truth. He argued in his *History of America* that although pagan Amerindian tribes believed in a future state, their inferior rational capacities proved that this notion had arisen from an innate feeling, a 'sentiment, resulting from a secret consciousness of its own dignity, from an instinctive longing for immortality'.[79] The non-rational foundation of this belief was evident from their corporeal conceptions of the afterlife, which were manifested in the custom of burying weapons, domestic goods, servants and wives with deceased warriors and hunters.[80] Robertson also argued that even the wisest pagan philosophers, the Stoics and the Brahmins, had been impeded by their lack of access to revelation, which had led them to adopt the false belief in the transmigration of the soul.[81]

Throughout the eighteenth century, therefore, the orthodox Presbyterian view that the natural powers of reason were perfectly capable of discovering the soul's immortality came under significant scrutiny. Pagan religion played an important role in this critique. For many of the literati, the pagans' views on the nature of the soul or the afterlife provided powerful historical evidence of the severe limits of human reason in attaining true knowledge of the supernatural. For the majority, this did not threaten their belief in a future state. On the contrary, it merely brought the superior nature of Christian supernaturalism, and the importance of divine revelation, into sharper perspective.

As we have seen, pagan visions of the supernatural world excited Scottish intellectuals throughout the eighteenth century. The pagans' oracles, gods and conceptions of the afterlife formed an important part of attempts to define and defend appropriate attitudes towards the supernatural. In the case of the oracles, the rise of naturalistic theories attributing their powers to human imposture contributed to the declining respectability of supernatural explanations that ascribed their pronouncements to demonic spirits. This explanatory shift furthered the banishment of demons from scholarly accounts of events in the natural world. It also meant that the oracles lost their previous significance in defending the supernatural realm against the aspersions of materialists and atheists.

In contrast, pagan beliefs in divine power and the afterlife continued to engage the Scottish literati throughout the century, and remained central to the religious debates of the Enlightenment. Here we see no shift from 'supernatural' to 'natural' explanation, but the deployment of *incorrect* pagan supernaturalism to vindicate *correct* Christian supernaturalism. For most Scottish thinkers, both orthodox and heterodox, the superstitious polytheism of the pagan masses proved that the supernatural assistance of divine revelation offered Christians a distinct advantage in reaching an accurate understanding of the supernatural world. Pagan religion thus demonstrated the virtues of revealed religion over the rational religion of the deists or the irreligion of the atheists.

Despite this general consensus, the Scots were deeply divided over the question of whether it was even possible for pagans to discover the fundamental principles of Christian supernaturalism through the natural powers of the human mind. According to orthodox Presbyterians, reason was able to guide all humans to knowledge of God and the soul's immortality. Pagans who failed to acknowledge these principles were therefore negligent or deliberately wicked. For these thinkers, natural religion thus represented an intermediate stage between complete ignorance of supernatural reality and the greater enlightenment provided by the Christian Scriptures – which, moreover, offered the only hope of salvation.

Yet for many heterodox thinkers, the inability of the pagan philosophers to deduce fundamental Christian principles through reason proved that natural religion was very difficult, if not impossible, to obtain. For a sceptic such as Hume, paganism demonstrated that the best course of action was to accept that knowledge of God and the afterlife must necessarily remain a mystery, beyond rational demonstration. Yet for the majority who disagreed with the orthodox position on natural religion, paganism demonstrated that the advantages of supernatural revelation were even greater than the Calvinist creed suggested. For this group, pagan beliefs in divine power and the afterlife widened the gulf they perceived between true and false supernaturalism. The findings of the present chapter therefore indicate that substantial modifications are required in existing accounts of the European Enlightenment, which trace a direct line between investigations of non-Christian religions and the devaluation of Christianity.[82] They also suggest that future scholarship on Enlightenment Scotland must engage seriously with Thomas Ahnert's recent work, which has shown that the literati's confidence in the powers of reason was far more circumscribed than has previously been recognised and that theological concerns continued to occupy a central place in contemporary debates.[83] Indeed, the Scots' histories of paganism reveal that a commitment to Christian supernaturalism remained a vital force in the intellectual life of the Scottish Enlightenment.

Notes

* I would like to thank Professor Thomas Ahnert, Professor Stewart J. Brown, Professor Colin Kidd and Dr Felicity Green for stimulating discussions on this topic.

1 Brian Hillyard, 'The Glasgow Homer', in Stephen W. Brown and Warren McDougall (eds), *The Edinburgh History of the Book in Scotland, Vol. 2: Enlightenment and Expansion, 1707–1800* (Edinburgh: Edinburgh University Press, 2012), pp. 69–88.
2 See, for example, Colin Kidd, 'The Scottish Enlightenment and the matter of Troy', *Journal of the British Academy*, 6 (2018), 97–130.
3 The classic study remains Frank E. Manuel, *The Eighteenth Century Confronts the Gods* (Cambridge, MA: Harvard University Press, 1959). See also Urs App, *The Birth of Orientalism* (Philadelphia, PA: University of Pennsylvania Press, 2010); Guy G. Stroumsa, *A New Science: The Discovery of Religion in the Age of Reason* (Cambridge, MA: Harvard University Press, 2010), pp. 77–123, 145–57; Burton Feldman and Robert D. Richardson, *The Rise of Modern Mythology, 1680–1860* (Bloomington, IN: Indiana University Press, 1972). On Britain, see Colin Kidd, *The World of Mr Casaubon: Britain's Wars of Mythography, 1700–1870* (Cambridge: Cambridge University Press, 2016). On Scotland, see Felicity Loughlin, 'Religion, Erudition, and Enlightenment: Histories of Paganism in Eighteenth-Century Scotland' (PhD thesis, University of Edinburgh, 2017).
4 Colin Kidd, 'The Scottish Enlightenment and the supernatural', in Lizanne Henderson (ed.), *Fantastical Imaginations: The Supernatural in Scottish History and Culture* (Edinburgh: John Donald, 2009), pp. 91–109.
5 Particularly influential was Cicero's *De Divinatione*. For a lucid overview of pagan and patristic discussions of the oracles, see Anthony Ossa-Richardson, *The Devil's Tabernacle: The Pagan Oracles in Early Modern Thought* (Princeton, NJ: Princeton University Press, 2013), pp. 13–45. For more on political prophecies see Michael B. Riordan, 'Scottish political prophecies and the crowns of Britain, 1500–1840', Chapter 7 this volume.
6 Ossa-Richardson, *The Devil's Tabernacle*, pp. 21–2.
7 I am grateful to Dr Martha McGill for drawing these lecture notes to my attention.
8 On Scottish concerns over materialism, see Kidd, 'The Scottish Enlightenment and the supernatural', pp. 94–5.
9 'Certus est ... angelos existere ... oracula ne vix quidem explicari possunt nisi substantias quasdam invisibles quas angelos vocamus aut Demones agnoscamus.' EUL, MS Dc.8.18, p. 9.
10 'Malos itaque Angelos ... probari poterit ex ... praedictione futurorum ab Oraculis Ethnicorum, in quibus nihil probabilius quam a Daemone datam fuisse responsionem.' St Andrews University Library, MS BC59.S1, fo. 264.
11 'Angelorum existentiam probant philosophi ... a miris effectis editis olim apud Ethnicos ab oraculis ... quodque ... saepe dici nequeant a Deo proficisci sed a malo aliquo agente, cui sit potentia supra vires humanas, hinc concludunt Angelos malos: si autem sunt mali etiam agnoscendi sunt boni; cum ipsi hi mali ab initio boni necessario sint agnoscendi.' Glasgow University Library, MS Murray 49, fo. 88. Loudon first gave this lecture at the University of St Andrews, where he taught from 1695 until he moved to Glasgow in 1699. See the notes of John Craigie (1695–96), St Andrews University Library, MS 37025, pp. 219–20.
12 Robert Millar, *The History of the Propagation of Christianity, and the Overthrow of Paganism*, 2 vols, 3rd ed. (London, 1731), I, p. 314.

13 *Ibid.*
14 James Bell, *The Excellency of the Christian Religion Above the Pagan and Mahometan* (Aberdeen, 1737), p. 82.
15 *Ibid.*, p. 5.
16 Thomas Blackwell, *An Enquiry into the Life and Writings of Homer* (London, 1735), pp. 186–204.
17 Bernard Le Bovier de Fontenelle, *The History of Oracles, in Two Dissertations* (Glasgow, 1753). I am grateful to Professor Thomas Ahnert for drawing this edition to my attention.
18 On which, see Ossa-Richardson, *Devil's Tabernacle*, pp. 188–268.
19 Walter Anderson, *The History of Croesus King of Lydia, In IV Parts* (Edinburgh, 1755), p. xv. For the discussion of the oracles, see pp. xii–xxiv, 80–9.
20 *Ibid.*, p. xix.
21 *Ibid.*, p. 82.
22 *Ibid.*, p. 82. See also pp. xvii–xviii.
23 *Ibid.*, p. 82.
24 Anon., 'Art. IX: *The History of Crœsus King of Lydia*', *Critical Review* (March 1756), p. 139.
25 *Ibid.*, pp. 139–40 (original emphasis).
26 William Robertson, 'Article I: *The History of Crœsus, King of Lydia*', *Edinburgh Review* (July 1755), p. 70.
27 *Ibid.*
28 William Robertson, *The History of America*, 2 vols, 2nd ed. (London, 1778), I, p. 389.
29 This position was enshrined in the opening lines of *The Westminster Confession of Faith*, the Calvinist creed to which the Church of Scotland subscribed.
30 On orthodox arguments of this kind, see Thomas Ahnert, 'The soul, natural religion, and moral philosophy', *Eighteenth-Century Thought*, 2 (2004), 235–50, at pp. 238–42.
31 *Westminster Confession*, ch. XIV.
32 On the difficulties involved in defining 'deism' as a unitary set of ideas, see Wayne Hudson, *The English Deists: Studies in Early Enlightenment* (London: Routledge, 2008), pp. 1–28.
33 *Ibid.*, pp. 12–13.
34 Thomas Ahnert, *The Moral Culture of the Scottish Enlightenment, 1690–1805* (New Haven, CT: Yale University Press, 2014), pp. 44–51.
35 *Ibid.*, pp. 96–105.
36 Duncan Forbes, *A Letter to a Bishop, Concerning Some Important Discoveries in Philosophy and Theology*, 3rd ed. (London, 1747), p. 87 (original emphasis).
37 Millar, *Propagation of Christianity*, I, p. 159.
38 NRS, GD18/5031, fo. 6, Sir John Clerk to Thomas Blackwell, 23 Sep. 1734.
39 For a discussion of these arguments, see Christopher Berry, 'Rude religion: the psychology of polytheism in the Scottish Enlightenment', in Paul Wood (ed.), *The Scottish Enlightenment: Essays in Reinterpretation* (Woodbridge: Boydell, 2000), pp. 315–34; and R. J. W. Mills, 'William Falconer's *Remarks on the Influence of Climate* (1781) and the study of religion in Enlightenment England', *Intellectual History Review*, 28 (2018), 293–315, at pp. 299–301.

40 See for instance Henry Home, Lord Kames, *Essays on the Principles of Morality and Natural Religion* (Edinburgh, 1751), pp. 138–40, 346–8; James Burnet, Lord Monboddo, *Antient Metaphysics: Volume Fourth: Containing the History of Man* (Edinburgh, 1795), pp. 367–70.
41 William Robertson, *An Historical Disquisition Concerning the Knowledge which the Ancients had of India* (London, 1791), p. 313.
42 Archibald Campbell, *The Necessity of Revelation: Or An Enquiry into the Extent of Human Powers with Respect to Matters of Religion* (London, 1739). On the overlooked significance of this work as a pioneering contribution to the Scottish science of human nature, see R. J. W. Mills, 'Archibald Campbell's *Necessity of Revelation* (1739) – the science of human nature's first study of religion', *History of European Ideas*, 41 (2015), 728–46.
43 Campbell, *Necessity*, pp. 406–8.
44 *Ibid.*, p. 408.
45 John Erskine, 'The law of nature sufficiently promulgated to heathens' (1741), reprinted in his *Theological Dissertations* (London, 1765), pp. 200–41.
46 *Ibid.*, p. 206.
47 *Ibid.*, p. 207.
48 *Ibid.*, pp. 220–1. Erksine cited Psalm 97:6, Romans 1:18–21 and Romans 2:12–15.
49 *Ibid.*, pp. 225–7.
50 Thomas Blackwell, *Letters Concerning Mythology* (London, 1748), p. 136.
51 *Ibid.*, pp. 361–2.
52 David Hume, *The Natural History of Religion*, in his *Four Dissertations* (London, 1757), p. 31.
53 *Ibid.*, pp. 33–4.
54 *Ibid.*, p. 34.
55 *Ibid.*, p. 33.
56 On the controversial features of Hume's work, see Lorne Falkenstein, 'Hume's project in the "Natural History of Religion"', *Religious Studies*, 39 (2003), 1–21; Peter J. E. Kail, 'Understanding Hume's *Natural History of Religion*', *Philosophical Quarterly*, 57 (2007), 190–211; R. J. W. Mills, 'The "historical question" at the end of the Scottish Enlightenment: Dugald Stewart on the natural origin of religion, universal consent and religious diversity', *Intellectual History Review*, 28 (2018), 529–54, at pp. 536–7.
57 On Robertson and pagan religion, see Thomas Ahnert, 'Fortschrittsgeschichte und Religiöse Aufklärung. William Robertson und die Deutung außereuropäischer Kulturen', *Geschichte und Gesellschaft*, 23 (2010), 101–22; Stewart J. Brown, 'William Robertson, early orientalism, and the historical disquisition on India of 1791', *SHR*, 88 (2009), 289–312; Stewart J. Brown, 'An eighteenth-century historian on the Amerindians: culture, colonialism and Christianity in William Robertson's *History of America*', *Studies in World Christianity*, 2 (1996), 204–22.
58 Robertson, *America*, I, p. 381.
59 Robertson, *Historical Disquisition*, p. 317.
60 *Ibid.*, p. 330.
61 *Ibid.*

62 On the importance of enquiries into the pagans' natural knowledge of the immortality of the soul for debates within the Scottish church over morality and divine justice, see Ahnert, *Moral Culture*, pp. 46–51, 100–3, 137–9.
63 Campbell, *Necessity of Revelation*, p. 95.
64 *Ibid.*, p. 107. Campbell's analysis was based on Socrates's defence of the immortality of the soul as reported by Plato in the *Phaedo* and *Republic*.
65 *Ibid.*, pp. 122–79.
66 *Ibid.*, pp. 385–6.
67 *Ibid.*, p. 411 (original emphasis).
68 Erskine, *Theological Dissertations*, pp. 206–12.
69 *Ibid.*, pp. 232–5.
70 *Ibid.*, pp. 237–8.
71 Ramsay argued that the wise pagans had in fact preserved some knowledge of all Christian mysteries in this way. See Andrew Ramsay, *The Philosophical Principles of Natural and Revealed Religion: Unfolded in a Geometrical Order*, 2 vols (Glasgow, 1748–49), II, pp. 7–15.
72 *Ibid.*, II, pp. 233–74.
73 *Ibid.*, II, pp. 215–16, 274–99.
74 *Ibid.*, II, pp. 318–48. See also Ramsay's unpublished manuscript on the souls of beasts, Bibliothèque Méjanes, Aix en Provence, MS 1188, 'Discours sur l'ame des bêtes'. Transcribed in Marialuisa Baldi, *Verisimile, non vero: filosofia e politica in Andrew Michael Ramsay* (Milan: F. Angeli, 2002), pp. 446–56.
75 Ramsay, *Philosophical Principles*, II, p. 364.
76 David Hume described Ramsay as an 'ingenious author' whose eccentric theology meant that he had 'thrown himself out of all received sects of Christianity'. See Hume, *Natural History*, p. 102n.
77 Blackwell, *Enquiry*, p. 77.
78 Hume, *Natural History*, p. 91.
79 Robertson, *America*, I, p. 387.
80 *Ibid.*, p. 388.
81 Robertson, *Historical Disquisition*, pp. 330–1.
82 For recent articulations of this argument, see Stroumsa, *New Science*, p. vii; App, *Birth of Orientalism*, pp. xiii–xiv. For the classic statement of this view, see Manuel, *The Eighteenth Century Confronts the Gods*, p. 6.
83 For this revisionist approach, see Ahnert, *Moral Culture*, pp. 4–5 and *passim*.

13

Eighteenth-century Scotland and the visionary supernatural

Hamish Mathison

> The sun had clos'd the *winter-day*,
> The Curlers quat their roaring play,
> And hunger'd Maukin taen her way
>   To kail-yards green,
> While faithless snaws ilk step betray
>   Whare she has been.[1]

The loss of light begins and ends this chapter. It proposes that the use and embodiment of the supernatural in eighteenth-century Scottish verse holds to the key term and opaque conjunction 'as if'. It proposes that the idea of the supernatural allowed people in eighteenth-century Scotland to wrestle with the idea of a new and elusive descriptor: British. Writing within an ethereal concept such as 'Britain' was always and already a complicated poetic and political gesture. This chapter will propose that Allan Ramsay and Robert Burns were using the idea of a supernatural vision to bring into being the expression of cultural absence at one and the same time as they acknowledged the immanence of deep civic and political loss.

What follows will take Robert Burns's poem 'The Vision' (1786) as its end point, and will look backwards through the eighteenth-century supernatural poetry of Burns (1759–96), John Pinkerton (1758–1826) and Allan Ramsay (1686–1758) in order to establish the changing ways in which Scottish poets could represent the supernatural. It examines popular literary tropes that began to emerge as a consequence of the Union debates around the turn of the seventeenth and eighteenth centuries, where the realm of the supernatural was invoked to resist the idea of Union. The chapter acknowledges the incorporation into elite literary parlance of a synthetic demotic voice that speaks of popular superstition as well as of popular biblical knowledge, more often than not premised upon representations of the other-worldly that looked back to medieval and Renaissance Scottish verse forms in order to overcome more recent challenges to Scottish literary authority. Building upon Ramsay's deeply politicised 1724 invocation of the supernatural realm in the wake of Union in 1707, the chapter, having situated a Scottish supernatural and preternatural voice in poetry towards the start of the century, will resolve itself in a turn to Robert Burns's 1786 'The Vision'. It argues that Burns's poem uses the supernatural to fashion a complex treatment of identity, faith, belief and doubt.

None of this would have been possible without the publication of one of the most remarkably figurative political speeches in British political history. Lord Belhaven's November 1706 'Speech in Parliament' has become much better known (in significant part through the offices of his critic Daniel Defoe) as 'The Vision'. Belhaven spoke against the Union of parliaments on the terms proposed, and his speech was printed. The most powerful trope within the printed speech is the phrase 'I think I see'. The condensation of imagination in that phrase, befitting the condensation behind any use of figurative language, remains moving and powerful to this day. For Belhaven, to pass the act enabling parliamentary Union will bring about, in vision, a cascade of loss:

> I think, I see *a Free and Independent Kingdom* delivering up ... A Power to Manage their own Affairs by themselves, without the Assistance and Counsel of any other.
>
> I think, I see *a National Church* ... voluntarily descending into a Plain, upon an equal level with *Jews, Papists, Socinians, Arminians, Anabaptists*, and other Sectaries ... should not the Consideration of these things vivifie these *dry Bones* of ours? Should not the Memory of our Noble Predecessors *Valour & Constancie*, rouse up our drouping Spirits? ... Are our Eyes so Blinded? Are our Ears so Deafned? Are our Hearts so Hardned? Are our Tongues so Faltered? Are our Hands so Fettered, that in this our day, I say, *My Lord, That in this our day, that we should not mind the things, that concern the very Being and Wellbeing of our Ancient Kingdom, before the day be hid from our Eyes.*[2]

Belhaven has two turns in the above passage: one to what you know and one to what you cannot. The first is effective enough – an appeal to historical and textual record. The second appeal is much the stronger by far: an appeal to prognostication – to what might happen. Prognostication was a staple of Scottish print culture by the early eighteenth century, a well-embedded form of popular print expression. Given the millennial feel of the times, perhaps Belhaven was right to tap into this populist function of print culture. Certainly, Belhaven's appeal is to popular print and prognostication as much as it is to the biblical overtone of prophecy.

Belhaven's speech, and its subsequent publication, led to a rebuttal by Daniel Defoe (1660?–1731), who was employed to publish in favour of the Union of the parliaments. Defoe responded in poetry to Belhaven's prose work, cementing the role of figurative language in the evolution of popular debate concerning the rights and wrongs of Union. Defoe's poem, itself published in 1706 as 'The Vision', begins with the invocation of the supernatural realm, and returns to it consistently as he seeks not only to rebut Belhaven's principal claims, but also to turn Belhaven's prophetic method back against the Scottish peer:

> Come hither ye Dreamers of Dreams,
> Ye Soothsayers, Vizards and Witches,
> That puzzle the World with hard Names,
> And without any meaning make Speeches:
> Here's a Lord in the North,
> Near *Edinburgh* Frith;
> Tho little has been said of his Name or his Worth;
> He's seen such a Vision, no Mortal can reach it,
> I challenge the Clan of *Egyptians* to match it.
>
> ...
>
> Then *Scotland* comes next on the Stage,
> For in Visions you must not be nice,
> And a skip of three thousand Years age,
> Is nothing where Men are Concise;
> I name it the rather
> Because you may gather,
> How that every Man is the Son of his Father,
> A Truth for the future no Mortal can doubt,
> Whatever they might, before he found it out.
> But heark, now the Wonders begin,
> And take care least the Vision should fright ye;
> For if it should make you unclean,
> He has not told how he would dight ye.[3]

Belhaven's speech, traductions of it, Defoe's response and numerous other interventions in pamphlet form circulated in the opening decades of the eighteenth century. The passage of these publications in 1706 is important for what follows, because at the inception of the century there is a clear and unambiguous alignment of a fraught political nationhood with a fraught visionary practice. The supernatural realm is not bolted on after the fact of political reality, it is constitutive of it, certainly in terms of the Union debate at the turn of the century. Literary practice, figurative practice, is not something that follows a high-political moment, but is rather the thing that constitutes the architecture and boundaries of the debates concerning the rights and wrongs of political union. The use of the supernatural realm is, in a sense, entirely appropriate. Janus-faced, it allows a writer or orator to look back upon time so immemorial as to be, well, immemorial, while anticipating in a prognostic or prophetic act that which is yet to come. In 1706, or at any other point at which the supernatural realm bodies forth into eighteenth-century quotidian Scottish experience, it holds at one and the same time the promise of what was once unrecorded and what soon will be recorded unless we guard against it.

This creates for Belhaven, and his literary antecedents, both an opportunity and a problem – which Defoe was perhaps the first to register. There is an opportunity, insofar as the discussion is lodged in a time not of the present, but of past and future. An unwritten future may be revealed by the emergence of a voice that thinks it sees; change can be effected on account of the persuasive power of that which is yet to be. On the other hand, there is a problem; located not in a moment of current agency, the supernatural realm can remind us of what was, what may be, but is condemned to avoid this moment, the moment that is. Hence, on the one hand, in the material by Belhaven there is an attention to the previous (to the 'Memory of our noble Predecessors' in the 'ancient Kingdom') and the future ('I think I see'), where even the present moment is made insubstantial by the use of a rhetorical question and an auxiliary verb: 'Are our Hands so fettered, that in this our Day, I say, my Lord, that in this our Day, we should not mind'. Defoe latches on to the ambivalence of 'should' in Belhaven's speech, turning it against him: 'For if it should make you unclean, / He has not told how he would dight ye'. It is thus a very specific moment in time – late 1706 – with which this chapter begins, for the consequences of Belhaven's speech and Defoe's rebuttal for Scottish poetic practice in the century that followed were deeply significant: echoes can be heard, as we shall see, through to at least the 1790s.

It was in 1792 that, in the first volume of the *Transactions of the Society of the Antiquaries of Scotland*, William Tytler of Woodhouselee (1711–92) named Allan Ramsay as the author of the 1724 poem 'The Vision'. Ramsay's poem had been written to respond to the Union of parliaments in 1707: a narrator engages with Scotland's essential muse and spirit, named 'Callidon'. The narrator's stupidity is both funny and, as he is an unknowing Scottish nationalist, deeply moving. He is excused in significant fact because the poem is meant to be a medieval piece, translated in the Renaissance, only published a generation after the dust had settled on the politics of 1707. Ramsay had included the poem in his 1724 collection *The Ever Green*. To be fair, in 1724 Ramsay had not tried terribly hard to hide his identity, finishing the poem with the attribution 'AR. SCOT.' despite the text's assertion in the colophon that it was 'Compylit in Latin be a most lernit Clerk in Tyme of our Hairship and Oppression, anno 1300, and translatit in 1524'.[4] In his attribution and review, Tytler made the firm observation that 'Ramsay's natural turn led him to drollery; and when the fit seized him, his vein of humour ran freely, and without control. Here he stood in need of a friend to have *pinched his ear*.'[5] Tytler praised Ramsay's capture of Scottish landscape and martial valour. However, like his peers, he responded less well to Ramsay's treatment in the poem of the supernatural Scottish muse Callidon's digressive excursion into the private lives of the gods, finding 'the guardian genii [i.e. spirits] of modern nations at their cups ... unsuitable to the solemn dignity of the subject'.[6] Pastoral dignity is brought about in a rather underhand way, as Callidon simply refuses to share his knowledge at key points. In stanza thirteen Callidon suggests, 'But its nocht fit an mortal Man / Sould ken all I can tell' and again refuses knowledge to our narrator and all 'Sauls rowit up in Clay' (those of us mere mortals condemned to roll around in flesh and bone) in stanza seventeen.

Now, Tytler was an acute reader of Ramsay; he was also on a mission to fillet out what he perceived to be the best bits of a poem written by an author whose standing was based, by the late eighteenth century, upon *The Gentle Shepherd*'s (1725) reputation as Scottish pastoral theatre. Tytler ignored what Ramsay absolutely grasps in 'The Vision' as well as in *The Gentle Shepherd*: the absurdity of the supernatural, specifically its intervention in Scottish politics. Callidon is, as obviously now as in 1724 or 1792, an absurd figure, a machine for the generation of reflections upon the honour of parliamentary Union a generation after the fact. In 1724 Ramsay had grasped the loss of what Tytler absurdly sought in 1792 to retain: the sonority of 'the guardian genii of modern nations'. Ramsay's poem is a dialogue, in substantial part, with the supernatural realm, and an unflinching exposure of its strengths and weaknesses.

The invocation of the muse, in the form of a vision, is important because it allows Ramsay to recollect Lord Belhaven's speech and the visionary discourses of the century's turn as well as allowing him to invoke an authority far higher than the temporal – higher even than the literary supernatural – specifically, to invoke the word of God. Behind the opening gestures of Ramsay's poem lies Psalm 137. Ramsay's narrator, exhausted, collapses into the embrace of lowland Scotland's countryside in the poem's second stanza. As if to confirm the nation's exceptional status, this post-Reformation poem that needs the Stuart King James's Bible in order to resonate fully is set in a pre-Reformation Scotland where the only bibles were handwritten in Latin and you could count the literate on the fingers of a few hands. As sleep takes the narrator to a realm in which he can meet Callidon, the nation's muse, so it takes the reader to Psalm 137:

Ther vexit, perplexit,
I leint me doun to weip,
In brief ther, with Grief ther,
I dottard owre on Sleip.[7]

The experience is of exile-in-place. The narrator is lost in memory and sleep as a nation as 'vexit, perplexit' as he himself has been lost to the English King Edward; an experience inverted from the geographical displacement of the Israelites in Psalms. And yet, as Tytler notes, the real loss in play here is not so much that of the medieval Scots but that of the young Ramsay whose parliament fled in 1707, a further trauma belatedly following abandonment by their king of 1603.[8] The Scots, unlike the Israelites, do not even have (in 1300, 1724 or the time of writing) the dignity of geographical exile with which to metaphorise this kind of complaint. The expression is one of self-loathing; an internalisation of exile brought about by supplication to England. Sleep blessedly brings about the dulling of the senses in the fourth stanza: 'Heir Somnus in his silent Hand / Held all my Sences at Command, / Quhyle I forzet my Cair'. Although the physical world may retreat in sleep, there is no time for blank desertion; instead, a supernatural being is on hand to trouble the narrator because he could see:

> A Man with Aspeck kynd,
> Richt auld lyke and bauld lyke,
> With Baird thre Quarters skant,
> Sae braif lyke and graif lyke,
> He seemt to be a Sanct.[9]

The poem as a whole is driven by a couple of the words in this passage, and the present chapter continues to examine their treatment as troublesome signifiers in Scottish supernatural verse for the remainder of the eighteenth century: 'seemt to be' and 'lyke'. The figure is not a saint, he just 'seemt to be a Sanct'. That is terribly important, because while on the one hand there is obviously scant theological place for elderly bald Scottish visionaries, by gifting the character the 'seeming' of a saint, Ramsay is able to incorporate his narrator's Christian world view into a treatment of an otherwise secular figure.[10] Given that the nation in exodus is Scotland, not Israel, the script for visionary exceptionalism can only be written with characters drawn from the supernatural and figurative.

This in turn generates the impetus behind Scottish poetry's commitment to the supernatural realm. Nothing worldly could deliver a religiously derived superlunary account for the being of the Scottish people (Gaelic and English speakers, all from every point of the compass) and their woes. Nothing in print could simultaneously account for oppression when nationhood had a principally Catholic past and principally Protestant present (and that's just the forms of faith expression that could afford print and the officials to disburse it). No single utterance, or bundle of utterances, could smooth over the events of the

Scottish Reformation and the cascade of outcomes that led to the Union of Crowns in 1603; only the supernatural in the form of a figure such as Callidon could hope to offer the flexibility of hope that was required.

As Tytler was inching towards recognising in 1792, there is something innately silly about Callidon, about this literary compromise, but the fault is not Ramsay's. What Ramsay is in the process of achieving in this poem is the realisation of a commitment to metaphoricity which places the realm of the literary, and more specifically the realm of the figurative, at the heart of post-Union negotiations of Scottish identity. The great strength of a commitment to a Scottish being that is always 'like' something else, or which only always 'seems to be', is that it skates above the limitations of the historical record. The great threat it brings is commensurate; that for post-Union Scotland, Scottishness – Callidon – can only ever be like something it is not, can only ever be a placeholder for an absence: a likeness and a seeming, not a being and a presence. The remainder of the poem lays down, as it imagines Scotland's future ('Of quhat sall afterwart befall, / In mair auspicious Tymes') the concerns about local governance – and wider British policy – that were to power the astonishingly rich treatment of the supernatural in eighteenth-century Scottish verse.[11]

One of Tytler's intuitions was that Ramsay's powerfully Scottish figure owes a significant debt to Alexander Pope's mock-heroic poetry, specifically the supernatural machinery that Pope introduced to *The Rape of the Lock* in its second (1714) edition:

> For aften far abufe the Mune,
> We watching Beings do convene,
> Frae round Eards outmost Climes,
> Quhair evry Warden represents
> Cleirly his Nations Case.[12]

As Ariel is to Belinda in Pope's now canonical poem, so Callidon is to Scotland (and so Pope will reappear below in relation to Robert Burns's 1786 iteration of 'The Vision'). Callidon and other 'watching Beings' guide and protect their charges, convening as if in a benign supernatural parliament that skates rather closely to Milton's infernal parliament of failed angels, but that clearly laments the transformation in 1707 of Edinburgh's Parliament Close into a misnomer. In lunar orbit, Callidon may bring succour to the somnolent, but would appear to have no more executive effect than Belinda's ethereal hairdresser-in-chief:

> With Air then sae fair then,
> That glanst like Rayis of Glory,
> Sae Godlyk and oddlyk
> He thus resumit his Storie.[13]

Ramsay's synthetic ancient lexis collapses the grammatical heft here of two powerful adjectives, and the nuance matters: 'Godlyk' and 'oddlyk'; they are either adjectives 'Godly' and 'oddly' or compound adjectives 'God-like' and 'odd-like'. The foregrounding of the compound, of the synthetic, is important; it emphasises the reliance of the moment not upon being but upon likeness.

Callidon offers some hope to the narrator, and then is called away by an unnamed 'wondir fair Etherial Dame' whose job it is, presumably, to round up errant male spirits. Despite the presumption that Callidon's words are awfully important, the narrator's attention is wandering; as the supernatural figure speaks, so 'methocht ther came':

> QUHYLE thus he talkit, methocht ther came
> A wondir fair Etherial Dame,
> And to our Warden sayd,
> Grit *Callidon* I cum in Serch
> Of zou, frae the hych starry Arch,
> The Counsill wants zour Ayd.[14]

Here, 'methocht' is the key, as the intercession of a second supernatural being has become little more than a piece of narrative housekeeping. The emotional affect is clear, however, and again the key term is 'methocht':

> With that my Hand methocht he schuke,
> And wischt I Happyness micht bruke,
> To eild be Nicht and Day;
> Syne quicker than an Arrows Flicht,
> He mountit upwarts frae my Sicht,
> Straicht to the milkie Way;
> My Mynd him followit throw the Skyes,
> Untill the brynie Streme
> For Joy ran trinckling frae myne Eyes,
> And wakit me frae Dreme.[15]

When we hear that 'my Hand methocht he schuke', the reader is tempted to think by now that Callidon did not; that there was no hand shaking, just 'methocht'. There is nothing in actuality: 'My Mynd him followit' is all. Meanwhile, explicitly, the narrator is deprived of sight twice in one stanza; both the presence of the supernatural being ('He mountit upwarts frae my Sicht') and the presence of the vision itself ('the brynie Streme / For Joy ran trinckling frae myne Eyes') are lost as the eyes betray the viewer, just as Belhaven feared in 1706. Yet now, as sight fades on politics and the wider nation so concrete, and actual sensation comes to return, sight and sound offer apolitical ease and pleasure:

> Then peiping, half sleiping,
> Frae furth my rural Beild,
> It eisit me and pleisit me
> To se and smell the Feild.[16]

Social and political determination, wealth, martial pride: these are not returned to Scotland at the poem's conclusion. What is returned is the capacity to know the body's own bounds: to see and smell, to 'se and smell the Feild'. It is worth recalling Belhaven's 1706 rhetorical questions, as Ramsay would appear in this poem to be directly addressing Belhaven's complaint: 'Are our Eyes so blinded? Are our Ears so deafned? Are our Hearts so hardened? Are our Tongues so flattered? Are our Hands so fettered, that in this our Day, I say, my Lord, that in this our Day, we should not mind the Things that concern the very Being and Well-being of our ancient Kingdom, before they be hid from our Eyes?'[17] In Ramsay's poem, the narrator's senses are dimmed and the world 'hid from our eyes' only to be relieved, the Heart affected and Tongue and Hands set free to make poetry 'in this our day'. That which was hid from the eye is brought about in Ramsay's poem as it enters into dialogue today with Belhaven's yesterday. And so as Callidon has to shoot off ('quicker than an Arrows Flicht') for a meeting, he leaves behind emotion and the capacity to feel once more, for 'Joy ran trinckling frae myne Eyes', alongside the poem's own narrative. Words and feeling in this world and age are the residue of a supernatural encounter with the next.

The legacy of the poem is a complex one. In it, Ramsay binds politics to literary form, uncovering Alexander Montgomerie's sixteenth-century 'Cherrie and Slae' stanza form and binding its allegorical whimsy to ancient and modern Scottish politics.[18] Furthermore, Ramsay's antiquarian impulse here (he reproduced Montgomerie's poem inside *The Ever Green*, in which his own poem appeared) serves to accommodate both the commitment to, and scepticism towards, the supernatural realm that the poem displays. Aside from the immediate subject matter, what Robert Burns takes from the poem is its scepticism towards the supernatural realm and its complex treatment of narrative authority.

Robert Burns's two signal contributions to supernatural verse in Scotland are his relentless combination, and recombination, of the temporal and the timeless alongside his combination and recombination of the local and the universal. This is witnessed in 'The Vision', to which this chapter now turns.

Burns knew what he was doing when he called his poem 'The Vision': it was no accident; it was always going to be a piece wherein his narrator's words were overtaken by the sophistication of the poet's broader figurative tropes and the reader's memory of recent verse. Thus it is that Burns achieves in here a polyphonic combination of the present and the real with the past and the remembered. He effects this both at the level of the propositional content of the piece (what it claims to be about) and the formal mechanism of the piece (how it is brought into print, formally). Both form and content in this poem function in harmony; they bring about the collapse of the present temporal and spatial moment into the supernatural gift of a dream and a dream figure. That figure brings about change in the mind of the narrator. It is tempting to write 'in the mind of the poet', but because the poem is so self-conscious of its form and antecedents, to a level where we will see it footnoting its own heritage upon the same page as its apparent truth telling, it is impossible to escape (nor is it intended that we escape) the fictional, wry and self-interrogatory method of the piece. The vision is the narrator's, not Burns's; otherwise, who owns the footnotes? This is witnessed early in the poem, in a couple of stanzas that Burns was to rework repeatedly in fragments over the next decade:

> There, lanely, by the ingle-cheek,
> I sat and ey'd the spewing reek,
> That fill'd, wi' hoast-provoking smeek,
> The auld, clay biggin;
> And heard the restless rattons squeak
> About the riggin.
>
> All in this mottie, misty clime,
> I backward mus'd on wasted time,
> How I had spent my *youthfu' prime*,
> An' done nae-thing,
> But stringing blethers up in rhyme
> For fools to sing.[19]

Backwards is the key impetus for this poem and for its most obvious successor, the 'Epistle to Hugh Parker' (1788). 'I backward mus'd on wasted time', writes Burns, musing backwards; there's a doubling of the reversal of memory here, for the narrator reflects (at a moment of writing) on the moment of looking backwards (as experienced previously). Strange things happen when you start reflecting upon reflecting, narratologically; not least the intervention of a supernatural muse who will help you make sense of it all. Crucially, the elision of place and time begins before the appearance of the supernatural figure that will gift the narrator his vision; notice how the poem clearly establishes, as Ramsay did, the act of unseeing as its key trope. It is not the unseen that is the key determinant of the poem, rather it is the experience of being unable to see; beside the 'ingle-cheek' nothing can be seen apart from the obscurant itself: 'I sat and ey'd the spewing reek, / That fill'd, wi' hoast-provoking smeek / The auld, clay biggin'. This establishes the core of the poem's supernatural relationships: the visible light spectrum takes you merely to smeek. There is nothing beyond, the smeek is all there is to the eye; painful, all encompassing, it morphs slowly into a metaphor for our place in this world – a deeply Protestant sense that the human eye can respond in only the shortest of ways to the full circumference of God's intentions about us. As quite imperfect simulacra of the divine, it is both the duty and compulsion of our flawed bodies to look beyond the 'smeek' (which we ourselves have brought about) in order to find the greater significance of things.

Beyond sight there appears to be only sound, and supposition: '[I] heard the restless rattons squeak / About the riggin'. This is a deeply visual poem, and as with much of Burns's work on the supernatural, the play of authenticity and credulity hinges on the relationship between the seen and the unseen. Hearing is not of the same order as seeing; to hear is merely to acquire the rights to a published sight that would come into being were the physical moment of sensual perception more propitious.[20] Burns makes this clearer in the 'Epistle to Hugh Parker'. There, the relationship between this world and others is even more explicitly brought about by the smeek of an ill-banked fire:

> Here, ambush'd by the chimla cheek,
> Hid in an atmosphere of reek,
> I hear a wheel thrum i' the neuk,
> I hear it – for in vain I leuk. –
> The red peat gleams, a fiery kernel,
> Enhusked by a fog infernal:
> Here, for my wonted rhyming raptures,
> I sit and count my sins by chapters.[21]

The fireside is a gateway to another realm in both poems. In the later 'Epistle to Hugh Parker' it facilitates a collapse into self-acknowledged poetic failure on all counts ('Tak this excuse as nae epistle') except the being of the words on the page. In 'The Vision', however, the domestic hearth, *pace* Freud, is most *unheimlich* (uncanny): it is at once familiar and then suddenly and unexpectedly unfamiliar; in being so, it is disturbing and worthy of note.

All hell would appear to break loose shortly after Burns's sightlessness in 'The Vision', as the door to his cottage is kicked open, not by Satan or one of his legion, but by a beautiful woman:

> When click! the *string* the *snick* did draw;
> And jee! the door gaed to the wa';
> And by my ingle-lowe I saw,
> Now bleezan bright,
> A tight, outlandish *Hizzie*, braw,
> Come full in sight.[22]

At the heart of this stanza is the confusion of 'bleezan bright'. On the one hand, the previously useless fire in the ingle is now 'bleezan bright'; the entry of the figure has supernaturally brought about the fire's reincarnation (alternatively, the draught of air introduced to the cottage gives the fire new impetus – on this reading the joke is embedded within the lethargic melancholy of the narrator's inability to stoke a fire). Alternatively, the 'Hizzie' is herself 'bleezan bright' – in the moment of the 'Now' a figure alight as an angel appears at the door. The logic of the stanza splits in two; given the description of the failed fire, offered at length in preceding stanzas, it surely must be the here and now of the fire that suddenly is bright. On the other hand, the rhyme of 'bright' with 'sight' seems to align what would have to be a supernatural brightness with the appearance of a figure who must thus be cast as supernatural. Seeming is all; before the poem enters into its sustained analysis of what it means to speak of inspiration as a writer, it is unclear whether that inspiration is a function of (literal) enlightenment in a material sense (a fire 'bleezan bright') or a visitation from another realm (a figure 'bleezan bright'). Again, sight and sightlessness are at the heart of the problem. Burns's genius lies in absolutely refusing to adjudicate between competing versions, and we must acknowledge the humour of this refusal to commit to one version of truth.

Burns was not the first writer, of course, to consider the sudden imposition of a supernatural figure upon a moment of writerly reflection. There has been considerable thought given to the antecedents to Burns's poem. This chapter would like to suggest a key text that has been somewhat neglected, John Pinkerton's *Craigmillar Castle: An Elegy*, of 1775. John Pinkerton's early piece deals its cards straight in front of Burns's poem.[23] Pinkerton writes of falling asleep, and in quatrains the supernatural element is quickly made the key matter of the text:

> While yielding thus to lenient grief, I deem'd
> A rushing noise I heard, and looking round,
> A sudden light effulgent on me beam'd,
> And all my soul in admiration bound.
>
> Upon the hill descended from on high,
> A BEING far transcending human kind:
> I gaz'd upon him as he glided nigh,
> His form engaging all my pensive mind.
>
> An azure robe, of a celestial dye,
> Around him wildly wanton'd in the breeze:
> Bare were his feet; his looks did seem to vye
> With new-fall'n snow that tips the aged trees.[24]

The young Pinkerton (1758–1826) finds himself drawn, as Burns was to be, to the visual impact of his spectre: he is 'looking' when 'A sudden light effulgent on me beam'd'. Whether or not the eyes are key to this piece, Pinkerton displays precisely the same terribly important caveat as Burns when push comes to credulous shove: seeming. Notice how 'his looks did seem', as we will find Coila pinned between the possible and impossible by the same 'seeming':

> Her *Mantle* large, of greenish hue,
> My gazing wonder chiefly drew;
> Deep *lights* and *shades*, bold-mingling, threw
> A lustre grand;
> And seem'd, to my astonish'd view,
> A *well-known* Land.[25]

This 'seeming' occurs repeatedly in Burns's text, and in both 'Duans'.[26] The next occurrence is in a stanza which Burns was to rework into his most canonical poem, *Tam o'Shanter*, here offered as:

> Here, DOON pour'd down his far-fetch'd floods;
> There, well-fed IRWINE stately thuds:
> Auld, hermit AIRE staw thro' his woods,
> On to the shore;
> And many a lesser torrent scuds,
> With seeming roar.[27]

Burns is building on what this chapter has established as Scottish poetic practice in the early eighteenth century: a play of seeming and likeness. It invites yet refuses an actual connection between the everyday and the supernatural even as, at the same moment, it invites and permits that connection in language and the realm of the imaginary. As Scotland's rivers flow with their eternal seeming, so Scotland's heroes 'seem'd to muse, some seem'd to dare'.[28] The seeming view and seeming sound of Scotland are followed shortly after by another moment of mis-sight, whereas with Ramsay's ambiguous commitment to the sainted quality of Callidon we find the actually heavenly teased by the seemingly supernatural:

> With musing-deep, astonish'd stare,
> I view'd the heavenly-seeming *Fair*;
> A whisp'ring *throb* did witness bear
> Of kindred sweet,
> When with an elder Sister's air
> She did me greet.[29]

Burns's deep indebtedness to Ramsay extends to his reinvigoration of Pope's supernatural machinery from *The Rape of the Lock*, as the narrator experiences the 'whisp'ring throb [that] did witness bear / Of kindred sweet'. As no angel can stand (or fall) alone, and as Callidon had his peers and meetings to attend in 1724, so this figure is embedded within a host in the course of 1786. Coila, for that is the name of this being, makes clear in the second 'Duan' or section of the poem (a nod to James Macpherson) that she really has been reading her Pope:

> 'Know, the great *Genius* of this Land,
> 'Has many a light, aerial band,
> 'Who, all beneath his high command,
> 'Harmoniously,
> 'As *Arts* or *Arms* they understand,
> 'Their labors ply.
>
> 'They SCOTIA'S Race among them share;
> 'Some fire the *Sodger* on to dare;
> 'Some rouse the *Patriot* up to bare
> 'Corruption's heart:
> 'Some teach the *Bard*, a darling care,
> 'The tuneful Art.[30]

The play of literary memory here is fully, and quite deliberately, complicated; Burns is unambiguously juggling two distinct, and coterminous, literary predecessors: Ramsay and Pope. The former, as we have seen, trades upon the invocation of a Renaissance verse form (the *Cherrie and Slae*) in order to open up the space for a patriotic supernatural response on the part of Callidon to grand political events in the teeth of which the narrator would otherwise be powerless. The latter grabs hold of Milton's *Paradise Lost* to prove the impossibility of epic poetry in a fallen age of material whiggery and the equal impossibility of appealing to a supernatural realm for a defence against such material's encroachment upon basic human values such as love, tolerance and forgiveness.

It is not that Burns does not know what he is doing, in fact the precise opposite. The painful collision highlights principally the singular capacity of a narrating voice to manage a performance, and it is unequivocally a Scottish narrating voice. The poem's collocation of literary inheritance firmly proposes not only that Scots can play with the folkloric, but that they can mediate between the highest – and most popular – expressions of national literary culture available within the British Isles in the eighteenth century. Adjudication between competing versions of literary culture and popular credulity is thus booted on to the shoulders of Coila, a supernatural figure. She is apparently well read in Ramsay and Pope, and her being depends not only upon the narrator not waking for a while but also upon his ability to remember what (he claims he thinks) he saw and what (he claims he recalls) she said. Towards the end of the poem James Thomson, William Shenstone and Thomas Gray (some of the most popular eighteenth-century poets) appear; ghostly presences all, helped along in their authority by the fact that they are all dead:

> 'Thou canst not learn, nor I can show,
> 'To paint with *Thomson's* landscape-glow;
> 'Or wake the bosom-melting throe,
> 'With *Shenstone's* art;
> 'Or pour, with *Gray*, the moving flow,
> 'Warm on the heart.[31]

This text, then, remembers at least two levels of ghostly presence in the literary afterlife: the acknowledged and the unacknowledged. The curious negative 'canst not learn, nor can I show' associated with the three worthies of that stanza indicate, of course, that Coila *has* shown and the narrator *has* learnt. It is in the unspoken realm of supernatural influence that meaning, and poetic power, lie; the level of Ramsay's 1724 visionary archaism and Pope's 1714 supernatural satire upon the contemporary world. That late stanza reinforces the commitment of Burns to the supernatural realm within his text; not a belief in the extramundane, but a keen appreciation of its power as a trope to interrupt the popular poetic and civic idioms Burns witnessed in Thomson, Shenstone and Gray.

Burns's 'The Vision' does not conclude, but it does end. In ending, it recalls rather the greatest English elegy of the seventeenth century, Milton's *Lycidas*:

> Yet once more, O ye laurels, and once more
> Ye myrtles brown, with ivy never sere,
> I come to pluck your berries harsh and crude,
> And with forc'd fingers rude
> Shatter your leaves before the mellowing year.[32]

For Burns, the momentary being of the collegial supernatural spirit is 'once more' (after Belhaven, Defoe, Ramsay, Pinkerton and others) lost, in 'light away'. In the concluding stanza, the final two words are the most difficult, as Milton's classical source and Christian framework are replaced by an intimation of absence that complements Milton's fear that amid worldly tumult Christ's immanence becomes ever less tangible:

> '*And wear thou this*' – She solemn said,
> And bound the *Holly* round my head:
> The polish'd leaves, and berries red,
> Did rustling play;
> And, like a passing thought, she fled,
> In light away.[33]

It was a dream: no holly was bound. James Kinsley, Burns's most acute editor, suggests that we look to Isaac Watts's treatment of Psalm 90 when we read these lines.[34] However, in light of the wider argument above concerning eighteenth-century Scottish supernatural verse, it is the actual King James text of Psalm 90 that strikes the clearest chord, not just for Burns's text but perhaps for our wider treatment of the superlunary in this chapter: 'For a thousand years in thy sight are but as yesterday when it is past, and as a watch in the night. Thou carriest them away as with a flood; they are as a sleep ... we spend our years as a tale that is told.' Burns was never to resolve whether his muse flies away in light, or flies 'in light away', bringing about darkness. The sense of the stanza suggests the former; a blaze of light accompanies the departure of the supernatural being. Yet the poem is quite clear that Coila's retreat signifies absence and loss, a moment of not-being; she takes light with her: 'light away'. This would be a terribly gloomy place to resolve the text, were it not for the fact that Burns, also in the final stanza, pulls out the recurrent ace in the pack of visionary cards: likeness. Coila flees, and with her flees light '*like* a passing thought' (my emphasis). It is 'as if' she fled, 'as if' she were present, 'as if' the light is drawn.

As we have noted, Lord Belhaven when faced with the greatest existential threat his political nation had faced did not see, but thought he saw. So too Allan Ramsay, who in 1724 did not see, but buried his narrative authority in layers of seeming. So Burns too, when pushed, flicks us back – not from the presence of the supernatural, but from its absence. Coila, the supernatural muse, has not left the poem but becomes a likeness, an approximation, a mark and measure of figurative language. The elusive quality of the realm of the supernatural in eighteenth-century Scottish verse is therefore best concluded by Burns's stanza, for while allowing the supernatural realm to speak of artistry and politics, invention and civil society, its reliance upon figuration and similitude allows it to fashion and maintain a place immune to the threats of improvement, enlightenment or even critical judgement. As the sun drops on the opening stanza with which the chapter began, so the light is taken away with the supernatural's retreat from presence at the end. That play of sleep and light, of revelation and narrative, is crucial to the establishment of a distinct Scottish literary voice within the eighteenth century. It marks the bringing about of a literary nation, the shaping of the supernatural realm as an enabler of a complex reflection upon Scotland's new being and new absence: 'like a passing thought, she fled, / In light away.'[35]

Notes

1 Robert Burns, *The Poems and Songs of Robert Burns*, ed. James Kinsley, 3 vols (Oxford: Oxford University Press, 1968), 'The Vision' (1786), I, p. 103, lines 1–6 (original emphasis).

2 *The Lord Beilhaven's Speech in Parliament Saturday the Second of November, on the Subject-Matter of an Union Betwixt the Two Kingdoms of Scotland and England* ([Edinburgh], 1706), pp. 1–6 (original emphasis).
3 From Daniel Defoe, *The Vision, a Poem: Being an Answer to the Lord Beilhaven's Speech* (Edinburgh, 1706), n.p. (original emphasis). I am grateful to Professor Julian Goodare for the suggestion that Defoe's reference to the 'Clan of Egyptians' in this context takes us to Exodus 7, in which Aaron and Moses engage in a contest of 'signs and wonders' with Pharaoh's magicians. Defoe's use of 'dight' at the end of this passage is complicated: it indicates both a cleaning (how he will make you clean again) as well as a shaping (how he will form/dress/shape you). The play between the signification of the words is, possibly and appropriately, between that of an indeterminate Scots and English usage at the end of the seventeenth century. For more on the exchange between Belhaven and Defoe, see Ralph McLean, '"Literary symbols": language and style in the 1707 Union debates', *Scottish Affairs*, 27:1 (2018), 20–6.
4 Allan Ramsay, *Works*, original eds Burns Martin and John Oliver, 6 vols (Edinburgh: STS, 1945–74), headnote to 'The Vision' in *The Ever Green* (1724), III, eds Alexander Kinghorn and Alexander Law, p. 81.
5 William Tytler of Woodhouselee, 'Observations on the Vision', in *Transactions of the Society of the Antiquaries of Scotland* (Edinburgh, 1792), 395–402, at p. 401 (original emphasis).
6 *Ibid.*
7 Ramsay, *Works*, stanza III of 'The Vision' in *The Ever Green* (1724), III, p. 82.
8 On the continuing literary trauma of Union, the best book remains Leith Davis, *Acts of Union: Scotland and the Literary Negotiation of the British Nation, 1707–1830* (Palo Alto, CA: Stanford University Press, 1998).
9 Ramsay, *Works*, stanza IV of 'The Vision' in *The Ever Green* (1724), III, p. 83.
10 Ramsay's figure, bearded and bald, is that of a saint depicted in statuary or glass, a pre-Reformation character in many ways.
11 Ramsay, *Works*, stanza XII of 'The Vision' in *The Ever Green* (1724), III, p. 87.
12 *Ibid.*
13 *Ibid.*, p. 89. This is a curious use: we might today use 'oddly' casually as an adverb, but here Ramsay is using 'oddlyk' as an adjective to signify division – Callidon is apart from the singular Godhead and thus is to be taken as a part of a whole as odd/oddly – much as for contemporary Christians the Son and Father may be thought of as apart yet single.
14 *Ibid.*, p. 94 (original emphasis).
15 *Ibid.*
16 *Ibid.*
17 *The Lord Beilhaven's Speech*, p. 3.
18 See Ian Ross, 'The form and matter of "The Cherrie and the Slae"', *Texas Studies in English*, 37 (1958), 79–91.
19 Burns, *Poems and Songs*, 'The Vision' (1786), I, p. 103, lines 13–24 (original emphasis).
20 Burns makes much of the sensual corroborations of sight and sound. The credulity of the narrator's grandmother in a poem such as the 'Address to the Deil' (1786), for example, hinges on the grandmother's (super)rationalisation

of unexplained aural phenomena. In what follows, this chapter acknowledges an uneasy debt to Freud's analysis of sight and the anxiety of seeing in his 1919 essay 'The Uncanny' as it has influenced the critical discussion of European 'gothic' literature over the last fifty years.
21 Burns, *Poems and Songs*, 'Epistle to Hugh Parker' (1788), I, pp. 412–13, lines 7–14.
22 Burns, *Poems and Songs*, 'The Vision' (1786), I, p. 104, lines 37–42 (original emphasis).
23 For some context, see Patrick O'Flaherty, *Scotland's Pariah: The Life and Work of John Pinkerton* (Toronto: University of Toronto Press, 2015), pp. 8–9. O'Flaherty notes Pinkerton's teenage correspondence with James Beattie on the topic of this poem. While Burns in his correspondence acknowledges Beattie's poem 'To Mr. Alexander Ross at Lochlee' as a source for the muse who kicks in his door (Beattie's muse is 'Scota'), and notwithstanding the deep English eighteenth-century literary points of supernatural contact from Pope through Gray to Beattie, the parallels between Pinkerton's 1775 text and Burns's are too pressing simply to set aside, despite Pinkerton's later reputation.
24 John Pinkerton, *Craigmillar Castle: An Elegy* (Edinburgh, 1776), p. 6.
25 Burns, *Poems and Songs*, 'The Vision' (1786), I, p. 105, lines 67–72 (original emphasis).
26 A 'Duan' is simply a chunk of verse, suggesting a passage of related narrative thoughts or stanzas. It tries to indicate an oral poetic origin before print and page or line numbers. It sounds odd and archaic deliberately. Here the use forms part of Burns's wry rejection of James Macpherson's well-meaning and interesting 'Ossianic' attempt to fake a Scottish oral poetic past.
27 Burns, *Poems and Songs*, 'The Vision' (1786), I, p. 105, lines 79–84.
28 *Ibid.*, I, p. 105, line 95.
29 *Ibid.*, I, p. 109, lines 133–8 (original emphasis).
30 *Ibid.*, I, pp. 109–10, lines 145–56 (original emphasis). What Coila identifies as 'this Land' flickers between meaning what the poet recalls, Scotland as a whole, local communities in the south-west, and all points in between. See Penny Fielding, 'Burns's topographies', in *Scotland and the Borders of Romanticism*, ed. Leith Davis, Ian Duncan and Janet Sorenson (Cambridge: Cambridge University Press, 2004), pp. 170–87. The 'great *Genius*' is God; but Burns, who was a Freemason, chooses to leaven the signification of the stanza with the frisson of craft by the use of the Masonic marker 'great *Genius*' here.
31 Burns, *Poems and Songs*, 'The Vision' (1786), I, p. 112, lines 247–52 (original emphasis).
32 John Milton, *Complete Shorter Poems*, ed. John Carey (London: Longman, 1981), 'Lycidas' (1638), pp. 239–40, lines 1–5.
33 Burns, *Poems and Songs*, 'The Vision' (1786), I, p. 113, lines 271–6 (original emphasis).
34 'Time like an ever-rolling stream / Bears all its Sons away; / They fly forgotten as a Dream / Dies at the opening Day.' Isaac Watts, *The Psalms of David Imitated in the Language of the New Testament* (London, 1719), p. 230.
35 Burns, *Poems and Songs*, 'The Vision' (1786), I, p. 113, lines 275–6.

Index

Note: page numbers in *italics* refer to illustrations.

Aaron, brother of Moses 237n.3
Abercromby, David, physician 140
Aberdeen 95, 169
   Aberdeen Doctors 148
   Aberdeenshire 12, 47, 96, 104n.45
   King's College (University of
      Aberdeen) 5, 139
   Marischal College 206
   synod of 59
Abraham 27, 204
Adam 32, 150, 162, 214
Adamson, Patrick, archbishop of
   St Andrews 42
afterlife 19–20, 180, 204, 205,
   208–9, 213–16
   see also Heaven; Hell
agriculture 15, 128, 129
   see also corn; famine; harvest
Agrippa, Cornelius, occult
   philosopher 132
Ahnert, Thomas 209, 216
Aird, Francis, minister of Dalserf
   144, 154
Aitkin, John, interrogator 75, 77
Albany, Duke of *see* Stewart, John
Albion *see* Britain
Alexander III, king of Scots 120
Allan, David 175n.61
'All Sons of Adam' (song) 96
almanacs 127, 137, 140
Alver, Bente 79
Amadas, Elizabeth, prophetess 112

American Psychiatric Association 57
Amerindians 215
amulets 183
Anabaptism 146, 222
Anaxagoras, ancient philosopher
   210, 213
an dà shealladh 178
Anderson, George, schoolmaster 166
Anderson, Walter, minister 207–8
angels 4, 12–13, 18, 58, 86–106 *passim*,
   87, 89, 90, 93, 94, 206, *232*
   as avengers 88, 98
   belief in 148, 192
   fallen 96, 153, 154, 163, 205–6,
      214, 227
      see also demons
   as guardians 87–8, 91–2, 99
   as intermediate spirits 98–9
   in sermons 15, 154–5
   see also Christsonday
anger 14, 50–1, 52, 97, 98, 129, 144,
   150, 165–8
animals 4, 5, 94, 136, 183, 214
   see also bats; birds; cats; cows;
      cryptozoology; dogs; fish;
      horses; insects; moles; newts;
      pigs; seals; shape-shifting;
      sheep; snails; snakes; toads;
      whales; worms
animism 13, 15, 58, 82
Annand, William, minister of
   Edinburgh 162

Anne de la Tour d'Auvergne 111, 120
Anne of Denmark, queen of Scots 91
Annunciation 89
Anstruther, Sir William, of
    Anstruther, senator of the
    college of justice 164
anthropology 7, 13, 23n.27, 40,
    56–7, 67
Antichrist 32, 108, 167
antiquarianism, antiquarians 19, 120,
    121, 208, 229
    see also folklore
ants 26
apocalypticism 19, 109, 135, 161, 167,
    169, 171, 172, 182, 192
    see also Antichrist; Last Judgement;
    millennialism
Apollo, ancient god 208
apparitions 95, 132, 137, 165, 179,
    183, 193
    see also spirits; visions
Appin 188, 201n.51
Arbuthnott, Robert 89
Argyll 32, 37n.56
    Argyllshire 185–6
    Earl of *see* Campbell, Archibald
Aristotle, ancient philosopher (and
    Aristotelianism) 4, 18, 139, 181
Arminianism 162, 163, 222
*Art of Good Lewing & Good
    Deyng, The* 89
Arthur's Seat 64
Arth, William, friar 38n.64
Asloan Manuscript 28–9, 30
astrology 15–16, 18, 79, 127–41
    passim, 181
astronomy 128, 131, 139
    see also comets; eclipses
atheism 6, 148, 157n.24, 164, 172,
    191, 215–16
Athelstaneford 146
Atholl 193
Aubrey, John, antiquary 178, 190
Augustine, St, early Christian
    scholar 185
Austin, James H. 60
Ayrshire 47, 178, 193

Baikie, Elspeth, accused witch 75
Bailey, Michael D. 17–18
Baillie, Robert, minister and Glasgow
    University professor 151

Baird, John, minister 150
Ball-Ley (Orkney) 74–5, 77, 82
Banastre, William, prophet 107
Bannatyne, George, merchant and
    compiler 30–2
    Bannatyne Club 121
    Bannatyne Manuscript 28, 29, 30
baptism 74
    see also Anabaptism
Barber, Theodore 57, 61
bards 208, 234
barnacle geese 5–6
Bassantin, James, mathematician
    135, 138
bats 12
Baxter, Richard, theologian 6
Beattie, James, poet and philosopher
    238n.23
Bede, historian and reputed
    prophet 111
beggars 47–8, 134
Belhaven, Lord *see* Hamilton, John
belief, definition of 7–9
Bell, James, minister 206
benandanti 56
Bever, Edward 2, 55–6
Bible 6, 89, 97, 132, 163, 209, 225
    see also Geneva Bible; Psalms;
    Scripture
Binning, Hugh, minister of Govan
    148, 150, 153, 154, 162
birds 136
    see also barnacle geese; cock,
    crow of; corbies; geese; hens;
    owls; wrens
Birrel, Robert, diarist 115
Bishops' Wars (1639–40) 117
blacksmiths 43, 134
Blackwell, Thomas, the elder, minister
    and Marischal College
    professor 161
Blackwell, Thomas, the younger,
    Marischal College professor
    206, 211, 213, 214
Blair, Hugh, minister and
    rhetorician 171
blast, blasting 64, 66, 189
Blears, Georgie 13
Blind Harry 28
blindness 98, 147, 222, 228–9,
    231–2
blood 6–7, 98, 116, 129, 165

Blount, Charles, freethinker 209
Boarhills 41, 45
bodies 79, 129, 152, 163, 165, 209, 214, 229, 231
   dead 6, 89, 91, 92, 164, 180
   physiology of 163–4
   subtle 59–60
   see also blood; cauls; corporeality; physiognomy; skeletons; souls
Boece, Hector, principal of Aberdeen University 5–6
bogles 26
Borders, Anglo-Scottish 6, 107–8
Borobie, John, prior 113, 121
Bothwell, Earl of see Stewart, Francis
Bourguignon, Erika 57
Bourignon, Antoinette, mystic and prophetess 203n.77
Bowndie, Barbara, accused witch 15, 72–85 passim
Boyle, Robert, natural philosopher 178, 190–1, 193, 203n.77
Boyman, Janet, visionary accused of witchcraft 60, 63–4, 66
Boyne, battle of (1690) 118
Brahmins 215
Breadalbane 193
Bridlington, John of, prophet 107
Britain 170, 208, 221
   in prophecy 107–26 passim
   see also Union of Crowns; Union of Parliaments
Britannia 114
   see also 'Rule Britannia'
Brock, Michelle D. 3, 15, 18
brooms 59
brownies 26, 144, 154, 155, 156n.2, 180
Brown, Jean, visionary accused of witchcraft 47, 50
Brown, John, minister of Wamphray 151, 153
Bruce, Edward, 1st Earl of Kincardine 117
Bruce, Michael, minister 153
Bruce, Robert, king of Scots 112
Bruce, Robert, minister of Edinburgh 151, 152
Bryson, James, printer 91
Buchanan, George, humanist 128, 130–1

burials 215
Burness, John, storyteller 121
Burnet, James, Lord Monboddo, judge and philosopher 210
Burns, Robert, poet 11, 86, 221–2, 227, 229–38 passim
Burntisland Parish Church 92
Bute 189

Cadwaladr, Welsh king 109, 116
Caledonian Mercury 99
calendar 96
   see also Christmas; Fastern's Eve; Halloween; Martinmas; May games; Michaelmas
Callidon, poetic muse 224–9, 233–4, 237n.10, 237n.13
Calvin, John, theologian 91, 94, 128–9, 130, 153, 162
Calvinism 18, 100, 155, 156, 213, 216
Cameron, Allan, of Loch Eil 188
Cameron, Euan 2, 18
Campbell, Archibald, 7th Earl of Argyll 185
Campbell, Archibald, minister and St Andrews University professor 210–11, 213, 220n.64
Campbell, Colin, minister of Achnaba 137
Campbell, Diarmid 186
Campbell, Duncan, visionary 62
Campbell, Iain Òg, of Cabrachan 185
Campbell, John, of Ardkinglas 185–6
Campbell, John, of Cawdor 185
Campbell, Margaret, accused witch 185–7
Campbell, Neil, bishop of Argyll 187
candles 62, 95–6
Cardano (Cardanus), Girolamo, physician and natural philosopher 132
Carluke 144, 154
Carmichael, Alexander, folklorist 95
Carnasserie Castle 187
Caro Baroja, Julio 83
Carpzov, Benedict, jurist 6
Carswell, John, bishop of Argyll 186
Cartesianism see Descartes, René
Castillo, Richard J. 63
Cathcart, James, astrologer 134, 140

Catholicism 112, 116–17, 160, 163, 184, 214
  angels in 88–91, 96, 100
  anti-Catholicism 6–7, 135, 136, 167, 169
  Catholic priests 43, 186
  pre-Reformation 11, 28–31, 88–91, 226
cats 180, 183
cauldrons 12
cauls 184
Celtic societies 50
Charles II, king of Great Britain 118, 139, 168
Charles IX, king of France 137, 143n.52
Charles Edward Stuart, Young Pretender 119
charming, charms 29, 36n.31, 95, 97, 133, 142n.37, 186
chastity 10
Chaucer, Geoffrey, poet 33, 36n.31
Chester-le-Street 113
childbirth 60
  see also monstrous births
children 43, 101, 165
  in pageants 88, 91
  predictions about 96, 112, 114, 137, 180
  prodigious 165
  as visionaries 64–5, 66, 97, 188
  witches and 74, 188
Christianity 48, 209, 211
  ancient philosophy and 162
  folklorised 181
  other religions and 108, 111, 204, 210, 212, 216
  supernatural aspects of 3–4, 14, 205
  see also Catholicism; Protestantism
Christis Kirk on the Grene (poem) 31
Christmas 88, 96, 184
Christsonday, folk angel 47, 60, 64–5, 95–7, 98, 100
chronology 135, 137
Church Fathers 204, 205
Church of Scotland *see* Kirk
Cicero, ancient statesman and philosopher 204, 215, 217n.5
clairvoyance *see* divination
Clark, James, minister of Dirleton 146
Clark, Stuart 4, 83
Cleghorn, William, Edinburgh University professor 170
Clement VII, pope 112
Clerk, Sir John, of Penicuik, antiquary 210
clothing 32, 60
  azure 232
  black 188
  bright 98, 233
  green 95, 100, 188, 233
  silk 95–6
  tartan 188
  white 95, 97, 98
  see also winding sheets
cock, crow of 180
Cock, Janet, accused witch 189
cognition 48, 63
Cohen, Elisabeth S. 81
Coila, poetic muse 233–6, 238n.30
Collace, Katharine, spiritual diarist 165
Collingwood, R. G. 79
Collins, Anthony, freethinker 209
Columba, St 91
Colvill, William, minister and principal of Edinburgh University 146–7
comets 130, 137, 165
Confession of Faith (1560) 91, 161
  see also Westminster Confession
Constans 108–11 *passim*
  see also Last World Emperor
Constantine, emperor 109, 110
Cooper, Richard, artist 86, *87*
Copenhagen 131
corbies 59
corn 74, 144, 180
corporeality 180, 215
  see also bodies
corruption *see* depravity
Corss, James, almanac-maker 137
Cossé, Timoléon de 130
Cotton, Robert, antiquary 116
court, royal 19, 31, 46, 107, 112, 114, 121
  entertainments at 30, 36n.39
  fairy court 33, 43, 45, 47, 49, 65
Covenanters 154, 178, 179, 190–4
  covenanting 16, 95, 98, 162, 166
  personal covenants 192

Cowan, Edward J. 108, 154, 155
Cowan, James, minister 98
Cowie, Janet, visionary 62
cows 8, 66
   cowhides 183
Craig, James, Glasgow University student 206
Craig, Thomas, jurist 114
cream 28
Creation 18, 88, 161, 163, 211, 212
Crie, Jean, visionary 59, 66
crime 14–15, 30, 31, 43, 131, 189, 191
   see also murder; witchcraft
Croesus, king of Lydia 207
Cromwell, Oliver, lord protector 110, 117, 119
crusades 109–10, 112, 117
'Crying of ane Playe, The' (poem) 25, 28–9, 30
cryptozoology 5
Culsetter, Elspeth, accused witch 73, 76
cunning-folk 189
   see also magical practitioners
cursing, curses 27, 29, 31, 112, 183

Dale, Antonie van, physician and preacher 207
Dalglish, Robert, of Lauriston 138
Dalkeith, presbytery of 134
Dalrymple, David, Lord Hailes, antiquary 120
Dalrymple, John, of Stair 193
Dalserf 149
damnation 31, 96, 153, 161, 214
   see also Hell; reprobation
dancing 8, 15, 50, 72–85 *passim*, 144
Davies, Owen 55
deafness 191, 222, 229
death 7, 78, 100, 165, 170, 209
   deathbeds 89, 92
   death penalty 43, 74, 82, 134
   predictions of 88, 91, 107, 134, 180–3
   transportation of dead souls 89, 92, 95
   see also bodies, dead; funerals; resurrection of the dead

Defoe, Daniel, author 222–4, 237n.3
deism 20, 206, 208, 209, 211, 213, 216, 218n.32
Delphi 205
demonic pact 14–15, 48–9, 74, 76, 78, 179, 188–9, 191–2
demonology 4, 73, 77–8, 82, 96, 181
demons 86, 90, 97, 183, 186, 205–6
   appearance of 29, 153
   belief in 148
   in poetry 27, 29, 31
   pre-Reformation 144
   scepticism about 17, 157n.24, 207, 215
   in sermons 15, 153–4, 155, 158n.58
   spirits interpreted as 14, 15, 16, 19, 82, 154, 155, 156n.5
   see also angels, fallen; possession, demonic
Denmark 183
depravity 144, 146, 147, 149, 151–3, 155, 166
   see also reprobation
Descartes, René, philosopher 139
   Cartesianism 57
Deskford Church, Moray 89
Devil 64, 98, 188, 192
   apocalypse and 169
   astrology and 132–3, 138, 140, 141
   fall of 95
   oracles and 207
   in poetry and literature 27, 109
   prophecy and 116, 117, 193
   in sermons 15, 144–5, 147–8, 150–6
   witches and 41, 49, 54n.27, 61, 72–7, 82, 95, 131, 189
   see also demonic pact
   see also demonology; demons; possession, demonic
devils *see* demons
Dickson, David, minister and professor 162, 163
discernment 146–8
   see also spirits, discernment of
disease 29–30, 33, 59, 66, 134, 136
   see also blast; eating disorders; melancholy; plague; smallpox

disenchantment 17–18, 204, 208
divination 16, 65, 132, 182, 183, 184, 189, 194, 200n.48, 206
  see also *an dà shealladh*; astrology; *fiosachd*; fortune-telling; *frìth*; *manadaireachd*; oracles; palmistry; physiognomy; prognostication; prophecy; scrying; Second Sight; seers; *slinneineachd*; *taibhsearachd*; *taghairm*; visions
dogs 32, 36n.39
  dog's ear 31
Domat, Bremond, artist and author 111
Doppelgänger 184
Douglas, Gavin, poet and bishop of Dunkeld 26
Douglas, Jean, wife of Robert Dalglish of Lauriston 138
Douglas, Jonet, accuser of witches 191–3
drama 9, 17, 30
  see also theatre
dreams 1, 45, 61–2, 118, 155, 179, 192, 208
  poetic dream-visions 25–6, 35, 58, 223, 228, 230, 236
  see also nightmare experience; visions
drought 167–8
druids 208
Drummond, William, of Hawthornden, poet 99
Dumbarton 191
Dumfries, presbytery of 98
Dunbar 32
Dunbar, William, poet 30–1, 34n.2, 58
Dunblane 32
Duncan, John, merchant of Edinburgh 98, 100
Dundee 88
Dunlop, Bessie, visionary accused of witchcraft 47–8, 49–50, 60–1, 66
Duns 98
Durham, James, minister at Glasgow 91, 147, 164, 166
dwarfs 30, 36n.39

each uisge 8
Earlston (Erceldoune) 107
earthquakes 98
eating disorders 59
eclipses 12, 128, 130, 136
economics 141, 171
Edinburgh 30, 42, 88, 91, 129, 130, 134, 139, 150, 167
  Castle 90
  Firth (Frith) 223
  Greyfriars Churchyard 94
  Holy Trinity Chapel 89
  market cross 29
  shops in 91
  University 139, 141
Edmonstone, Archibald, brother of William Edmonstone 192
Edmonstone, William, of Duntreath, prophet 191, 192
Edward I, king of England 107
Edward VI, king of England 110, 115
eggs, eggshells 200n.48
Egypt, Egyptians 43, 204, 207, 210, 223, 237n.2
  see also gypsies
Eil, Loch 188
elect, election 15, 92, 99, 149, 150, 151, 152, 153, 161, 166
elf shot *see* elves, elf shot
Elgin 62
Elizabeth I, queen of England 115, 135
Elliot, Isobel, visionary 59–60
elrich 11, 25–38 *passim*
elves 1, 12, 25, 32, 36n.39, 50, 61, 66, 121, 154
  elf queen 27, 43, 47, 64
  elf shot 29–30, 189
  see also fairies
emotions 13–14, 39–54 *passim*, 97, 165, 228
  see also anger; fear; jealousy; love; sympathy; trust and distrust
empire 19, 111, 171
  see also Last World Emperor
enchantment 155
  see also disenchantment
Endor, Witch of 12, 181
England 63, 98, 168–9
  perceptions of Scottish supernaturalism in 190, 207

poetry from 1, 235, 238n.23
prophecies and 107–26 *passim*, 135
scholarship on 2–3, 18, 86, 92, 99, 160
Scottish subjugation to 226
  see also Union of Parliaments
Enlightenment 16, 17, 19, 122, 148, 161, 170–1, 204–5, 215–16, 236
enlightenment, spiritual 192, 209
enthusiasm, religious 58, 195
Epicurus, ancient philosopher 162
Episcopalianism 97, 98, 162–3, 203n.77
Erskine, John, Popular party minister 211, 213
Erzählkultur 183
Essinquoy 77
Europe 2, 18, 213
  angels in 88
  antiquity and 204, 207, 216
  divination in 181–5
  millennialism in 136
  mysticism in 194
  popular culture in 55, 60, 181–5, 189
  prophecies and 19, 107, 108, 114, 116
  Scottish relations with 110, 112
Eusebius, early Christian scholar 206
Eve 151, 214
Evelyn, John, diarist 190
Evil Eye 194
Ewart, David, astrologer 134
Exclusion Crisis (1679–81) 194
excommunication 27, 31, 33
  see also cursing

fairies 59, 78, 82, 188
  angels and 94, 95–7, 98, 100
  encounters with 39, 42–51 *passim*, 60, 61, 63, 65, 74, 189
  fairy-hills 28
  fairy king and queen in poetry 1, 9–11, 20, 25, 27, 32, 33
  fairyland 33, 39, 43, 49, 51, 59, 65
  fairy queen in popular culture 39, 45, 47–8, 50, 51, 64–5
  morality of 44, 97
  prophecies and 110
  Scottish belief in 3, 50
  Second Sight and 184
  sent to Hell 45, 97
  unorthodoxy of 15, 145, 148, 154–6
  see also elves
Fall of Man 88, 148, 151, 163, 214
familiars 180, 181, 208
famine 98, 128, 136, 182
fantasies 41, 43, 44, 51, 52, 55, 57, 60–2, 66–7, 77
  literary fantasy 1, 11, 25–8, 31–3
Fastern's Eve 58
fasting 59, 167, 168, 191
  see also eating disorders
Fates 33
Favret-Saada, Jeanne 7–8
fear 114, 131, 140, 165, 207, 211
  of angels 100
  of atheism 16
  of fairies 50
  of magic 18
  of other-worldly evil 12, 26–7, 82
  of portents 130, 132, 150
  of spirit-guides 14, 44–5, 49–50
Feochan, Loch 185
Fergesson, John, second-sighted prophet 119
Ferguson, Adam, philosopher 170, 171
Fian, John, visionary accused of witchcraft 59, 66, 95
Fife 14, 41
Finlay, son of Black Duncan MacFadyen 32
fiosachd 182
fire 98, 150, 151, 184, 231–2
  angels and 92, 95, 98
  divination and 65, 180
  in fairyland 44
  in Hell 95, 153
First Book of Discipline (1561) 139
fish 180
Fleming, Robert, the elder, minister 163
Flodden, battle of (1513) 110
Flood, biblical 211, 214
Flood, Victoria 108
flying 59, 63, 98
folklorists 183–4
folk tales 47–8, 80, 82, 121, 183
Fontenelle, Bernard le Bovier de, author 207

Forbes, Duncan, of Culloden, judge and politician 210
Forbes, John, song collector 96
Forbes, Robert, university regent 139
fortune-telling 134, 188, 193–4
Foulis Press 204
France 6, 7, 111–14, 137, 157n.24
 French Revolution 171
Francis II, king of France 114, 170
Fraser, John, minister and writer on Second Sight 62, 178
Fraser, Jonet, visionary 97, 98
Freemasonry 16, 179, 189–90, 192–3, 238n.30
freethinking 24n.42, 205, 206
 see also deism; scepticism
free will 162, 167
Freiris of Berwik, The (poem) 31
Freud, Sigmund 231, 238n.20
friars 107
 anti-fraternalism 32
friendship 46, 67, 181
frìth 183
funerals 183, 184
 see also burials; gravestones; graveyards; winding sheets

Gaelic language, Gàidhealtachd 96, 180, 182–8, 194–5
Gall, James, poem in memory of 190
Garden, George, episcopalian minister of Aberdeen 203n.77
Garden, James, episcopalian minister and Aberdeen University professor 190, 203n.77
Gaskill, Malcolm 81
geese 27, 31
gender 55, 195, 202n.62
Geneva Bible 132
Gentiles 108, 117, 210
George I, king of Great Britain 119
Germany 183–4, 195
ghosts 148, 156, 205
 ghostly armies 165
 ghost stories 121
 in poetry 27, 235
 as spirit-guides 14, 39, 42, 45, 47, 49
 see also afterlife; apparitions
giants 26, 27, 29, 30, 32, 43

Gibson, Marion 81
Gillespie, Archibald, minister of Kilmartin Glassary 165
Ginzburg, Carlo 56
Glasgow 59, 135, 149, 204, 207
 University 169, 206
God 4, 88, 145, 149–50, 155
 belief in 7, 157n.24
 see also atheism
 as creator 4, 32, 79, 209, 212
 see also Creation
 as deliverer 100, 144, 147–54 *passim*, 169, 192
 see also grace; Holy Spirit; salvation
 human relationship with 47, 51, 57
 imparting knowledge 6–7, 135, 136, 192
 knowledge of 209, 210–14, 216
 law of 27
 other spirits and 44, 47, 88, 92, 94, 95–7
 in poetry 26, 27, 32, 225, 228, 238n.30
 prophecy and 107, 118
 as punisher 79, 98, 129–30, 137, 144, 149–50, 153, 165, 167, 171
 in sermons 15, 144–59 *passim*
 as sovereign 18–19, 129, 132, 138, 148, 160–77 *passim*
 see also Holy Trinity; Jesus Christ; miracles
'God and Sanct Petir' (poem) 25
Goes, Hugo van der, artist 89
Goodare, Julian 2, 10, 13–14, 55, 56, 63–4, 133, 154
good neighbours *see* fairies
Gordon, John, parish clerk of Mortlach 201n.51
Gordon, William, treasurer of Caithness 201n.51
Gormshuil Mhòr na Maighe, reputed witch 188
Gowdie, Isobel, visionary accused of witchcraft 59–60
Gowrie, Earl of *see* Ruthven, John
grace 138, 145, 147–50, 152, 166, 167
Grandtully 92
Grant, Anne MacVicar, folklorist 100
Grant, Francis, advocate 168

Grant, Marion, accused witch 95
grasshoppers 26
gravestones 91, 92, *94*, 100
graveyards 184
Gray, Thomas, poet 234–5, 238n.23
Greece, Greeks, ancient 10, 79, 204, 207, 210–13
  Greek sea 32
green kirtles 59
Gregory, David, mathematician 139
Gruffydd, Rhys ap, conspirator 111–12
Guild, William, minister 92
Gunpowder Plot (1605) 168
Guthrie, William, minister of Fenwick 164
gypsies 43
Gyre Carling, The (poem) 25, 27, 29, 32

Haddington 32
Hadley Williams, Janet 11
hægtessan 29
Hailes, Lord *see* Dalrymple, David
Haldane, Isobel, visionary accused of witchcraft 49
Halloween 8, 64
hallucinations, hallucinogens 40, 52, 57, 58, 61–2
Hamilton, John, 2nd Lord Belhaven 222–5, 229, 236
Hamilton, John, archbishop of St Andrews 88
hammermen 88
  see also blacksmiths
Hanoverian dynasty 119–20
Harington, John, courtier 116
Harris 90
harvest 26, 95, 167, 186
health and healing 10, 42–3, 44, 65–7, 164, 183
  see also charming; disease; medicine
heart-work 192
heathens 98, 110, 132, 210, 211
Heaven 26, 45, 153, 162, 165, 166
  angels in 88, 92, 97, 99
  the heavens 127, 128, 129, 130, 132, 136, 137, 164
  see also paradise

Hebrides 181
Hecate, ancient goddess 12
Helena, mother of Constantine 109
Hell 58, 133, 140, 153, 158n.58
  see also fairies sent to Hell
HEMPE prophecy *115*, 116, 119
Henderson, Alexander, minister 151–2
Henderson, Bessie, visionary accused of witchcraft 59
Henderson, Lizanne 3, 47–8, 154, 155
Henry VII, king of England 109, 110
Henry VIII, king of England 19, 110, 111, 114–15, 116
Henry Frederick, son of James VI 167
Henryson, Robert, poet 31
hens, chickens 26, 32, 61
heraldry 89, *113*
herbs 14, 42, 44, 60
Herodotus, ancient historian 204
Highlands 8–9, 16, 110, 170, 178–203 *passim*, 208
  Highlanders 32–3, 50, 119, 178, 193–4
  Highland Host 193
  Highlandism 184
  see also Celtic societies; Gaelic language
Hobbes, Thomas, materialist philosopher 206
Hog, James, of Humbie 134
Holland 119
holly 235
holy days 184
Holy Rood (Cross) 109, 112, 117
Holyrood Abbey and Palace 117
Holy Spirit 146, 155, 164
Holy Trinity 47
Home, Henry, Lord Kames, philosopher 210
Homer, ancient poet 204
Hood, Robin, outlaw 30
Horace, ancient poet 204
horses 8, 63, 95, 132, 165, 180
hospitality 47–8
hosts, consecrated *89*
Hoy 15, 72, 78
Hudson, Wayne 209
Hume, Alexander, minister 161, 163, 164

Hume, David, philosopher 209, 210, 211–13, 214–16, 220n.76
Hume, Patrick, of Polwart, poet 33, 37n.56
Hungary 112
Hunter, Michael 24n.42, 178, 190
Hutcheson, George, minister of Edinburgh 147
Hutton, Ronald 50
hypnosis 57, 61, 63

iconoclasm 91
imagination 2, 10, 12, 77, 78, 213, 222, 233
　in visions 42, 57, 61, 65
　see also fantasies
incubi 25
India 204, 212
insects 12
　see also ants; grasshoppers
Iona 91, 186
Ireland 109, 118–19
　Irish language 114
Irvine, presbytery of 151
Israel, Israelites 169

Jacobitism, Jacobites 19, 98, 117, 118–20, 121, 168, 171
James I, king of Scots 89
James II and VII, king of Great Britain 117–18
James IV, king of Scots 28, 89, 110
James V, king of Scots 19, 28, 43, 112–14
James VI, king of Scots, later James VI and I, king of Great Britain 5, 19, 28, 38n.65, 131
　Daemonologie 60, 91–2, 95, 116, 131–3, 135–6, 156n.2, 163
　prophecy and 109, 114, 116, 117
　public celebrations and 167–8
James Edward Stuart, Old Pretender 118
jealousy 51, 137
Jehosophat, Valley of 112
jeremiads 171
Jerusalem 108, 109, 110, 112
Jesus Christ 145–7, 149, 152, 154, 155
　celebrations of 88
　coming of 206
　encounters with 97, 165
　in poetry 235
　prophecy and 108, 116
　as punisher 92
Jews 32, 37n.53, 108, 117, 222
　see also Israel
John, St 96
Johnston, Archibald, of Wariston, advocate 165
Johnstones, of Annandale 91
judgements, divine 90, 92, 98, 100, 137, 144, 150, 172, 214
　see also Last Judgement
Julius Caesar, ancient statesman 111

Kames, Lord see Home, Henry
Kidd, Colin 147, 205
Kieckhefer, Richard 27
Kilwinning Lodge 192–3
Kincardine, Earl of see Bruce, Edward
Kinsley, James 236
Kintyre 98
Kirk 97, 167, 169
　divisions within 209
　kirk sessions 14, 134, 156
　kirkyards see graveyards
　orthodox supernaturalism and 3–4, 139, 147, 149, 155, 161
　popular belief and 36n.31, 135, 145, 148
　pre-Reformation 30, 31, 32
　see also Catholicism
　role in community 16, 17, 150, 152
　Scripture and 132
　see also Christianity
Kirk, Robert, minister of Aberfoyle 55, 62–3, 66, 98–9, 178, 190
Kirkwall 73, 77, 188
Kirmayer, Laurence J. 58
Kittok, poetic protagonist 26
Klaniczay, Gábor 55
Knipoch 185
Knox, John, minister and Reformer 38n.64, 132, 169, 170
　Book of Common Order 186

Lactantius, early Christian scholar 108
Laird of Cool's Ghost, The 99
landscape 15, 78–80, 82, 88, 225, 235
　see also trees
Lasswade 59

Last Judgement 13, 89–98 *passim*, 90, 93, 94, 108, 112, 150, 154, 214
Last World Emperor 108–10
Lauder, Sir John, of Fountainhall, judge 133–4, 140, 191–2
Lauderdale, Earl and Duke of *see* Maitland, John
laurel 235
Lauriston Castle 138
Lauriston, Lord *see* Napier, Alexander
Law, John, Glasgow University professor 206
Law, Robert, minister 191–3
Lazarus 89
Lee, Nathaniel, playwright 193–4
legends 5, 10, 107, 183
legislation 31, 133–4
Leith 131
Lewington, Thomas, translator 89
Lewis 8
Leys, Thomas, accused witch 96
Lhuyd, Edward, ethnographer 8–9, 23n.30
Lichtoun's 'Quha doutis dremis is bot phantasye?' (poem) 25, 31
Lindsay (Lyndsay), Sir David, of the Mount, poet and playwright 33, 90
Linlithgow Palace 89
Lismore 185–6, 188
Lochaber 188
Loch Ness Monster 5
Logan, John, minister of Leith 166
London 112, 113–14, 115, 116, 182, 193–4
Lord Fergus Gaist (poem) 25, 27, 31
Lorn 185–6
Lothian 42, 44
Loudun 6
Loudun, John, Glasgow University professor 206, 217n.11
Loughlin, Felicity 19
Lovat, Simon, 11th Lord 118
love 234
  of God 100, 149, 150, 154, 165, 192
  ladies' love 9–10
  love magic 200n.48
  predictions about 134, 137
  pursuit of 101
  for spirit-guides 47, 48, 64
Love, Grizell, visionary 58, 97, 98

Lowlands 16, 178, 179, 190–4, 225
Lucifer *see* Devil
Luhrmann, Tanya 57, 65
Lutheranism 163
Lydgate, John, poet 31

Macbeth *ii*, 12
MacDonald, Alasdair A. 108
Macduff 12
MacGillereacht, Donaldus More, parishioner of Mortlach 201n.51
McGill, Martha 3, 12–13, 18, 155
McGreiger, Donald, daughter of, visionary 97
Mackellar of Cruachan, charmer 186
Mackenzie, Sir George, of Rosehaugh, advocate 6–7, 162, 193
Mackenzie, George, of Tarbat 191, 193
Mackenzie, Kenneth, 3rd Earl of Seaforth 193
Maclaurin, Colin, mathematician 141
Macleod, Alexander 90
Macpherson, James, poet 12, 234, 238n.26
MacQueen, Patrick, minister and alleged magician 186
McWard, Robert, minister 192
Madeleine of Valois, queen of Scots 112–13
magic 2, 17, 18, 24n.42
  learned discussion of 131, 133, 134, 140
  magic circles 12, 31
  magic numbers 43, 72, 76, 79–80
  in poetry 10, 27, 29, 32, 140
  popular interest in 79
  see also amulets; apparitions; charming; divination; flying; love magic; portents; rituals
magical practitioners 41–3, 56, 60
  see also cunning-folk; seers
magicians, learned 132, 134–5, 140, 143n.68, 237n.3
  see also druids; necromancy
Màiri Mhòr, second-sighted seer 186–7
Maitland, John, 2nd Earl and 1st Duke of Lauderdale 6, 193
Maitland, John, of Thirlestane, chancellor 30

Maitland, Sir Richard, of
    Lethington 30
Maitland Folio Manuscript
    28, 29, 30
maleficium 189, 194
Mallet, David, poet 99
manadaireachd 183
Man, Andrew, visionary accused of
    witchcraft 47, 50, 51, 60–2,
    64–6, 95–7, 100
Margaret Tudor, queen of Scots 88,
    89, 110, 111
Maria Clementina Sobieska, wife of
    James, Old Pretender 118
Marischal College *see* Aberdeen
marriage 27, 32, 46, 50, 54n.27, 137,
    165, 215
    predictions about 112, 114, 134, 179
    between supernatural
        creatures 27, 32
Marshall, Peter 92, 99
Martin, Lauren 80
Martin, Martin, physician and
    ethnologist 8, 65, 91, 178,
    179–82, 195
Martinmas 96
Mary I, queen of England 110, 115
Mary of Guise, queen of Scots 88, 112
Mary, Queen of Scots 28, 91, 114, 116,
    135, 170
Mary, Virgin 109
    see also Annunciation
Mason Word 190
materialism 191, 206, 208, 215
mathematics 17, 79, 131, 135, 137, 141
    see also magic numbers
Mathison, Hamish 11–12
Maurice, William, of Clennenau 116
Maxwell, George, of Pollok 192
Maxwell, James, writer on
    prophecies 116–18
Maxwell, John, 8th Lord 90–1, 100
Maxwell-Stuart, P. G. 134
May games 30
medicine 42, 128, 129, 131
    see also health and healing
Meek, Donald 187
melancholy 59, 232
Melanchthon, Philip, Reformer 135
Melrose Abbey 88, 107
Melville, Sir James, courtier 135

Melville, Robert, courtier 135, 138
memory 52, 61
    literary memory 229, 230, 234–5
    national memory 222
Merlin, prophet 107, 109, 111–14
metaphysics 1, 4, 88, 205
Michaelmas 91
Michael, St, archangel 89, 91, 96
Middle-Earth 45
midnight 61, 184
Millar, Robert, minister of Paisley
    Abbey 206, 210
millennialism 136, 222
Miller, Hugh, folklorist 100
Miller, Joyce 79
Milton, John, poet 227, 234, 235
Minos, king of Crete 206–7
mint 26
miracles 4, 155, 163, 168, 205, 206,
    207, 208, 209
    see also wonders
Moaness 72, 75, 75–8, 80–3
Moderate party 171, 209
moles 27
Monboddo, Lord *see* Burnet, James
Monmouth, Geoffrey of, chronicler
    109, 110, 116
monstrous births 33, 165
Montgomerie, Alexander, poet 32–3,
    37n.56, 37n.57, 229
moon 26, 130, 210
Moranski, Karen 108
Moray, Sir Robert, politician and
    natural philosopher 117
Mortlach 201n.51
Moses 237n.3
Muhammed 32
murder 6–7, 185
Murray, John, Earl of
    Tullibardine 138
Murray, Margaret 104n.51
Murthlie 188
muses 11, 224–5, 230, 236, 238n.23
    see also Callidon; Coila
music 17, 64, 88–9, 101
    see also bards; piping; trumpets
Muslims 111
mutism 74, 83, 98, 188, 191, 193
'My gudame wes a gay wyf'
    (poem) 25, 26
mysticism 79, 179, 194, 195

Naiden, James 131
Napier, Alexander, Lord Lauriston 138
Napier, John, of Merchiston 136, 138
natural philosophy 4, 128, 129, 135, 139, 141, 211
natural religion 208–13
nature 4, 9, 20, 78–9, 146, 148, 162, 163, 170
   laws of 1, 10, 17, 79, 129, 137, 145, 210, 212
      see also God, law of
   light of 208, 210
   see also landscape
nature spirits 76, 82, 154, 155
necromancy 31, 131, 133, 140
Neoplatonism 190
Nesmith, James, minister 149
Netherlands 183, 195
   see also Holland
neurobiology 13, 55–6, 60, 67
   see also cognition
Newmills 6
Newton, Humphrey, informer 110
Newton, Isaac, natural philosopher 137, 139
newts 26
Nicneven, sobriquet of supposed witch 33
'Nicricherts, twa', alleged witches 186
night 8, 58, 60–2, 79, 98, 180
   night battles 56
   see also midnight
nightmare experience 5
Nisbet, James, Covenanter 193
Nithsdale 97
Nixon, Robert, prophet 107, 119
Noah 211, 213, 214
   Noah's Ark 26
noon 91, 136
Normans 109
North Berwick Law 29, 32
North Berwick witch trials 131
novels 208

oatcakes 50
Oates, Titus, informer 118
occult 3, 15, 179, 181, 182, 184, 186, 191, 192
O'Flaherty, Patrick 238n.23
Ogilvie, William, minister of East Lothian 99

ointments 44
Oldmixon, John, printer 119
Oldridge, Darren 2–3, 87
Ong, Walter J. 81–2
oracles 19–20, 205–8, 215
orality 81–2
Orkney 15, 46, 72–85 *passim*, 104n.45, 188, 200n.46
Orpheus 27, 140
Ossian 12, 238n.26
Ostling, Michael 56
Ottomans *see* Turks
owls 12

paganism, pagans 14, 120, 121
   in ancient world 19–20, 108, 204–20 *passim*
   see also heathens; Gentiles
Paisley 191
palmistry 134
Paplay, Marjorie, accused witch 73–5, 80, 82
paradise 214
paranormal 5–6
Paris 135
parliament of England 114, 116, 117–18, 168
parliament of Scotland 167
   see also legislation; Union of Parliaments
Paterson, Laura 78, 83
patrons and clients 14, 46–8, 50, 51
Pearson, Alison, visionary accused of witchcraft 14, 41–5, 47–52 *passim*, 60–2, 65
Pencaitland 59
Pennant, Thomas, traveller 91
Pepys, Samuel, diarist 178
Perseus of Macedonia 130
Persia 204
Perth 49, 88, 190
   Perthshire 50, 97
Philip II, king of Spain, husband of Mary I 115
Phoebus, sun god 10
physiognomy 134
pigs 180
pilgrimage 109
Pillans, James, university regent 139
Pindar, ancient poet 204

Pinkerton, John, poet 221, 232–3, 238n.23
piping 44, 201n.51
Pitcairn, Alexander, minister 169
Pitcairne, Archibald, physician 21n.1
Pitcairn, Robert, antiquary 60
plague 92, 98, 129–30, 168
Plato, ancient philosopher 94, 210, 213, 215
Plutarch, ancient historian 204
Pócs, Éva 55–6
poetry 1, 9–12, 25–38 *passim*, 58, 99, 101, 114, 128, 190, 221–38 *passim*
Polwart *see* Hume, Patrick
polytheism 108, 209–10, 215
Pont, Robert, minister and Reformer 135–6
Poor Law Act (1575) 134
Pope, Alexander, poet 227, 233–5, 238n.23
Popish Plot (1678–81) 118
portents 136, 150, 179, 193, 194
  see also apparitions; comets; eclipses; monstrous births; prodigies
possession, demonic 2, 6, 132, 152, 191, 193
  spirit 179, 192, 194
pound keepers 26
prayer 56, 57
  to angels 88, 91
  as defence 44, 191
  exhortations to 97, 147, 151, 191
  fasting and 167
  invocation and 64, 186
  prayer books 88, 89
Presbyterianism 97–8, 162–9 *passim*, 182, 208, 211, 214, 215, 216
  presbyteries 73, 76, 134, 156
  see also Covenanters
Presocratics, ancient philosophers 204
Prestonpans, battle of (1745) 118
preternatural 4, 127, 145, 147, 163
Princess of Cleve, The (play) 193
print culture 114–15, 118, 204, 222
prodigies 118, 165, 208
prognostication 111, 112, 128, 136, 150, 180, 195, 222, 224
prolactin 61
prophecy 19, 107–26 *passim*, 113, 115, 182, 192, 194, 195, 222, 224

by angels 91, 206
condemnation of 132, 142n.37
by Fates 33
by ministers 164, 171
by oracles 205–7
prophets 56, 191
  see also seers
Protestantism 7, 14, 28, 187, 226, 231
  angels in 18, 88, 91, 94, 99, 100
  astrology and 129
  miracles and 163
  prophecy and 110, 112, 116
  providence in 160, 162–3, 167, 169, 170
  scholarship on 3, 17–18
  see also Anabaptism; Arminianism; Calvinism; Episcopalianism; Lutheranism; Presbyterianism; Puritans; Quakerism; Reformation
proverbs 31
providence 3, 16, 18–19, 118, 129, 138, 160–77 *passim*, 192, 211
  angels and 99
  predictions and 118, 150, 184
Psalms 92, 98, 147, 165, 169, 225–6, 236
  see also Wode Psalter
psychology 40–1, 52, 56, 57, 58, 65
  psychoanalysis 55
  see also neurobiology
Ptolemy, ancient astronomer 128, 139
Puritans 116
Purkiss, Diane 55
Pythagoras, ancient philosopher 94

Quakerism 146
Quietism 203n.77

Rae, Peter, Glasgow University student 206
Raffe, Alasdair 3, 18, 157n.24
Ramsay, Allan, poet and playwright 11, 99, 221, 224–30, 233–6
Ramsay, Andrew, Catholic writer 214, 220n.71, 220n.76
reason 20, 55, 132, 136, 147, 166, 208–16
Reddy, William M. 48, 51–2
Reformation 3–4, 11, 15–18, 43, 179, 186–7, 194

angels and 88, 91–2, 96–8, 100
astrology and 127, 132, 133, 135
literature and 29, 31–2, 225, 227
providence and 160, 167, 169
sermons and 144–8, 154–5
Reid, Christian, accused witch 95
Reid, John, printer 118
Reid, Thom, spirit-guide 47–8, 49, 50, 60, 66
Renaissance 10, 79, 87, 187, 221, 234
Renfrewshire 178, 193
Reoch, Elspeth, visionary accused of witchcraft 46–7, 50, 60–1, 188–9
repentance 98, 146, 167, 171, 172
reprobation 153, 161
Restoration (1660) 97, 117, 164
resurrection of the dead 110, 164
revelation, divine 20, 147, 206, 209, 211–16
Revolution (1688–89) 98, 118, 119, 168, 169
Ridder-Patrick, Jane 15, 17, 18
Rimour, Thomas, of Erceldoune, prophet 107–8, 110, 111–14, 117, 118–20
   see also Thomas of Erceldoune; Thomas the Rhymer
Riordan, Michael B. 10, 19
rituals 14, 42, 56, 64, 132, 181, 183, 185
   in poetry 25, 27
   Protestantism and 17, 18
Robertson, Alexander, minister of Fortingall 20–1n.1
Robertson, William, minister and historian 170, 208, 210, 212–13, 215
Roderick the Impostor, seer 181
Rohault, Jacques, natural philosopher 139
Rollock, Robert, minister and Edinburgh University professor 92, 146, 155
romanticism 10, 12, 16, 121, 195
Rome, Romans 112
   ancient 121, 204, 210, 211, 214
Roper, Lyndal 55
Rosa, Salvatore, painter 12
Rosicrucianism 190, 201n.59
Rosslyn Chapel 88

Roule's 'Devyne poware of michtis maist' (poem) 25, 27, 29–30, 31, 33
Royal Society 181
'Rule Britannia' (song) 99
Runciman, Alexander, painter 12
Russell, John, advocate 168
Rutherfoord, William, visionary 98
Rutherford, Samuel, minister and St Andrews University professor 95, 149, 153
Ruthven, Alexander, Master of Ruthven 167
Ruthven, John, 3rd Earl of Gowrie 167

St Andrews 42, 88
   University 217n.11
St Andrews, parish of (Orkney) 77
St Clements Church, Rodel 90
St Kilda 181
saints 32, 96, 109, 112, 117, 192, 226, 237n.10
Salem witch trials 189
salvation 17, 148, 149, 161, 209, 216
   see also Heaven
Sampson, Agnes, accused witch 131
Sandyford 110
Sangha, Laura 86–7, 99
Satan see Devil
Scandinavia 183, 184
Scarborough 113
scepticism 24n.42, 211, 229
   about astrology 130–1
   about bleeding corpse 6
   about powers of reason 209, 213
   about Second Sight 179, 194
   about witchcraft 157n.24, 205
Scientific Revolution 16, 17
Scotland, identity of 11–12, 222, 227
   see also Highlands; Lowlands
Scot, Michael, astrologer 140, 142n.68
Scot, Reginald, writer on witchcraft 157n.24
Scott, Alexander, poet 114
Scott, Sir Walter, novelist and antiquary 120–1
Scribner, Bob 18
Scripture 147, 149, 151–2, 154, 206, 209, 211, 213, 216
   astrology and 132, 134, 136

Scripture (*continued*)
  providence and 166, 169, 172
  visionaries and 97
scrying 183
Seaforth, Earl of *see* Mackenzie, Kenneth
Seal, astrologer 134
seals 95
Second Sight 3, 16, 18, 119, 145, 178–203 *passim*
  etymology of 185–6
Secret Commonwealth, The see Kirk, Robert
seely wights 56, 63
seers 13, 56, 57, 62–6, 107, 179–84, 195, 202n.62, 208
Seligman, Rebecca 58
Sempill, Robert, poet 42
Seneca, ancient philosopher and playwright 215
sermons 15, 18, 91, 92, 144–59 *passim*, 166, 167, 170, 171
  attendance at 195
servants 63, 186, 195, 215
Seton Palace 114
sex 10, 47, 48, 50, 82, 109
Sextus, king in prophecy 109
Shakespeare, William, playwright 12
shamanism 63–4
shape-shifting 10, 28
Sheba, Queen of, prophetess 109, 110–11
sheep, ewes 66
  divination by shoulder-blade of 65, 183
sheets 98
  see also winding sheets
Shenstone, William, poet 234–5
Shetland 73–4, 78, 95
Shipton, Mother, prophetess 107
Shony, god in Lewis 8
shrouds *see* winding sheets
Sibbald, James, Aberdeen Doctor 148, 149
Sibyls, Sibylline prophecies 108, 110, 112, 118, 121
sight, theories of 63, 148, 185, 237–8n.20
  see also blindness; Evil Eye; Second Sight
Simpson, William, spirit-guide 14, 42–3, 45, 47, 65

sin, sins 14, 32, 134, 140, 147–53 *passim*, 162–3, 171, 172, 231
  forgiveness of 30
  original sin 15, 148
    see also Adam; Fall of Man
  punishment of 31, 88, 97, 129, 137, 101, 165
  see also depravity
Sir Colling the Knycht (poem) 26
skeletons 12
Skene, Alexander, chronicler 169
Skeyne, Gilbert, royal physician 129–30
Skye 91
sleep 58, 60–2, 225–6, 232, 236
  sleepwalking 45
  see also dreams
slinneineachd 183
Sloane, Hans, physician and collector 181
Sluhovsky, Moshe 179
smallpox 100
Smith, Adam, economist 170–1
Smith, David 79–80
Smith, Wilfred Cantwell 7, 8
snails 26
snakes 40
Society in Scotland for Propagating Christian Knowledge (SSPCK) 170, 171
Socinianism 162, 163, 222
sociology 40–1, 48
Socrates, ancient philosopher 210, 213, 220n.64
  see also Presocratics
Solomon 109
Solway Sands 112, 117
souls 4, 13, 44, 56, 79, 130, 146, 148–9, 153
  angels and 89, 90, 92, 94–5
  immortality of 208–9, 213–16
  pre-existence of 214
  transmigration of 94, 213, 214–15
  see also spirit, human
Spanish Armada (1588) 170
Spinoza, Baruch, philosopher 206
spirit-guides 14, 39–54 *passim*, 66, 188–9
  sex with 10, 48, 50, 188
spirit, human 59–60, 63, 79, 117, 130, 164, 166
spirits 4, 5, 83, 133, 190, 207, 208, 225

depiction of 91
discernment of 2, 6, 14, 27
encountered by seers 13, 180–1, 184, 191, 194
intermediate 99
reformation of 3
spirit doubles 181
summoning of 27, 41, 49, 64, 183
see also necromancy
see also angels; bogles; brownies; demons; *Doppelgänger*; dwarfs; elves; fairies; familiars; Fates; ghosts; giants; green kirtles; Holy Spirit; incubi; muses; nature spirits; seely wights; trolls; water-bulls; water-horses
spiritualism 101
Standsfield, Philip, murderer 6–7
stars 118, 128–9, 131–2, 134, 138, 140
as deities 210
shooting stars 130, 137, 165
see also astrology
Steward, Simeon, poet 20n.1
Stewart dynasty 107, 109, 110, 114, 121
see also Jacobitism
Stewart, Francis, 5th Earl of Bothwell 131
Stewart, John, Duke of Albany, regent of Scotland 111, 112, 120, 121
Stewart, John, of Baldynneis, poet 31
Stewart, John, spirit-guide 47
Stirling 42
Castle 43
Stirling, Alexander, visionary 165
Stiùbhart, Domhnall Uilleam 3, 16
Stobo, John, astrologer 138
Stoicism, Stoics 162, 215
Strabo, ancient geographer 204
Strathspey 65, 188
straws 59, 62
sun, sunrise, sunset 44, 97, 98, 130, 136, 165, 186, 210, 221, 236
Sunday 96, 200n.48
supernatural, definition of 1–9, 145–6, 148, 163
see also nature; occult; paranormal; preternatural
superstition 2, 14, 15–16, 26, 133, 149, 182, 221
astrology as 130, 135, 140, 141

bleeding corpse as 6
Catholicism as 136
Jacobites and 119
necromancy as 31
prophecy as 120, 121, 208
religion as 209
swords 13, 62, *90*, 95, 98
sympathy 14, 50, 100

taghairm 183
taibhsearachd 178
taibhsearan 181
Tàillear Dubh na Tuaighe, legendary hero 188
tarbh-feirigh 8
tarbh-uisge 8
Taylor, Rupert 107
Thales of Miletus, philosopher 213
theatre 193–4, 225
Thetis, sea nymph 10
Thomas of Erceldoune (romance) 109–10
Thomas, Keith 2
Thomas the Rhymer 115, 182
see also Rimour, Thomas
Thomism 181
Thomson, James, poet 99, 234–5
Thomson, Peggy, sweetheart of Robert Burns 86
Thornton, Tim 108
Thrummy Cap and the Ghaist 121
thunderbolts 98
Tibbermore 59
Tindal, Matthew, freethinker 209
toads 12
Toland, John, freethinker 209
Tonge, Israel, informer 118
Trall, Jonet, visionary accused of witchcraft 95
trances 13, 55–71 *passim*, 95
trauma 43, 49, 53n.2, 57–8, 65, 188
in literature 226
trees 5, 180
see also holly; laurel
Trinity Altarpiece 88–9
trolls 79
trumpets 89, 92, *93*, *94*, 100, 207
trust and distrust 47, 50, 108, 118, 131–2, 146–7, 149, 151
Tudor dynasty 107, 109, 121
Tullibardine, Earl of see Murray, John

Turks 109, 110, 112, 117
Tweed, river 208
Tytler, William, of Woodhouselee 224–5, 227

Union of Crowns (1603) 19, 107, 114–17, 121, 135, 168, 227
Union of Parliaments (1707) 11, 119–20, 168, 221–5, 227, 236
universities 4, 42, 147, 204, 205
   and astrology 16, 17, 127, 128, 135, 139, 140
   see also Aberdeen; Edinburgh; Glasgow; St Andrews
'Upon a tyme the faierie elves' (poem) 1, 3, 9–11, 20

vapours 205
Veitch, Marion, diarist 165
Virgil, ancient poet 204
   Aeneid 26
visionaries 14, 39–54 *passim*, 194–5, 100, 164, 194, 195, 226
   see also seers; *taibhsearan*
visions 55–71 *passim*, 83, 97–8, 109, 118, 165, 179–88 *passim*, 195
   belief in 155, 192
   in poetry 25–6, 221–38 *passim*
   see also apparitions; hallucinations

Wales 107, 109, 110, 112, 116
   Welsh language 23n.30, 114
Walker, Patrick, chronicler 164
Wallace, Margaret, visionary 59, 66
Walsham, Alexandra 18
Waltheof, St, abbot of Melrose, prophet 107
wars 63, 171, 182
   Anglo-Scottish 110–11, 120, 168
   see also Bishops' Wars
   predictions of 110, 118, 119, 120, 128, 132, 136, 165, 195
water 95, 183, 200n.48
   dew 98
   holy water 27, 31
   spas 98
water-bulls 8
water-horses 8

Watson, Isobel, visionary accused of witchcraft 50, 95
Watts, Isaac, hymn writer 236
weapons 185, 215
weather 10, 15, 128, 129, 131, 136, 140, 151
   see also drought; thunderbolts; whirlwinds
Weber, Max 17
Webster, James, minister 146, 150, 154
Webster, Tom 56
Wedderburn, Alexander, minister of Kilmarnock 99, 146, 166
Wehr, Thomas 61
wells 28, 95
   elrich wells 26
   holy wells 18
Welsh, John, minister of Ayr 151, 153, 164
Westminster Confession (1646) 161, 162–3, 218n.29
whales 26
Whatley, Stephen, translator 207
Whigs 19, 119
whirlwinds 29, 41, 45, 46, 64, 129, 150
Whole Prophesie of Scotland, The 107–26 *passim*
Wigtownshire 47
Wilby, Emma 55–6, 59, 80
William III, king of Great Britain 119, 168
Willumsen, Liv Helene 15
Wilson, Sheryl 57, 61
winding sheets 180, 184
witchcraft 7, 49, 61, 130, 131, 132, 148, 156, 182
   consulting witches 140, 185–6
   in poetry and drama 12, 27, 32, 33, 223
   visions of witches 97
   Witchcraft Act (1563) 30, 133–4
   witches' sabbat 61, 76
   see also cursing; Endor, Witch of; *maleficium*
witch-hunting, witchcraft trials 3, 11, 17, 29, 39–41, 51, 95, 157n.24, 188–9, 191

confessions to witchcraft 55, 56–7, 59–60, 63–4, 72–85 *passim*, 131, 185–9, 200n.46
scholarship on 2
Wode Psalter 96
Wodrow, Robert, minister of Eastwood 164, 169
wonders 4, 5, 147, 163, 223

Wood, John, of Humbie 134
worms 5–6
wrens 8–9, 36n.39

Yeoman, Louise 155, 194
Yorkshire 107, 112
Young Pretender's Destiny Unfolded, The 119

EU authorised representative for GPSR:
Easy Access System Europe, Mustamäe tee 50,
10621 Tallinn, Estonia
gpsr.requests@easproject.com

www.ingramcontent.com/pod-product-compliance
Lightning Source LLC
Chambersburg PA
CBHW051607230426
43668CB00013B/2015